Unprepared

Unprepared

America in the Time of Coronavirus

Compiled and Edited by Jon Sternfeld

Introduction by Timothy Egan

BLOOMSBURY PUBLISHING

NEW YORK • LONDON • OXFORD • NEW DELHI • SYDNEY

BLOOMSBURY PUBLISHING
Bloomsbury Publishing Inc.
1385 Broadway, New York, NY 10018, USA

BLOOMSBURY, BLOOMSBURY PUBLISHING, and the Diana logo are trademarks of Bloomsbury Publishing Plc

First published in the United States 2020

ISBN: HB: 978-1-63557-720-4; eBook: 978-1-63557-721-1

LIBRARY OF CONGRESS CATALOGING-IN-PUBLICATION DATA IS AVAILABLE

2 4 6 8 10 9 7 5 3 1

Typeset by Westchester Publishing Services
Printed and bound in the U.S.A. by Berryville Graphics Inc., Berryville, Virginia

Everyone now asks: When will things get back to normal? But, as a physician and researcher, I fear that the resumption of normality would signal a failure to learn. We need to think not about resumption but about revision.

—SIDDHARTHA MUKHERJEE,
AUTHOR AND PHYSICIAN

CONTENTS

INTRODUCTION

THE PAGES THAT follow are the tick-tock of a tragedy, perhaps the greatest collapse of American society in so short a time, ever. You can read it and weep—for the dead, those family and friends you thought had ten more good years but instead did not have ten days. You can read it and rage—at the idiocy, the indifference, the defiance of science. You can read it and feel humbled, even powerless, at the predatory power of a new virus to bring down the human species. Or you can read it and learn. It's all here without filter, the words of people who tried to save us from ourselves, and the words of those who betrayed us.

We know what happened. There's no need to wait for the forensics from future historians. Why it happened on such a scale is the harder, more worthwhile question. The first reports came out of China in the last gasp of 2019. The government announced seven cases of an unusual flu or pneumonia, traced to the Huanan Seafood Market. No need for alarm, the authorities said; most likely, it did not spread from human to human. Within three weeks, the disease had officially arrived in the United States, a lone case, and had a name: a coronavirus for the year it appeared, Covid-19. A month or so later, the United States reported fifty-three cases. The spread of this murderous respiratory ailment, said President Donald Trump on February 24, "is very much under control." Three days later, he said it would disappear, "like a miracle."

By the time the World Health Organization declared a global pandemic, on March 11, the coronavirus had leaped to 114 countries, with 118,000 reported cases. From there, we became all too familiar with the word "exponential." The first known death in the United States was announced on February 29. Barely four months after that, as the sun set on the longest day in the year, the disease had taken the lives of nearly 120,000 Americans—more than twice the number of all United States deaths from the Vietnam War. The toll hit people of color hardest. It ravaged those without health care, those who lived paycheck-to-paycheck, those who nested in close quarters, those who had to slaughter hogs, nurse the sick, or bathe the elderly, those who had to ride buses or subways to work.

Usually, it began with a cough or tickle in the throat, followed by fever and chills, muscle soreness and fatigue. But it could feel like no other flu or cold. The sick hallucinated, sweated through bed sheets, went weeks without being able to sit up. They compared it to an anvil on the chest. Hospitals filled. Doctors discovered that blood clots, strokes, neurological disorders, and organ failure were associated with the disease. There was a run on hand sanitizer and toilet paper, and a shortage of surgical masks and cotton swabs, things no longer made in America. Under lockdown, with stores, bars, and restaurants shuttered, playgrounds closed, courts and town halls empty, society began to break. By June, nearly one in six working Americans had lost a job.

Those who couldn't afford to stay home took their sickness to work, until they showed up in hospital emergency rooms and took a number. "I can't breathe" was a common complaint of the ill. And then it became a street chant, after the Memorial Day murder of a Black man pinned under the knee of a white policeman in Minneapolis. People took to the streets in small towns and downtowns, a tsunami of social upheaval unseen in fifty years. It was as if the vast, fetid reservoir holding every inequity of the last four hundred years had suddenly burst. The Covid crackup was not an American moment. It was the American condition, laid bare by a virus.

"Somebody picked up our country and just shook it and turned it upside down," said Governor Andrew Cuomo of New York, one of the first political leaders to take the disease seriously, though even he did not act quickly at first. It was like a snow globe, he told us. "And it's all chaotic and things are flying all over."

Oh, but we would rise to meet the challenge, it was said. This is our Pearl Harbor. Our 9/11. Our Great Depression. Our Hurricane Katrina. The comparisons did not work. For this pandemic felt like nothing else. In the 1930s, you could take hold of your mother's hand as she lay dying in a dust storm. In the dystopia of 2020, your last glance was through a plexiglass partition, if you were lucky. Human touch could be fatal. You could bury the dead but not celebrate the life, for there was no certainty that the gathering would not imperil those close to the deceased.

How did this happen? How did a lethal pandemic, an economic depression, and civil unrest, all of historic magnitude, come together at a time when America was supposedly great again? It's tempting to quote Hemingway's explanation on going broke: "Two ways. Gradually and then suddenly." But that isn't quite expansive enough. The granularity in these pages tells the story of the gradual and sudden, both symptoms of something much larger. There's no master narrative in this tale of a nation brought to its knees, no voice of God in the telling. It is *us*, in a tangle of contradiction, the leaders and followers, the experts and the crackpots, told without comment.

Several big themes emerge in the day-by-day statements presented herein. The overriding one is how utterly unprepared the nation was for a wave of disease and death. Many smart people had warned of the likely arrival of a swift and incurable new virus with no respect for borders. And many smart people had warned that the obesity, diabetes, hypertension, addiction, and other pathologies of despair that are prevalent in a nation where twenty-eight million people have no health insurance would make the United States particularly vulnerable to such a pandemic. A person with no health care wakes up sick, can't go to a doctor, but instead goes to work and infects everyone.

We'd been lucky. But luck was no match for the hard task of building an infrastructure of prevention and treatment. With little notice, the pandemic preparation team was dismantled in the White House. When the contagion took hold, the response from leaders at the highest level was chaotic and disastrous. Hospitals did not have adequate plans, supplies, equipment, or guidance. A country that had turned out eight combat aircraft every hour at the peak of World War II could not even produce enough seventy-five-cent masks or simple cotton nasal swabs.

The second thread is denial, a natural human reaction, which explains much of the above. The excuses were many. It's only China. It's only a few nursing homes. It's only the elderly and frail, people with one foot in the grave. It's only in the winter months. It's just like the flu. No reason to panic. Go about your daily lives.

The virus exposed class divides, which were always there but not always self-evident. In mid-March, people were told to stay home for two weeks or more—to work remotely or take a hiatus. Who couldn't do this? People without childcare. People without paid family leave. People who did not have two weeks' pay in the bank. Nearly eighty million workers, almost 60 percent of the workforce, are hourly employees. Staying home would push some into homelessness. Others were deemed "essential." They *had* to go to work. Grocery clerks, meatpackers, delivery drivers. Going to work without proper guidance on masks and distancing, without adequate precautions in the store or on the factory floor, meant many of these vital workers got sick and died.

And not far from class, but related, is race. Why did people of color get sick at a much higher rate than whites? Blacks and Native Americans were five times more likely than whites to die or be hospitalized from coronavirus, by one government measure. Hispanics were not far behind. The explanation for this disparity, from the Centers for Disease Control, was "longstanding systemic health and social inequities."

Finally, there was the failure to mount a national response. Most of Europe locked down early. Italy went into mandatory hibernation on March 9, just two days after Robert Redfield, director of the CDC, said, "the general risk to the American public remains low." The United States dithered, argued, and delayed as months passed without a plan. Fifty states went fifty ways. The federal government sent conflicting signals. Wear masks. Don't wear masks. Anyone who wants a test could get a test, except there were never enough tests. Close the stores, bars, hair salons, restaurants, but "LIBERATE" the states that ordered such a thing, as the president tweeted. Don't mess with freedom, even if one person's liberty meant could mean another's death. One day Trump proclaimed that his "authority is total." Another day he said he bore no responsibility for the human wreckage in the nation he governed. He wanted all of the control but none of the blame.

This tragedy unfolded in five stages, each revealing a broader failure. In the arrival phase, through January, the Chinese seemed more concerned with containing information than containing the spread. This changed by the third week of January, when Wuhan, a city of ten million people, went into lockdown. "We might leave a bad name in history," said the mayor.

The United States and South Korea each reported their first cases on January 21. The Koreans launched an immediate program of testing, monitoring, and tracing. The Americans were dismissive. Within five weeks, South Korea had tested sixty-five thousand while the U.S. had yet to reach five hundred. "We have it totally under control," said President Trump, a phrase he would use over and over. "It's going to be just fine." By the end of April, new cases in South Korea were down to less than ten a day. In the United States, the pandemic raged at a daily rate of more than twenty-five thousand newly sick.

The emergency phase was chaos, misdirection, and a woeful misreading of what was about to swamp the world in misery. Though the federal government declared a public health emergency on January 31, those in charge continued to downplay the crisis. "We have contained this," said Larry Kudlow, director of the National Economic Council, on February 25. "I won't say airtight, but pretty close to airtight. We have done a good job in the United States." Was there a national plan? An army of contact tracers at the ready? Test kits deployed to every county in the land? Nothing of the sort was evident. The imperative from the top was to protect the stock market and the economy, the guarantors of reelection.

Hubris was in the air. The initial cases could be wished away. "When you have fifteen people, and the fifteen within a couple of days is going down to close to zero, that's a pretty good job we've done," said Trump on February 26. He bragged, two days later, that there were no deaths from Covid-19 in the United States On February 29 came the contradiction: the first official death in the United States, in Washington State, though there may have been earlier, undetected fatalities.

The missteps mounted. Soon, the United States was the hotspot, the sad, piteous giant. On March 27, the BBC reported a milestone in American exceptionalism: the United States had more cases than any other country, surpassing China. In response, the White House blamed global health experts and announced plans to withdraw funding from the World Health Organization in the middle of a pandemic. By early May, an American was dying of Covid-19 every forty-nine seconds. The United States, with less than 5 percent of the world's population, had more than 30 percent of the sick. In two months' time, the nation had gone from zero deaths to more than any nation on earth. No other country was even close.

The inevitable lockdown, the third phase, came in fits and starts. It was borne by the startling realization that infected people without symptoms, those who seemed perfectly healthy, could make others sick. The quickest way to prevent a disease that could kill upward of two million Americans was to put the nation in a deep freeze. It would require patience—not weeks, but maybe months, without contact. And it would be a huge hit to the economy. Millions of businesses might go under. This was hard for many people to accept. When Governor Gavin Newsom of California declared on March 15 that all bars, nightclubs, breweries, and in-dining restaurants would be closed, the governor of Oklahoma, Kevin Stitt, bragged about eating in a packed restaurant. Spring breakers headed for the beaches of Florida and Texas. Party on!

We took some solace in cleaner air, the hush that fell over cities, the bread-making skills of many a competitive bro. Still, even the palliative of nature was not enough to stem loneliness and depression, the pain of isolation. And the pandemic had another soundtrack as well: the blare of sirens coming and going as people fell mortally ill. Many counted on the avuncular authority of a veteran virologist, Dr. Anthony Fauci, director of the National Institute of Allergy and Infectious Diseases since 1984. He tried to be an anchor for a ship of state that was woefully adrift. And when he didn't make a public appearance for several days, people worried that he'd been silenced. Others, in the darkest corners of conspiracy theory, blamed him for the chaos.

When Wisconsin voters went to the polls in April, after the Supreme Court ruled that they could not be delayed, voting itself became a perilous act. People were forced to choose between the basic duty of citizenship in a free nation and putting their lives in danger. Democracy, like so many other elements of society, was sick.

Congress passed the largest rescue package in American history, a $2 trillion–dollar lifeline. It provided relief for average Americans but was heavily weighted toward the well connected and well off. Even with checks on the way, people became increasingly anxious, tired, and fatigued. Trump mused about opening up for Easter. "We cannot let the cure be worse than the problem," he said.

The fourth phase, the opening, started with a bang and fizzled into a fog of dread and uncertainty. It revealed more about our politics, particularly the red-blue divide, than it did about the pandemic. The virus had no political bias, but wearing a mask was seen as evidence of one. Consumers of far-right media were found to be less likely to exercise caution, one study found. The rapid spread of misinformation added another word to the national lexicon: infodemic.

Georgia, Florida, and Texas gave consumers a green light, while states like Michigan, Washington, and New York kept most of their cities and towns shuttered. When Senate Majority Leader Mitch McConnell suggested that Democratic states were a problem, Governor Cuomo despaired at what had become of us. "How ugly a thought," he said. "People died. 'Fifteen thousand people died in New York, but they were predominantly Democrats. So why should we help them?' . . . That's not who we are." Sadly, it was.

One of the most bizarre statements to come out of the White House was the suggestion by Trump on April 23 that cleaning disinfectants and sunlight might be used to treat Covid-19 patients. Though he was rebuffed by medical authorities, it marked a low point in guidance from a government where no one seemed to know what they were doing. A nation that had once shown the world how to defeat polio was promoting quack remedies from the presidential podium.

Something shattered on Memorial Day, the start of the final phase, the reckoning. The country was already raw and ready to boil over when George Floyd had the life slowly snuffed out of him by a white police officer. Things that had been brewing for centuries were added to a toxic mix of indifference, incompetence, and state-backed cruelty. When upward of twenty-six million took to the streets in the month of June, it felt like no other expression of political rage—and may have been the largest concentrated protest in the nation's history. Those who'd been in lockdown, who'd watched the response of the highest office in the land devolve into nonsense and non sequiturs, now saw on their screens an endless replay of the mortal result of systemic racism. At the same time, the number of American COVID-19 deaths passed one hundred thousand. The year was not even half over.

Through the summer, as the daily count of the dead and newly infected fell in the European Union and much of Asia, cases spiked in the U.S.—for days on end, enough new victims to fill a stadium were added to the toll. And here's the tragedy within a tragedy: most of those who died would still be alive had the United States taken the kind of decisive early action that other nations did, according to several studies. It's a fair question to ask if willful negligence led to the deaths of those people. The consequences of being unprepared were catastrophic.

You can think of this volume as a time capsule, some artifact that will be opened in a hundred years to the horror of those who read it. They will wonder what we were thinking. They will reflect on how things changed, if at all. They will look to see if those responsible for losing the war against the coronavirus paid a price. They will find, in the tragic consistencies, an answer to the "why it happened" question. But this document also burns for the here and now. It's history on the fly, an owner's manual for the outraged, a call to arms for the vigilant.

— Timothy Egan
July 2020

AUTHOR'S NOTE

In late May, while I was turning in the first draft of this manuscript, George Floyd was murdered by a Minneapolis police officer while two others held him down and a third looked on. The outrage, protests, government response, police reaction, and grassroots activism that emerged from Floyd's murder (along with Ahmaud Arbery's and Breonna Taylor's) are included at the end of this book not just because of a coincidence of timing. True, it was the biggest story since the start of the Covid-19 crisis, a period of collective pause when the nation seemed incapable of focusing on anything else. But here was another public health issue, one that was also disproportionately affecting Black and Brown communities in America, and it was caught on video in a way that didn't allow for any spinning or both-siding, a rare feat these days. It spoke so loudly that even an international pandemic couldn't drown it out. The two stories were inextricably linked and anyone who had been watching America in 2020 could see that. Floyd's murder, at the hands of men sworn to protect him, didn't change the story of this book so much as serve as its inevitable climax.

By the end of May, everything that we had been tracking day to day regarding the coronavirus's arrival in this country and the effects it had on the public seemed to emerge in this crystallized form. The pandemic that disproportionately affected minority communities, the competing forms of mass communication that presented diametrically opposed (but not equally true) versions of events, the built-up tension and frustration of months in quarantine, the people out of work and in fear for their livelihoods, the people who had to go to work in fear for their lives, the outrage at an incompetent and unprepared government seemingly indifferent to public health, and the collective uprising of citizens who felt the system had failed them all came together in a crescendo.

THE ORIGINAL IDEA for this book came from my editor, Anton Mueller, who suggested putting together a narrative of the pandemic (or what was clearly the first wave) through the words of our leaders: the president, his cabinet and task force members, health officials, governors, senators, and mayors. During those months, their words were like satellites beamed in to a suddenly confusing and foreign world. They spoke in press conferences, public statements, interviews, and, some more than others, on Twitter. There was something so pure and direct about the concept, with its echoes of a previous era. It would be an attempt to hold leaders accountable for their words in an inarguable way: *you said this on this date.*

But it became clear to us that this perspective was too narrow, like viewing the epidemic through a soda straw. Something was missing: an agreed-upon set of facts. So we began including the tally from the Coronavirus Resource Center (at Johns Hopkins University), the COVID Tracking Project (at the *Atlantic*), prominent scientists, and then news outlets to provide a factual grounding; later, we sought the voices of individual journalists to provide witness of what was happening on the ground and behind doors. Their research and reporting were invaluable to making the story feel more complete. Of all the damage the current administration (and its media apparatus) has done, its destruction of the value of truth is perhaps the most demoralizing and dangerous. Something tells me everything poisonous about them comes from that tree.

So, *Unprepared* is a patchwork: voices from the public space, happening in real time, at the speed of history. As many of us were stuck at home, this is a record of what we heard, a version of the national voice, which, of course, wasn't a monolithic thing. It was a voice in direct conflict with itself, reckoning with what it wanted to say and what the people needed to hear. These pages capture a nation that first thought it was frozen, only to realize it was actually in transition. It's a snapshot of the change occurring before we knew what would come out the other end. In 2020, we had to stop so that we could take in what was happening around us, feel helpless so we could find our agency, lose hope so we could create it again.

In selecting what quotes to include, I have done my best to be a fair arbiter, but this is not "objective" in the classic (and I believe outdated) journalistic sense. There was no effort to both-sides this story. The quotes chosen were representative of the speakers and events, and I attempted in good faith to capture that reality. The resulting book is part oral history and part eavesdropping, a radio on the mantel broadcasting the voices coming through to our various living rooms and bedrooms, backyards and patios, places we have known far too intimately these past months. As the coronavirus and its effects spread around us, these were the words that informed, enraged, comforted, and provoked us.

This book is not meant to be some overarching history of this period, as it is limited to mostly public figures: government leaders, journalists, prominent officials, health experts, academics, and leading scientists. Of course, the Covid crisis played out in millions of ways through brave and hardworking individuals, people without microphones, media platforms, and Twitter followings, those on the front lines in emergency rooms, ambulances, nursing homes, factories, plants, post offices, labs, morgues, and prisons. Their voices need to be heard as well and will no doubt be magnified in time.

BECAUSE OF THE realities of book publishing, I am writing this from early July, so you know more about how this story turns out than I do. Though everyone at Bloomsbury has worked incredibly hard and quickly, books just take time. Some argue it's the reason they're obsolete. I'm not sure: I think, as everything becomes compact and faster, it's why they remain valuable.

Nevertheless, I wouldn't venture to guess about the America you are currently reading this from. The first Covid months felt like some kind of temporary hold, which you'll see is how just about everyone thought of them. Back then, we couldn't conceive how quickly America could or would change. It seems obvious in hindsight how this country was bursting at the seams. These months turned out to be a door to something else, a portal, to what I can't say. Things seem like they could go either way right now and I wouldn't venture to guess.

But maybe you are closer to having some idea.

—Jon Sternfeld
New York
July 2020

Unprepared

THE ARRIVAL

DECEMBER 31–JANUARY 30

TUESDAY, DECEMBER 31, 2019*

Dr. Li Wenliang, Wuhan Central Hospital, Wuhan, China: 7 confirmed cases of SARS were reported from Huanan Seafood Market, isolated in the Emergency Department of Houhu District of our hospital. The latest news is that the coronavirus infection is confirmed and the virus is being typed . . . Don't spread the word, let family members and relatives take precautions.†

Wuhan Municipal Health Commission, Wuhan, China: Recently, some medical institutions found that multiple pneumonia cases received were related to South China Seafood City. After receiving the report, the Municipal Health Commission immediately carried out a case search and retrospective investigation in the city's medical and health institutions related to South China Seafood City. Twenty-seven cases have been found, of which seven are severely ill, and the remaining cases are stable and

---

* Note: Any condensing of a quote is indicated with an ellipsis. All quotes are *sic*.

† WeChat message to colleagues

controllable . . . The investigation so far has found no obvious person-to-person transmission, and no medical personnel have been infected.

JANUARY 2, 2020

***Beijing News Express*:** According to official Weibo news from the Jianghan District Government Office in Wuhan City, due to the emergence of pneumonia patients of unknown causes in the South China Seafood Market in Wuhan City, the South China Seafood Wholesale Market was closed for environmental sanitation on January 1.

JANUARY 3

Via *Chutian Dushi Bao*,* Wuhan, China: According to a report by the Wuhan Public Security Bureau of Xinhua News Agency on the 1st, some untrue information about "Wuhan Viral Pneumonia" was circulating on the Internet a few days ago, and the public security department investigated it. At present, eight people† have been dealt with by the police in accordance with the law because of dissemination of false information . . . Wuhan police reminded that posting information and remarks on the Internet should comply with laws and regulations. The police will investigate and deal with illegal acts of fabricating, spreading, and spreading rumors and disturbing social order. The police urged netizens not to create rumors, believe or spread rumors, and to build a harmonious and clear cyberspace.

JANUARY 5

Wuhan Municipal Health Commission: As of 8:00 on January 5, 2020, a total of 59 patients with unexplained viral pneumonia diagnosis were

---

* Wuhan newspaper

† One of the arrested was Dr. Li Wenliang

reported, including 7 severely ill patients . . . Epidemiological investigation shows that some patients are operating households in South China Seafood City (South China Seafood Wholesale Market) in Wuhan. As of now, preliminary investigations have shown that no clear evidence of human-to-human transmission has been found.

JANUARY 6

***Stat News*:** The cause of mysterious pneumonia cases in the Chinese city of Wuhan remains unknown, health authorities in the city said Sunday, as the number of infected people rose to 59 from 44 on Friday.

JANUARY 9

World Health Organization (WHO): Chinese authorities have made a preliminary determination of a novel (or new) coronavirus, identified in a hospitalized person with pneumonia in Wuhan . . . In the coming weeks, more comprehensive information is required to understand the current status and epidemiology of the outbreak, and the clinical picture.

JANUARY 16

Ministry of Health, Labor and Welfare, Japan: According to the risk assessment of WHO and the National Institute of Infectious Diseases for new coronavirus-associated pneumonia, at present, there is an undeniable case in which the possibility of limited human-to-human transmission of this disease, such as between families, has been reported. However, there is no clear evidence of persistent human-to-human transmission.

MONDAY, JANUARY 20

Dr. Zhong Nanshan, Former President, Chinese Medical Association: According to the current data, the new type of coronavirus pneumonia is definitely transmitted from person to person. There are two cases in Guangdong, they had not been to Wuhan, but their family members have been infected with new coronavirus pneumonia after going to Wuhan. We can say now, yes, there is a human-to-human phenomenon.

JANUARY 21

National Public Radio (NPR): The World Health Organization will convene an emergency meeting tomorrow about a virus that has infected almost 300 people, most of them in China. It's a type of virus known as a coronavirus.

Centers for Disease Control and Prevention (CDC): Coronaviruses are a large family of viruses, some causing respiratory illness in people and others circulating among animals including camels, cats, and bats. Rarely, animal coronaviruses can evolve and infect people and then spread between people, such as has been seen with Severe Acute Respiratory Syndrome (SARS) and Middle East Respiratory Syndrome (MERS). When person-to-person spread has occurred with SARS and MERS, it is thought to happen via respiratory droplets with close contacts, similar to how influenza and other respiratory pathogens spread. The situation with regard to 2019-nCoV is still unclear.

Korea Centers for Disease Control, South Korea: As of today, 21 January 2020, the first confirmed case of novel coronavirus, currently receiving treatment in isolation, is stable with no signs of pneumonia. In-depth epidemiological investigation on the case has been undertaken, and the contacts of the patient are under active monitoring. According to the investigation, there are 44 contacts who are either passengers or airport staff. Out of 44 contacts, nine of them have left the country and the rest are under active monitoring through local health facilities. They will be monitored for 14 days from the last day of contact with the patient and receive a call from health authority on first, second, and seventh day for fever or respiratory symptoms. If showing any signs or symptoms of illness, they will be isolated and tested.

CDC: The Centers for Disease Control and Prevention today confirmed the first case of 2019 Novel Coronavirus (2019-nCoV) in the United States in the state of Washington.

Governor Jay Inslee (WA):* From November to January 15, we had a Washington State resident, a man in his 30s, who was in Wuhan, China . . . On January 20, samples were confirmed by the CDC in Atlanta that, in fact, he carried the novel coronavirus, and he was hospitalized.

CDC: While originally thought to be spreading from animal-to-person, there are growing indications that limited person-to-person spread is happening. It's unclear how easily this virus is spreading between people.

Gov. Inslee (WA): This is certainly not a moment for panic or high anxiety. It is a moment for vigilance.

JANUARY 22

President Donald Trump: We have it totally under control. It's one person coming in from China, and we have it under control. It's going to be just fine.

JANUARY 23

Dr. Sylvie Briand, Director, Global Infectious Hazard Preparedness, WHO: Currently, we use the name of 2019 Coronavirus, but we will convene a committee to decide on the official name.

---

* No party affiliations are affixed to the names of elected officials.

Dr. Michael Ryan, Executive Director, Health Emergencies, WHO: The data we presented was referring to what we were reported [up] to today, which was 291 cases.

Dr. Tedros Adhanom Ghebreyesus, Director-General, WHO: Make no mistake. This is an emergency in China, but it has not yet become a global health emergency. It may yet become one.

JANUARY 25

International Air Transport Association (IATA): IATA is closely monitoring developments related to the Coronavirus outbreak in Wuhan (China) and is actively engaged with the World Health Organization Secretariat, ICAO and the US Centers for Disease Control. WHO is advising measures to limit the risk of export or import of the disease, without unnecessary restrictions on international traffic.

JANUARY 26

Ma Xiaowei, Minister, National Health Commission, China: Experts from the World Health Organization are invited to visit Wuhan, and experts from Hong Kong, Macao, and Taiwan are arranged to conduct field trips to Wuhan. After an assessment, the World Health Organization has announced that the epidemic situation will not be identified as a "public health emergency of international concern" for the time being . . . An epidemic is an order, and prevention and control is our responsibility. We will go all out to do a good job in prevention and control, give full play to the institutional advantages of socialism with Chinese characteristics, use our accumulated experience in the prevention and control of major public health events, and rely on the majority of medical workers and the people to fight an epidemic. In the People's War, we have the confidence, determination, and ability to win the epidemic.

JANUARY 27

Mayor Zhou Xianwang, Wuhan, China: We understand that the public is unsatisfied with our information disclosure. On one hand, we failed to disclose relevant information in a timely manner; on the other, we did not make sufficient use of valid information to improve our work. As for the late disclosure, I hope the public can understand that it's an infectious disease, and relevant information should be released according to the laws. As a local government, we can only disclose information after being authorized . . . It's unprecedented to lockdown a city with more than 10 million people in human history. However, faced with the current situation, we've closed the city gate and possibly besieged the virus within the city. We might leave a bad name in history.

Dr. Scott Gottlieb, Former Commissioner, Food and Drug Administration (FDA): Global spread appears inevitable. So too are the emergence of outbreaks in the U.S., even if a widespread American epidemic can still be averted. When pockets of the outbreak arrive on our shores, we shouldn't have undue panic. But we need to be ready.

Bavarian Ministry of Health, Germany: A man from the district of Starnberg has been infected with the novel coronavirus . . . the patient is clinically in good condition, monitored medically and isolated. The close contact persons are informed in detail and informed about possible symptoms, hygiene measures and transmission channels.

The "Task Force Infectiology" of the LGL and the Robert Koch Institute (RKI) currently consider the risk for the Bavarian population to become infected with the new type of coronavirus to be low.

JANUARY 28

President Xi Jinping, China: The virus is a devil and we cannot let the devil hide. China will strengthen international cooperation and welcomes the WHO participation in virus prevention . . . China is confident of winning the battle against the virus.

Senator Elizabeth Warren (MA): With well over 2,000 people infected and a rising death toll, China has restricted the movement of 56 million people . . . Instead of building capacity to combat these problems, Donald Trump has deprioritized global health security and risked putting us on our heels in a crisis. Trump has repeatedly tried to nickel and dime federal programs essential to health security, proposing billions of dollars in cuts so drastic that even a leading House Republican thought they would leave Americans vulnerable. Trump eliminated the key position that coordinates global health security across the many federal agencies that work to keep us safe.

Dr. Michael Osterholm, Director, Center for Infectious Disease Research and Policy, University of Minnesota: The idea that we could create this seal around China is just totally unrealistic. I think at that point, you have to assume we're going to see widespread transmission around the world.

Former Vice President Joe Biden: The outbreak of a new coronavirus, which has already infected more than 2,700 people and killed over 80 in China, will get worse before it gets better. Cases have been confirmed in a dozen countries, with at least five in the United States. There will likely be more . . . I am concerned that the Trump administration's shortsighted policies have left us unprepared for a dangerous epidemic that will come sooner or later.

Federal Open Market Committee, the Federal Reserve: The threat of the coronavirus, in addition to its human toll, had emerged as a new risk to the global growth outlook, which participants agreed warranted close watching.

JANUARY 30

Dr. Tedros, Director-General, WHO: I'm declaring a public health emergency of international concern over the global outbreak of novel coronavirus. In total, there are now 7,834 confirmed cases, including 7,736 in China, representing almost 99% of all reported cases worldwide. 170 people have lost their lives to this outbreak, all of them in China. We must remember that these are people, not numbers . . . [T]here is no reason for measures that unnecessarily interfere with international travel and trade. So, WHO doesn't recommend limiting trade and movement. We call on all countries to implement decisions that are evidence-based and consistent.

Prime Minister Giuseppe Conte, Italy: We have two confirmed cases of coronavirus in Italy. We have already prepared all the precautionary measures to isolate these two cases. There is no reason to create social alarm or panic.

Wilbur Ross, U.S. Secretary of Commerce: I don't want to talk about a victory lap over a very unfortunate, very malignant disease. But the fact is, it does give businesses yet another thing to consider when they go through their review of their supply chain. On top of all the other things, you have SARS, you have the African swine virus there, now you have this. It's another risk factor that people need to take into account . . . So, I think it will help accelerate the return of jobs to North America—some to the US, probably some to Mexico as well.

CDC: The 2019 Novel Coronavirus (2019-nCoV) has spread between two people in the United States, representing the first instance of person-to-person spread with this new virus here. Previously, all confirmed U.S. cases had been associated with travel to Wuhan, China, where an outbreak of respiratory illness caused by this novel coronavirus has been ongoing since December 2019. However, this latest 2019-nCoV patient has no history of travel to Wuhan, but shared a household with the patient diagnosed with 2019-nCoV infection on January 21, 2020.

President Trump: We only have five people. Hopefully, everything's going to be great. They have somewhat of a problem, but hopefully, it's all going to be great. But we're working with China, just so you know, and other countries very, very closely. So it doesn't get out of hand.

Dr. Tedros, Director-General, WHO: There are now 98 cases in 18 countries outside China, including eight cases of human-to-human transmission in four countries, Germany, Japan, Vietnam, and the United States of America. So far, we have not seen any deaths outside China, for which we must all be grateful . . . We don't know what sort of damage this virus could do if it were to spread in a country with a weaker health system.

Dr. Li, Wuhan Central Hospital, China: After receiving the new coronavirus pneumonia patients, I started to have cough symptoms on January 10, fever on the 11th, and hospitalization on the 12th. At that time, I was still wondering why I still said that there was no person to pass on, no medical infection, and later I lived in the ICU. I had a nucleic acid test before, but showed negative, yet I still have difficulty breathing and cannot move. My parents are also in hospital. In the ward, I also saw a lot of netizens' support and encouragement to me and my mood will be easier. Thank you for your support. I would like to clarify in particular that I have not had my license revoked. Please rest assured that I will actively cooperate with the treatment and strive to be discharged early!

THE EMERGENCY

JANUARY 31–MARCH 14

JANUARY 31

Alex Azar, Secretary of Health and Human Services (HHS): I have today declared that the coronavirus presents a public health emergency in the United States . . . In accordance with the declaration, beginning at 5:00 P.M., Eastern Standard Time; Sunday, February the 2nd, the United States government will implement temporary measures to increase our abilities to detect and contain the coronavirus proactively and aggressively . . . The President has signed a presidential proclamation, using his authority pursuant to Section 212(f) of the Immigration and Nationality Act, temporarily suspending the entry into the United States of foreign nationals who pose a risk of transmitting the 2019 novel coronavirus. As a result, foreign nationals, other than immediate family of U.S. citizens and permanent residents, who have traveled in China within the last 14 days will be denied entry into the United States for this time.

FEBRUARY 1

Salvador Illa, Health Minister, Spain: Yesterday, after 10 pm, the National Center for Microbiology confirmed that one of the five samples from La

Gomera has tested positive* . . . The person who has tested positive is isolated and receiving medical attention. We are in contact with the Minister of Health of the Canary Islands, Teresa Cruz, and we want to convey a message of confidence in the national health system.

Dr. Li, Wuhan Central Hospital, China: Today the nucleic acid test result is positive, the dust has settled and the diagnosis has finally been confirmed.

FEBRUARY 2

Governor Andrew Cuomo (NY): We take a situation like this very seriously. We understand the density of New York, the complexity of New York. Whatever happens internationally it winds up at our doorstep relatively quickly. So we've been through situations like this before. We're very proactive. I don't take anything for granted. Precaution is always the best practice.

President Trump: We pretty much shut it down coming in from China. But we can't have thousands of people coming in who may have this problem, the coronavirus. So, we're going to see what happens, but we did shut it down, yes.

Donald G. McNeil Jr., science and health reporter, *New York Times*: The Wuhan coronavirus spreading from China is now likely to become a pandemic that circles the globe, according to many of the world's leading infectious disease experts.

The prospect is daunting. A pandemic—an ongoing epidemic on two or more continents—may well have global consequences, despite the extraordinary travel restrictions and quarantines now imposed by China and other countries, including the United States.

---

* First confirmed positive Covid-19 case in Spain

FEBRUARY 4

CNN: The total number of confirmed cases in China stands at 20,438 as of today, an increase of 3,235 from the previous day—a jump of over 18%. The death toll is now at 425 in mainland China, an increase of around 65 from Sunday. The numbers have been jumping by huge margins in recent weeks. Less than a month ago, the first coronavirus patient died in China on January 9. By January 28, the death toll had topped 100; by January 31 it topped 200; the very next day, February 1, it topped 300. Today it topped 400.

President Trump: Protecting Americans' health also means fighting infectious diseases. We are coordinating with the Chinese government and working closely together on the coronavirus outbreak in China. My administration will take all necessary steps to safeguard our citizens from this threat.*

FEBRUARY 5

Dr. Nancy Messonnier, Director, National Center for Immunization and Respiratory Diseases (NCIRD), CDC: The total number of confirmed positives in the United States remains at 11. Right now, 206 persons under investigation or PUIs have tested negative for infection with this Novel virus . . . This is the beginning of what could be a long response. Right now we're aggressively intervening to contain introduction into the United States.

Jennifer Nuzzo, Associate Professor, Johns Hopkins Center for Health Security: All of the evidence we have indicates that travel restrictions and quarantines directed at individual countries are unlikely to keep the virus out of our borders. Simply put, the virus is spreading too quickly and too silently and our surveillance is too limited for us to truly know which countries have active transmission and which don't.

---

* State of the Union address

FEBRUARY 7

President Trump: Just had a long and very good conversation by phone with President Xi of China. He is strong, sharp, and powerfully focused on leading the counterattack on the Coronavirus . . . he will be successful, especially as the weather starts to warm & the virus hopefully becomes weaker, and then gone. Great discipline is taking place in China, as President Xi strongly leads what will be a very successful operation.

Alex Azar, Secretary of HHS: Although the virus represents a potentially very serious public health threat, and we expect to continue seeing more cases here, the immediate risk to the American public is low at this time.

U.S. Bureau of Labor Statistics, Department of Labor: Nonfarm payroll employment rose by 225,000 in January 2020. Construction, health care, and transportation and warehousing added jobs over the month. Average hourly earnings of all employees on private-sector payrolls rose by 7 cents or 0.2 percent in January. Over the year, hourly earnings have risen by 3.1 percent.

CNBC: Economists surveyed by Dow Jones were looking for payroll growth of 158,000 and the jobless rate to stay at 3.5%, its lowest in more than 50 years.

Wuhan Central Hospital: In the fight against the pneumonia epidemic of the new coronavirus infection, our hospital's ophthalmologist, Li Wenliang, was unfortunately infected. He passed away after all the efforts we've taken to resuscitate him. We deeply mourn his passing.

MONDAY, FEBRUARY 10

CDC: CDC today confirmed another infection with 2019 Novel Coronavirus (2019-nCoV) in the United States that was detected in California. The patient who was under a federal quarantine order recently returned from

Wuhan, China, where an outbreak of respiratory illness caused by this novel coronavirus has been ongoing since December 2019. This brings the total number of 2019-nCoV cases in the United States to 13.

President Trump: They're working hard. Looks like by April, in theory when it gets a little warmer, it miraculously goes away. I hope that's true, but we're doing great in our country. China, I spoke with President Xi and they're working very, very hard and I think it's going to all work out fine.

Dr. Tedros, Director-General, WHO: There've been some concerning instances of onward #2019nCoV spread from people with no travel history to China. The detection of a small number of cases may indicate more widespread transmission in other countries; in short, we may only be seeing the tip of the iceberg.

President Trump: I had a long talk with President Xi . . . two nights ago and he feels very confident. He feels very confident. And he feels that, again, as I mentioned, by April or during the month of April, the heat, generally speaking, kills this kind of virus.

FEBRUARY 11

Dr. Tedros, Director-General, WHO: First of all, we now have a name for the disease and it is Covid-19 and I will spell it: C-O-V-I-D-19. Co—C-O—stands for corona, as you know; V-I stands for virus; D for disease, so Covid . . . We had to find a name that did not refer to a geographical location, an animal, an individual or group of people and which is also pronounceable and related to the disease.

Dr. Briand, Director, Global Infectious Hazard Preparedness, WHO: Scientists have done some phylogenetic studies and they have identified that this virus is very similar to a coronavirus that can be found in bats. But when they did some sampling in the Wuhan Seafood Market, they didn't find so many bats and so it's very likely that there is an intermediate host that has been contaminated.

Princess Cruises: Princess Cruises confirms an announcement, from the Japanese Ministry of Health, of 39 new positive cases of Coronavirus onboard Diamond Princess. We are following guidance from the Japan Ministry of Health on plans for disembarkation protocols to provide medical care for these new cases.

Dr. Tedros, Director-General, WHO: The number of cases in the rest of the world [besides China] is less than 400 and there is only one death. That's a window of opportunity so I'm reminding: there is time, the time is ticking and time is of the essence in this outbreak.

Dr. Ryan, Executive Director, Health Emergencies, WHO: If fires are left unchecked, they can burn down a lot of the forest and one can speculate how far a fire like this can burn.

FEBRUARY 14

Dr. Messonnier, Director, NCIRD, CDC: There are more than 600 people still under quarantine in the United States because of their recent return from the epicenter of this outbreak in China . . . Based on what we know now, we believe this virus spreads mainly from person to person among close contacts, which is defined at about six feet. Through respiratory droplets produced, which an infected person coughs or sneezes. People are thought to be the most contagious when they're most systematic. That's when they're the sickest.

FEBRUARY 18

Dr. Tedros, Director-General, WHO: In the past 24 hours, China has reported 1,800 new cases, including both clinically and lab confirmed cases.

Outside China, there are now 804 cases in 24 countries with three deaths. In the past 24 hours, there have been 110 new cases outside China, including 99 on the Diamond Princess cruise ship.

Dr. Anthony Fauci, Director, National Institute of Allergy and Infectious Diseases (NIAID), National Institutes of Health (NIH): People on a large ship, all together, at the same time, all the time—you couldn't ask for a better incubator for infection.

Dr. Ryan, Executive Director, Health Emergencies, WHO: It takes a huge effort on behalf of a health system to have people in hospital on average for 20 days at the level of intensive care. So, the system becomes over driven by so many people requiring such long-term care.

Dr. Fauci, Director, NIAID: Well, it's even more disturbing, because not only do we not have an appreciation of the magnitude, even more disturbing is that we don't have an appreciation of where the magnitude is going . . . So what we're doing to mitigate that is that we're taking five cities, representative cities—Los Angeles, San Francisco, New York, Chicago, and Seattle—and going into clinics where people present with flu-like symptoms but don't have the flu.

FEBRUARY 19

Kristalina Georgieva, Chair and Managing Director, International Monetary Fund (IMF): The coronavirus is our most pressing uncertainty: a global health emergency we did not anticipate in January. It is a stark reminder of how a fragile recovery could be threatened by unforeseen events. There are a number of scenarios, depending on how quickly the spread of the virus is contained.

Peter Oppenheimer, Goldman Sachs: We believe the greater risk is that the impact of the coronavirus on earnings may well be underestimated in current stock prices. While a sustained bear market does not look likely, a near-term correction is looking much more probable.

Stephen Roach, Yale School of Management: Irrational exuberance never makes sense . . . If the global economy is as weak as I think it is in the first half of this year, that points to a pretty serious reckoning for frothy financial markets.

FEBRUARY 20

S&P 500: 3,373.23,–12.92(–0.38%)
Dow 30: 29,219.98,–128.05(–0.44%)
Nasdaq: 9,750.96,–66.21(–0.67%)
Stamps.com Inc. was among stock's biggest gainers, closing at 157.99 +62.53 (+65.50%).

Bloomberg News: U.S. equities slumped on concern that the coronavirus that originated in China will take a heavy toll on corporate earnings.

FEBRUARY 21

James Bullard, President and CEO, Federal Reserve Bank, St. Louis: There's a high probability that the coronavirus will blow over as other viruses have, be a temporary shock and everything will come back.

FEBRUARY 22

Bloomberg News: Authorities in northern Italy temporarily closed some universities after a surge in coronavirus cases left the country with the most infections in Europe, including two cases in the financial hub of Milan. The number of reported cases rose to 60 on Saturday, including 47 in the Lombardy region, which borders Switzerland and includes Milan, Italy's second-biggest city.

Giulio Gallera, Acting Health and Welfare Minister, Lombardy, Italy: The contagiousness of this virus is very strong and pretty virulent . . . [but] today it's not a pandemic.

Prime Minister Conte, Italy: I've wondered myself why so many cases in Italy . . . and the answer is in the rigorous and meticulous controls our country has adopted from the start.

FEBRUARY 23

Peter Navarro, Director, White House Office of Trade and Manufacturing Policy:* There is an increasing probability of a full-blown Covid-19 pandemic that could infect as many as 100 million Americans, with a loss of life as many as 1–2 million souls. To minimize economic and social disruption and loss of life, there is an urgent need for an immediate, supplemental appropriation of at least $3.0 billion dollars to support efforts at prevention, treatment, inoculation, and diagnostics.

President Trump: We have it very much under control in this country . . . it's a big situation going on throughout the world. And I can say, the United States, we've very much closed our doors in certain areas, in about certain areas, through certain areas. And we'll see what happens. But we have the greatest doctors in the world. We have it very much under control. We accepted a few people—a small number of people. They're very well confined and they should be getting better fairly soon. Very interestingly, we've had no deaths. We have a—I mean, you know, we've had a great practice. We had 12, at one point. And now they've gotten very much better. Many of them are fully recovered . . . I think President Xi is working very, very hard. I spoke to him. He's working very hard. I think he's doing a very good job. It's a big problem. But President Xi loves his country. He's working very hard to solve the problem and he will solve the problem.

---

* Memo to the President (published by *Axios* on April 7)

MONDAY, FEBRUARY 24

Dr. Tedros, Director-General, WHO: The sudden increase of cases in Italy, the Islamic Republic of Iran and the Republic of Korea are deeply concerning. There is a lot of speculation about whether this increase means that this epidemic has now become a pandemic. I have spoken consistently about the need for facts, not fear. Using the word pandemic now does not fit the facts, but it may certainly cause fear. This is not the time to focus on what word we use.

Dr. Ryan, Executive Director, Health Emergencies, WHO: Pandemic comes, I think, from the Greek *pan demos*, which means everybody. There must be the population, *pan* meaning everyone. So pan demos is a concept where there's a belief that the whole world's population would likely be exposed to this infection and potentially a proportion of them fall sick . . . so we're in a phase of preparedness for a potential pandemic.

MONDAY, FEBRUARY 24

Mayor Ron Nirenberg, San Antonio, TX: The quarantine has been managed with great care by experts of highly trained professionals. We have had a total of six positive cases to date [in the city] and every precaution has been taken to keep them properly isolated, ensuring that the chances of exposure for others is extremely low. Let's be clear, the most dangerous, damaging infectious disease is hysteria and so what we're trying to do is make sure we have a compassionate human response to a crisis that's happening.

President Trump: The Coronavirus is very much under control in the USA. We are in contact with everyone and all relevant countries. CDC & World Health have been working hard and very smart. Stock Market starting to look very good to me!

Dr. Michael Osterholm, Director, Center for Infectious Disease Research and Policy: It's now clear that the epidemic was never going to be contained.

At most, its spread was slowed by the lockdown imposed in China and other countries' efforts to identify infected people and anyone they might have been in contact with . . . In light of the disease's features, the quarantine of the passengers and crew members on the Diamond Princess cruise ship in Yokohama Bay in Japan looks like a cruel experiment: While confined, these people were forced to breathe recycled air for two weeks. The measure achieved little except to prove just how effective the virus is at spreading. Trying to stop influenza-like transmission is a bit like trying to stop the wind.

FEBRUARY 25

Mayor LaToya Cantrell, New Orleans, LA:* As Mayor of the great City of New Orleans, I invite you to visit our city to experience the excitement of Mardi Gras!

***New Orleans Times-Picayune*:** While large crowds watched the long-running Rex and Zulu parades on the uptown routes, scores of revelers instead chose to spend their Tuesday in a place many maintain is the only one to experience the true Mardi Gras: the French Quarter.

Alex Azar, Secretary of HHS: As of this morning, we still have only 14 cases of the China coronavirus detected here in the United States, involving travel to China or close contacts with those travelers. We have three cases among Americans repatriated from Wuhan and we have 40 cases among American passengers repatriated from the Diamond Princess in Japan.

Larry Kudlow, Director, National Economic Council: We have contained this. I won't say airtight, but pretty close to airtight. We have done a good job in the United States.

---

* This announcement was posted at the start of the season in late January. February 25 was Fat Tuesday, the culmination of Mardi Gras festivities.

Senator Brian Schatz (HI), Subcommittee on Appropriations on Labor, HHS, and Education: The president's budget cuts the infectious disease rapid response reserve fund, the public health preparedness and response fund, hospital preparedness program and the epidemiology and laboratory capacity program. So given everything that's happened over the last 50 days, I want to give you* an opportunity, and given the context here, which is last night, you proposed a $25 billion supplemental, do you want to rescind those cuts to the base budget of your agencies that deal with this problem?

Dr. Anne Schuchat, Principal Deputy Director, CDC: Of course, we've been watching the situation in China closely. And then of course the recent emergence of community spread in Italy and Iran and South Korea have raised questions with people of what might happen here. We want people to be ready in terms of if we do see community spread, what would that mean to you?

President Trump: We have very few people with it, and the people that have it are—in all cases, I have not heard anything other. Maybe there's something new, because for two days, I haven't been seeing too much of that news, of very much news, because [my trip to India] has been very all-encompassing.

Dr. Schuchat, Principal Deputy Director, CDC: Now, it's not so much a question of if this will happen anymore, but rather more a question of exactly when this will happen, and how many people in this country will become infected and how many of those will develop severe or more complicated disease? . . . Based on what we know right now, we believe the immediate risk here in the United States remains low.

---

* Sen. Schatz is questioning HHS Secretary Alex Azar.

Dr. Fauci, Director, NIAID: A standard flu season, seasonal flu, the lethality is 0.1%. Right now, depending upon what the denominator is, the lethality for the current coronavirus infection is somewhere around 2% . . . When you get to the 1918 [flu pandemic], it's 1.5 to 2%.

Alex Azar, Secretary of HHS: We're trying to engage in radical transparency with the American public as we go through this. Each of those messages is accurate but addresses a particular aspect of what we're talking about. So for instance, abroad, this is spreading quite rapidly. In the United States, thanks to the president and this team's aggressive containment efforts, this disease, as Dr. Schuchat said, is contained. We are now two weeks with no additional US-based cases. 14 cases on February 11th, 14 cases today. That is a remarkable level of containment here in the United States.

President Trump: I think that whole situation will start working out. A lot of talent, a lot of brainpower is being put behind it. Two and a half billion dollars we're putting in. I see that Chuck Schumer criticized that. He thought it should be more. And if I gave more, he'd say it should be less. It's automatic, you know, with these characters. They're not—they're just not good for our country. If I gave more, he'd say "it should be less."

FEBRUARY 26

Prime Minister Conte, Italy: It's time to turn down the tone, we need to stop panic . . . Panic is a completely unjustified reaction that compromises the overall efficiency of the system and triggers regrettable speculations on the prices of some products . . . Calm is brought back through punctual and transparent communication.

CDC: The Centers for Disease Control and Prevention (CDC) has confirmed an infection with the virus that causes Covid-19 in California in a person who reportedly did not have relevant travel history or exposure to another known patient with Covid-19. At this time, the patient's exposure is unknown. It's possible this could be an instance of community spread of Covid-19, which would be the first time this has happened in the United States. Community spread means spread of an illness for which the source of infection is unknown.

University of California Davis Health: Today we learned a patient we are treating here at UC Davis Medical Center for the novel coronavirus (Covid-19) is being investigated by the Centers for Disease Control and Prevention (CDC) as possibly the first patient to have received the infection from exposure in the community . . . We requested Covid-19 testing by the CDC, since neither Sacramento County nor the California Department of Public Health is doing testing for coronavirus at this time. Since the patient did not fit the existing CDC criteria for Covid-19, a test was not immediately administered.

Alex Azar, Secretary of HHS: As of today, we have 15 cases of Covid-19 that have been detected in the United States, with only one new case detected in the last two weeks. We also have three cases among Americans repatriated from Wuhan, and 42 cases among Americans repatriated who had been stuck on the Diamond Princess in Japan. The President's early and decisive actions, including travel restrictions, have succeeded in buying us incredibly valuable time.

President Trump: We're rapidly developing a vaccine and they can speak to you, the professionals can speak to you about that. The vaccine is coming along well, and then speaking to the doctors, we think this is something that we can develop fairly rapidly, a vaccine for the future, and coordinate with the support of our partners.

Dr. Fauci, Director, NIAID: So although this is the fastest we have ever gone from a sequence of a virus to a trial, [a vaccine] still would not be applicable to the epidemic unless we really wait about a year to a year and a half. We can't rely on a vaccine over the next several months to a year.

President Trump: Johns Hopkins, I guess, it is a highly respected, great place. They did a study, comprehensive, "The Countries Best and Worst Prepared for an Epidemic" and the United States, we're rated number one. We're rated number one for being prepared.

Johns Hopkins Bloomberg School of Public Health:* National health security is fundamentally weak around the world. No country is fully prepared for epidemics or pandemics, and every country has important gaps to address.

Dr. Messonnier, Director, NCIRD, CDC: As more and more countries experience community spread, successful containment at our borders becomes harder and harder. Ultimately, we expect we will see community spread in this country. It's not so much a question of if this will happen anymore but rather more a question of exactly when this will happen and how many people in this country will have severe illness.

President Trump: I don't think it's inevitable. It possibly will [spread in the U.S.]. It could be at a very small level or it could be at a larger level. Whatever happens, we're totally prepared. It may get bigger, it may get a little bigger. It may not get bigger at all. We'll see what happens, but regardless of what happens, we're totally prepared . . . When you have fifteen people, and the fifteen within a couple of days is going to be down to close to zero, that's a pretty good job we've done.

Rep. Nancy Pelosi (CA), Speaker of the House: I don't think the president knows what he's talking about. Once again.†

---

* This is the study referenced in the President's preceding quote.

† Response to CNN's Manu Raju asking: "Coronavirus is under control, according to the president. Your reaction to that?"

President Trump: I hope that it's going to be a very little problem, but we have to work together instead, [Nancy Pelosi] wants to do that. Same thing with "Cryin'" Chuck Schumer. He goes out and he says, "The president only asked for two and a half billion dollars. He should have eight and a half." This is the first time I've ever been told that we should take more. Usually, it's we have to take less, and we should be working together. He shouldn't be making statements like that, because it's so bad for the country. And Nancy Pelosi—I mean, she should go back to her district and clean it up, because it's the number one—if you look at percentage down, that was one of the finest in the world, and now you look at what's happening. And I'm just saying, we should all be working together. She's trying to create a panic, and there's no reason to panic because we have done so good. These professionals behind me and over here, and over there, and back here, and in some conference rooms—I just left a group of forty-five people that are the most talented people in the world. Parts of the world are asking us, in a very nice way, can they partake and help them. So Nancy Pelosi shouldn't—and she knows it's not true. She knows—all—all they're trying to do is get a political advantage. This isn't about political advantage.

FEBRUARY 27

Governor Gavin Newsom (CA): As of today, at this hour we have 33 confirmed positive tests for the virus. Five individuals have subsequently moved out of state, so there are 28 people that we know in the state of California that are positive . . . We have just a few hundred testing kits in the state of California, and that's surveillance testing as well as diagnostic testing. That's simply inadequate to do justice to the kind of testing that is required to address this issue head on.

President Trump: It's going to disappear. One day—it's like a miracle—it will disappear. And from our shores, we—you know, it could get worse before it gets better. It could maybe go away. We'll see what happens. Nobody really knows.

Gov. Newsom (CA): It's very easy for me, I mean, we're involved [in] 68 lawsuits with the Trump Administration, to find daylight and politicize this. But first and foremost, I'm an American citizen. I'm a father of four. Politics has no place at this moment. We have to meet this moment with a sense of urgency and conviction that transcends politics and transcends pettiness.

Dr. Tedros, Director-General, WHO: This narrowing window of opportunity . . . It's getting even more narrow. Let's use this window of opportunity to mobilize all things. We should do everything, starting from containment, to preparedness for any eventualities, even worst scenario, and give it our best.

Gov. Newsom (CA): The testing protocol is so important. You don't know what you don't know unless you're testing. And so this point cannot be emphasized enough. We should have caregivers, doctors, have the capacity in real time on demand to advance these testing protocols.

Dr. Ryan, Executive Director, Health Emergencies, WHO: I think Maria [Van Kerkhove, WHO Head of Emerging Diseases] spoke about hands to face. I've been looking around the room here. I can't tell you the number of you who've put your hands to your face in the last 20 minutes or half an hour.

Gov. Inslee (WA): I just received a call from @VP Mike Pence, thanking Washington State for our efforts to combat the coronavirus. I told him our work would be more successful if the Trump administration stuck to the science and told the truth.

Stephanie Buhle, Spokesperson, New York City Department of Health: Testing for coronavirus is not available yet in New York City. The kits that were sent to us have demonstrated performance issues and cannot be relied upon to provide an accurate result.

FEBRUARY 28

ProPublica: As the highly infectious coronavirus jumped from China to country after country in January and February, the U.S. Centers for Disease Control and Prevention lost valuable weeks that could have been used to track its possible spread in the United States because it insisted upon devising its own test. The federal agency shunned the World Health Organization test guidelines used by other countries and set out to create a more complicated test of its own that could identify a range of similar viruses. But when it was sent to labs across the country in the first week of February, it didn't work as expected. The CDC test correctly identified Covid-19, the disease caused by the virus. But in all but a handful of state labs, it falsely flagged the presence of the other viruses in harmless samples.

President Trump: I'm going to South Carolina, a big rally. A lot of people—thousands of people outside and it's going to be very exciting . . . We're at the same number [of Covid-19 cases]. A lot of people are getting better. Very much better. The 15 number.

***Science* magazine:** The World Health Organization (WHO) has shipped testing kits to 57 countries. China had five commercial tests on the market 1 month ago and can now do up to 1.6 million tests a week; South Korea has tested 65,000 people so far. The U.S. Centers for Disease Control and Prevention (CDC), in contrast, has done only 459 tests since the epidemic began.

Governor Gretchen Whitmer (MI): While there have been no confirmed cases in Michigan yet, and the current risk of getting coronavirus in the United States is low, we must take an abundance of caution to ensure the safety of our families . . . By activating the State Emergency Operations

Center, we're ensuring that every branch of state government is on alert, and actively coordinating to prevent the spread of Coronavirus if it comes to Michigan. We are taking this step out of an abundance of caution.

Mick Mulvaney, White House Chief of Staff: We took extraordinary steps four or five weeks ago. Why didn't you hear about it? What was going on four or five weeks ago? Impeachment and that's all the feds wanted to talk about. The real news was happening and we were dealing with it in a way that I think you folks would be extraordinarily proud of and serving the nation extraordinarily well. The press was covering it because they thought it would bring down the president. The reason they pay so much attention today it's because this will bring down the president. That's what it's all about.

President Trump: There have been no deaths in the United States at all. A lot of that is attributable to the fact that we closed the border very early. Otherwise, it could be a different story. So we'll—we'll just keep doing a good job. We're ordering a lot of supplies. We're ordering a lot of—a lot of elements that, frankly, we wouldn't be ordering unless it was something like this. But we're ordering a lot of different elements of medical. We are working on cures and we're getting some very good results. As you know, they're working as rapidly as they can on a vaccine for the future.

Senator Kelly Loeffler (GA): Democrats have dangerously and intentionally misled the American people on #Coronavirus readiness. Here's the truth: @realDonaldTrump & his administration are doing a great job working to keep Americans healthy & safe.

President Trump: Well, I think that the media is—yes, I think that CNN is a very disreputable network. I think they're doing everything they can to instill fear in people and I think it's ridiculous. And I think they're very disreputable. And some of the Democrats are doing it the way it should be, but some of them are trying to gain political favor by saying a lot of untruths . . . it's political. It's politics. So, speaking of politics, I'm going to South Carolina. I think we're going to do fantastically there and it will be very interesting to see what happens tomorrow.*

Gov. Cuomo (NY): To be prepared, you have to mobilize multiple systems, right. Just start to run the video tape in your mind. People are coming in to the airport at JFK. They're coming from a place that may have the virus. You now have more countries that have the virus. So more people are coming in.

Governor Kate Brown (OR): Let me be clear, as of today there are zero confirmed cases of coronavirus in Oregon, and the risk to Oregonians of contracting the coronavirus remains low. However, in an escalating global health crisis, we must make sure we are as ready and informed as we can be. The purpose of the Coronavirus Response Team is to ensure we are taking every precaution necessary, in coordination with local health authorities, hospitals, community health partners, and school districts, to make sure that Oregon is fully prepared to respond to any outbreaks of the coronavirus and that Oregonians know how they can keep their families safe.

President Trump: One of my people came up to me and said, "Mr. President, they tried to beat you on Russia, Russia, Russia." That didn't work out too well. They couldn't do it. They tried the impeachment hoax. That was on a perfect conversation. They tried anything. They tried it over and over. They'd been doing it since you got in. It's all turning. They lost. It's all turning. Think of it. Think of it. And this is their new hoax. But we did something that's been pretty amazing. We have fifteen people in this massive country and because of the fact that we went early. We went early,

---

* The South Carolina Democratic Primary was held on February 29.

we could have had a lot more than that. We're doing great. Our country is doing so great. We are so unified. We are so unified.

FEBRUARY 29

Dr. Jeffrey Duchin, Public Health Officer, Seattle, WA: Today Public Health of King County is announcing three new presumptive positive cases of novel coronavirus (Covid-19), including one person who died* . . . two of the current cases are associated with Life Care Nursing Facility, a long-term care facility, in Kirkland, WA. In addition, we are aware of a number of individuals associated with the long-term care facility who are reportedly ill with respiratory symptoms or pneumonia and we're in the process of investigating these symptoms as an outbreak.

Gov. Inslee (WA): I know this news is alarming, but we are doing everything possible to make sure the public is safe. Earlier today I declared an emergency proclamation directing state agencies to use all resources necessary to prepare for and respond to the outbreak. The best thing people can do to help is remain informed and take routine health precautions.

President Trump: We've taken the most aggressive actions to confront the coronavirus. They are the most aggressive taken by any country and we're the number one travel destination anywhere in the world, yet we have far fewer cases of the disease then even countries with much less travel or a much smaller population. As an important part of our efforts, on Monday, I'll be meeting with the largest pharmaceutical companies in the world, actually. They'll be coming to the White House, and we're talking about a vaccine and developing, very quickly—and they've already started working

* At the time, this was thought to be the first U.S. death attributed to Covid-19. A February 6 death in Santa Clara County would later be determined to be the first.

on it—developing, very rapidly, a vaccine for the virus, to combat the virus. And we're having very good initial feedback. But these companies will be coming to the White House on Monday. Tremendous amounts of supplies are already on hand. We have 43 million masks, which is far more than anyone would have assumed we could have had so quickly, and a lot more are coming.

Vice President Mike Pence: And as the President just described, the President took unprecedented action to suspend all travel into the United States from China. Simply had never been done before by any previous administration . . . We are urging Americans to not travel to the areas in Italy and the areas in South Korea that are most affected by the coronavirus.

President Trump: At this moment, we have twenty-two patients in the United States currently that have coronavirus. Unfortunately, one person passed away overnight. She was a wonderful woman, a medically high-risk patient in her late fifties. Four others are very ill, thankfully fifteen are either recovered fully or they're well on their way to recovery.

Alex Azar, Secretary of HHS: The risk to any average American is low from the novel coronavirus. The risk remains low thanks to the unprecedented actions President Trump has taken and the actions he's announcing today. That risk remains low, but this can change rapidly.

Dr. Robert Redfield, Director, CDC: We're going to continue to be transparent in relating that to the American public. But at this stage, again, the risk is low. We need to go on with our normal lives.

MARCH 1

Gov. Cuomo (NY): This evening we learned of the first positive case of novel coronavirus—or Covid-19—in New York State. The patient, a woman in her late thirties, contracted the virus while traveling abroad in Iran, and is currently isolated in her home. The patient has respiratory symptoms, but is not in serious condition and has been in a controlled situation since arriving to New York . . . There is no reason for undue anxiety—the general risk remains low in New York. We are diligently managing this situation and will continue to provide information as it becomes available.

Larry Kudlow, Director, National Economic Council: The virus is not going to sink the American economy. What is, or could, sink the American economy is the socialism coming from our friends on the other side of the aisle. That's the biggest fear that I have.

MONDAY, MARCH 2

Dr. Ryan, Executive Director, Health Emergencies, WHO: Here we have a disease for which we have no vaccine, no treatment. We don't fully understand transmission. We don't fully understand case fatality . . . the [Director-General] said it in this speech, it's not influenza and it's not behaving like influenza. It is behaving like Covid-19. The problem is we don't know exactly how Covid-19 behaves, but we know it's not transmitting in exactly the same way that influenza was . . . You're purely moving in that sense to save as many lives as you can.

Gov. Cuomo (NY): We're extrapolating from what happened in China and other countries. We have the best healthcare system in the world here. And excuse our arrogance as New Yorkers, I speak for the Mayor also on this one, we think we have the best healthcare system on the planet right here in New York. So, when you're saying what happened in other countries vs. what happened here, we don't even think it's going to be as bad as it was in other countries. We are fully coordinated, we are fully mobilized, this is all about mobilization of a public health system.

Dr. Oxiris Barbot, New York City Health Commissioner: We know that there's currently no indication that it's easy to transmit by casual contact, there's no need to do anything special anything in the community. We want New Yorkers to go about their daily lives, ride the subway, take the bus, go see your neighbors.

***MarketWatch*:** Though health officials have warned Americans to prepare for the spread of the novel coronavirus in the U.S., people shouldn't wear face masks to prevent the spread of the infectious illness, according to the Centers for Disease Control and Prevention, the U.S. Department of Health and Human Services and the U.S. surgeon general.

Dr. Tedros, Director-General, WHO: I remember once, this is long time ago. I was very, very young actually. And there was a lot of destabilization in the world, and somebody was asking a question, "When do human beings stand as one?" was the question. And another one was responding—this is in school—"When we have a common enemy from another planet." Why do we need another enemy from another planet to be one, when we have in the same planet a common enemy that could affect us all equally?

Vice President Pence: At the present moment, we have 43 domestic cases of the coronavirus, 48 cases of individuals who've returned to the United States. Of the domestic cases, 29 of the 43 are either in California or Washington State and we have communities that are facing what the experts tell us could potentially be a cluster in those communities. Sadly today, there were four additional fatalities, raising the number that six Americans have lost their life to the coronavirus.

Dr. Ryan, Executive Director, Health Emergencies, WHO: We spend quantums more, thousands, millions times more preparing for every type of other security challenge except a public health one. And we may be paying a heavy price for ignoring preparedness as one of the central measures of human security on this planet.

Dr. Redfield, Director, CDC: The risk to the American people is low . . . And I think the American public should rest assured, we have one of the finest public health programs in the world, when you look at the state and local, territorial.

Dr. Fauci, Director, NIAID: If you talk about the entire country, the whole 360 million people in this country, the risk is a low risk. I think the point you're making is that since we haven't done yet, but will happen really soon, the testing into the community, how do we know the risk is low? I would imagine it's still going to be low regardless of that. What happens in real time, which is the reason why we do this so frequently, is that things can change. But right now, today, on this day, Monday, if you look at the country as a whole, the risk is low.

President Trump: I don't think you'll need that* because I really think we're in, you know, extremely good shape. We're prepared for anything and we could always do that at a later date if we need it, but I don't think we need that at this stage. You know, interestingly, we were discussing—and a question I get asked a lot by people is, on average, you lose from 26,000 to 70,000 or so and even some cases more from the flu. We lose—we have deaths of that per year. Worldwide, it's hundreds of thousands of deaths from the common flu. And they ask, you know, what's the difference and how does this differ, and I guess there are things that are similar and things that are different. Every one of them is different. It might not be a bad question to ask. Because I get that all the time. So, so far we have six here. You have, in other countries, very—I mean, China, obviously, got hit the hardest. I noticed that South Korea is hit very hard. Italy is being hit very hard. But I—I would like to maybe know—because I—I am oftentimes asked—we

---

* Response to unidentified reporter asking: "Are you also considering a national emergency declaration that would allow states and local governments to tap FEMA aid?"

average, I suspect—Tony,* I think you said from around 26 to 27,000, up to 60 or 70,000 deaths per year. That's a lot of deaths. And here we're talking about a much smaller range. Now, hopefully, it stays at a much smaller range. And, again, we're prepared for anything.

MARCH 3

Senator Lamar Alexander (TN), Chair, Committee on Health, Education, Labor and Pensions: Around the world, the spread of the novel Coronavirus is alarming. 90,000 cases in 65 countries, 3,000 deaths, according to the World Health Organization, but most people in the United States are at low risk . . . According to our trade representative, more than 20% of everything we import is from China. Medicines, car parts, cell phones, televisions. China's shut down factories and locked down 16 cities where 760 million people live. Think about that for a moment. 760 million people is more than twice as many people as live in the United States, and they've been locked down in China as China tries to grapple with this.

Dr. Messonnier, Director, NCIRD, CDC: Over the weekend, multiple states announced new presumptive positive cases of Covid-19. As of Monday evening, there were 60 cases.

Dr. Ryan, Executive Director, Health Emergencies, WHO: WHO has no national authority in this area in legal terms. We don't have the right to punish member states for exceeding our travel advice. What we do have is scientific evidence. What we do have, if anything, is a moral authority to advise countries how to best use that evidence. If countries decide to exceed that evidence, there's not a whole lot we can do about that. We can only challenge them, and continue to challenge them on that. But clearly, travel measures by themselves do not represent an adequate response to the spread

---

* Dr. Anthony Fauci

of any infectious disease, and that has increasingly been proven to be true in this event.

Senator Patty Murray (WA), Ranking Member, Committee on Health, Education, Labor and Pensions: And is as so often the case, this public threat will have hidden and higher costs for those who are low wage workers, who don't have affordable childcare, who don't have health insurance, and who are experiencing homelessness. In my home state, people are being told to stay home for two weeks if they are sick. There are no tests, so they can't get tested. Guess who can't stay home? If you don't have childcare, if you're a low wage worker, if you don't have sick leave. When those people's basic needs are not met, they cannot make choices to protect themselves, which means they can't make choices that best protect others too, because one person getting sick has repercussions for all of those around them.

Paul Molinaro, Chief, Operations Support and Logistics, WHO: We're obviously concerned. We're seeing the first initial panic reaction around PPE (Personal Protective Equipment), which we're still frantically trying to address.

National Nurses United: High percentages of hospitals do not have plans, isolation procedures, and policies in place for Covid-19; that communication to staff by employers is poor or nonexistent; that hospitals are lacking sufficient stocks of personal protective equipment (PPE) or are not making current stocks readily available, and have not provided training and practice to staff on how to properly use PPE.

Bonnie Castillo, RN, Executive Director, National Nurses United: This crisis highlights our country's completely fractured health care system and failure to invest in public health. Facilities don't have a plan, or they haven't explained the plan, or they don't have the supplies, equipment, and training to carry out any plan. The outcome of this chaos is that health care workers, patients, and the entire community are exposed to this virus and needlessly put at risk.

Sen. Murray (WA): The administration has had months to prepare for this, and it is unacceptable that people in my state and nationwide can't even get an answer as to whether or not they are infected. To put it simply, if someone at the White House or in this administration is actually in charge of responding to the coronavirus, it would be news to anybody in my state . . . I'm very frustrated at the steps the President has taken, from repeatedly contradicting experts' advice to downplaying the seriousness of this threat, and to appointing a politician to lead the response.

Senator Chris Murphy (CT): I do think it's worth saying that it is pretty extraordinary that we have to have our medical and health professionals counter-message the President of the United States, that they have to spend their time trying to correct the record. We have become normalized to this administration's, to this president's, loose association with the truth, but it becomes particularly dangerous in the middle of a pandemic response.

Senator Tina Smith (MN): We've heard so much misinformation. I mean it's been said that this virus was developed as a tool to wage economic war on the United States. It's been said that this is part of a strategy to try to bring down the economy. It's ridiculous and it's harmful . . . My point is that there's consequence to this misinformation that makes it more difficult for public health professionals to respond and to take care of the population in the ways that we need to. That's what worries me.

Dr. Fauci, Director, NIAID: There are always conspiracy theories when there's a new disease that people are afraid of and that is really novel to them. I have to say, I'm thinking back now about 35 or 37 years ago, I sat in this room trying to explain to the committee then that HIV was not a virus that was developed by the CIA to essentially eliminate certain populations. It's crazy, but this is what happens when you have outbreaks. There's a lot of misinformation.

Senator Pat Roberts (KS): There's a lot of partisan elbows out there right now. We don't need to politicize a pandemic. I would recommend that we monitor what people say . . . maybe we ought to quarantine people for 14 days if they just shut up about the politics and tossing around the partisan things.

Dr. Fauci, Director, NIAID: This is a brand-new virus with which we have no experience. Even though the concept that when warm weather comes, many respiratory viruses diminish, we have no guarantee at all that this is going to happen with this virus.

Senator Mitt Romney (UT): Should our flight attendants not on our instruction tell them not just to fasten in their seatbelt, but that if you cough or sneeze you should cough into fabric or into your sleeve or whatever? I mean, I keep going on an airplane, someone coughs or sneezes and I hear it barking out. It's like my goodness. In a condition like this, just the general flu, given the fact we have the flu going on and colds, should we not be telling people on airplanes, "You may not cough or sneeze unless you're covering your mouth." I think I know the answer to that.

MARCH 4

Gov. Newsom (CA): The number of cases in the state of California is 53. That includes 24 individuals who were repatriated in the state of California, 29 individuals that have subsequently been tested positive . . . We have accordingly, with this new ICU patient that passed away, entered into this new phase. And that has required me under the circumstances to advance a proclamation of a state of emergency in the state of California.

Gov. Cuomo (NY): There is a lot of overlap and this is the most complex case that we have had in terms of the number of interactions. There was the attorney, as you know, who works at the law firm in Manhattan. Family in Westchester, they had attended schools—both Yeshiva University and the SAR school. They had been to synagogue services that had a large number of people. So it is the most complex detective investigation matter . . . And, again, all off this one attorney, 50-year-old, who is the only person to date who is hospitalized because he also had a respiratory illness and we said that is the target, problematic population, right. Senior citizens, immune compromised or underlying illness and especially an underlying respiratory illness.

Rep. Lois Frankel (FL), House Subcommittee on Labor, Health and Human Services, Education, and Related Agencies: I know you're not supposed to touch your face, but is it any part of your face? Where are the germs going? And if someone gets quarantined, how long do they have to get quarantined for? And can there be repeated quarantines? I guess the better question is, do you think this is going to be a widespread issue in our country?*

Rep. Tom Cole (OK), Ranking Member, House Subcommittee on Labor, Health and Human Services, Education, and Related Agencies: The current challenge that we have, frankly, is a reminder that you need to do these things and you need to do them on a regular basis. You can't just show up on game day and think you're going to be able to deal with something. You have to have made the commitments, the investments over a long period of time to have the infrastructure to do it.

***Business Insider*:** Microsoft has asked employees in the Seattle area and San Francisco Bay Area to work from home until March 25, according to

---

* Questioning Dr. Fauci at a hearing held by the House Appropriations Subcommittee on the National Institutes of Health 2021 budget request

an email reviewed by *Business Insider.* Microsoft Executive Vice President Kurt DelBene sent an email asking "all employees who are in a job that can be done from home" to work from home after King County—where Microsoft is based—advised employers on Wednesday to allow remote work.

MARCH 5

Rep. Pelosi (CA): When the President says they're only fifteen and they're four or five times that many at that time, they're more now, that's just not right. And when the President said, go to work, no, there are other guidances that should be out there. And when the President said and he did say, precisely, the Obama administration made a decision on testing that turned out to be very detrimental to what we're doing. He said that Wednesday at a meeting addressing the virus outbreak and we did that decision a few days ago so that the testing can take place in a much more rapid and accurate fashion. While the aid to Senator Lamar Alexander, who's the chair of the committee of jurisdiction said "The administration, the Obama administration made no such rule change" and a policy expert at the association of public health laboratories said, "We aren't sure what rule he was referencing."

Neel V. Patel, *MIT Technology Review*: While other countries have been able to run millions of tests, the CDC has tested only 1,235 patients. Speed is of the essence when dealing with an epidemic early, and the CDC's mistakes are already proving costly to tracking the outbreak in the US.

President Trump: Well, actually, we were given—I think really given tremendous marks—if you look at Gallup poll, you look at other polls—for the way we've handled it. And one of the things I did is I closed down the borders to China and to other areas that are very badly affected and really having a lot of troubles—I mean, countries and areas of countries that have had a lot of problem. And I closed them down very early, against the advice of almost everybody, and we've been given rave reviews. And that's why we have only, right now, 11—it's a lot of people, but it's still 11 people—versus tremendous numbers of thousands of people that have died all over the world. We have 11. We have 149 cases, as of this moment. This morning, it was 129. And I just see—right now it's about 149 cases. There are 100,000 cases all over the world. So we were really given tremendous marks for having made the decision.

Rep. Pelosi (CA): We're very proud that yesterday we came to forehead, a very strong bipartisan piece of legislation, much improved on what was sent to us originally in terms of the appropriation for the Coronavirus.*

President Trump: It's going to all work out. Everybody has to be calm. It's all going to work out.

MARCH 6

President Trump: So I told Mike not to be complimentary of the governor [of Washington State] because that governor is a snake. Okay. Inslee. And I said, "if you're nice to him, he will take advantage." And I would have said no. Let me just tell you, we have a lot of problems with the governor and the governor of Washington that's where you have many of your problems. Okay. So Mike may be happy with him, but I'm not, okay? And he would say that† naturally. And as I said last night at the town hall, if we came up with a cure today, and tomorrow everything is gone, and you went up to this governor—who is a, you know, not a good governor, by the way—if you went up to this governor, and you said to him, "How did Trump do?"—he'd say, "He did a terrible job." It makes no difference.

South by Southwest Festival, Austin, TX: The City of Austin has cancelled the March dates for SXSW and SXSW EDU. SXSW will faithfully follow

---

* H.R. 6074: Coronavirus Preparedness and Response Supplemental Appropriations Act, 2020: This bill provides $8.3 billion in emergency funding for federal agencies to respond to the coronavirus outbreak. (Source: congress.gov)

† See Inslee tweet on February 27

the City's directions. We are devastated to share this news with you, "The show must go on" is in our DNA, and this is the first time in 34 years that the March event will not take place. We are now working through the ramifications of this unprecedented situation.

Maria Morris, Senior Staff Attorney, National Prison Project: Once a contagious illness enters, conditions in correctional facilities are highly conducive to it spreading . . . People in government custody, including in prisons, jails, and civil detention, are often forgotten in emergencies. This creates unnecessary suffering and loss of life. We have the opportunity to take steps now to limit the spread of the virus in prisons, jails, and detention centers. But the time to act for the health of those incarcerated, and for the broader community, is now.

President Trump: They would like to have the people come off [the Grand Princess]. I'd rather have the people stay, but I'd go with them. I told them to make the final decision. I would rather it because I like the numbers being where they are, I don't need to have the numbers double because of one ship that wasn't our fault, and it wasn't the fault of the people on the ship either.

Vice President Pence: As I said yesterday, we've been able to provide tests to all the state jurisdictions and labs that have requested it and I'm pleased to report that all state labs have the test. And now because of the change that President Trump implemented at the FDA a week ago, now state labs can actually conduct coronavirus tests themselves. Beyond that, between March 2nd and 5th, we distributed more than 900,000 tests across the country, including 200,000 that could allow 75 individual patients, 75,000 individual patients to be tested. As the secretary of HHS just described, by tomorrow another 200,000 tests will be shipped, and by the weekend another million tests will be shipped around the country, with the expectation that at the end of next week, four million tests will be shipped.

President Trump: Anybody that wants a test can get a test. That's what the bottom line is.

Robinson Meyer and Alexis C. Madrigal, *Atlantic*: *The Atlantic* could only verify that 1,895 people have been tested for the coronavirus in the United States, about 10 percent of whom have tested positive. And while the American capacity to test for the coronavirus has ramped up significantly over the past few days, local officials can still test only several thousand people a day, not the tens or hundreds of thousands indicated by the White House's promises.

U.S. Bureau of Labor Statistics: Total nonfarm payroll employment rose by 273,000 in February, and the unemployment rate was little changed at 3.5 percent, the U.S. Bureau of Labor Statistics reported today. Notable job gains occurred in health care and social assistance, food services and drinking places, government, construction, professional and technical services, and financial activities.

Sarah Chaney, *Wall Street Journal*: The spread of the novel coronavirus threatens to trigger a sharp pullback in U.S. hiring after the labor market showed signs of picking up earlier this year. Services industries that help drive the U.S. economy—including air transportation, restaurants, entertainment and retail—would suffer the most from the spread of the virus, according to economic research firm Capital Economics. Some of those sectors saw particularly strong job gains in February before cases of the infection began rising in the U.S., according to Friday's jobs report from the Labor Department. Leisure-and-hospitality companies added 51,000 jobs in February, and restaurants added 53,000 to payrolls.

MARCH 7

Jason Horowitz, *New York Times*: Italy's government early Sunday took the extraordinary step of locking down much of the country's north, restricting movement for about a quarter of the Italian population in regions that serve as the country's economic engine. The move represents the most sweeping effort outside China to stop the spread of the coronavirus, and is tantamount to sacrificing the Italian economy in the short term to save it from the ravages of the virus in the long term.

Tim Killian, Public Liaison, Life Care Center, Kirkland, WA: As of February 19, we have 120 residents at Life Care Kirkland. 54 of them have been transferred to various hospitals throughout the area. The numbers of deaths since February 19 associated with this facility are 26 . . . The current number of residents that remain in the facility are 63. Of those, 6 are currently showing symptoms . . . On 2/19 there were 180 employees associated with Life Care Kirkland. Of that number, 70 now show symptoms.*

President Trump: No, [the testing system is] performing very well, and it has been performing very well. And as you said, you had two of the three that worked perfectly. And that's all you need is two of the three. In fact, you could have one of the three and it will work. So he had two of the three, but now it's performing perfectly in all places . . . Anybody that wants a test can get a test. That's what the bottom line is.

Alex Azar, Secretary of HHS: You may not get a test unless a doctor or public health official prescribes a test. That is our medical system in the United States, in the same way that you may not get a cardiac medicine if your doctor doesn't prescribe that.

Dr. Stephen Hahn, Commissioner, FDA: There were manufacturing problems with the CDC test. While those issues have been resolved, at the time, this created complications for expanding access for public health

---

* The number of Covid deaths at Life Care Center rose to forty by April 2. According to *Business Insider*, "At one point, the [nursing] home in Washington-state accounted for 60% of the US virus death toll by itself."

laboratories and other developers who might use the CDC test as the basis for development of their own test . . . As of today, the CDC test shipped to public health labs has been able to test more than 3,500 specimens from 1,583 patients.

Dr. Redfield, Director, CDC: We still have only around 200 cases that we've diagnosed in the United States. We're going to see more cases because we're getting more diagnostics out there. But I would say that—again, what I said before that—that, at the present time, the general risk to the American public remains low.

MARCH 8

Gov. Cuomo (NY): The other confusion that has been created and I think which fuels fear in people. President of the United States says, "Anyone who wants a test can have a test." Vice President of the United States says, "We don't have the testing capacity." People say, "How can you say both things?" You can't say both things. We don't have the testing capacity that we need. Not everyone who wants a test can have a test.

Reporter #1:* Are you going to continue hold rallies and are you taking any precautions with the White House staff?

President Trump:† Well, we'll have tremendous rallies. And we're doing very well. And we've done a fantastic job with respect to that subject on the virus. Yeah.

Reporter #2: How concerned are you that coronavirus—

President Trump: We've had tremendous cooperation with other countries and all over the world. And we've made it very, very tough. Very strong. Very stringent borders.

---

* White House Press Corps reporters were off camera (at Mar-a-Lago) and unidentified.

† Direct exchanges

Reporter #3: Are you concerned that the virus is getting closer to the White House and D.C.?

President Trump: No, I'm not concerned at all. No, I'm not. No, we've done a great job. Thank you very much.

Mayor Bill de Blasio, New York City: As of yesterday, we had twelve positive cases since the beginning of this crisis. There is one new one and I'm going to say up front we are gathering information on this new case. We need a little more time to get all the facts 100 percent clear. So, we'll have an update on the new case later on today. I can only tell you, tell you in New York City, in the Bronx, but I want to get all the facts straight before we give you more. So, twelve as of yesterday plus one, thirteen as of today, seven new cases since Friday.

Gov. Cuomo (NY): We are trying to contain the spread of the virus. How do you contain the spread of the virus? By testing as many people as you can. Find the positives and then isolate the positive people. That is how you contain the spread of the virus.

MONDAY, MARCH 9

Prime Minister Conte (Italy): I am about to sign a decree that we can describe as "stay at home." All movement across the country is to be avoided unless motivated by three specific circumstances. Reasons of work, reasons of necessity, or health reasons. It is prohibited to gather in and outside bars open to the public.

Dr. Tedros, Director-General, WHO: Over the weekend we crossed 100,000 reported cases of Covid-19 in 100 countries. It's certainly troubling that so many people and countries have been affected so quickly. Now that the virus has a foothold in so many countries, the threat of a pandemic has become very real. But it would be the first pandemic in history that could be controlled. The bottom line is we're not at the mercy of the virus.

Governor John Bel Edwards (LA): Just minutes ago while I was on a conference call with Vice President Mike Pence on the coronavirus, I learned that we have a presumptive positive case here in Louisiana . . . Now is the time for seriousness, there is no place for panic or hysteria.

Vice President Pence: As I stand before you today, the risk of contracting the coronavirus to the American public remains low, and the risk of serious disease among the American public also remains low . . . My mother is 88 years young. My stepfather is about the same age. This is just a really good time, what Dr. Fauci tells us, what the experts tell us is, is to look after family members, loved ones who are senior citizens, and particularly those who have serious underlying health conditions.

Alex Azar, Secretary of HHS: We now have a total of 2.1 million tests that are available, either shipped, or waiting to be shipped, or waiting to be ordered. We, by the end of this week, expect to be able to be producing up to four million tests per week in the United States.

Robinson Meyer and Alexis C. Madrigal, *Atlantic*: Nearly two weeks after the new coronavirus was first found to be spreading among Americans, the United States remains dangerously limited in its capacity to test people for the illness, an ongoing investigation from *The Atlantic* has found. After surveying local data from across the country, we can only verify that 4,384 people have been tested for the coronavirus nationwide, as of Monday at 4 P.M. eastern time. These data are as comprehensive a compilation of official statistics as currently possible.

President Trump: So last year 37,000 Americans died from the common Flu. It averages between 27,000 and 70,000 per year. Nothing is shut down, life & the economy go on. At this moment there are 546 confirmed cases of CoronaVirus, with 22 deaths. Think about that!

Mayor de Blasio, New York City: Certainly a lot of people would say all over this country that we haven't gotten the answers we would have liked to have seen from our federal government. But that being said, I think there's a bigger truth about the coronavirus and what we're experiencing here, which is that ultimately the people will be the solution.

Senator Bernie Sanders (VT): Think about the insanity of a system where today somebody wakes up and maybe they think they have the symptoms of a Coronavirus, yet they cannot afford to go to a doctor. What does that mean? So they're going to go to work and make a serious epidemic even worse . . . Trump's people were saying just a little while ago, that, yeah, we're working on a vaccine. Hopefully, they are. But, this is how crazy it is. We couldn't guarantee that when that vaccine is developed, they couldn't guarantee that people would be able to afford it. This is how sick this system is. Let me tell you, if elected president, everybody in this country will get that vaccine, absolutely free.

MARCH 10

President Trump: This was something that came out of China, and it hit us and many other countries. You look at the numbers; I see the numbers with just by watching you folks. I see it—it's over one hundred different countries. And it hit the world. And we're prepared, and we're doing a great job with it. And it will go away. Just stay calm. It will go away.

Rep. Hakeem Jeffries (NY): Thousands have died #Coronavirus. The stock market has collapsed. Recession may be imminent. And the so-called President spent the weekend at a Florida golf resort. Pathetic.

Rep. Rosa DeLauro (CT), Chair, Subcommittee on Labor, Health and Human Services, Education, and Related Agencies: The Executive Office for Immigration Review, which falls under the Department of Justice, told all judges and staff members in an email Monday that all of the Coronavirus posters, which explain in English and Spanish how to prevent catching and spreading the virus, had to be removed immediately. I just wanted to say that whatever one's view is on any issue that we face in this nation, whatever your personal views are, whatever your ideology is, that we cannot, we cannot in this public health crisis play fast and loose with people's health, no matter what we believe. It is a moral responsibility for us to make sure that everyone is protected.

Dr. Redfield, Director, CDC: We obviously got first notification of this new disease on, actually New Year's Eve, December 31st, in Korea and China. And the Chinese fairly rapidly published the genetic sequence at the end of the first week of January. We actually worked at CDC based on that, and it created a diagnostic test that really, I think, tested the first person in January 17th. So fairly quickly, we had a diagnostic test up and running at the CDC, which is our job, to get that technology available for the public health laboratories of the country.

Rep. DeLauro (CT): I'm very concerned, and I think we all are, about our nation's testing capabilities for Coronavirus. Other countries have been testing thousands of people for weeks, but the US is woefully behind the curve. The low number of positive tests in the US is likely a byproduct of under testing, as opposed to an accurate count of the prevalence of Coronavirus in the United States. My understanding is that the testing kits are now being distributed across the country, and commercial firms are involved as well, but the delay has been unacceptable.

Dr. Fauci, Director, NIAID: As of this morning, there was 712 [cases], I believe, with 27 deaths guaranteed by the time of this evening, that's going to be up, and there'll be several more, and tomorrow there'll be several more. And there are a number of things that one can do in order to blunt it. If you look at the curves of outbreaks, they go big peaks and then they come down. What we need to do is flatten that down . . . [Y]ou have to start taking seriously what you can do now that if and when the infections will come, and they will come, sorry to say, sad to say they will, but when you're dealing with an infectious disease, we always have that metaphor that people talk about that Wayne Gretzky, he doesn't go where the puck is, he's going where the puck is going to be. Well, we want to be where the infection is going to be as well as where it is.

Alex Azar, Secretary of HHS: As of noon Pacific, we had 548 individuals who have been offloaded from the [Grand Princess]. 228 Canadians are already back in Canada, flown there, I believe it was overnight. 171 Californians were taken by the government of California and are now at Travis Air Base. 26 individuals were sick and they are being treated for various, it could be from the novel Coronavirus. It could also just be we had some frail individuals who are sick that needed treatment.

Dr. Jerome Adams, U.S. Surgeon General: Know your circumstances. Are you in an environment where you can telework? Are you planning on going to large gatherings, like church? Do you live in a community that is being particularly impacted by the coronavirus? You can find out this information from your state or local health department. Does your state have a hotline that you can call into to help you assess symptoms? Again, knowing your circumstances.

Vice President Pence: As the President said, anyone who, on a doctor's order, wants to be tested can at a doctor's indication be tested now. We're working to fill that need and we're making great progress every single day . . . We would be in a very different place if President Trump had not suspended all travel from China. And we would also, I suspect, be in a very different place if we hadn't issued travel advisories for portions of Italy, or portions of South Korea and initiated a screening of all passengers on all direct flights into the United States from both of those countries.

Dr. Fauci, Director, NIAID: I mean I think for the country right now to say we're going to close all the schools in the country, I don't think would be appropriate. Would school closures be appropriate depending upon not whether you have already the horse is out of the barn, but when you start to see we're getting a little bit danger here, so let's do it.

Larry Kudlow, Director, National Economic Council: Let me just say, coming into this difficult period, the economy is in fundamentally good shape. We saw a blockbuster jobs report last Friday . . . The unemployment remains low at 3.5%. Other indicators look pretty good. We had a lot of momentum in the first quarter, good thing . . . And again, I will repeat the President's words. It just struck me as his determination. He intends to bring the full power of the federal government to deal with these health and economic challenges.

Gov. Cuomo (NY): We have 173 cases. Only 14 people are in the hospital. Well, how can that be? Because people are at home recovering from flu-like symptoms. 14 out of 173. If you look at the 14, most of the 14 are members of that vulnerable community. Again, you want to put this all in perspective, the single best way to put it in perspective is the Johns Hopkins tally, which has tallied all of the cases since China. 114,000 cases. That's China, that's South Korea, that's Italy, that's the United States. 4,000 deaths, again, in the vulnerable population. 64,000 people recovered. 46,000 cases still pending, people getting treatment, or people at home. That's the entirety of the universe . . . Much of the transmission tends to happen on a geographic basis. Kids go to school, kids go to a store, parents go to a store, parents walk down the block, shake hands with someone. Parent is walking the dog, meets somebody, says hello, has a conversation.

Vice President Pence: Well, look, as the President has said in our line of work, you shake hands when someone wants to shake your hand and I expect the President will continue to do that. I'll continue to do it.

Gov. Cuomo (NY): The period would be from March 12 this Thursday, a two-week period where facilities within that area [of New Rochelle, a suburb of New York City] and schools within that area would be closed for two weeks. We'll go in, we'll clean the schools, and assess the situation. This will be a period of disruption for the local community. I understand that. Local shop owners don't like the disruption. Nobody does. Local politicians don't like the disruption. I get it. This can't be a political decision this is a public health decision. It's not a decision that I am making. I'm making, accepting the recommendation of [New York State Health Commissioner] Dr. Zucker. In a situation like this, whether you're president, mayor, governor, let the experts decide and let the science drive the decision. When you politically interfere in science, that's when you tend to make a mistake.

MARCH 11

Dr. Tedros, Director-General, WHO: In the past two weeks, the number of cases of Covid-19 outside China has increased 13-fold, and the number of affected countries has tripled. There are now more than 118,000 cases in 114 countries, and 4,291 people have lost their lives. Thousands more are fighting for their lives in hospitals. In the days and weeks ahead, we expect to see the number of cases, the number of deaths, and the number of affected countries climb even higher. WHO has been assessing this outbreak around the clock and we are deeply concerned both by the alarming levels of spread and severity, and by the alarming levels of inaction. We have therefore made the assessment that Covid-19 can be characterized as a pandemic. Pandemic is not a word to use lightly or carelessly. It is a word that, if misused, can cause unreasonable fear, or unjustified acceptance that the fight is over, leading to unnecessary suffering and death.

Prime Minister Angela Merkel, Germany: When the virus is out there, the population has no immunity and no therapy exists, then 60 to 70% of the population will be infected . . . The process has to be focused on not overburdening the health system by slowing the virus's spread. It's about winning time.

Rep. Gerry Connolly (VA), House Committee on Oversight and Reform: Was it a mistake, Dr. Fauci, do you believe, to dismantle the office within the National Security Council charged within global health and security?

Dr. Fauci, Director, NIAID:* I wouldn't necessarily characterize it as a mistake. I would say we worked very well with that office. It would be nice if the office was still there.

Dr. Osterholm, Director, Center for Infectious Disease Research and Policy: We are worse off today than we were in 2017 because the health care system is stretched thinner now than ever. There is no excess capacity. And public health funding has been cut under this administration . . . In the US—and in other upper and middle-income countries—we may expect to see a case fatality rate equal to or higher to what we see in China.

Dow Constantine, County Executive, King County, WA: Governor Inslee has ordered the prohibition of gatherings of more than 250 people. In addition, we also agreed that gatherings smaller than that should not happen unless very clear Public Health-recommended steps are taken Our Public Health Officer, Dr. Jeff Duchin, will be signing an order that prohibits smaller events of 250 people or less in King County, unless they meet public health guidelines to ensure social distancing, adequate sanitation, regular health checks of employees, and other measures designed to prevent the virus from being transmitted.

Mayor de Blasio, NYC: You don't get this disease by eating food in a restaurant or you know, eating takeout or drinking something. It is neutralized in your digestive system. You get it through cough, sneeze, or spit and you know, through people talking in spit coming out inadvertently for example. And it has to go directly into your mouth, nose, or eyes. So people

---

* Direct exchange

should go out and continue to live life, should go out to restaurants, and obviously we don't want any discrimination.

Gov. Cuomo (NY): While the risk to New Yorkers remains low, we are taking a number of steps out of an abundance of caution to protect public health . . . At the same time, we're continuing to prioritize ramping up testing capacity because the more people you identify as having the virus, the better you can contain it. We're also leading by example and providing paid leave to all state workers who are quarantined as a result of the virus—and we encourage businesses to voluntarily do telecommuting to the extent possible. Again, I want to remind people to keep this in perspective: the facts do not justify the fear in this situation and the facts here should actually reduce anxiety.

Marc Perrone, President, United Food and Commercial Workers (UFCW): Nearly 80 million American workers—or 59 percent of the entire U.S. workforce—are hourly employees who only get paid for the hours they work. As the financial impact of the coronavirus is felt across every community, these hard-working men and women are on the front lines. I am urging each of our nation's elected leaders to develop immediate policies that ensure that workers—salaried and hourly—do not have to choose between work and their health. These policies should not only protect workers against financial loss (from loss of hours or job loss), but should further ensure that workers seek out immediate medical attention if they feel sick or believe they have been exposed to the coronavirus.

Dr. Fauci, Director, NIAID, NIH: I think you set the gauges that this is a really serious problem, we have to take seriously.* People always say, "well, the flu, you know, the flu does it, the flu does that." The flu has a mortality

* In reply to Rep. Michael Cloud (TX): "I'm trying to assess where the American people should set their gauges."

of 0.1%. This is ten times that. That's the reason I want to emphasize we have to stay ahead of the game.

Former Governor Matt Bevin (KY): Chicken Little has just confirmed that the sky IS indeed falling . . . Everyone is advised to take cover immediately and to bring lots of toilet paper with them when they do so.

Office of the Mayor, San Francisco, CA: Mayor London N. Breed today announced that the Health Officer of the City and County of San Francisco will issue a Public Health Order prohibiting all large group events of 1,000 or more persons. This measure is necessary to slow the spread of novel coronavirus (Covid-19) in the community and builds on the City's March 6th public health recommendations.

Golden State Warriors, National Basketball Association: Due to escalating concerns about the spread of the coronavirus, and in consultation with the City and County of San Francisco, tomorrow night's game vs. the Nets at Chase Center will be played without fans. Fans with tickets to this game will receive a refund in the amount paid.

President Trump: Taking early intense action, we have seen dramatically fewer cases of the virus in the United States than are now present in Europe. The European Union failed to take the same precautions and restrict travel from China and other hot spots. As a result, a large number of new clusters in the United States were seeded by travelers from Europe. After consulting with our top government health professionals, I have decided to take several strong but necessary actions to protect the health and well-being of all Americans. To keep new cases from entering our shores, we will be suspending all travel from Europe to the United States for the next 30 days.* The new rules will go into effect Friday at midnight. These restrictions will be adjusted subject to conditions on the ground.

---

* The actual order from DHS, which is less broad, follows.

U.S. Department of Homeland Security: Today President Donald J. Trump signed a Presidential Proclamation, which suspends the entry of most foreign nationals who have been in certain European countries at any point during the 14 days prior to their scheduled arrival to the United States. These countries, known as the Schengen Area, include: Austria, Belgium, Czech Republic, Denmark, Estonia, Finland, France, Germany, Greece, Hungary, Iceland, Italy, Latvia, Liechtenstein, Lithuania, Luxembourg, Malta, Netherlands, Norway, Poland, Portugal, Slovakia, Slovenia, Spain, Sweden, and Switzerland. This does not apply to legal permanent residents, (generally) immediate family members of U.S. citizens, and other individuals who are identified in the proclamation.

MARCH 12

Governor Mike DeWine (OH): We have today again consulted with experts, so we are announcing today that children in the state will have an extended spring break of 3 weeks. We will review it afterwards. This will begin on Monday. We will continue to consult with educators on this. We have to take this action. We have to do everything we can to slow down the spread of this virus. We know Covid-19 will spread, but by slowing it down it'll allow our healthcare system to work. We don't want our healthcare providers to have to make the decision of who lives and who dies. We know this will impact families. We understand the sacrifice this will entail, but this is the right thing to do. We have a responsibility to save lives. We could have waited to close schools, but based on advice from health experts, this is the time to do it.

Mayor Steve Fulop, Jersey City, NJ: The logic here is simple, if the conversation federally and at the state level is around closing schools, or what we would classify as controlled environments, in order to limit the spread of the virus, wouldn't logic lead us to make sure we are also thinking about large uncontrolled environments until we have more answers? . . . We are going to be saying to a nightclub or a bar that it's lights out at 10 P.M., before the big crowds start to get there at 11, 12, 1 and 2. Jersey City has started to attract a lot of people for nightlife from New York, from elsewhere. We're going to put some restrictions on that, because we think it's a reasonable and it's in best interest of the public health.

Mayor Mike Duggan, Detroit: I said yesterday the key to slowing the spread of the coronavirus is with us, being responsible neighbors to each other. And today the Detroit Pistons showed us what being responsible neighbors really is. The steps they took today were just extremely positive. And so many of you know what happened last Saturday night. The Utah Jazz played the Pistons at Little Caesars Arena. Two Jazz players, Rudy Gobert and Donovan Mitchell subsequently were diagnosed with Covid-19 . . . Playing in the NBA, up against the player, is exactly the kind of high-risk activity that can lead to the spread of the disease. The NBA did the right thing in suspending the season.

Dr. Fauci, Director, NIAID: The system is not really geared to what we need right now, what you are asking for.* That is a failing. Let's admit it. The fact is, the way the system was set up, the public health component that Dr. Redfield was talking about, was a system where you put it out there in the public and a physician asks for it and you get it. The idea of anybody getting it easily the way people in other countries are doing it—we're not set up for that. Do I think we should be? Yes. But we're not.

President Trump: They have a million tests out now. They're going to have—over the next few days, they're going to have 4 million tests out. And, frankly, the testing has been going very smooth. If you go to the right agency, if you go to the right area, you get the test.

***Time* magazine:** As of March 11, CDC, state and public health labs have conducted more than 11,000 tests since mid-January. By comparison,

---

* Representative Debbie Wasserman Schultz (FL) was questioning CDC director Redfield: "I'm asking for a name. Who is in charge of making sure that people who need to get tested who are indicated to be tested can get a test? Who?" Dr. Fauci responded.

South Korea has tested more than 200,000 of its population of 51 million since January.

Sen. Mitt Romney (UT): Our system has just not been up to snuff and I think a lot of people are frustrated by it. I'm one of them.

Senator Richard Blumenthal (CT): I am appalled and astonished that we have lost a critical two months there's still no plan, no strategy, for testing for ventilators, for the basics that are required for people to survive. We're talking about life and death and there's still no plan.

Senator Marco Rubio (FL), Chair, Senate Committee on Small Business and Entrepreneurship: One of the reasons why we've struggled to produce the testing kits is because we rely on foreign producers for the chemicals that are needed to make them. And there's a growing shortage because more people are testing, and as I said earlier, the countries that have it are going to be less willing to provide it . . . Today, 80% of the active pharmaceutical ingredients in the United States and the drugs that are here are sourced somewhere else, and a lot of that is China. And now, in the face of the pandemic, as I said, the absence of this capacity in the medical sector is endangering our healthcare system.

Alexandre de Juniac, Director-General and CEO, IATA: These are extraordinary times and governments are taking unprecedented measures. Safety—including public health—is always a top priority. Airlines are complying with these requirements. Governments must also recognize that airlines—employing some 2.7 million people—are under extreme financial and operational pressures. They need support.

Disney World Resorts: While there have been no reported cases of Covid-19 at Disneyland Resort, after carefully reviewing the guidelines of the Governor of California's executive order and in the best interest of our guests and employees, we are proceeding with the closure of Disneyland

Park and Disney California Adventure, beginning the morning of March 14 through the end of the month.

***Wall Street Journal*:** U.S. stocks plunged Thursday in their worst day since the 1987 crash. The Dow Jones Industrial Average fell 10%, and the S&P 500 and Nasdaq tumbled nearly as much to join the Dow in a bear market.

MARCH 13

President Trump: To unleash the full power of the federal government in this effort today, I am officially declaring a National Emergency. Two very big words. The action I am taking will open up access to up to 50 billion dollars of very important and a large amount of money for states and territories and localities in our shared fight against this disease.

Rep. Pelosi (CA): Sadly and prayerfully, we have learned of the tragic deaths of at least 41 Americans from this public health emergency so far. The American people expect and deserve a coordinated science-based and whole of government response to keep them and their loved ones safe. A response that puts families first to stimulate the economy. To put families first, last week the House passed a strong bipartisan 8.3 billion dollar emergency funding package of entirely new funds.

***Washington Post*:** Senate Majority Leader Mitch McConnell (R-Ky) was absent from negotiations on a coronavirus relief package, spending Friday in Kentucky at a judicial event with Supreme Court Justice Brett M. Kavanaugh. As a pandemic sweeps the globe, creating economic and health care panic, McConnell shuttered the Senate for the weekend on Thursday, leaving it to House Speaker Nancy Pelosi (D-Calif.) and Treasury Secretary Steven Mnuchin to reach a deal on legislation in response to the crisis.

President Trump: Today we are announcing a new partnership with* private sector to vastly increase and accelerate our capacity to test for the Coronavirus. We want to make sure that those who need a test can get a test very safely, quickly and conveniently . . . We therefore expect up to a half a million additional tests will be available early next week. The FDA's goal is to hopefully authorize your application within 24 hours. It'll go very quickly. It's going very quickly. Which will bring additionally 1.4 million tests on board next week and five million within a month. I doubt we'll need anywhere near that.

Vice President Pence: After you tapped me to lead the White House Corona Task Force, Mr. President, you said this is all hands on deck and you directed us to immediately reach out to the American business sector, commercial labs to meet what we knew then would be the need for testing across the spectrum. And today, with this historic public-private partnership, we have laid the foundation to meet that need. For Americans looking on, by this Sunday evening, we'll be able to give specific guidance on when the website will be available. You can go to the website, as the President said. You'll type in your symptoms and be given direction whether or not a test is indicated. And then at the same website you'll be directed to one of these incredible companies that are going to give a little bit of their parking lot so that people can come by and do a drive by test. And they're going to literally make, literally make hundreds and thousands of tests available and being processed with results to patients in the very near future.

Covid Tracking Project: U.S. Tests as of March 13: 16,665.

President Trump: Google is helping to develop a website. It's going to be very quickly done, unlike websites of the past, to determine whether a test is warranted and to facilitate testing at a nearby convenient location. And

* *Sic*

we have many, many locations behind us, by the way. We cover this country and large parts of the world, by the way. We're not going to be talking about the world right now. But we cover very, very strongly our country. Stores in virtually every location. Google has 1,700 engineers working on this right now. They've made tremendous progress . . . We can learn, and we will turn a corner on this virus. Some of the doctors say it will wash through and will flow through, in interesting terms, very accurate. I think you're going to find in a number of weeks, it's going to be a very accurate term.

Dr. Fauci, Director, NIAID: The containment, the mitigation, so that as I've said, many times, that curve that I refer to that goes up. We don't want to have that curve. We want to suppress it down to that small mound and I think what we've done today is something that is going to be a very important element in having us be successful in doing that. We still have a long way to go. There will be many more cases, but we'll take care of that.

Kristen Welker, NBC News: Dr. Fauci said earlier this week that the lag in testing was in fact, failing. Do you take responsibility for that? And when can you guarantee that every single American who needs a test will be able to have a test? What's the date of that?

President Trump:* Yeah. No, I don't take responsibility at all because we were given a set of circumstances, and we were given rules, regulations and specifications from a different time. It wasn't meant for this kind of an event with the kind of numbers that we're talking about. And what we've done is, redesigned it very quickly with the help of the people behind me. We're now in very, very strong shape. I think we'll be announcing, as I said, Sunday night. This will start very quickly. We'll have the ability to do in the millions [tests] over a very, very quick period of time.

* Direct exchange

President Trump: If you go back to the swine flu, it was nothing like this. They didn't do testing like this. And actually, they lost approximately 14,000 people. And they didn't do the testing. They started thinking about testing when it was far too late. What we've done and one of the reasons I think people are respecting what we've done, we've done it very early. We've gotten it very early, and we've also kept a lot of people out. Well, ask them how they did. with the swine flu. It was a disaster . . . They had a very big failure with swine flu, a very big failure.

Yamiche Alcindor, PBS: My first question is, you said that you don't take responsibility, but you did disband the White House pandemic office and the officials that were working in that office left this administration abruptly, so what responsibility do you take to that? The officials that worked in that office said that the White House lost valuable time because that office wasn't disbanded. What do you make of that?

President Trump:* I just think it's a nasty question, because what we've done is—and Tony [Fauci] had said numerous times that we've saved thousands of lives because of the quick closing. When you say "me," I didn't do it. We have a group of people I could ask, perhaps in my administration, but I could perhaps ask Tony about that, because I don't know anything about it. You say we did that. I don't know anything about it.

Alcindor: You don't know about the reorganization that happened at the National Security Council?

Trump: It's the administration. Perhaps they do that. People let people go. You used to be with a different newspaper than you are now. Things like that happen.

---

* Direct exchange

MARCH 14

Prime Minister Pedro Sánchez, Spain: On March 11, 2020, the World Health Organization elevated the public health emergency situation caused by Covid-19 to an international pandemic. The rapid evolution of events, at the national and international levels, requires the adoption of immediate and effective measures to face this situation. The extraordinary circumstances that arise constitute, without a doubt, an unprecedented health crisis and of enormous magnitude both due to the very high number of citizens affected and the extraordinary risk to their rights . . . In order to face this serious and exceptional situation, it is essential to proceed to the declaration of the state of alarm.

Gov. Cuomo (NY): From my point of view, the main negative on closing the New York City school system is the possible effect on losing workers because they have to stay home and take care of their children. The most pressing issue of workers staying home are healthcare workers. Again, this is all going to come down to a hospital crisis, assuming we can't get the spread rate of the disease down.

President Trump: I was honored to see that the stock market, you were mostly there with us, set a record in a short period of time, over a 45 minute period that we had the press conference yesterday in the Rose Garden. That was a record, all time record. I think we should do one of them every day perhaps. How about five times a day? We'll do one five times a day. But that was something to watch and I had no idea. We walked back. I said, "So how did that work out?" They said, "Sir, you just set a new record in the history of the stock market." So that was pretty good.

THE LOCKDOWN

MARCH 15–APRIL 19

MARCH 15

Dr. Fauci, Director, NIAID: I think Americans should be prepared that they're going to have to hunker down significantly more than we as a country are doing.

Gov. Newsom (CA): We are calling for the home isolation of all seniors in the State of California . . . We recognize that social isolation for millions of Californians is anxiety inducing, but we recognize what all of the science bears out and what we recognize around the rest of the world that we need to meet this moment head on and lean in, not isolate ourselves to this moment, but lean in and own this moment and take actions that we think are commensurate with the need to protect the most vulnerable Californians.

Mayor de Blasio, New York City: This is a decision that I have taken with no joy whatsoever, with a lot of pain, honestly, because it's something I could not in a million years have imagined having to do. But we are dealing with a challenge and a crisis that we have never seen in our lifetimes and is only just begun. So, I regret to have to announce that as of tomorrow, our public schools will be closed. In other words, to all parents who are hearing this now, there was no school tomorrow and we will be suspending our public schools until after the spring vacation . . . I have been very honest about the fact that there is a real possibility that by closing our schools now we may not have the opportunity to reopen them in this full school year.

Gov. Newsom (CA): Number two, we are directing at all bars, nightclubs, wineries, brewpubs and the like be closed in the State of California. We believe that this is a non-essential function in our state, and we believe that is appropriate under the circumstances to move in that direction. As it relates to restaurants, we have more nuanced concerns and considerations. Some have suggested just shutting down all of our restaurants. We don't believe ultimately that is necessary at this moment.

Governor Kevin Stitt (OK): Eating with my kids and all my fellow Oklahomans at the @CollectiveOKC. It's packed tonight!

Rep. Devin Nunes (CA): There's a lot of concerns with the economy here, because people are scared to go out. But I will just say, one of the things you can do, if you're healthy, you and your family, it's a great time to just go out, go to a local restaurant, likely you can get in, get in easily. Let's not hurt the working people in this country that are relying on wages and tips to keep their small business going.

MONDAY, MARCH 16

Imperial College London, UK: In the (unlikely) absence of any control measures or spontaneous changes in individual behaviour, we would expect a peak in mortality (daily deaths) to occur after approximately 3 months. In such scenarios, we predict 81% of the GB and US populations would be infected over the course of the epidemic . . . In total, in an unmitigated epidemic, we would predict approximately 510,000 deaths in [Great Britain] and 2.2 million in the US, not accounting for the potential negative effects of health systems being overwhelmed on mortality.

Dr. Deborah Birx, White House Coronavirus Response Coordinator: So, we had new information coming out from a model, and what had the biggest impact in the model is social distancing, small groups, not going in public in large groups. But the most important thing was if one person in the household became infected, the whole household self-quarantined for 14 days. Because that stops 100 percent of the transmission outside of the household. And as we talked about early on, it's silent.

Dr. Nasia Safdar, Medical Director of Infection Control, University of Washington: Social distancing is the practice of limiting contact with others. It's a recommended measure and really important to prevent the spread of Covid-19. The U.S. is just in the beginning phases of Covid-19 and as we have seen from other countries, social distancing has been a measure that has helped to interrupt or slow or prevent the transmission of the disease. It is one thing that is in our control today and it requires that you limit your contact with other people. The distance that's necessary to achieve social distancing is at least six feet . . . for Covid-19, and influenza, where the transmission is via droplet, this is likely to be a very effective measure.

Dr. Tedros, Director-General, WHO: You cannot fight a fire blindfolded. And we cannot stop this pandemic if we don't know who is infected . . . We have a simple message for all countries: test, test, test. Test every suspected case.

Sen. Romney (UT): Every American adult should immediately receive a one-time check for $1,000 to help ensure families and workers can meet their short-term obligations and increase spending in the economy. Congress took similar action during the 2001 and 2008 recessions. While expansions of paid leave, unemployment insurance, and SNAP benefits are crucial, the check will help fill the gaps for Americans that may not quickly navigate different government options.

MARCH 17

Gov. Cuomo (NY): Remember those snow globes when you were a kid and you shook the globe and this snow went all over and the whole picture changed as soon as you picked up and shook that snow globe? Somebody picked up our country and just shook it and turned it upside down and it's all chaotic, and things are flying all over, and there's new information and there's mixed information and people don't know what to do and businesses are closing and the rules change every minute.

President Trump: I've always known this is a—this is a real—this is a pandemic. I've felt it was a pandemic long before it was called a pandemic. All you had to do is look at other countries. I think now it's in almost 120 countries all over the world. No, I've always viewed it as very serious. There was no difference yesterday from days before. I feel the tone is similar, but some people said it wasn't.

Gov. Cuomo (NY): I said to the President, who is a New Yorker, who I've known for many, many years, I put my hand out in partnership. I want to work together 100 percent. I need your help. I want your help . . . [The Federal Government] has been responsive late at night, early in the morning, and they've thus far been doing everything that they can do, and I want to say thank you and I want to say that I appreciate it and they will have nothing but cooperation and partnership from the state of New York. And we're not Democrats and we're not Republicans, we are Americans, at the end of the day. That's who we are and that's who we are when we are at our best.

President Trump: I think our economy will come back very rapidly. So it's fifteen days from yesterday. We'll see what happens after that. If we do this right, our country and the world frankly, but our country can be rolling again pretty quickly, pretty quickly. We have to fight that invisible enemy that I guess unknown,* but we're getting to know it a lot better.

---

* *Sic*

Gov. Cuomo (NY): Is it three months? Is it six months? Is it nine months? I don't know, but it's this much time. We will get through this much time. Understand what we're dealing with, understand the pressures that we're feeling, but we will get through this much time. Be a little bit more sensitive, understand the stress, understand the fear, be a little bit more loving, a little bit more compassionate, little bit more comforting, a little bit more cooperative and we will get through this time.

President Trump: If you look at a swine flu, the whole thing in, I guess it was 2009, and what they did and the mistakes they've made, they were terrible. They were horrific mistakes. 17,000 people died. I'll be honest, they shouldn't be criticizing because we've done a fantastic job. The only thing we haven't done well is to get good press. We've done a fantastic job, but it hasn't been appreciated.

Gov. Cuomo (NY): There is something to this lack of ability to connect. Don't hug, don't kiss, stay six feet away. We are emotional beings and it is important for us, especially at times of fear, times of stress, to feel connected to someone, to feel comforted by someone. I mentioned my daughter, I haven't seen my daughter in over two weeks. It breaks my heart, breaks my heart, and then this concept of maybe I can't get next to her because of this virus. There's a distance between me and my daughter because of this virus.

President Trump: By the way, for the markets, for everything. It's very simple, very simple solution. We want to get rid of it. We want to have very, as few deaths as possible. This is a horrible thing. You look at what's going on with Italy. We don't want to be in a position like that but a much larger because we're a much larger country. We don't want to be there and I think we've done really well. I think we've done well. I think the states have done well. We're all working together. The best thing we can do is get rid of the virus. Once that's gone, it's going to pop back like nobody's ever seen before. That's my opinion but I think it will pop back like nobody's ever seen before.

Gov. Cuomo (NY): Realize the time frame that we're expecting. Make peace with it. And find a way to help each other through this situation because it's hard for everyone. And the goal for me, socially distanced but spiritually connected. How do you achieve socially distanced but spiritually connected? I don't have the answer, but I know the question.

President Trump: I don't think in terms of recession. I think in terms of getting it out, because when we're finished with the virus, we will win. We will win, and when that victory takes place, our economy's going to go through the roof. It is so pent up. It is so built up. It is so ready to go in an upward direction, but we have to knock out this enemy. This is a really tough enemy, but we have to knock out, all of us. That's all of us. I don't think in terms of recession, not recession, it's words. We have to knock out this and we will have an economy. I actually think we'll have an economy like we've never had before. It's all pent up.

Gov. Cuomo (NY): This is an extraordinary time in this nation's history. It will go down in the history books as one of those moments of true crisis and confusion and chaos. I lived through 9/11. I remember the fear and the panic that existed in 9/11 where a single moment, your whole concept of life and society can be shaken, where you need to see government perform at its best, you need to see people at their best. Everybody's afraid. Everybody's nervous. How you respond, how you act, this is a character test for all of us individually. It's a character test for us collectively as a society. What did you do at that moment when all around you lost their head, right? Rudyard Kipling. That is this moment.

Vice President Pence: Our task force received a report this morning on the progress that the US Public Health Service and FEMA are making, working closely with state governments and also partners in the private sector like CVS, Target, Walgreens, and Walmart to expand remote testing sites around the country and we'll have a full report later this week as those come online . . . It's important the American people understand the testing is happening all over the country.

Governor J. B. Pritzker (IL): Frankly, we're focused as much as anything on the supply chain for testing, which, like I said, we're not getting any help from the federal government on. So we're literally, I'm calling CEOs at 10:00 at night and 6:00 in the morning and every other hour of the day to try to get ahold of supplies that we need in order to make our tests effective in the state of Illinois, because we're not getting help from the federal government.

President Trump: We've ordered massive numbers of ventilators. We have by any normal standards, we have a lot of respirators, ventilators. We have tremendous amounts of equipment but compared to what we're talking about here, this has never been done before. Yesterday I gave the governors the right to go order directly if they want, if they feel they can do it faster than going through the federal government.

Governor Larry Hogan (MD): I can tell you that there's quite a bit of frustration on the part of all of the governors that we don't have answers to those questions. And the first answer is no, we don't have enough test kits and neither does any other state. And no, the federal government does not have an answer. And we are behind. And that's going to continue to be a problem that we're all trying to address. So we're all trying to take decisions in our own states to ramp up whatever capabilities we can without the federal government, and we're also trying to push the federal government to be able to speed up their response. Some states have opened up testing facilities with no ability whatsoever to do the test. They have drive-thrus overloaded with thousands of people with no ability to do the test.

MARCH 18

Prime Minister Merkel, Germany: Since German unification—no, since the Second World War—no challenge to our nation has ever demanded such a degree of common and united action.

Gov. Gretchen Whitmer (MI): There are people right now who are out of a paycheck. They're terrified of losing their home in the coming weeks. I will not sit back and let them live in fear. So today I signed an executive order banning tax foreclosures while we work to mitigate the spread of coronavirus. Starting today, no one will lose their home due to tax for closure until this epidemic has abated.

President Trump: I would like to begin by announcing some important developments in our war against the Chinese virus. We'll be invoking the Defense Production Act, just in case we need it. In other words, I think you all know what it is, and it can do a lot of good things if we need it.

Gov. Jay Inslee (WA): We know that something like 70 to 90% of the fatalities that have been experienced have been in people of over the age of 60 and those with serious underlying health conditions. And we know that, if we were going to think of all the things we could do as Washingtonians today, it would be to encourage our parents, our grandparents, our uncles, our aunts to shelter in place so that they can save themselves from this scourge . . . I was kind of reminded of this a couple of hours ago. I called my old basketball coach, Walt Milroy. He was my coach at Ingram High School. And he is a hundred years of age. And he's great health, totally with it, as knowledgeable about what's going on in the world as he was when he was our coach. And it was just really fun talking to him. And I want to keep that for years. And, if we can all protect him, and his generation, and frankly my generation by reducing our social exposure, that's going to be a really good thing.

Dr. Patricia Powell, Director, Montefiore Einstein Center for Bioethics: You might not get access to a ventilator if you get a prognosis that no matter what, you probably won't get better. That's not a circumstance that people in America are used to thinking about.

MARCH 19

Kianush Jahanpur, Ministry of Health (Iran): Based on our information, every 10 minutes one person dies from the coronavirus and some 50 people become infected with the virus every hour in Iran.

Associated Press (AP): China has exonerated a doctor who was officially reprimanded for warning about the coronavirus outbreak and later died of the disease, a startling admission of error by the ruling Communist Party that generally bodes no challenges to its authority. The party's top disciplinary body said the police force in Wuhan had revoked its admonishment of Dr. Li Wenliang that had included a threat of arrest.*

It also said a "solemn apology" had been issued to Li's family and that two police officers, identified only by their surnames, had been issued "disciplinary punishments" for the original handling of the matter.

President Trump: I have to say I think with social distancing that the media has been much nicer. I don't know what it is. All these empty, these in-between chairs . . . You probably shouldn't have anybody sitting behind you either. You should probably go back, but I love it. It's so much nicer, but I shouldn't say that because you'll get me now. Thank you all for being here, and we continue our relentless effort to defeat the Chinese virus.

Mayor London Breed, San Francisco: I really thought that we were already past the xenophobia that has existed since the beginning of learning of the Coronavirus and its origin. It is very unfortunate that this continues to be an issue and it is offensive not only to our Chinese community here in San Francisco, it's offensive to our city as a whole where we pride ourselves on our diversity. We know that this disease is not discriminating against someone based on race. We know that people who are

---

* See January 3 entry

being diagnosed are of all races and backgrounds... So, sadly, this continues to be a problem where the President continues to stand by his messaging around his labeling of the Coronavirus and we want to make it clear that that is not something that's acceptable or tolerated here in San Francisco.

President Trump: First of all, governors are supposed to be doing a lot of this work and they are doing a lot of this work. The federal government is not supposed to be out there buying vast amounts of items and then shipping. We're not a shipping clerk. The governors are supposed to be, as with testing, the governors are supposed to be doing it.

Governor Charlie Baker (MA): I think every governor in the United States has been banging on the door of the federal government with respect to the stockpile. We certainly have, and we're going to continue to. Getting the supply chain running with respect to that, so that we have the ability to be sure that even once the stockpile is dealt with, there's a supply chain there with a regular distribution of additional gear is going to be critically important, not just for Massachusetts providers, but for providers all over the country and for first responders and others.

President Trump: I have to say if chloroquine or hydroxychloroquine works or any of the other things that they're looking at that are not quite as far out, but if they work, your numbers are going to come down very rapidly. So we'll see what happens, but there's a real chance that they might work.

Gov. Baker (MA): Look, I haven't seen my father in a month. I can't remember the last time I went a month without seeing my dad. But I absolutely believe it is in his best interest for me to give him space. I mean, I'm in my 60s, but I'm a healthy person, and if I were to end up contracting this, I really do believe for me it would be like the flu. But my dad's 91 years old, and the people that he spends most of his days with are, generally speaking, in the same age category that he is in . . . that physical presence for them at this point in time is exactly the wrong thing to do. And I think we just all have to come up with alternative ways of trying to create the connectivity that, for all of us when it comes to our parents and our grandparents, that's so fundamental.

MARCH 20

Gov. Cuomo (NY): The number one opportunity to make a difference here is to flatten the curve, flatten the increase in the number of cases, as we've talked about. Flatten the increase of the number of cases coming into the hospital system. And the best way to do that is by reducing density. Density control. Density control valve, right? And that's what we have been doing all along. We're going to take it to the ultimate step, which is we're going to close the valve, all right? Because the rate of increase in the number of cases portents a total overwhelming of our hospital system. So we're going to put out an executive order today, New York State on PAUSE. Policies that Assure Uniform Safety for Everyone. Uniform Safety for Everyone. Why? Because what I do will affect you and what you do will affect me. Talk about community and interconnection and interdependence. This is the very realistic embodiment of that. We need everyone to be safe, otherwise, no one can be safe.

Dr. Michael Ryan, Executive Director, Health Emergencies, WHO: We can say 10,000 deaths and sounds like a lot, and then other people say, well, people die of other things too. But take one look at what's happening in some health systems around the world. Look at the intensive care units. Completely overwhelmed. The doctors and nurses awfully exhausted. This is not normal.

Amy Campanelli, Cook County Public Defender, Chicago, IL: We've gotten a hundred [inmates] out. That's not enough. There are too many people in the jail who don't belong there even before. There are people there now that absolutely should be home with their families.

President Trump: We're going to be talking to the governors about [new drug treatments], and the FDA is working on it right now. The advantage is that it has been prescribed for a totally different problem, but it has been described for many years. Everybody knows the levels of the negatives and the positives. But, I will say that I am a man that comes from a very positive school when it comes to, in particular, one of these drugs. We'll see how it works out, I'm not saying it will, but I think that people may be surprised. By the way, that would be a game changer.

Peter Alexander, NBC News: What do you say to Americans who are scared, though? I guess, nearly 200 dead; 14,000 who are sick; millions, as you witness, who are scared right now. What do you say to Americans who are watching you right now who are scared?

> **President Trump:*** I say that you're a terrible reporter. That's what I say . . . I think it's a very nasty question, and I think it's a very bad signal that you're putting out to the American people. The American people are looking for answers and they're looking for hope. And you're doing sensationalism, and the same with NBC and "Con-cast." I don't call it—I don't call it "Comcast," I call it "Con-cast." Let me just—for who you work—let me just tell you something: That's really bad reporting, and you ought to get back to reporting instead of sensationalism. Let's see if it works. It might and it might not. I happen to feel good about it, but who knows. I've been right a lot. Let's see what happens . . . You ought to be ashamed of yourself.

MARCH 21

Prime Minister Jacinda Ardern, New Zealand: Stay home, save lives . . . We're going hard and we're going early. We only have 102 cases, but so did Italy once.

---

* Direct exchange

AP: Italy, at the heart of Europe's rampaging outbreak, announced nearly 800 new deaths and 6,600 new cases—its biggest day-to-day increase yet. Local authorities in Italy's northern regions have been pleading with the national government to enact ever stricter measures. The most hard-hit region, Lombardy, accounts for more than 60% of Italy's rapidly surging death toll.

Gregg Gonsalves, Epidemiologist, Yale School of Public Health: What is happening in Florida with spring break partying-on by students oblivious to the epidemiological implications of their actions is nothing short of tragic. While many of us have been hunkering down to try to break the chains of infection in our communities, these young people have decided the pleasures of the moment are worth bringing back the coronavirus to their friends and family.

MARCH 22

***U.S. News and World Report*:** As the number of U.S. coronavirus cases soared past 26,000 and the death count eclipsed 300 on Sunday, millions of Americans spent their first weekend under stay-at-home orders. The huge spike in cases propelled the United States to a position no country would want: America has now overtaken Germany as the country with the fourth-highest number of cases.

President Trump: I'm really happy with the job we're doing. And I'm glad that this team and me are here for this horrible thing. I mean, it's—a number of people have said it, but—and I feel it, actually: I'm a wartime president. This is a war. This is a war. A different kind of war than we've ever had.

Lloyd Blankfein, CEO, Goldman Sachs: Extreme measures to flatten the virus "curve" is sensible—for a time—to stretch out the strain on health infrastructure. But crushing the economy, jobs and morale is also a health issue-and beyond. Within a very few weeks let those with a lower risk to the disease return to work.

Gov. Bel Edwards (LA): Today I'm issuing a stay at home order for the entire state of Louisiana . . . There are some basic facts that we simply cannot deny or ignore: two weeks ago today there were zero confirmed cases of Covid-19 in Louisiana. One week ago, last Sunday morning, we had 91 confirmed cases. As of this morning we now have 837 confirmed cases and 20 deaths so that's a ten time increase in seven days.

President Trump: WE CANNOT LET THE CURE BE WORSE THAN THE PROBLEM ITSELF.

Dr. Amy Acton, Director, Ohio Department of Health: This is a war on a silent enemy. I don't want you to be afraid. I am not afraid. I am determined, but I need you to do everything. I want you to think about the fact this is our one shot in this country. All of us are going to have to sacrifice, and I know someday we will be looking back and wondering what was it we did in this moment.

MONDAY, MARCH 23

Dr. Tedros, Director-General, WHO: The pandemic is accelerating. It took 67 days from the first reported case to reach the first 100,000 cases, 11 days for the second 100,000 cases and just four days for the third 100,000 cases.

Gov. Bel Edwards (LA): We know that the growth in trajectory of cases has us right where Spain and Italy were, for example. I can't tell you why, but we're quite certain that it's true.

Bonnie Castillo, RN, Executive Director, National Nurses United: It is outrageous for the CDC to tell hospitals that nurses and other health care workers don't need the maximum protective gear to prevent them from getting sick during this pandemic . . . When nurses and doctors get sick from this virus who is going to be left to take care of the public? If they don't want the entire health care system to collapse, Congress must act immediately to protect the frontline health care providers.

Lt. Governor Dan Patrick (TX): And you know, Tucker,* no one reached out to me and said, "As a senior citizen, are you willing to take a chance on your survival in exchange for keeping the America that all America loves for your children and grandchildren?" And if that's the exchange, I'm all in . . . I'm going to do everything I can to live but, if you said, "Are you willing to take a chance?" You know if I get sick I'll go and try to get better but if I don't, and I don't try to take this in any kind of morbid way, but I'm just saying that we got a choice here, and we are going to be in a total collapse or recession/depression/collapse in our society. If this goes another several months there won't be any jobs to come back to for many people.

Gov. Whitmer (MI): In just 13 days, we've gone from zero to 1,232 confirmed cases of the coronavirus Covid-19. It has doubled over the weekend. This virus is spreading exponentially . . . The only tool that we have to fight it at the moment and to support our healthcare system to respond is to give them the opportunity by buying some time. And let me tell you why that's so important. We have roughly 10 million people in our state. There is a model that anticipates that if we stay on our current trajectory, just like Italy, over 70% of our people could get infected with Covid-19. Of that 7 million people projected, about a million of them would need to be hospitalized. We have about 25,000 acute care beds in Michigan. Think about that. That's where we are headed currently. So stopping the spread of this virus is really the most important tool that we have right now to keep our communities safe. That means without aggressive additional measures, more people will get sick, more people will die, and our economy will suffer longer.

* Fox News's Tucker Carlson, who is interviewing him.

MARCH 24

President Trump: And we're going to be opening relatively soon. And we are—our time comes up on Monday or Tuesday, our—you know, the allotted two weeks, but we'll stay a little bit longer than that. But we want to get open very soon . . . we're opening up this incredible country because we have to do that. I'd love to have it open by Easter, okay. I would love to have it open by Easter.* I will tell you that right now. I would love to have that. It's such an important day for other reasons, but I'll make it an important day for this too. I would love to have the country opened up and they're just raring to go by Easter.

Rep. Liz Cheney (WY): There will be no normally functioning economy if our hospitals are overwhelmed and thousands of Americans of all ages, including our doctors and nurses, lay dying because we have failed to do what's necessary to stop the virus.

Gov. Newsom (CA): The question of whether California will open in April, let me be sober about that. I'm not Pollyannaish about any of these things . . . As of 10:00 AM this morning, we've lost 40 lives in the state of California related to Covid-19. We have lost over 2,100, or rather we have 2,100 positives in the state of California, 2,102 which was 17.5% higher than the previous day. Again, that's a 10:00 AM number, those numbers change in real time, but a 17 and a half percent increase and now a loss of a young person's life.†

President Trump: Look: Easter's a very special day for me. And I see it sort of in that timeline that I'm thinking about. And I say, wouldn't it be great to have all the churches full? . . . So I think Easter Sunday and you'll

---

* April 12

† A teenager from Lancaster, CA, had passed away after testing positive for Covid, though later reports indicated "extenuating circumstances" surrounding his death.

have packed churches all over our country. I think it would be a beautiful time, and it's just about the timeline that I think is right.

Eliza Orlins, Public Defender, New York City: What we're seeing at Rikers Island is that the numbers of people who have tested positive for Covid-19 are going up exponentially. I also don't think the numbers we're seeing begin to reflect the full number of people exposed or infected. This is not a natural disaster where we don't know the numbers . . . this is something we can model out in real time and see exactly how many people will be infected if we don't act today.

New York City Corrections Officers' Benevolent Association: New York City jails are the epicenter of the epicenter. Every day, more COs and more inmates are testing positive. The city is asking COs to put out an inferno without even a fire extinguisher.

MARCH 25

Senator Chuck Schumer (NY), Senate Minority Leader: After sleep-deprived nights and marathon negotiating sessions, we have a bipartisan agreement on the largest rescue package in American history. This bill is far from perfect, but we believe the language has been improved significantly to warrant its quick passage . . . This is not a moment of celebration, but one of necessity. To all Americans, I say, "Help is on the way."

Dr. Jennifer Avegno, Director, New Orleans Department of Health: We remain very concerned about the number of known cases of Covid-19 that we have in New Orleans . . . Compared with other counties around the country, what we know is that we have one of the highest infection rates behind several counties in New York City and a handful of others . . . What these numbers continue to tell us is that we have substantial community spread. Each of us needs to act as if we have been exposed to this virus.

Gov. Bel Edwards (LA): The first case confirmed 13 days after [Mardi Gras] and happened in New Orleans. I happen to think a fair amount of it was seeded then if that's the word.

Gov. Cuomo (NY): Now you have to ask yourself why? Why does New York have such a high number? And again, in the totality, we understand what it means, but why does New York have such a high number? This is my personal opinion, I like to make sure that I separate facts from personal opinion. The facts I give you the best facts I have and again, the data changes day-to-day, but I give you exactly what I have on a day-to-day basis. Personal opinion, why does New York have so many more cases than any other state? How can it be you're 15 times the number of California . . . Answer one is, because we welcome people from across the globe. We have people coming here, we have people who came here from China, who came here from Italy, who came here from countries all around the globe. We have international travelers who were in China, and who were in Italy, and who were in Korea and who came here. I have no doubt that the virus was here much earlier than we even know, and I have no doubt that the virus was here much earlier than it was in any other state because those people come here first. That's the first answer.

Paula Reid, CBS News: Sir, lawmakers and economists on both sides of the aisle have said that reopening the country by Easter is not a good idea. What is that plan based on?

President Trump: Just so you understand—are you ready? I think there are certain people that would like it not to open so quickly. I think there are certain people that would like it to do financially poorly because they think that would be very good as far as defeating me at the polls. And I don't know if that's so, but I do think it's so that a lot of—that there are people in your profession that would like that to happen.

Reid: But your own medical experts did not endorse that plan yesterday.

President Trump: I think it's very clear—I think it's very clear that there are people in your profession that write fake news. You do. She does. There are people in your profession that write fake news. They would love to see me, for whatever reason—because we've done one hell of a job. Nobody has done the job that we've done. And it's lucky that you have this group here, right now, for this problem, or you wouldn't even have a country left.

Dr. Birx, White House Coronavirus Response Coordinator: [President Trump] has been so attentive to the scientific literature and the details and the data. I think his ability to analyze and integrate data that comes out of his long history in business has really been a real benefit during these discussions about medical issues.

Gov. Kate Brown (OR): We need substantially more PPE. Right now, what is available is being prioritized for hot spots like New York, California and Washington, leaving a state like Oregon with few options. So here's the deal. We have the ability to make more. Right here in Oregon, companies have the experience, the facilities and the equipment, to scale up manufacturing of PPE right now. So the question is, what's the barrier? And from our perspective, for what we're seeing, it's frankly the federal government.

Gov. Cuomo (NY): The second answer is because we are close, because we are close. We talk about the virus and how it transfers in a dense area. It's literally because we are close, because we live close to one another, because we're close to one another on the street, because we live in close communities, because we're close to one another on the bus. We're close to one another in the restaurant, we're close to one another in the movie theater and we have one of the most dense close environments in the country and that's why the virus communicated the way it did. Our closeness makes us vulnerable. Our closeness makes us vulnerable. That spatial closeness makes us vulnerable. But it's true that your greatest weakness is also your greatest strength and our closeness is what makes us who we are. That is what New York is, our closeness is what makes us special, our acceptance, our openness is what makes us special.

Former Vice President Biden: I have no doubt that all of us, including the younger generation, younger people, are going to step up and make the sacrifices of a few weeks or even a few months for our normal lives to be able to return, in order to beat this virus because this is who we are. That's the spirit that has defined America. We see it in the millions of young people who are working every day to make their communities better, serving others, teaching kids to read, feeding hungry families, mowing the lawn or they're buying groceries for the elderly neighbor next door.

Gov. Cuomo (NY): I can see how New Yorkers are responding, I can see how New Yorkers are treating one another. I see the 6,000 mental health volunteers, I see the 40,000 healthcare workers stepping up. I see the vendors calling me saying, "I can help." That's New York, that's New York and that my friends is undefeatable and I am glad in some ways that we're first with this situation because we will overcome and we will show the other communities across this country how to do it. We'll be there for them, we want them to be there for us and we will be there for each other as we always have been. Any questions?

MARCH 26

***Live Science*:** Although both countries reported their first cases of Covid-19 on the same day (Jan. 20), South Korea's testing rate is already six times higher than the test rate in the U.S. So far, the U.S. test rate is about 1,048 tests per million people and South Korea's is 6,764 tests per million people.

Sen. Warren (MA): Widespread diagnostic testing is necessary to control coronavirus—as we've seen, countries that instituted widespread testing early on have thus far stemmed the spread of Covid-19 and aided their economies by getting healthy people back to work. South Korea, for example, developed an expansive testing system. As a result, it has been able to track, isolate, and quarantine infected people without shuttering its cities or forcing its citizens to stay inside. It's no secret that the U.S. missed its chance to control Covid-19 through early testing. The Trump Administration profoundly mishandled its coronavirus response, leaving public health officials without diagnostic tests in the early days of the pandemic. Public and private labs are racing to catch up.

Lori Bassani, President, Association of Professional Flight Attendants: It is with deep sadness we report that one of our own . . . has passed away from Covid-19. Paul [Frishkorn] is the first of our colleagues to lose his life as a result of this deadly virus. We are deeply saddened and are reminded that no precaution is too much to take during this horrible time.

Jesse Drucker, *New York Times*: The federal government's planned $2 trillion economic rescue package includes financial aid for individuals and industries that are struggling to survive the coronavirus pandemic. It also includes a potential bonanza for America's richest real estate investors. Senate Republicans inserted an easy-to-overlook provision on page 203 of the 880-page bill that would permit wealthy investors to use losses generated by real estate to minimize their taxes on profits from things like investments in the stock market. The estimated cost of the change over 10 years is $170 billion.

Mayor Muriel Bowser, Washington, D.C.: It's wrong. It's outrageous. We're not a territory. We pay more taxes—unlike the territories—than 22 states. We have a larger population than several states and we are treated as a state by thousands of federal laws and programs. It's unconscionable to give DC the least amount of funding of any state, especially given the unique challenges we take on as the seat of the federal government.

MARCH 27

Gov. Baker (MA): No, we're not going to be up and running by Easter. No.

Governor Phil Murphy (NJ): We have now lost a total of 108 precious lives. We mourn with these families and indeed with our entire state every precious life that has been lost. God rest their souls . . . My thoughts and indeed our thoughts are also with the women and men in our hospitals, working valiantly to save lives, and I can only imagine the emotional toll on them as well when they lose a patient. In fact, it isn't easy on any of us. These aren't abstract numbers. These are our neighbors, our family, our friends, all of us. We are in this together and we mourn together.

President Trump: We've had great success over the last month. We've, as you know, the millions and millions of pieces of equipment have been delivered successfully by us, purchased and delivered, and we've made it available to the states and the governors have been very gracious, for the most part, I would say. A couple that aren't appreciative of the incredible job, they have to do a better job themselves. That's part of the problem.

BBC: The US now has more confirmed cases of coronavirus than any other country, with more than 86,000 positive tests. According to the latest figures collated by Johns Hopkins University, the US has overtaken China (81,897 cases) and Italy (80,589).

Gov. Murphy (NJ): I mentioned at the end of my remarks [to the AARP], I said, "Listen, this is a war." And I said, "We all know what the ingredients are to winning a war," and I referred to WWII. And it struck me as I was saying that to this particular group, and I think I acknowledged it that we were speaking to folks, if they were 80 or 85 years old or older . . . this wasn't abstract. They lived it. They might have been on the young side but they lived it. So, I was born in '57. I know this from my dad, my uncles, my aunts, my grandparents, but we've got a lot of folks in this state and

Judy [Persichilli, NJ Health Commissioner] and I spoke to a lot of them this morning who were there and who saw with their own eyes what it takes to win a war. And it doesn't take panic. That's the last thing we need. And just as equally so, it isn't business as usual. We're in a war footing.

Rep. Alexandria Ocasio-Cortez (NY): I represent one of the hardest hit communities in the hardest hit cities in this country: Queens, New York. Thirteen dead in a night in Elmhurst Hospital alone. Our community's reality is this country's future if we don't do anything. Hospital workers do not have protective equipment. We don't have the necessary ventilators. But we have to go into this vote* eyes wide open. What did the Senate majority fight for? One of the largest corporate bailouts, with as few strings as possible, in American history. Shameful. The greed of that fight is wrong—for crumbs, for our families, and the option that we have is to either let them suffer with nothing or to allow this greed, and billions of dollars, which will be leveraged into trillions of dollars, to contribute to the largest income inequality gap in our future. There should be shame for what was fought for in this bill and the choices that we have to make.

Rep. Denver Riggleman (VA): Government can do some things for the American people. The CARES Act is not perfect, but it provides much needed funds for medical equipment, support for small businesses, and additional tools to fight this crisis . . . Almost nothing perfect comes out of government. Service, however, demands that we put forth a perfect effort to do the best we can.

Rep. Hakeem Jeffries (NY): The House just passed the #CARESAct to address the #coronavirus pandemic. America is a resilient nation. We defeated the Great Depression. We defeated Nazi Germany. We defeated Jim Crow. We will defeat #COVID19 as well #FlattenTheCurve #ForThePeople.

---

* The economic stimulus bill (the CARES Act) would go for a House vote later that day.

President Trump: I think they [Democratic governors] should be appreciative because you know what? When they're not appreciative to me, they're not appreciative to the Army Corps. They're not appreciative to FEMA. It's not right. These people are incredible. They're working twenty-four hours a day. Mike Pence—I mean, Mike Pence, I don't think he sleeps anymore. These—these are people that should be appreciated. He calls all the governors. I tell him—I mean, I'm a different type of person—I say, "Mike, don't call the governor of Washington. You're wasting your time with him. Don't call the woman in Michigan.*" All—it doesn't make any difference what happens . . . You know what I say? If they don't treat you right, I don't call. He's a different type of person.

Mayor de Blasio, New York City: 25,573 cases in the city of New York. We remain the epicenter of the Covid-19 crisis in the United States of America. I look forward to a day where I can tell you that's no longer true, but today that is true. 366 New York City residents have been lost. 366 of our neighbors have been lost and I want to note that this is becoming personal for all of us in our neighborhoods.

President Trump: So look, hydroxychloroquine is a very powerful drug for certain things. And it's a very successful drug. There's reason to believe that it could be successful here. Now, the reason I disagree with you, and I think Tony [Fauci] would disagree with me, but the reason I disagree with you is that we have a pandemic. We have people dying now. If we're going to go into labs and test all of this for a long time, we can test it on people right now, who are in serious trouble, who are dying. If it works, we've done a great thing. If it doesn't work, we tried. But this is not something that's going to kill people.

Mayor de Blasio, New York City: [I] want to take a moment to just offer my sorrow and condolences to the families of some of our public servants

---

* Gov. Gretchen Whitmer

that we've lost. Dennis Dickson, the custodian I mentioned at 1 Police Plaza. Irene Weiss, a community assistant in the Parking Meter Collections Department at Department Transportation. David Perez, an investigator at the Department of Correction. Kious Kelly, a nurse manager at Sinai West... And Dez-Ann Romain, principal at Brooklyn Democracy Academy, everyone's feeling these losses deeply. We look forward to the day when we don't have to talk about fallen comrades, but that day is still a way off and we have to be clear about that. The human toll is what matters and for everyone who says it's about the economy and getting the economy back up, that's just wrong. It's about saving lives first.

Gov. Baker (MA): Boy, I follow a lot of the photography that's on social media from people around the Commonwealth. And for the most part, all I see are empty streets and empty parking lots. And we obviously talked to the folks at the T* every day about what's going on with their volume, which is pretty much created almost across the board. And lieutenant governors talking to mayors every single day and city managers about what they're seeing in their communities. And the message from almost everybody is, it's really quiet out there.

President Trump: Just finished a very good conversation with President Xi of China. Discussed in great detail the CoronaVirus† that is ravaging large parts of our Planet. China has been through much & has developed a strong understanding of the Virus. We are working closely together. Much respect!

***Gothamist*:** On Friday at 7 P.M., New Yorkers cheered on the city's essential workers from their homes. The #ClapBecauseWeCare campaign was a success, and as such will continue every night at 7 P.M. until... however long this takes.

---

* The Massachusetts Bay Transportation Authority, which serves the Greater Boston area

† *Sic*

MARCH 29

President Trump: When we discussed, back in a room—we were in a conference room—a very nice one, actually; it's called the Cabinet Room—that statement was made that they've been delivering for years, ten to twenty thousand masks. Okay, it's a New York hospital. Very—it's packed all the time. How do you go from ten to twenty, to three hundred thousand? Ten to twenty thousand masks to three hundred thousand? Even though this is different, something is going on, and you ought to look into it as reporters. Where are the masks going? Are they going out the back door?

***Healthline*:** The Covid-19 outbreak was identified in South Korea and in the United States on the same day. In the more than 2 months since then, South Korea has reduced its rate of new daily cases to one-tenth of its peak while the United States likely won't see that peak for weeks . . . The reasons for the disparity in the two countries' outcomes have to do with more than just size, experts say. It has more to do with the United States missing a critical window to ramp up testing and implement precautionary procedures to get on top of the virus. The United States has more than six times the population of South Korea, but it's reporting more than 15 times the number of confirmed Covid-19 cases and deaths.

Johns Hopkins Coronavirus Resource Center:
U.S. cases: 139,099
U.S. deaths: 2,438
South Korea cases: 9,478
South Korea deaths: 152

President Trump: Because the "Ratings" of my News Conferences etc. are so high, "Bachelor finale, Monday Night Football type numbers" according to the @nytimes, the Lamestream Media is going CRAZY, "Trump is reaching too many people, we must stop him." said one lunatic. See you at 5:00 P.M.!

MONDAY, MARCH 30

Captain Brett Crozier, USS *Theodore Roosevelt*:* The environment most conducive to the spread of the disease is the environment the crew of the TR is in right now, both aboard ship and ashore . . . Keeping over 4,000 young men and women on board the TR is an unnecessary risk and breaks faith with those Sailors entrusted to our care. There are challenges associated with securing individualized lodging for our crew. This will require a political solution but it is the right thing to do. We are not at war. Sailors do not need to die. If we do not act now, we are failing to properly take care of our most trusted asset—our Sailors. Request all available resources to find NAVADMIN and CDC compliant quarantine rooms for my entire crew as soon as possible.

Gov. Cuomo (NY): Most impacted states. New York you see is at 66,000, New Jersey is next with 13, California 6,000. So we have 10 times the problem that California is dealing with. 2,739 deaths in the state of New York. Total of 148,000 cases. 2,739 deaths. That's a lot of loss. That's a lot of pain. That's a lot of tears. That's a lot of grief that people all across the state are feeling. 1,200 is up from 965 deaths yesterday.

Letitia James, Attorney General (NY): It is disgraceful that Amazon would terminate an employee who bravely stood up to protect himself and his colleagues. At the height of a global pandemic, Chris Smalls and his colleagues publicly protested the lack of precautions that Amazon was taking to protect them from Covid-19. Today, Chris Smalls was fired. In New York, the right to organize is codified into law, and any retaliatory action by management related thereto is strictly prohibited. At a time when so many New Yorkers are struggling and are deeply concerned about their safety, this action was also immoral and inhumane.

---

* Email to naval superiors, leaked to the *San Francisco Chronicle*. Note: "The TR" is the nickname of the USS *Roosevelt*.

Mayor Sylvester Turner, Houston, TX: Let me just make my plea. Until the coronavirus is resolved, criminals take a break, ok! Stay home, ok? Stay home. And don't commit any crimes! And that way, they'll stay safe and out of jail, and police officers can stay safe and go home to their families, ok? So everybody chill! Crooks, criminals, you chill! Wait until the coronavirus is over! Ok, and then we'll all be ok.

MARCH 31

Central Pollution Control Board, Government of India: The nationwide Janta Curfew on March 22, 2020 and lockdown since March 24, 2020, have resulted in significant improvement in air quality in the country, as revealed by data analysis and comparison of data for time before enforcement of restrictions . . . As a result of stringent travel restrictions and shutting down of non-essential activities including those of air polluting sectors, air quality improvement has been noted in many towns and cities across the nation.

Dr. Redfield, Director, CDC: One of the [pieces of] information that we have pretty much confirmed now is that a significant number of individuals that are infected actually remain asymptomatic. That may be as many as 25%. That's important, because now you have individuals that may not have any symptoms that can contribute to transmission, and we have learned that in fact they do contribute to transmission.

President Trump: I want every American to be prepared for the hard days that lie ahead. We're going to go through a very tough two weeks. And then hopefully as the experts are predicting, as I think a lot of us are predicting after having studied it so hard, you're going to start seeing some real light at the end of the tunnel, but this is going to be a very painful, very, very painful two weeks.

Las Vegas and Clark County: Due to the closure of Catholic Charities, the city of Las Vegas, Clark County and area homeless providers are setting up a temporary shelter for the homeless on the upper parking lot of the Cashman Center.

Jace Radke, Press and Information Office, Las Vegas: The marked squares are to help meet social distancing requirements. We'll continue to provide this temporary respite, while practicing necessary social distancing, for anyone who is suffering from homelessness.

President Trump: I've had many friends, business people, people with great, actually common sense, they said, "Why don't we ride it out?" A lot of people have said. A lot of people that thought about it, ride it out, don't do anything, just ride it out, and think of it as the flu. But it's not the flu. It's vicious. When you send a friend to the hospital and you call up to find out how is he doing, it happened to me, where he goes to the hospital and he says goodbye, he's sort of a tough guy, a little older, a little heavier than he'd like to be frankly, and you call up the next day, how's he doing, and he's in a coma. This is not the flu. So we would have seen things had we done nothing. But for a long while, a lot of people were asking that question, I think, right?

Gov. Cuomo (NY): In general, I am tired of being behind this virus. We've been behind this virus from day one. The virus was in China. We knew where it was in China. Unless we assume there's some immune system variation with Asian people, it was coming here. And we have been behind it from day one since it got here. And we've been playing catch up. You don't win playing catch up. We have to get ahead of it.

Dr. Fauci, Director, NIAID: In a perfect world, it would have been nice to know what was going on [in China and Italy]. We didn't, but I believe that we acted very, very early in that.

Gov. Cuomo (NY): And also we need a social acceptance of the time expectation. We're all anxious. We're all tired. We're all fatigued. It's been all bad news for a long time. Our whole lifestyle has been disrupted. Everybody wants to know one thing: when is it over? Nobody knows. Well, President said by Easter. This one said by this. Nobody knows. You can have a hypothesis, you can have a projection. You can have an opinion, but nobody knows. But I can say this, it is not going to be soon.

President Trump: Fifteen days ago we published our nationwide guidelines to slow the spread of the virus. On Sunday, I announced that this campaign will be extended until April thirtieth. In a few moments, Dr. Birx will explain the data that formed the basis for our decision to extend the guidelines and Dr. Fauci will explain why it's absolutely critical for the American people to follow the guidelines for the next thirty days. It's a matter of life and death, frankly. It's a matter of life and death.

Gov. Cuomo (NY): So you have 50 states competing to buy the same item. We all wind up bidding up each other and competing against each other. Where do you now literally will have a company call you up and say, "Well, California just outbid you." It's like being on eBay with 50 other States bidding on a ventilator. You see the bid go up because California bid, Illinois bid, Florida bid, New York bids, California rebids. That's literally what we're doing. I mean how inefficient. And then FEMA gets involved and FEMA starts bidding. Now FEMA is bidding on top of the 50. So FEMA is driving up the price. What sense does this make?

Coronavirus Death Toll, United States:
March 1, 2020: 2
March 31, 2020: 3,768*

---

* The CDC, along with many nonpartisan health and science experts, agreed that this count is low.

APRIL 1

Prime Minister Silveria Jacobs, St. Maarten: Simply. Stop. Moving. If you do not have the type of bread you like in your house, eat crackers. If you do not have bread, eat cereal, eat oats, sardines.

Governor Brian Kemp (GA): Over the past forty-eight hours, the modeling and data has dramatically changed for Georgia and many other states around the country. The CDC has announced that individuals can be infected and begin to spread coronavirus earlier than previously thought even if they have no symptoms. From a public health standpoint, this is a revelation and a game changer. In addition, new models show that Georgia will need more time to prepare for hospital surge capacity, and while we are making excellent progress with our team, we have got to be more aggressive. For those reasons and in accordance with Dr. Toomey's recommendation, I will sign an executive order today closing K-12 public schools for the rest of the school year.

Rep. Devin Nunes (CA): I mean, look, the schools were just canceled out here in California, which is way overkill. I mean, it's possible kids could have went back to school in two weeks to four weeks, but they just canceled the rest of the schools. Look, I'm optimistic here. I think that the drugs that are on the market now . . . Look how quick we were able to get this approved, this new malaria drug that you've been talking about every night [hydroxychloroquine]. There's a lot of optimism here that we have in some of these drugs that are coming on line. The vaccines are going to take a while. But look, we have this bill that we just passed last week, $2.2 trillion worth. We have to focus on keeping people employed. I will tell you this, if we don't start to get people back to work in this country over the next week to two weeks, I don't believe we can wait until the end of April.

Rep. Karen Bass (CA), Chair, Congressional Black Caucus: To drive down the street and none of the businesses are open, the small businesses.

And to see lines in front of our grocery stores. And unfortunately in my district, in one part of my district, in front of a gun shop, going down the street—a line . . . This is a strong gun control state, so to see people lined up here. I mean this is not Texas, this is not, you know, the South, so to see people lined up at the gun store is pretty frightening here.

Gov. Murphy (NJ): Let me just put on the Uncle Sam hat. We need you. If you're watching and you're a healthcare worker who may have retired, from out of state, a doctor from out of the country. I know this is not covered by my executive order because it didn't have to be, but we're also unleashing nurses and doctors and others who are studying in their last semester of studies. We need you. We need you in a big way.

President Trump: I have hundreds of millions of people, number one on Facebook. Did you know I was number one on Facebook? I just found out I'm number one on Facebook.* I thought that was very nice, for whatever it means.

APRIL 2

Rep. Carolyn Maloney, Chair, House Committee on Oversight and Reform: The new documents we are releasing today confirm the urgent warnings we have been hearing from our nation's governors and health care professionals for weeks—they do not have enough personal protective equipment and medical supplies, and the administration has provided only a tiny fraction of what they desperately need. Unfortunately, President Trump spent months downplaying the coronavirus crisis and wasting precious time as thousands of Americans tested positive, got sick, and died.

---

* On Facebook, Donald Trump has around 27 million followers. The top FB followers, according to Statista, are: Christian Ronaldo (122 million), Shakira (100 million), Vin Diesel (96.8 million), and Leo Messi (90.2 million).

Rather than casting doubt on the gravity of this pandemic, the administration should have been working around the clock to prepare and execute plans to obtain desperately needed personal protective equipment and medical supplies.

Jared Kushner, Senior Advisor to the President: So, it's a very simple formula. The states should know how many ventilators they have in their states. And by the way, some governors you speak to or senators and they don't know what's in their state. Some governors I'll speak to and they'll know to the number how many ventilators they have in their state because that's the first thing a good manager will do.

Gov. Baker (MA): More beds will still be needed for both intensive care and for acute care, here in Massachusetts. And based on our projections, we believe we need to expand capacity of ICU beds by approximately five hundred beds in the coming weeks and based on our projections, we also know we need more ventilators and as we've said before, we've been chasing supplies from the federal government—and through other sources to—deliver ventilators that we've requested.

Jared Kushner: What a lot of the voters are seeing now is that when you elect somebody to be a mayor or governor or president, you're trying to think about who will be a competent manager during the time of crisis. This is a time of crisis and you're seeing certain people are better managers than others. So, what I would say is that the way that the federal government's trying to allocate it as they're trying to make sure, A.) you have your data. Don't ask us for things when you know that when you don't know what you have in your own state.

Marylou Sudders, Massachusetts Secretary of Health and Human Services: We have repeatedly requested for ventilators from the federal government, and we've actually increased our ask today. So we have not yet received any ventilators. And of course, any ventilators that come in will immediately go to hospitals to be tested before that they would be utilized.

Jared Kushner: You also have a situation where in some states, FEMA allocated ventilators to the states and you have instances where in cities they're running out, but the state still has a stockpile and the notion of the federal stockpile was, it's supposed to be our stockpile. It's not supposed to be state stockpiles that they then use.

Senator Cory Booker (NJ): Senator Menendez and I are fighting in line with our governor to get critical PPE for our state, ventilators for our state, and other things to empower our first responders in this crisis. We are continuing to demand that this president step up and use his power and authority to help people in New Jersey and across this nation. That means everything from using the Defense Production Act to better marshal federal resources. And to end really the agony of having governors be bidding against each other for critical resources.

Rep. Carolyn Maloney (NY): The President must act immediately to take all steps within his authority to get personal protective equipment and medical supplies to our nation's frontline responders who are risking everything to save their fellow Americans. The administration should utilize the Defense Production Act and other legal authorities to maximize domestic production, ensure suppliers are prioritizing U.S. needs before exporting critical supplies, and ensure that cities, states, and the federal government are working together, rather than competing to procure scarce supplies. The documents released today are from FEMA Region III, which includes Delaware, the District of Columbia, Maryland, Pennsylvania, Virginia, and West Virginia. The documents reveal that as of March 30, 2020, FEMA had provided only a fraction of each jurisdiction's request for personal protective equipment and medical supplies, leaving massive shortfalls.

Rep. Ayanna Pressley (MA) and Sen. Elizabeth Warren (MA): It is critical that the federal government make a concerted effort to account for existing racial disparities in health care access and how persistent inequities may exacerbate these disparities in the weeks and months to come as our nation responds to this global health pandemic. We urge HHS to work with states, localities, and private labs to better collect data on health disparities as we continue to respond to this pandemic.*

Emily Baumgaertner and James Rainey, *Los Angeles Times*: Two months before the novel coronavirus probably began spreading in Wuhan, China, the Trump administration ended a $200 million pandemic early-warning program aimed at training scientists in China and other countries to detect and respond to such a threat. The project, launched by the U.S. Agency for International Development in 2009, identified 1,200 different viruses that had the potential to erupt into pandemics, including more than 160 novel coronaviruses. The initiative, called PREDICT, also trained and supported staff in 60 foreign laboratories—including the Wuhan lab that identified 2019-nCoV, the new coronavirus that causes Covid-19.

Alphonso David, President, Human Rights Campaign: Our country is in crisis. Americans are finding themselves jobless, lying awake at night trying to find ways to make ends meet and put food on their tables. The last thing people should worry about in a pandemic is access to health care. Over 20 million Americans and almost one-in-five LGBTQ people lack health coverage. By not reopening the ACA exchange, Trump is making the LGBTQ community, and every marginalized community across this nation, more vulnerable to the virus. Yet again, Trump has failed us when we needed presidential leadership most.

---

* Letter to HHS

Sen. Booker (NJ): We are the wealthiest country on the planet earth. Everyone here in a health crisis should have access to healthcare. The simple request that this president open up the enrollment for the Affordable Care Act is common sense. To not do so is cruel.

Mayor Marty Walsh, Boston: On Monday we announced a pen pal program for veterans who may be feeling lonely or isolated. Right now we have seen an outpouring of interest. 450 people have reached out. We have so many volunteers that we're going to be able to not just fill that program but add volunteers to our food deliveries and other programs for veterans. It's a testament to Boston's respect and gratitude for those who served our country.

APRIL 3

Pope Francis: Let us try, if we can, to make the best use of this time: let us be generous; let us help those in need in our neighborhood; let us look out for the loneliest people, perhaps by telephone or social networks; let us pray to the Lord for those who are in difficulty in Italy and in the world. Even if we are isolated, thought and spirit can go far with the creativity of love. That is what we need today: the creativity of love.

President Trump: So with the masks it's going to be, really, a voluntary thing. You can do it, you don't have to do it. I'm choosing not to do it, but some people may want to do it and that's okay. It may be good, probably will. They're making a recommendation. It's only a recommendation, it's voluntary . . . I just don't want to wear one myself. It's a recommendation. They recommend it. I'm feeling good. I just don't want to be doing, I don't know, somehow sitting in the Oval Office behind that beautiful Resolute Desk, the great Resolute Desk. I think wearing a face mask as I greet presidents, prime ministers, dictators, kings, queens. I don't know, somehow, I don't see it for myself. Maybe I'll change my mind, but this will pass and hopefully it'll pass very quickly.

Karestan Koenen, Psychiatric Epidemiologist, Harvard's T. H. Chan School of Public Health: Many of the ways we as individuals, and communities and societies, cope with grief, we will not be permitted to do. And that seems more important than the numbers.

U.S. Bureau of Labor Statistics: In March, the unemployment rate increased by 0.9 percentage point to 4.4 percent. This is the largest over-the-month increase in the rate since January 1975, when the increase was also 0.9 percentage point. The number of unemployed persons rose by 1.4 million to 7.1 million in March. The sharp increases in these measures reflect the effects of the coronavirus and efforts to contain it. In March, unemployment rates rose among all major worker groups . . . The number of unemployed persons who reported being on temporary layoff more than doubled in March to 1.8 million. The number of permanent job losers increased by 177,000 to 1.5 million.

President Trump:* No. Me sign? No. There's millions of checks. I'm going to sign them? No. It's a Trump administration initiative, but do I want to sign them? No. The people are getting their money. There's a lot of stimulus going in a lot of different ways. There's also a stimulus going for companies that, if it weren't for our government, would not and some companies that were very strong a month ago.

Transportation Security Administration (TSA): A federal TSA employee passed away due to Covid-19 on April 2, 2020. The passing of Francis "Frank" Boccabella III, a valued friend and colleague of the entire Transportation Security Administration family at Newark Liberty International Airport and the larger TSA canine community, saddens all of us deeply. His passing represents a personal loss to all of us who knew him and

---

* David Jackson, a *USA Today* reporter, asked about multiple reports that Trump's name would appear on the stimulus checks being mailed to Americans.

cherished both his friendship and professionalism . . . Frank was dedicated to protecting the traveling public with his canine partner, Bullet, a 6-year-old German Short-haired Pointer and his previous canine partner, Zmay. Frank and his canine partners screened hundreds of thousands of passengers, keeping them and the transportation network safe. He is the first federal TSA employee who we have lost to Covid-19.

Stephen Weil, Attorney, Cook County, Chicago: A rapidly escalating public health disaster is unfolding behind the walls of the Cook County Jail. In the 11 days since March 23, the number of confirmed cases of Covid-19, the disease caused by a deadly coronavirus for which there is no vaccine and no cure, has risen from one to at least 167. A total of 46 corrections staff are also known to have Covid-19. These numbers will continue to rise dramatically because of the circumstances alleged in this complaint . . . The first infection was detected two weeks ago. One out of every 20 detainees now has coronavirus. That's an astronomically higher rate than the infection rate as the population as a whole, and that seems to be growing.

President Trump: The previous administration, the shelves were empty. The shelves were empty. So what you should do is speak to the people from the previous administration, Jim, and ask them that question* because the shelves were empty. You know what else? The military shelves were also empty. We had no ammunition, literally, and that was said by one of your favorite generals. Sir, we have no ammunition. Guess what? We had very little medical supply also.

Factcheck.org: More than once, President Donald Trump has falsely claimed that the federal stockpile of emergency medicine and supplies he

* CNN's Jim Acosta asked HHS Secretary Azar: "If you were preparing for a pandemic, if this government were preparing for a pandemic, why is it we don't have enough masks? Why is it we don't have enough medical equipment in this country?" Trump responded.

inherited from his predecessor was an "empty shelf." While the government does not publicize all of the contents of the repository, at the time Trump took office, the Strategic National Stockpile, as it is formally known, reportedly contained vast amounts of materials that state and local health officials could use during an emergency, including vaccines, antiviral drugs, ventilators and protective gear for doctors and nurses.

Akilah Johnson and Talia Buford, [*] ProPublica: As the disease spread at a higher rate in the black community, it made an even deeper cut. Environmental, economic and political factors have compounded for generations, putting black people at higher risk of chronic conditions that leave lungs weak and immune systems vulnerable: asthma, heart disease, hypertension and diabetes. In Milwaukee, simply being black means your life expectancy is 14 years shorter, on average, than someone white.

APRIL 4

Dr. Fauci, Director, NIAID: I came to NIH and I spent about five to eight years in the very early years of the AIDS epidemic, which was just the darkest years of my life because almost every single one of my patients died. And yet, as we knew epidemiologically that there was very little risk, there was a small risk, but very little risk of getting infected from a patient to see now, with these brave warriors are doing in the hospitals, not only giving life-saving treatment to people, but every single day putting themselves at risk for themselves and their family. I just think that the American public owe a phenomenal debt of gratitude for these people.

President Trump: And I hope they use the hydroxychloroquine, and they can also do it with Z-Pak, subject to your doctor's approval, and all of that. But I hope they use it because I'll tell you what: What do you have to lose? In some cases, they're in bad shape. What do you have to lose? It's been out there for a long time, and I hope they use it. And they're going to look at the—with doctors. Work with doctors. Get what you have to get. But we have it stockpiled, and it's—we have a lot of it, and we're getting more of it.

Gov. Cuomo (NY): Personal opinion, look, I want this all to be over. It's only gone on for 30 days since our first case. It feels like an entire lifetime. I think we all feel the same. This stresses this country, this state in a way nothing else has, frankly, in my lifetime. It stresses us on every level. The economy is stressed. This social fabric is stressed. Social systems are stressed. Transportation is stressed. It's right across the board, but the most difficult level is the human level. It is for me, anyway. It's every day, and it's everywhere.

Dr. Fauci, Director, NIAID: Remember Washington State was the first to get hit, but they put in a really good program of mitigation. And if you look at the charts that Dr. Birx showed the other day, they're still down there doing well. And the reason is, again, what I've said before, but I think it's worth reiterating, that we have two opposing forces here. The virus, which wants to do what the virus wants to do, viruses transmit from people to people. When people are separated from each other, virus does not transmit. It doesn't go anywhere.

***New York Times*:** Since Chinese officials disclosed the outbreak of a mysterious pneumonialike illness to international health officials on New Year's Eve, at least 430,000 people have arrived in the United States on direct flights from China, including nearly 40,000 in the two months after President Trump imposed restrictions on such travel, according to an analysis of data collected in both countries.

President Trump: I don't know much about [the removal of Naval Captain Brett Crozier]. I can only tell you this. Here we have one of the greatest ships in the world, nuclear aircraft carrier, incredible ship with thousands and thousands of people. And you had about 120 that were infected. Now, I guess the captain stopped in Vietnam and people got off in Vietnam.

Perhaps you don't do that in the middle of a pandemic or something that looked like it was going to be. History would say you don't necessarily stop and let your sailors get off, number one. But more importantly, he wrote a letter . . . I mean, this isn't a class on literature. This is a captain of a massive ship that's nuclear powered, and he shouldn't be talking that way in a letter.

APRIL 5

Queen Elizabeth II: Across the Commonwealth and around the world, we have seen heartwarming stories of people coming together to help others . . . It reminds me of the very first broadcast I made in 1940, helped by my sister. We as children spoke from here at Windsor to children who had been evacuated from their homes and sent away for their own safety. Today, once again, many will feel a painful sense of separation from their loved ones, but now as then, we know deep down that it is the right thing to do. While we have faced challenges before, this one is different. This time we join with all nations across the globe in a common endeavor.

Federal Bureau of Prisons (BOP): Given the surge in positive cases at select sites and in response to the Attorney General's directives, the BOP has begun immediately reviewing all inmates who have Covid-19 risk factors, as described by the CDC, starting with the inmates incarcerated at FCI Oakdale, FCI Danbury, FCI Elkton and similarly-situated facilities to determine which inmates are suitable for home confinement.

MONDAY, APRIL 6

Gov. Whitmer (MI): Like everyone, this is a challenging time and I see it in my kids' eyes and in my husband's eyes as they're all trying to figure out what is the right thing to do? How do we navigate this one? Will life ever get back to normal? Are we going to be okay? And we don't have the added pressures that I know a lot of Michiganders do about how are they going to keep a roof over their heads. And so I am reminded every day how great the sacrifices that so many people are making right now. I am always searching for sources of inspiration and I see it in the people that we've highlighted today and the people on the front line who are putting their own lives at risk to take care of others.

Kristen Clarke, President and Executive Director, Lawyers' Committee for Civil Rights Under Law: This Administration's alarming lack of transparency and data is preventing public health officials from understanding the full impact of this pandemic on Black communities and other communities of color . . . We are concerned that Black communities are being disproportionately impacted by the pandemic, and have lower access to Covid-19 testing which may cause delayed care, an increased risk of high mortality rates, and the acceleration of the spread of the disease in our communities.

Gov. Bel Edwards (LA): Disturbingly, this information is going to show you that slightly more than 70% of all the deaths in Louisiana are of African-Americans. And so that deserves more attention and we're going to have to dig into that and see what we can do to slow that trend down.

***New York Times*:** Chronic absenteeism is a problem in American education during the best of times, but now, with the vast majority of the nation's school buildings closed and lessons being conducted remotely, more students than ever are missing class—not logging on, not checking in or not completing assignments. The absence rate appears particularly high in schools with many low-income students, whose access to home computers and internet connections can be spotty. Some teachers report that fewer than half of their students are regularly participating.

President Trump: States can do their own testing. States, they're supposed to be doing testing. Hospitals are supposed to be doing testing. Do you understand that? We're the federal government. Listen, we're the federal government. We're not supposed to stand on street corners doing testing. They go to doctors, they go to hospitals, they go to the state.

Sen. Warren (MA): The White House is just simply wrong on the notion that somehow the states can manage this on their own. We need a national response. Think about what I was just talking about. It is the federal government that can order the tests. It is the federal government that can use the Defense Production Act in order to force companies to produce the test kits, the masks, the gowns, the kinds of things that we actually need in a crisis. The states don't have the power to do that. Only the federal government does. Look at what's happening when the states are out there trying, for example, to buy these masks in a market with no rules. What happens is states end up bidding against each other. New York bids against Massachusetts and they both are bidding against Arizona and California. That's great for whoever is sitting on a couple of million masks, but it's sure not good for the states that desperately need these masks and are paying more and more and more just to get basic supplies. It is the federal government that can allocate these masks not based on who bids the highest price, but where there's a real need. That is what a federal government that has a plan can do.

Gov. Whitmer (MI): While fighting Covid-19, we've seen an unprecedented rise in unemployment claims. When this first started a month ago, I took steps to expand benefits for Michiganders who are out of work because of Covid-19, and ease rules to make it easier to apply for unemployment. Now, the high volume that we have seen outpaces any even in the toughest week during the great recession. The hardest week during the great recession, for perspective, was 77,000 claims. Two weeks prior to Covid-19 first presenting in Michigan, we were averaging around 5,000 claims for a week. Now just for perspective, to know that that's what it was and now since Covid-19, the week of March 15th through the 21st there were 127,000 new claims. It was 5,000 and now it's 127,000. The week of March 22nd through 28th it was 300,000 new claims. These numbers are staggering, and they will continue to climb.

City of Hialeah, FL: Due to the overwhelming demand with the need for unemployment benefits, the City of Hialeah . . . will be opening 4 locations to give unemployment applications and assistance to all who are in need to apply, and due to high demand has not been able to get through the State of Florida unemployment website or 1-800 hotline number. Beginning Wednesday, April 8, 2020, the new schedule for collecting unemployment and assistance applications will be from 10:00am to 3:00pm until further notice. This is a drive-thru event. You must be in a vehicle to receive the unemployment application. If you do not meet these requirements, unfortunately, you will not be served.

Gov. Whitmer (MI): We've heard stories from people across the state who hold on to the little things to help them cope. Healthcare professionals, like Lori, who is a nurse at St. Mary Mercy in Lavonia, who sings "Amazing Grace" to her patients. Or Katie, a nurse at Sparrow Hospital, who uses dry erase markers to draw pictures on her face shield. Or the eighth-grade math teacher who writes problems on students' driveways in chalk, as they go for their jog. Or Colleen, from Hamtramck, who created a theater, where she performs from her balcony and streams on social media, to share laughter with people.

Dr. Amy Acton, Director, Ohio Department of Health: People at home: You are moving mountains. You are saving lives. I get emotional when I talk about this. This is no small thing we are doing together. It is so incredibly hard to shut down our lives the way we have. I am absolutely certain you will look back and know that you helped saved each other in this state. The impact is profound. Please at home: don't stop.

Governor Tony Evers (WI): Today, I signed an executive order suspending in-person voting for tomorrow's election. Frankly, there's no good answer to this problem. I wish it were easy. I had hoped that the Legislature would do its part—just as the rest of us are—to help keep people healthy and safe. But as municipalities are consolidating polling locations, and absent legislative or court action, I cannot in good conscience stand by and do nothing. The bottom line is that I have an obligation to keep people safe, and that's why I signed this executive order today.

United States Supreme Court: Wisconsin has decided to proceed with the elections scheduled for Tuesday, April 7. The wisdom of that decision is not the question before the Court. The question before the Court is a narrow, technical question about the absentee ballot process . . . Extending the date by which ballots may be cast by voters—not just received by the municipal clerks but cast by voters—for an additional six days after the scheduled election day fundamentally alters the nature of the election.*

Gov. Evers (WI): Tomorrow in Wisconsin, thousands will wake up and have to choose between exercising their right to vote and staying healthy and safe. In this time of historic crisis, it is a shame that two branches of government in this state chose to pass the buck instead of taking responsibility for the health and safety of the people we were elected to serve.

Sherrilyn Ifill, President, NAACP Legal Defense and Educational Fund: It is unconscionable. It is among the most cynical decisions I have read from this Court—devoid of even the pretense of engaging with the reality that this decision will mean one of two things for many WI voters: either they will risk their health & lives to vote, or they will be disenfranchised.

APRIL 7

***Milwaukee Journal Sentinel*:** The city has only five voting centers that are open Tuesday, a dramatic drop from the 180 polling places typically open on election day.

---

* The majority opinion was unsigned, but experts believe Justice Brett Kavanaugh wrote it.

Emilio De Torre, Director of Community Engagement, American Civil Liberties Union (ACLU) of Wisconsin: People seem to literally be taking their life into their hands to attempt to vote.

Neil Albrecht, Executive Director, Milwaukee Election Commission: We have moved forward with an election, but we have not moved forward with democracy in the state of Wisconsin.

President Trump: We want to look into it, World Health Organization, because they really are—they called it wrong. They called it wrong. They missed the call. They could've called it months earlier. They would have known, and they should've known. And they probably did know. So we'll be looking into that very carefully, and we're going to put a hold on money spent to the WHO. We're going to put a very powerful hold on it, and we're going to see. It's a great thing if it works. But when they call every shot wrong, that's no good.

Michael Lewis, author and journalist: So far, we've been talking about Trump as if he cares about risk and he wants to manage it well. I don't think that's true. I think that his whole life is about doing whatever his impulses tell him to do. And then, after the fact, telling a story that renders him the hero of the story—the person who saved the day. He's always done this, no matter the facts. I actually think he moves through life thinking, whatever happens, I can undo it with a story.

***Stamford Advocate* (CT):** An apparent wiring short in a crematory chamber appears to be the cause of a fire that broke out at Cognetta's Funeral Home in Stamford early Monday evening . . . Funeral home owner Nicholas Cognetta blamed the malfunction on the current health crisis. With its two crematory chambers, his facility has been serving families of the deceased in the state, but also assisting Westchester County to keep up with the demand there in dealing with the dead.

Mayor Lori Lightfoot, Chicago: Since the Covid-19 crisis first reached our city's doorstep we've been working around the clock to ensure our residents, all of our residents, are not only secure from the Covid virus, but are supported against the economic fallout of this terrible disease, both of which have impacted our entire city. While the federal government hasn't made all of its Covid related benefits available to our nation's immigrants, the executive order I signed ensures all Chicagoans including our immigrants and refugees, have equal access to these programs regardless of status.

APRIL 8

Mayor Eric Garcetti, Los Angeles: I know a lot of people have compared this to a kind of sudden shock, a moment like a Pearl Harbor or an earthquake or a 9/11. And yet I think it's not quite the right metaphor because this isn't about one single day and then rebuilding from it. It's a threat that gets worse every single day. I want to thank our bus drivers, our train operators who are doing incredible and heroic work. I stopped in at a safe distance with my mask on and his mask on. I was talking to a bus driver on the street on the way to work yesterday. They're proud of what they're doing. There's an amazing video I think that Metro put out that shows heroes don't just wear surgical masks in an operating room. They sometimes drive the bus and take those hospital workers there, take people who are feeling sick to a hospital because that's the only transportation that they have.

Mayor Mike Duggan, Detroit: I used to run a hospital. If you have a five hundred–person hospital, you'd like to have a hundred people be admitted and a hundred people being discharged every day. If you had that, you'd have the same number of beds and the same amount of staffing. When more people get admitted than are discharged, you start to run into crowding and what we had here was 125 people admitted a day, 100 being discharged, 150 people admitting a day, 100 being discharged. That was the anxiety you were hearing from the hospital is that Covid-19 was driving up the admissions to the point where we were getting crowded where people change surgery suites to patient beds. What they are telling me now is we're starting to see a shift.

Stacy Dean, Vice President for Food Assistance Policy, Center on Budget and Policy Priorities: I've never seen anything like it. People love the phrase "the perfect storm," but nothing is built for this . . . It's a highly flexible system, but it is not a system designed to absorb ten million people in one month.

Rep. Sheila Jackson Lee (TX): One wonders if you begin to identify this as a "Black virus." The facts speak for themselves.

President Trump: The Radical Left Democrats have gone absolutely crazy that I am doing daily Presidential News Conferences. They actually want me to STOP! They used to complain that I am not doing enough of them, now they complain that I "shouldn't be allowed to do them." They tried to shame the Fake News Media into not covering them, but that effort failed because the ratings are through the roof according to, of all sources, the Failing *New York Times*, "Monday Night Football, Bachelor Finale" type numbers (& sadly, they get it $FREE).

Mayor Duggan, Detroit: The men and women on the front line all along, in addition to the police who've done such a great job, have been the firefighters and the EMTs. They've gotten more and more work. They've had to work overtime. You've never heard any drama, you haven't heard about ambulance delays, you haven't heard about people not showing up for work. You haven't heard about sick calls. These men and women just show up every single day and protect you without any drama. Sometimes when you don't squeak, you don't get attention but I don't ever lose sight for a second of what they mean to us.

APRIL 9

Gov. Pritzker (IL): All across Illinois, individuals, and communities, and nonprofits, and grassroots organizations have stepped up to meet this moment. I am very, very proud of each and every one of them, and I hope you are, too. Know that everywhere that you look, there are helpers . . . Over 45,000 people have now answered our call to volunteer through Serve Illinois, our State Commission on Volunteerism, or Illinois Helps, our volunteer network of health professionals.

President Trump: The Wall Street Journal always "forgets" to mention that the ratings for the White House Press Briefings are "through the roof" (Monday Night Football, Bachelor Finale, according to @nytimes) & is only way for me to escape the Fake News & get my views across. WSJ is Fake News!

Gov. Whitmer (MI): This has been a hard month. We've got to take the lessons that we've learned from it and use them for the betterment of our state and the betterment of our people. A couple of important observations that we're seeing play out nationally, but we're seeing right here at home. 14% of our population is African-American, yet over 40% of the Covid-19 deaths in Michigan are African-Americans. This virus is holding up a mirror to our society and reminding us of the deep inequities in our country, from basic lack of access to care, to access to transportation, to lack of protections in the workplace. These inequities that hit people of color and vulnerable communities the hardest. Over the past four weeks, I've signed a number of executive orders to help ensure safety and security of the people of our state; especially focusing on the most vulnerable. We've banned evictions and tax foreclosures. We've expanded unemployment benefits. We've taken an action to get water restored.

Gov. DeWine (OH): Now I've told you this before, I'm a fan of the *Back to the Future* movies, Michael J. Fox, still like to watch them, but if you recall in those movies there's sometimes an alternative future. If you go down one track, you go here, and things happen. You make a separate decision here, and you go down a different track. And as I recall the movies, one of the tracks was usually a good track and the other one was a bad track, and that's based upon what we do.

Gov. Pritzker (IL): I am worried about people throwing caution to the wind and seeing a nice day outside and thinking that they're not in danger. You heard Doctor Ezike* talking about how some young people think that they're invincible, that this virus won't affect them. So everybody needs to know that if we are improving and it's still up in the air, but if we are improving here in the state, it is because people are staying at home. That is something to keep in mind.

Gov. Whitmer (MI): I think that it's important to be clear that while we could come up with all sorts of scenarios where we could make an argument that someone's safe and in whatever activity it is they want to do, every single exception to a stay home, stay safe order makes this more porous. Golf landscaping, and I've heard these seem to be the ones that we hear the most from the legislature, some of the Republican legislators, you know what, it's not critical infrastructure. It's just not. They are not necessary to sustain life. And to be candid, just by engaging in it can expose people to risk, serious risk. Every time you ask a low-income person to come out and fill up their gas tanks, go get food. It's additional opportunity for exposure and for spread.

Gov. DeWine (OH): Well, first of all, my wife Fran and I grew up in Yellow Springs. All the time we were growing up, there's on Saturday morning, it was people who were protesting. We're big believers in the first amendment.

* Illinois Department of Public Health Director Dr. Ngozi Ezike

And the folks who are outside have every right to be out there . . . The last thing we need is this thing to, is I've likened this to a monster and it's sort of on the floor, but it's still obviously claiming lives. We can't let it up and we can't feed it. And the way you feed it is by coming out and exposing yourself and exposing other people.

Rep. Carolyn Maloney (NY): The Postal Service is holding on for dear life, and unless Congress and the White House provide meaningful relief in the next stimulus bill, the Postal Service could cease to exist.

Rep. Brenda Lawrence (MI): Every day, the dedicated employees of the Postal Service are on the front lines of the Covid-19 pandemic to ensure all Americans receive their mail and packages, as well as critical medical supplies that are being shipped across the country. During a Census and election year, it is imperative that we have a fully functional Postal Service to ensure Americans across the country can participate in our democracy.

***San Antonio Express-News*:** In perhaps the most sobering reminder yet of the economic fallout caused by the coronavirus pandemic, the San Antonio Food Bank aided about 10,000 households Thursday in a record-setting giveaway at a South Side flea market . . . Thursday's drive-thru at Traders Village was the fourth such event for the Food Bank since March 31.

APRIL 10

Marc Perrone, President, UFCW: To help reduce the spread of this killer virus, it is absolutely critical that all Easter weekend grocery shoppers wear a mask while shopping, practice social distancing throughout the store, safely discard gloves and masks in trash cans, limit the number of trips and shoppers to an absolute minimum, and respect special shopping times for seniors. All Americans have a responsibility to help protect these essential workers and their fellow shoppers.

Rep. Rashida Tlaib (MI): At the onset of the Covid-19 crisis, around 2,800 families in Detroit had no running water. Now they and many more across my district and Michigan are being forced to face it without the ability to wash their hands and help safeguard themselves and their loved ones from this virus. Water has become more and more unaffordable, inaccessible and contaminated because we are not prioritizing the critical importance of water being a human right. The barriers and continued lack of investment are components of increased poverty and structural racism that many in our community have been facing their whole lives.

Gov. Whitmer (MI): Since I addressed the public yesterday afternoon, more than 200 people have died due to Covid-19. This is the highest number of Covid-19 deaths we have had in one day to date. These people were husbands, wives, grandparents, sons, and daughters. We are not out of the woods yet.

State Senator Mike Shirkey (MI), Majority Leader: OUR Governor IS DESTROYING OUR HEALTH BY KILLING OUR LIVELIHOODS!

New York Police Department: 7,096 uniformed members of the NYPD were on sick report [today] which accounts for 19.6% of the Department's uniformed workforce. Currently, 2,314 uniformed members and 453 civilian members tested positive for the coronavirus.

Governor Greg Abbott (TX): Next week I will be providing an executive order talking about what will be done in Texas about reopening Texas businesses also in a way that will be safe for that economic revitalization. We will focus on protecting lives while restoring livelihoods. We can and we must do this, so we can do both, expand and restore the livelihoods that Texans want to have by helping them return to work. One thing about Texans is they so much enjoy working and know they want to get back into the workforce.

President Trump: Because the T.V. Ratings for the White House News Conference's* are the highest, the Opposition Party (Lamestream Media), the Radical Left, Do Nothing Democrats &, of course, the few remaining RINO'S, are doing everything in their power to disparage & end them. The People's Voice!

APRIL 11

Governor Michelle Lujan Grisham (NM): Today, New Mexico's public health order banning mass gatherings has been amended to include houses of worship. The risk is simply too great. In-person services risk spreading #COVID19, potentially affecting thousands. This year, home is holy. Please, you MUST stay home.

Senator Ted Cruz (TX): I'm going to go play T-Ball, on a paddle board, at the beach, with my kids, while worshiping God on Easter Sunday.† Fortunately, I live in Texas—where we protect public safety, but aren't authoritarian zealots—so they won't arrest me!

Gov. Pritzker (IL): There are the additional stressors of either quarantine or having a loved one hospitalized that they cannot interact with. Although there are reasons to see hope and a lot of examples of people helping one another, all of which should lift us up, there are also circumstances that may cause you to feel despair, to find yourself swimming in the stress and uncertainty of it all. First, I want to say to all of you, feel all of it. We are living in a deeply unprecedented moment, and holding the emotional ramifications of that inside will only be harder on you. It's okay to feel. Please know that you don't have to feel it all alone. I want you to know that we're here to help, and here's how. The Illinois Department of Human Services

---

* *Sic*

† During the stay-at-home period, there had been reports of arrests for each of these activities.

Mental Health Division has launched a free of charge emotional support text line for Illinoisans experiencing stress related to Covid-19, Call for Calm . . . It's OK to feel, and please know you don't have to feel it all alone.

APRIL 12*

Pope Francis: In these weeks, the lives of millions of people have suddenly changed. For many, remaining at home has been an opportunity to reflect, to withdraw from the frenetic pace of life, stay with loved ones and enjoy their company. For many, though, this is also a time of worry about an uncertain future, about jobs that are at risk and about other consequences of the current crisis. I encourage political leaders to work actively for the common good, to provide the means and resources needed to enable everyone to lead a dignified life and, when circumstances allow, to assist them in resuming their normal daily activities.

Pastor Trey Haddon, Bloomington, IL: In a world where there's nothing but doom and gloom all over the TV, all over Facebook and Twitter and whatever platform you look at it—really, we felt there was a need for hope. And sharing that hope with anyone who had a vehicle that was able to drive up with an FM radio seemed like the best way to make that happen. The entire Easter event was full of chaos. It was full of disorder. It was full of confusion. It was full of isolation. Everybody was scared. I mean, does that not sound like the world we live in now? The Easter story is a reminder that even in death, there is still life. Even in isolation, there is still community.

CNN: The US now has the world's highest number of deaths from Covid-19, with at least 21,692 losing their lives to the virus as of Sunday afternoon . . . New York State alone has more cases than any other country.†

---

* Easter Sunday

† New York State had approximately 162,000 cases at the time.

Gov. Andrew Cuomo (NY): Somebody asked the question once, can you ever get numb to seeing these numbers? Unfortunately, no. Seven hundred fifty-eight people lost their lives in a twenty-four-hour period. I speak to many families who are going through this. Many people who lost loved ones. Everyone is a face and a name and a family that is suffering on this weekend, which for many people in this state and in this nation is a high religious holiday. Which is already distorted because we have churches closed, we have temples closed.

Kenneth Sullivan, CEO, Smithfield Foods: The closure of this facility,* combined with a growing list of other protein plants that have shuttered across our industry, is pushing our country perilously close to the edge in terms of our meat supply. It is impossible to keep our grocery stores stocked if our plants are not running . . . We have a stark choice as a nation: we are either going to produce food or not, even in the face of Covid-19.

Gov. Andrew Cuomo (NY): Again, to put it in context, 9,385 lives lost when you add those from yesterday. But in the context of 9/11 which was supposed to be the tragedy of my lifetime, 2,753 lives lost, we're now at 9,385. Big question for everyone is when do we reopen? People want to get on with their lives. People want to get out of the house, cabin fever, we need the economy working. People need a paycheck. Life has to function. When do we reopen? When do we reopen? Look, the answer is, we want to reopen as soon as possible. Everyone does. On a societal level, everyone does. On a personal level, let's just end this nightmare. Groundhog Day, you get up every day, it's the same routine. You almost lose track of what day of the week it is because they don't even have meaning anymore. And there's all sorts of anxiety and stress that we're all dealing with, so we want to reopen as soon as possible. The caveat is, we need to be smart in the way we reopen.

* A plant in Sioux Falls, South Dakota, which produces 4 to 5 percent of U.S. pork

MONDAY, APRIL 13

Dr. Amy Acton, Director, Ohio Department of Health: These masks are actually now being viewed in the studies that are done as yet another weapon to get back to normalcy. This is a culture change for us to do this. But it's actually acting very much like the other social distancing actions we took. This is like another layer, for those of you who have been following along, of swiss cheese; not having mass gatherings so we don't spread the disease. Or the closing of schools, another very, very hard policy decision.

Melissa Ackison, State Senate Candidate (OH): In a time where full-on unconstitutional tyranny is on display, the president is doing exactly what the patriots elected him to do, and I knew it was only a matter of time before he would flex his muscle and authority to save Ohio from unprecedented overreach. Patriots who love and respect our liberties and the Constitution are sick and tired of the fear-mongering while the governor and Dr. Acton continue to hide the numbers from the public.

State Senator Andrew Brenner (OH): We need to get the economy open, even if that means social distancing of some sort for months to come. We can't stay like this much longer, and the hundreds of thousands of Ohioans who've lost their jobs or the thousands of small business owners can't keep doing this either, or their lives will be irreparably destroyed.

Peter Navarro, Director, White House Office of Trade and Manufacturing Policy: It's disappointing that so many of the medical experts and pundits pontificating in the press appear tone deaf to the very significant losses of life and blows to American families that may result from an extended economic shutdown.

Gov. Jay Inslee (WA): I'm glad to be able to have basically a statement of broad principles that will abide across the West Coast. And those basic principles are, we know we have to have measures of testing and contact tracing in the ability to come out of this in a rational, thoughtful, scientifically based way. And I think that those principals were invited by with this agreement that you saw today.

Governor Ned Lamont (CT): One thing that's undeniable is that this virus does not stop at the border of any county, state, or country, but the impact is the same when it comes to our respective economies and healthcare systems. Working as a regional coalition to make the right decisions will lead to the best public health results for all of our residents. We must solve these problems together.

President Trump: When you say my authority, the president's authority, not mine, because it's not me. This is when somebody is the President of the United States, the authority is total and that's the way it's got to be. It's total. It's total and the governors know that.

Gov. Inslee (WA): As far as who has the legal authority to make decisions about the Stay Home, Stay Healthy Initiative, which I issued as governor of the State of Washington, there really is no question about that. That is in the singular purview of the State of Washington and the governor of the state of Washington. There is no legal authority that would give any president, of any party, the ability to countermand a health-based decision that is issued pursuant to Washington State law.

Kaitlan Collins, CNN: A quick question on something you just said. You said when someone is President of the United States, their authority is total. That is not true. Who told you that?

> **President Trump:*** You know what we're going to do? We're going to write up papers on this. It's not going to be necessary because the governors need us one way or the other, because ultimately,

---

* Direct exchange

it comes with the federal government. That being said, we're getting along very well with the governors and I feel very certain that there won't be a problem. Yeah please, go ahead.

Collins: Has any governor agreed that you have the authority to decide when their state opens back up?

President Trump: I haven't asked anybody. You know why? Because I don't have to.

Collins: But who told you the president has the total authority?

President Trump: Enough. Please.

APRIL 14

Gov. Cuomo (NY): We also have to be clear on who is responsible for each element of the opening. The president said last night that he has total authority for determining how and when states reopened. That is not an accurate statement in my opinion.

President Trump: The plans to reopen the country are close to being finalized and we will soon be sharing details and new guidelines with everybody. I will be speaking to all 50 governors very shortly and I will then be authorizing each individual governor of each individual state to implement a reopening and a very powerful reopening plan of their state at a time and in a manner as most appropriate.

Gov. Cuomo (NY): This has been a topic discussed since our founding fathers first decided to embark on this entire venture, right? This is basic federalism, the role of the states and the role of the federal government, and it is important that we get this right. Our founding fathers understood, and we have to remember today, that the balance between the state and the federal, that magnificent balance that is articulated in the Constitution is the essence of our democracy. We don't have a king in this country. We didn't want a king, so we have a constitution and we elect the president.

President Trump: The day will be very close because certain states, as you know, are in much different condition and in a much different place than other states. It's going to be very, very close, maybe even before the date of May 1st. So that will be for some states. Actually, there are over 20 that are in extremely good shape and we think we're going to be able to get them open fairly quickly and then others will follow.

Gov. Cuomo (NY): Let me make a personal point, not necessarily a factual point. President did his briefing last night and the president was clearly unhappy. President did a number of tweets this morning where he's clearly unhappy. He did a tweet about mutiny on the *Bounty* and governors are mutineers. I didn't follow the exact meaning of the tweet. But the basic essence of the tweet was that he was not happy with governors and that this was a mutiny. The president is clearly spoiling for a fight on this issue. The worst thing we can do in all of this is start with political division and start with partisanship. The best thing we have done throughout this past 44 days is we worked together and we haven't raised political flags even in this hyper-partisan environment, even though it's an election year, even though the politics is so intense, we said not here, not in this.

Former President Barack Obama: Let me start by saying the obvious, these aren't normal times. As we all manage our way through a pandemic unlike anything we've seen in a century, Michelle and I hope that you and your families are safe and well. If you've lost somebody to this virus or if someone in your life is sick or if you're one of the millions suffering economic hardship, please know that you're in our prayers. Please know that you're not alone. Because now's the time for all of us to help where we can and to be there for each other, as neighbors, as coworkers, and as fellow citizens. In fact over the past weeks, we've seen plenty of examples of the kind of courage, kindness, and selflessness that we're going to need to get through one of the most difficult times in our history.

Gov. Cuomo (NY): Sometimes it takes more strength frankly, to walk away from a fight, than engage in. The president will have no fight with me. I will not engage it. I've sat here every day for 44 years asking New Yorkers to remember that this is not about me, it's about we. I understand you're personally inconvenienced. I understand you're frustrated and stressed and anxious and you're feeling pain. Think about we.

Former President Obama: If there's one thing we've learned as a country from moments of great crisis, it's that the spirit of looking out for one another can't be restricted to our homes or our workplaces, or our neighborhoods, or our houses of worship. It also has to be reflected in our national government. The kind of leadership that's guided by knowledge and experience; honesty and humility, empathy and grace. That kind of leadership doesn't just belong in our state capitols and mayors' offices. It belongs in the White House. And that's why I'm so proud to endorse Joe Biden for President of the United States.

President Trump: Today, I'm instructing my administration to halt funding of the World Health Organization while a review is conducted to assess the World Health Organization's role in severely mismanaging and covering up the spread of the coronavirus. Everybody knows what's going on there . . . The WHO pushed China's misinformation about the virus, saying it was not communicable and there was no need for travel bans. They told us when we put on our travel ban, a very strong travel ban, there was no need to do it. Don't do it. They actually fought us. The WHO's reliance on China's disclosures likely caused a twenty-fold increase in cases worldwide, and it may be much more than that.

Gov. Cuomo (NY): Fifty years ago, this week, Apollo 13 gets damaged 220,000 miles from earth. Somehow they figure out how to get a spaceship back 220,000 miles 50 years ago. That's America. Okay, figure out how to do testing. Figure out how to use technology to do tracing. That's what we have to work on and we have to do that together. We have to do as a government what our people have done, right? . . . I look forward to working with the president in partnership and cooperation, but he has no fight here. I won't let it happen and look, unless he suggested that we do something that would be reckless and endanger the health or welfare of the people of the state. Then I would have no choice. But shy of that, I put my hand out to say, "Let's do this together."

NBC News: The number of "probable" coronavirus deaths in New York City would push its death toll over 10,000, according to NYC Department of Public Health Data obtained by NBC News. The data showed that the city's 6,589 confirmed coronavirus deaths would jump by 3,778 with "probable" fatalities included, raising the total death toll to 10,367. The department defines a "probable" victim as someone who had not tested positive, but whose death certificate lists that they were killed by Covid-19, the disease associated with coronavirus.

Dr. Barbot, New York City Health Commissioner: Behind every death is a friend, a family member, a loved one. We are focused on ensuring that every New Yorker who died because of Covid-19 gets counted . . . What New Yorkers are interested in, and what the country is interested in, is that we have an accurate and complete count. It's part of the healing process that we're going to have to go through.

Governor Ron DeSantis (FL): Obviously, WWE (World Wrestling Entertainment), there's no crowd so it's a very small number of people. We look at it on a case-by-case basis.* We haven't had a huge amount of requests . . . The one thing I do support is, we do need to support content, especially sports and events. We're not going to have crowds there, I get that. If NASCAR does a race and can televise it, I think that's a good

* On April 9, Gov. DeSantis classified live sporting events with a national audience (but no spectators), including wrestling, as "essential services" in the state of Florida.

thing. I'd like to see [Tiger] Woods and [Phil] Mickelson golf. That's social distance. I think people are starved for content. We haven't had new content since the middle of March. If people are told to say closer to the house, it sure does help to have fresh things to do . . . I mean, if you think about it, we've never had a period like this in modern American history where you've had such little new content, particularly in the sporting realm. I mean, people are watching, we're watching, like, reruns from the early 2000s.

APRIL 15

President Trump: So we have a lot of patients who recover, and they're so happy to have recovered that the first thing they do is say we want to give our blood. And they do that. It's incredible. We have thousands of people that are doing that. They recover, they feel they have an obligation because they've gotten such great care, and a lot of them didn't think they were going to make it.

Gov. Newsom (CA): Our numbers yesterday were the highest recorded, but so are the nation's. And so by no stretch of the imagination are we out of the woods, despite the fact that we put forward a framework yesterday to begin to consider the prospects of reopening certain sectors of our economy. I want folks to know we need to maintain our vigilance and we need to maintain the path that we are on, a path that is producing results. But again, we are not yet in a place where we need to be so that we could start reopening.

Operation Gridlock, Michigan: Everyone, every citizen, every business owner needs to get out of their house, out of their chair and get in their car, or truck, or anything that is legal to drive on taxpayer funded roads. Then drive to Lansing to circle the Michigan Capitol Building at 100 N. Capitol Avenue at noon on April 15.

Gov. Whitmer (MI): I was really disappointed to see people congregating and not wearing masks. We know that this rally endangered people. This kind of activity will put more people at risk and sadly, it could prolong the amount of time that we have to be in this posture.

Kellyanne Conway, Counselor to the President: This is Covid-19, not Covid-1, folks.* You would think that people charged with the World Health Organization facts and figures would be on top of that. This is just a pause right now. So there is an investigation, examination to what happened. But people should know the facts.

APRIL 16

Dr. Amy Acton, Director, Ohio Department of Health: This is a big part of our future. We're not going back to life just the way it was before, but we are moving forward in the most amazing ways. And once we accept it, and I'm telling you everyone, we're accepting this slowly. Every day I go through stages of grief. I go through denial. I go through a little anger. I go through a little bargaining: *I don't have to wear this [mask]. I might not need it. This isn't true.* I get a little down, and then I come to a different kind of acceptance. And at that stage, I start to imagine how things could be, how they could be better than they've been, how we could do things differently.

Rep. Steny Hoyer (MD), House Majority Leader: This morning's unemployment figures, which show that over 22 million Americans—or one in eight working adults in our country—have lost their jobs in the past month, reinforce just how critical it is that our nation take appropriate steps to be able to safely reopen our economy. In order to do that, we must get this pandemic under control so it is safe for people to return to work. That means a concerted federal effort to significantly increase the amount of testing being done and the availability of personal protective

---

* The "19" in "Covid-19" refers to 2019, the year it was first discovered.

equipment for frontline workers. So far, the Trump Administration is failing dismally to do that.

Kristalina Georgieva, Chair and Managing Director, IMF: We simply cannot take social cohesion for granted. We got a lot of support from the membership to help countries' efforts in calibrating their social policies to reduce inequality, protect vulnerable people, and promote access to opportunities for all. We are in this crisis together.

Gov. J. B. Pritzker (IL): As you know, Covid-19 and the lack of federal organization of the supply chain have truly warped the market. As a result, we rarely have the luxury of going directly to a manufacturer or even a distributor to place an order. Under the current circumstances, procurements are often made now through multiple layers of connections. One distributor in the U.S. will know another distributor in another country who knows someone with a warehouse of masks and gloves. Our state procurement team has to track down these leads, vet the source in a very short time, because they're competing to get the available goods first. And then they have to figure out how to ship the goods from point A to point B.

Sen. Chris Murphy (CT): What we're watching, potentially, is Trump using the same tools domestically that he used internationally. What he did to Ukraine he is arguably doing to Michigan, New York, and Connecticut today. He sees the money at his disposal as a mechanism to advance his political agenda. We should have removed him from office because he showed no contrition after his extortion campaign in Ukraine, suggesting that he was willing to use those same tactics domestically.

Marc Perrone, President, UFCW: This is now a matter of life and death. Amazon and Whole Foods must take immediate action to keep their workers safe from the rapidly growing coronavirus outbreak. With six more Whole Foods worker infections just reported, and countless Amazon workers exposed across the country, it is stunning that Amazon

CEO Jeff Bezos is more focused on silencing brave whistleblowers than actually taking the action needed to protect these grocery and warehouse workers.

Gov. Newsom (CA): I'll confess, myself included, sometimes we go to a grocery store, we're not always our best selves because of the stress all of us are bringing to bear in those lines, some large, some short, long and short. I just want to compliment you for holding that line and continuing to help us reduce our own stresses. You're not spending as much time with your kids and your families and I just want you to know, I heard a few grocery workers say this, "We're called essential workers, but increasingly we feel like we're disposable." I want you to know you're not disposable. You are essential and you're valued and I want from the bottom of my heart to extend my deep admiration and appreciation to you, those farm workers and everybody else that every day are unsung heroes that need to be called out at this moment for, yes, meeting this moment.

Rep. Lauren Underwood (IL): In our suburban communities, so many people are working from home if they are working. But we're also seeing significant increases in unemployment—like 1,000%. It's not necessarily like that in all of our rural communities where day-to-day life hasn't necessarily changed in terms of requirements to stay home and things like that. Certainly the agriculture industry has suffered. The leadership challenge for us is to navigate that dual experience.

President Trump: We're going to be helping with testing. They're going to be doing the testing. It's got to be a localized thing and it really has been since I'd been involved because I came in and federal government's supposed to do testing of parking lots in the middle of a certain state that's 2000 miles away.* It's ridiculous, but the testing has been so incredible. Two

---

* See Vice President Pence's comments on March 13.

things, testing and ventilators. Ventilators are really tough. They are very complex, they're very expensive, they're very sophisticated machines.

Gov. Inslee (WA): It's been confirmed by the President that he will not be interfering with our "Stay Home, Stay Healthy" initiative. He has decided to follow the Constitution, which is always a good thing to make sure that we could make our decisions for what is best for Washington here in Washington . . . By the way, he did not authorize us to make decisions. What authorized us to make decisions are the US Constitution and our state constitution and the people of the state of Washington.

President Trump: Based on the latest data, our team of experts now agrees that we can begin the next front in our war, which we are calling Opening Up America Again. And that's what we're doing. We're opening up our country, and we have to do that. America wants to be open and Americans want to be open. As I have said for some time now, a national shutdown is not a sustainable long-term solution.

Senator Lindsey Graham (SC): On what we need to do better, I think the key to me is testing. I can't really blame the president, but we are struggling with testing on a large scale. You can't really go back to work until we have more tests that shows who has it and who doesn't, and we're beginning to turn the corner on that.

Gov. Inslee (WA): We are a thousand miles away from having enough testing equipment in the United States and in the state of Washington . . . Let me give you an example of how desperate that situation was. About a week ago, we had to have a person drive from our lab in Shoreline to Spokane to pick up 40 vials of transport, virus transport medium, and drive it back 150 miles to Yakima for use at an outbreak going on in a long term-care facility because we didn't have enough swabs or test medium. That's how precarious this situation is. To remedy this, we need the federal government to cause a full-scale mobilization of the industrial capacity of the United States.

Mayor Lenny Curry, Jacksonville, FL: As of 5 P.M. tomorrow, we will be reopening the beaches and parks, throughout Duval County for essential activities only . . . This can be the beginning of the pathway back to normal life.

APRIL 17

Kaiser Family Foundation: There have been 3,423,034 total Covid-19 tests with results in the United States, with over 1 million added since last week. 19% of the total tests were positive. There were 10.4 tests with results per 1000 people.

Gov. Cuomo (NY): The only thing [President Trump's] doing, to be honest, "It's up to the states to do reopen." It was always up to the states. What, are you are going to grant me what the Constitution granted me before you were born? It's called the 10th Amendment. And I didn't need the president of the United States to tell me that I'm governor. And I didn't need the president of the United States to tell me the powers of a state. People did that. Alexander Hamilton, Thomas Jefferson, James Madison. They are the ones who gave me the power. And I don't need the president of the United States to read the Constitution for me. Maybe he should have read the Constitution before he said he had the power to open the states.

President Trump: Governor Cuomo should spend more time "doing" and less time "complaining". Get out there and get the job done. Stop talking! We built you thousands of hospital beds that you didn't need or use, gave large numbers of Ventilators that you should have had, and helped you with testing that you should be doing. We have given New York far more money, help and equipment than any other state, by far, & these great men & women who did the job never hear you say thanks. Your numbers are not good. Less talk and more action!

Gov. Cuomo (NY): Let's respond to the president. First of all, if he's sitting home watching TV, maybe he should get up and go to work, right? Second, let's keep emotion and politics out of this and personal ego, if we can, because this is about the people and it's about our job.

President Trump: So we're helping people. Even with swabs, we get ventilators. We're now the king of ventilators. We have hundreds of thousands under construction. We don't need them ourselves. The governors are in great shape.

Gov. Cuomo (NY): I don't know what I'm supposed to do—send a bouquet of flowers? Thank you again, Mr. President, for the Javits. Thank you for the U.S. Navy ship *Comfort*, which is just doing your job as president. It's not really thank you like you wrote a check yourself, but thank you.

President Trump: There's a tremendous amount of unused capacity in the states available for governors to tap. We have tremendous unused capability within those laboratories, and I hope the governors are going to be able to use them. The governors are responsible for testing, and I hope they're going to be able to use this tremendous amount of available capacity that we have. It's up to one million additional tests per week. When you think of that, in the next few weeks, we'll be sending out 5.5 million testing swabs to the state. Swabs can be done easily by the governors themselves. Mostly it's cotton. It's not a big deal.

Gov. Cuomo (NY): The president doesn't want to help on testing. I said the one issue we need help with it is testing. He said eleven times, "I don't want to get involved in testing. It's too complicated. It's too hard." I know it's too complicated and it's too hard. That's why we need you to help. I can't do an international supply chain. He wants to say, "Well, I did enough."

Yeah, none of us have done enough. We haven't, because it's not over . . . I don't do China relations. I don't do international supply chain and that's where the federal government can help. Also remember the federal government at the same time is developing testing capacity. So we wind up in this bizarre situation that we were in last time, fifty states all competing for these precious resources. In this case it's testing and then the federal government comes in and says to those companies, "I want to buy the tests also." This is mayhem. We need a coordinated approach between the federal government and the states.

***New York Times*:** As some governors consider easing social distancing restrictions, new estimates by researchers at Harvard University suggest that the United States cannot safely reopen unless it conducts more than three times the number of coronavirus tests it is currently administering over the next month . . . An average of 146,000 people per day have been tested for the coronavirus nationally so far this month, according to the Covid Tracking Project, which on Friday reported 3.6 million total tests across the country.

Gov. Cuomo (NY): Well, this is an important moment. [Trump's] saying he doesn't want to provide funding to the states and he doesn't want to help on testing and I can tell you the states can't do it otherwise. And if this testing doesn't work, that's a serious problem. I don't care about his politics but, if we don't have federal help on testing, that's a real problem. And I'm not going to go through the chaos that was created last time on PPE. Where people who were genuine heroes couldn't get PPE because there was a lack of coordination and because everything was made in China. We're looking at that situation with testing again. I can tell you that. I know enough to know that.

Gov. Hogan (MD): I want to remind Marylanders that beginning tomorrow morning, when inside retail establishments, including grocery stores, pharmacies, and convenience stores, or when riding any form of public transportation, the wearing of masks or face coverings will be necessary. Now, some people have said that covering their faces infringes on their rights, but this isn't just about your rights or protecting yourself, it's about protecting your neighbors. And the best science that we have shows that people might not know that they're carriers of the virus and, through no fault of their own, they could infect other people. And spreading this disease infringes on your neighbor's rights.

President Trump: LIBERATE MINNESOTA!

Governor Tim Walz (MN): If we just said let's go back to the way we were in January in operating, we would kill lots of people, especially those on the front line . . . I called [Trump] to ask what are we doing differently about moving toward getting as many people back into the workforce without compromising the health of Minnesotans or the providers. That will probably take longer than a two-word Tweet.

President Trump: LIBERATE MICHIGAN!

Gov. Whitmer (MI): I hope that it's not encouraging more protests. One of the things that I think in this moment right now is to acknowledge that people are feeling very anxious. People are worried about the business that they built, took a lifetime to build, and the employees who are counting on them. People are worried about making the rent payment because they are out of work. There's a lot of anxiety. I think the most important thing that anyone with a platform can do is to try to use that platform to tell people we're going to get through this.

President Trump: LIBERATE VIRGINIA, and save your great 2nd Amendment. It is under siege!

Governor Ralph Northam (VA): As the Governor of the Commonwealth of Virginia, I along with this staff is fighting a biological war. I do not have time to involve myself in Twitter wars. I will continue to make sure that I do everything that I can to keep Virginians safe and to save lives.

Mayor Muriel Bowser, Washington, D.C.: Let me just say a few things, and I know the chancellor will add to this, about what we have been doing around learning at home. We as a city and as a public education system and as a nation need to continue to address the digital divide. This pandemic has put a huge spotlight on one of the great inequities in our country, not everybody being able to access information quickly and in the same way.

Governor Tate Reeves (MS): I wanted to come here today and announce that we can all ease up and reopen, but we can't. We can't stay in this position for much longer. But we are still in the eye of the storm. I made a vow to protect the people of Mississippi. I have to do what the best information and wisdom I have tells me. Right now, it tells me I have to ask you to stay vigilant for one more week.

Governor Kristi Noem (SD): In South Dakota it looks different how we implement that because we took a different path. We did not mandate that our businesses would close. We gave them the opportunity to be innovative, to take care of their customers while they protected their employees going through the spread of this virus. Now we trusted the people of South Dakota to take personal responsibility for those actions and they overperformed in a really big way.

Robert F. Hill, Superintendent, Springfield City School District, OH: We made it through another week of remote learning! You are doing a wonderful job with your children and I cannot stress enough how grateful we are for the ongoing partnership with the families in our district. I know there are days when you feel like nothing got accomplished, but it did. You and your student may have stumbled through a math assignment, but playing Yahtzee with them later in the evening, was math. There are probably days when you feel like you cannot get your student to write one sentence in reply to an assigned reading lesson. It's ok. When you read them that story at bedtime, the one you have read a million times, that was reading. What about science? Remember when you went outside to observe the supermoon? It was so big and you talked about how it was closer to earth that night? That was science. Some days are better than others and some lessons are more structured than others. It may be hard, but keep trying. Do the best that you can and encourage your children to do the best that they can.

APRIL 18

Gov. Cuomo (NY): Good morning. Okay, let's start with some indisputable facts today. Today is Saturday, that is a fact, indisputable. Somebody probably could dispute it, but I will stand by that factual determination . . . We still have about 2,000 people yesterday who were new admissions to a hospital or new Covid diagnoses. That is still an overwhelming number every day, 2,000 new. If it wasn't for the relative context that we've been in, this would be devastating news, 2,000 people coming into the hospital system or testing positive.

President Trump: You don't hear anymore about ventilators. What happened to the ventilators? And now they're giving you the other. It's called testing, testing, but they don't want to use all of the capacity that we've created. We have tremendous capacity. Dr. Birx will be explaining that. They know that, the governors know that. The Democrat governors know that. They're the ones that are complaining.

Gov. Cuomo (NY): We did 500,000 tests in a month. That's great news. Bad news is it's only a fraction of what you need. The more you test, the more information, the more you can reopen society . . . These [test machine] manufacturers are regulated by the federal government, and the federal government clearly has a role in addressing this crisis, but we need two things from the federal government. We need help on that supply chain, especially when it becomes international, and we need coordination and basic partnership.

President Trump: My administration has also been speaking frequently with many of the governors to help them find and unlock the vast unused testing capacity that exists in their states. Dr. Birx discussed yesterday the commercial and academic laboratories in the states have tremendous unused capability which they can use. The governor should use it. Tremendous unused capability. They're waiting for business from these governors that some of them complain. I must tell you, for the most part we're getting along great with them, but some of them like to complain, but I still go back because the hardest thing of all by far by a factor of 20 is the ventilators. And now we're the king of ventilators.

Gov. Cuomo (NY): Last point, personal opinion. This is not a fact. This is just my opinion. You can throw it in the garbage. The emotion in this country is as high as I can recall. People are frustrated. We're anxious. We're scared. We're angry. We've never been through this before. And, on every level, this is a terrible experience. It's disorienting. It threatens you to your core. It makes you reflect on your whole life. It's mentally very difficult. It's emotionally difficult. Economically, it's disastrous. I mean, the market goes down. Your retirement funds go down. You're not getting a paycheck. It is as tumultuous a time as we have ever seen . . . And, look, if you have partisan division splitting this nation now, it's going to make it worse. Abraham Lincoln, "A house divided itself against itself cannot stand." 1858. Where did Abraham Lincoln get it from? "If a house is divided against itself, the house cannot stand," Mark 3:25. Okay, so this is accepted wisdom, Let us say. House cannot stand. Not to mention, a house cannot rise up from the greatest challenge it has seen since World War II. This is no time and no place for division. We have our hands full as it is. Let's just stay together and let's work it through. That's why we're called the United States. And the unity was key. Going back to Abraham Lincoln, it was always about the unity. Going back to the framers of the Constitution, it was always balance of power to ensure unity. And we need that unity now more than ever before. Questions?

President Trump: We have a tremendous lab capability, laboratory capability all over the country. And for some reason, the governors, a lot of them are. For some reason the governors, they're not, a lot of them are, but some of the governors like to complain and they're not using it. We have tremendous capability.

Gov. Hogan (MD): This has been the number one stumbling block in America, the lack of availability of testing, and you really can't get to any point where you can reopen the country until, not just in my state, but across the country, until we can do much, much larger-scale testing.

Gov. DeSantis (FL): I've always promoted essential activities with recreation. You've just got to do it in a way that's going to have low risk. I get a kick out of somebody jogging on the beach in California, like all by his lonesome, and you have a fleet of cops go out there. He's just jogging. Going forward, I think we've got to be promoting people to get exercise.

Jim Curcio, Surrogate, Atlantic County (NJ): Atlantic County Officials need to sound the alarm. Reopen New Jersey immediately with sensible restrictions. Trust American freedom ingenuity and the US Constitution. Untie the hands of the Private Sector so it can rescue NJ from this nightmare.

Gov. Murphy (NJ): That is irresponsible. We "untie" the system right now, there will be blood on our hands. And I want to make sure folks understand that. This is literally life and death.

APRIL 19

Gov. Cuomo (NY): Today is Sunday. That is a fact. I know these days tend to run one into the other, but today is Sunday. I like to focus on the facts in this situation because facts are what's most important. A lot of people have opinions and a lot of theories. But Senator Daniel Patrick Moynihan, who was a great senator from the state of New York, liked to say, "Everyone is entitled to their own opinion, but not his own facts." So let's give the people of the state the updated facts. This is the chart of total hospitalizations. We've been watching this twenty-four hours a day for it seems like most of our lives, but it's only been about 40 days.

Dr. Deborah Birx, White House Coronavirus Response Coordinator: [T]here are three ways we want to monitor this virus community by community. The first way is really understanding ER visits and the symptoms associated with Covid-19. And we're tracking and tracing those every day all across the country. The second way is really understanding influenza like illness and converting that entire surveillance program and monitoring program to Covid-like illness, which we can throughout the summer months because we don't have flu. And the third critical leg with those other two legs is testing. But testing needs to be focused critically where you start to see early evidence because no test is 100 percent specific and 100 percent sensitive.

Vice President Pence: The federal government at the President's direction will continue to support governors as they deploy the testing resources in the time and manner of their choosing. But we believe today, as Dr. Deborah Birx has confirmed, is we have a sufficient capacity of testing today for any state in America to move into phase one and begin the process of reopening their state and their economy.

Gov. Northam (VA): That's just delusional to be making statements like that. We—we have been fighting every day for PPE. And we have got some supplies now coming in. We have been fighting for testing. It's not a straightforward test. We don't even have enough swabs, believe it or not. And we're ramping that up. But for the national level say that we have what we need, and really to have no guidance to the state levels, is just irresponsible, because we're not there yet.

President Trump: One's a swab, one's a Q-tip. It's actually different. It's very sophisticated actually, but it's a little bit like, so this is the swab, and we've ordered a lot of them. They have a lot of them, some of them, some of the states, they were shipped to states and the states don't know where they are, but that's it.

Gov. Hogan (MD): It's not accurate to say there's plenty of testing out there, and the governors should just get it done. That's just not being straightforward.

President Trump: Some people believe in testing very strongly and other people believe in it less strongly, but still it's a very good thing to have. I think we can say that. Some people believe in it like they can't exist without testing and other people don't believe in it nearly as much . . . You must remember that the governors wanted to have total control over the opening of their states, but now they want to have us, the federal government, do the testing. And again, testing is local. You can't have it both ways.

Gov. Hogan (MD): To try to push this off to say that the governors have plenty of testing and they should just get to work on testing, somehow we aren't doing our job, is just absolutely false. Every governor in America has been pushing and fighting and clawing to get more tests. Not only from the federal government, but from every private lab in America, and from all across the world.

President Trump: I've seen the [protesters]. I've seen the interviews of the people. These are great people. Look, they want to get, they call cabin fever, you've heard the term. They've got cabin fever. They want to get back. They want their life back . . . And when the virus passes, I hope we're going to be sitting next to each other and baseball games, football games, basketball games, ice hockey games. I hope we're going to be sitting next to each other. I hope you have golf. The Masters is going to have 100,000 people, not 25 people watching at the course.

Gov. Cuomo (NY): I don't want to have gone all through this and then just say we are reopening. No, no, no. We have to open for a better future than we have ever had, and we have to learn from this. As we go through this, remember, I know people are eager to get on with life.

THE OPENING

APRIL 20–MAY 24

MONDAY, APRIL 20

Gov. Kemp (GA): Given the favorable data, enhanced testing and approval of our health care professionals, we will allow gyms, fitness centers, bowling alleys, body art studios, barbers, cosmetologists, hair designers, nail care artists, aestheticians, their respective schools and massage therapists to re-open their doors this Friday, April 24 . . . Theaters, social clubs and restaurant dine-in services will be allowed to open on Monday, April 27 . . . The private sector is going to have to convince the public that it's safe to come back into these businesses.

Brian Maloof, Owner, Manuel's Tavern, Atlanta (GA): My phone has been blowing up with tons of questions from staff and regular customers asking if we're going to open on Monday. The answer is no. All of our experience and the wisdom of some really smart people that work at the tavern think it's way too early. As much as I would like to be open, it's not happening. Being closed has not been fun, but it's been the safest, best thing we could do for our staff and our customers . . . We will continue doing to-go only until I'm convinced that it's safe to open the tavern back up completely; it may be several weeks or longer. Don't hate us for being safe. I look forward to selling you something to go.

Gov. Andrew Cuomo (NY): If you're looking for the optimist's view, it's not as bad as it was, but 478 New Yorkers died yesterday from this terrible virus. Everyone is anxious to reopen. Everyone is anxious to get back to work. So am I. Question is: What does that mean? How do we do it? When do we do it? Nobody disagrees that we want to get out of this situation. Nobody. You don't need protests to convince anyone in this country that we have to get back to work and we have to get the economy going and we have to get out of our homes.

Governor Henry McMaster (SC): South Carolina's business is our business. When this began, we were outrunning the competition in many of the races with our competition. We want to be able to continue to do that when this virus is gone, and as we're pulling out of it. So what I'm doing is—We want to be able, if you can imagine a race, we want to be able to slingshot around the competition and get back up to full speed as soon as we can. To that end, I have created an organization called Accelerate South Carolina. We must be ready to stomp on the gas when the green flag, when the green light comes up.

Mayor LaToya Cantrell, New Orleans: To the citizens of the city of New Orleans, please know that I will and have always continued to put the health of the people first. They are the priority. You can be reassured that I will not be bullied . . . These are the things I have to think about as being mayor of the city, and it's not driven by the dollar.

Lt. Gov. Patrick (TX): What I said when I was with you* that night is there are more important things than living. And that's saving this country for my children and my grandchildren and saving this country for all of us. I don't want to die, nobody wants to die, but man we've got to take some risks and get back in the game and get this country back up and running.

---

* Tucker Carlson, who is interviewing him on Fox News. (See March 23 for the interview to which he is referring.)

Gov. Whitmer (MI): Who in this great state actually believes that they care more about jet skiing then saving the lives of the elderly, or the vulnerable? This action isn't about our individual right to gather. It's about our parents' right to live. President Trump called this a war, and it is exactly that, so let's act like it. In World War II, there weren't people lining up at the Capitol to protest the fact that they had to drop everything they were doing, and build planes, or tanks, or to ration food. They rolled up their sleeves, and they got to work.

President Trump: As the experts have explained, this capacity is sufficient to allow states to conduct diagnostic testing to treat patients, as well as contact tracing to contain outbreaks and monitoring to pinpoint potential hotspots during phase one. And there are some hotspots and we have them pinpointed, and they can really cover it very, very nicely when they know exactly where to go, and they're being told where to go. And also these locations where they're going, and some of them are federal, some of the governors didn't realize they were allowed to use federal locations. They are. And we have a booklet of the federal locations. We can hold it up. I think you'll show that. Maybe we'll hold it up now. Yeah. Okay, fine. But you see the number of things. These are all locations where they can go, which is really pretty amazing. This is just one page out of many. Look at this. These are all locations. That's a lot of locations. And they can all . . . What is it, 5,000?

Edmond J. Safra Center for Ethics, Harvard University: We need to deliver 5 million tests per day by early June to deliver a safe social reopening. This number will need to increase over time (ideally by late July) to 20 million a day to fully remobilize the economy. We acknowledge that even this number may not be high enough to protect public health. In that considerably less likely eventuality, we will need to scale-up testing much further. By the time we know if we need to do that, we should be in a better position to know how to do it. In any situation, achieving these numbers depends on testing innovation.

Gov. Hogan (MD): This weekend we took an exponential, game-changing step forward on our large-scale testing initiative. We've been quietly working for a number of weeks on a confidential project . . . On Saturday the first lady and I stood on the tarmac at BWI airport to welcome the first ever Korean Air passenger plane, a Boeing 777, which had no passengers, but which was carrying a very important payload of LabGun Covid-19 PCR test kits from a South Korean company called LabGenomics, which will now give Maryland the capability of performing a half a million Coronavirus tests.

President Trump: We'll give you the details, but hundreds and hundreds of labs are ready, willing, and able. Some of the governors, like as an example, the governor from Maryland didn't really understand the list. He didn't understand too much about what was going on . . . By the way, not everybody agrees that we have to do that much testing. We're going maximum.

Gov. Hogan (MD): The 500,000 test capacity which we have just acquired is equal to the total amount of testing which has been completed by four of the top five states in America combined . . . the administration made it clear over and over again, they want the states to take the lead, and we have to go out and do it ourselves. And so that's exactly what we did.

President Trump: Some states have far more capacity than they actually understand, and it is a complex subject, but some of the governors didn't understand it. The governor, as an example, Pritzker from Illinois, did not understand his capacity, not simply ask the federal government to provide unlimited support. I mean you have to take the support where you have it, but we are there to stand with the governors and to help the governors, and that's what we're doing and they have a tremendous capacity that we've already built up and you'll be seeing that.

APRIL 21

Gov. Pritzker (IL): The truth of the matter is that the president doesn't seem to understand the difference between testing capacity and getting testing results. Testing capacity, what he's referring to is, hey, you've got enough machines in each of your states to run tests that will give you, you know, hundreds of thousands of results. But what he's not right about is we don't have the supplies to run those tests . . . So, what we needed was for the federal government—still need—for the federal government to enact the Defense Production Act to make it easier for us to obtain the swabs and the VTM and the reagent that we need. None of that has been done at the federal government level. That's the mistake that has been made all along here. We could have organized this and led this at a federal level. You know, everybody, including libertarians, would tell you that the purpose of the federal government at a minimum is to manage a national emergency. And this is a national emergency, and it's not being managed well from the White House.

Former State Rep. Stacey Abrams (GA): There's no legitimate reason for reopening the state except for politics, and I think it's deeply disingenuous [Governor Kemp] would pretend otherwise.

Mayor Keisha Lance Bottoms, Atlanta: We really are at a loss and I am concerned as a mother and the mayor of our capital city. I am perplexed that we [in Georgia] have opened up in this way . . . As I look at the data and as I talk with our public health officials, I don't see that it's based on anything that's logical.

Kareen Troitino, President of the Correctional Officer Union, Miami, FL: There's no social distancing. It's like what you see when you have a big exposé at some sweatshop in China. We're being made to keep producing these military jackets, which are not necessary at this moment. It's just pure greed.

ACLU Ohio: Black people represent 43 percent of Covid-19 deaths in Illinois, but make up only 14 percent of the state's population. In Louisiana, Black people make up 32 percent of the state but represent almost 60 percent of Covid-19 related deaths. Similarly alarming, in Mississippi, Black people make up 38 percent of the population but represent 52 percent of Covid-19 cases and 63 percent of reported deaths. Cities with larger Black and Latino communities are especially seeing the inequalities in Covid-19 cases and deaths. In Milwaukee, Black people make up 53 percent of people who have died from Covid-19, while making up only 39 percent of the city's population. In New York City, which now has more confirmed cases than anywhere else in the world, Latinos make up 29 percent of the population but 34 percent of Covid-19 deaths and Black people make up 22 percent of the population but 28 percent of deaths.

Former Vice President Biden: The Trump Administration is currently responsible for one of the most significant failures of governance of any administration in modern history. It failed to heed warnings and adequately prepare our nation. It has failed to sufficiently ramp up the production of critical equipment, like ventilators, masks, and other personal protective equipment through the Defense Production Act (DPA). It has not only left governors on their own to scramble for supplies, it has actively stood in the way of some of those efforts. And the Trump Administration has failed to surge Covid-19 tests nationally, which public health officials say is necessary to safely reopen our country.

National Nurses Association: To highlight the lack of transparency regarding the supply of personal protective equipment (PPE), management's refusal to meet and discuss the hospital's staffing plan should a surge in infected Covid-19 patients occur, and to describe current conditions and the need for more N95 respirators and other protective gear required to safely treat Covid-19 patients, registered nurses at Enloe Medical Center are holding a candlelight vigil and media availability at 8:00 P.M., April 22nd.

President Trump: Since we announced our guidelines on opening up America, as we call it, we say opening up America and we add the word "again." I think we can add the word probably "again," but that's what it is. We're opening up America again. 20 States representing 40% of the US population have announced that they are making plans and preparations to safely restart their economies in the very near future.

Sen. Ron Wyden (OR), Ranking Member, Senate Committee on Finance: I am concerned by reports that Economic Impact Payments to Americans will be delayed by the unprecedented decision to print "President Donald J. Trump" on the checks, as well as conflicting reporting on how this decision was made . . . I am concerned that the decision to gratuitously affix the president's name to checks disbursing taxpayer funds may have delayed delivery of money urgently needed by millions of Americans to meet basic needs.

Steve Mnuchin, Secretary of the Treasury: Now let me make just one more comment on the [Paycheck Protection] Program. We have over a million companies that have received this with less than 10 workers. So there is very broad participation in really small business. I will comment, there have been some big businesses that have taken these loans. I was pleased to see that Shake Shack returned to the money . . . There is a certification that people are making and I asked people just make sure the intent of this was for business that needed the money.

Dr. Redfield, Director, CDC: There's a possibility that the assault of the virus on our nation next winter will actually be even more difficult than the one we just went through. When I've said this to others, they kind of put their head back, they don't understand what I mean.

APRIL 22

Johns Hopkins Coronavirus Resource Center:
Global cases: 2,620,579
U.S.: 837,947

Spain: 208,389
Italy: 187,327
France: 157,125
Germany: 150,062
United Kingdom: 134,638
Iran: 85,996
China: 83,868

Gov. Murphy (NJ): I'd like to remember three more of those we've lost. John Carreccia. There's John. He was born in New York City, but called the Ford section of Woodbridge Township home for the past 40 years. For three decades, John worked for the Port Authority of New York and New Jersey at Newark Airport and the World Trade Center, retiring as operations supervisor in human services. Since his retirement, he remained active and was serving as the Chief of the Woodbridge Township Ambulance and Rescue Squad. John was also active in the life of St. James Roman Catholic Church in Woodbridge. He's being remembered by his family, friends and colleagues as a leader, teacher and mentor.

Gov. Newsom (CA): We've actually directed beyond just Santa Clara,* go back as far as December, to request the coroner's autopsy to dig even deeper. We are very pleased with the work that was done in Santa Clara County to make public that information, and know that we are doing the same across the state and other counties as well to ultimately help guide a deeper understanding of when this pandemic really started to impact California directly.

---

* A woman from Santa Clara who died in early February was determined to be the first U.S. fatality from Covid-19.

Mayor Carolyn Goodman, Las Vegas, NV: I'd love everything open because I think we've had viruses for years that have been here.

Dr. Fauci, Director, NIAID: If you jump the gun and go into a situation where you have a big spike, you're gonna set yourself back. So as painful as it is to go by the careful guidelines of gradually phasing into a reopening, [opening too soon] is going to backfire. That's the problem.

ACLU: The government models fail to consider the impact of the virus on the incarcerated population, who will be infected and die at higher rates. And any prison or jail outbreak is bound to spill over into the broader community—causing more people to die in the general public, too. The ACLU partnered with epidemiologists, mathematicians and statisticians to create a first-of-its-kind epidemiological model that shows that as many as 200,000 people could die from Covid-19—double the government estimate—if we continue to ignore incarcerated people in our public health response. But we have the power to change this grim outcome. We can save as many as 23,000 people in jail and 76,000 in the broader community if we stop arrests for all but the most serious offenses and double the rate of release for those already detained.

Dr. Rick Bright, Former Director, Biomedical Advanced Research and Development Authority (BARDA): Yesterday, I was removed from my positions as the Director of the Biomedical Advanced Research and Development Authority (BARDA) and HHS Deputy Assistant Secretary for Preparedness and Response . . . I believe this transfer was in response to my insistence that the government invest the billions of dollars allocated by Congress to address the Covid-19 pandemic into safe and scientifically vetted solutions, and not in drugs, vaccines and other technologies that lack scientific merit. I am speaking out because to combat this deadly virus, science—not politics or cronyism—has to lead the way . . . I also resisted efforts to fund potentially dangerous drugs promoted by those with political connections . . . Sidelining me in the middle of this pandemic and placing politics and cronyism ahead of science puts lives at risk and stunts national efforts to safely and effectively address this urgent public health crisis.

Rep. Adam Schiff (CA), Chair, House Intelligence Committee: We all hope, again and again, that we've seen the worst this President has to offer. And then he sinks lower. If Trump is punishing scientists who insist our coronavirus response be based on science, not hype, he is putting more lives in danger. Congress must find out.

Senator Mitch McConnell (KY), Senate Majority Leader: I think this whole business of additional assistance for state and local governments needs to be thoroughly evaluated. There's not going to be any desire on the Republican side to bail out state pensions by borrowing money from future generations . . . I would certainly be in favor of allowing states to use the bankruptcy route. It saves some cities. And there's no good reason for it not to be available. My guess is their first choice would be for the federal government to borrow money from future generations to send it down to them now so they don't have to do that. That's not something I'm going to be in favor of.

APRIL 23

Gov. Cuomo (NY): [McConnell] represents the state of Kentucky. Okay? When it comes to fairness, New York state puts much more money into the federal pot than it takes out. Okay? At the end of the year, we put into that federal pot $116 billion more than we take out. Okay? His state, the state of Kentucky, takes out 148 billion more than they put in. Okay? So he's a federal legislator. He's distributing the federal pot of money. New York puts in more money to the federal pot than it takes out. His state takes out more than it puts in. Senator McConnell, who's getting bailed out here? It's your state that is living on the money that we generate. Your state is getting bailed out. Not my state.

Vice President Pence: I think by Memorial Day Weekend, we will largely have this coronavirus epidemic behind us.

Dr. Fauci, Director, NIAID: I agree you don't need to test everybody, but you should at least be able to test the people in which you have to test to be able to do containment, and right now I think there's still some gaps there. I mean, on paper it might look OK, but we absolutely need to significantly ramp up not only the number of tests, but the capacity to actually perform them, so that you don't have a situation where you have a test, but it can't be done because there's not a swab, or not an extraction media or not the right vial—all of those things got to be in place. I am not overly confident right now at all that we have what it takes to do that.

President Trump: No, I don't agree with them on that. No, I think we're doing a great job in testing. I don't agree. If [Dr. Fauci] said that, I don't agree with it.*

Rep. Frank Pallone Jr. (NJ), Chair, House Energy and Commerce Committee: Removing Dr. Bright in the midst of a pandemic would raise serious concerns under any circumstances, but his allegations that political considerations influenced this decision heighten those concerns and demand full accountability . . . I have been particularly concerned by the Trump Administration's politicization of public health agencies. This most recent action, if true, further raises serious questions about the

---

* Trump's response to CBS News's Weijia Jiang: "Do you agree with Dr. Fauci that we're just not there yet?"

commitment of President Trump and his Administration to science and the public good as the government and the nation work to combat an unprecedented global health pandemic.

U.S. Bureau of Labor Statistics: In the week ending April 18, the advance figure for seasonally adjusted initial claims was 4,427,000 . . . The total number of people claiming benefits in all programs for the week ending April 4 was 12,506,993, an increase of 4,300,016 from the previous week. There were 1,757,864 persons claiming benefits in all programs in the comparable week in 2019.

CNBC: Shares of Zoom closed 12.5% higher on Thursday after the company announced its number of daily users grew 50% in the past month. More than 300 million people used Zoom's videoconferencing software on April 22, CEO Eric Yuan announced in a webinar. Zoom has seen a spike in users since the Covid-19 pandemic has pushed many companies and schools to remote work. Zoom announced on April 1 it had 200 million people using its software in March, after several stay-at-home mandates were implemented, from about 10 million in December.

Senator Ben Sasse (NE): Last month, Congress didn't fix a crummy formula for emergency benefits, and now bad policy is hurting America's workers. It's hard for small businesses to serve their communities when Washington pits them against a system that pays more for unemployment than work. Tim Scott, Lindsey Graham, Rick Scott, and I warned about this in March, but Speaker Pelosi and Senator Sanders decided to ignore reality. They said that this wouldn't happen. They were wrong. They ought to admit it, apologize to the small businesses they hurt, and join us in fixing this.

Governor Pete Ricketts (NE): I'd just encourage everybody if you are thinking, "Oh gee I'm just going to stay home and collect unemployment benefits because it's paying me more than my job was." If your employer calls you back, take that job, because if you don't, you will lose your benefits. That's how it works here in Nebraska.

Sen. Warren (MA): My oldest brother, Don Reed, died from the coronavirus on Tuesday evening. He was charming and funny, a natural leader. What made him extra special was his smile. He had a quick, crooked smile that seemed to generate its own light—and to light up everyone around him. I'm grateful to the nurses and frontline staff who took care of him, but it's hard to know that there was no family to hold his hand or to say "I love you" one more time—and no funeral for those of us who loved him to hold each other close.

Rep. Maxine Waters (CA), Chair, House Financial Services Committee: I'm going to take a moment to dedicate this legislation to my dear sister who is dying in a hospital in St. Louis, Missouri right now, infected by the coronavirus. This legislation provides $370 billion in funding for small businesses, as well as $100 billion for hospitals and coronavirus testing.

Gov. Cuomo (NY): Senator McConnell, who is the head of the Senate, we've been talking about funding for state and local governments, and it was not in the bill that the house is going to pass today. They said, "Don't worry, don't worry. Don't worry, the next bill." As soon as the Senate passed it, this current bill, Senator Mitch McConnell goes out and he says, "Maybe the states should declare bankruptcy." Okay. This is one of the really dumb ideas of all time.

Rep. Ocasio-Cortez (NY): It is a joke when Republicans say they have urgency around this bill. The only folks that they have urgency around are folks like Ruth's Chris Steakhouse and Shake Shack. Those are the people getting assistance in this bill. You are not trying to fix this bill for mom and pops. And we have to fight to fund hospitals? Fighting to fund testing? That is what we're fighting for in this bill. It is unconscionable. If you had urgency, you would legislate like rent was due on May 1st.

President Trump: It is interesting that the states that are in trouble do happen to be blue. It is interesting.

Gov. Cuomo (NY): Vicious is saying, when Senator McConnell said, this is a blue state bailout, what he's saying is if you look at the states that have coronavirus problems, they tend to be democratic states. New York, California, Michigan, Illinois. They are Democratic states. So if you fund states that are suffering from the coronavirus, the Democratic states, don't help New York state because it is a Democratic state. How ugly a thought. I mean, just think of what he's saying. People died. "Fifteen thousand people died in New York, but they were predominantly Democrats. So why should we help them?" I mean, for crying out loud, if there was ever a time for you to put aside your pettiness and your partisanship and this political lens that you see the world through Democrat and Republican and "we help Republicans, but we don't help Democrats." That's not who we are.

Department of Homeland Security: Recent incidents and arrests nationwide illustrate how the Covid-19 pandemic is driving violent actors—both non-ideologically and ideologically motivated—to threaten violence . . . the pandemic has created a new source of anger and frustration for some individuals. As a result, violent extremist plots will likely involve individuals seeking targets symbolic to their personal grievances.

President Trump: Supposedly when we hit the body with a tremendous, whether it's ultraviolet or just very powerful light, and I think you said that hasn't been checked, but you're going to test it.* And then I said supposing

* Bill Bryan, acting undersecretary of science and technology for the Department of Homeland Security, had just given a presentation on Covid-19's reaction to light and heat.

you brought the light inside the body, which you can do either through the skin or in some other way. And I think you said you're going to test that too. Sounds interesting, right? And then I see the disinfectant, where it knocks it out in one minute. And is there a way we can do something like that by injection inside or almost a cleaning because you see it gets in the lungs and it does a tremendous number on the lungs, so it'd be interesting to check that so that you're going to have to use medical doctors, right, but it sounds interesting to me. So, we'll see, but the whole concept of the light, the way it kills it in one minute. That's pretty powerful.

Stephen Hahn, Commissioner, FDA: I certainly wouldn't recommend the internal ingestion of a disinfectant.

APRIL 24

Patrice A. Harris, President, American Medical Association: It is unfortunate that I have to comment on this, but people should under no circumstances ingest or inject bleach or disinfectant.

Mayor Keisha Lance Bottoms, Atlanta: In addition to advising people to please stay home now I have to add to that list and don't inject your body with Lysol. It's like we're living in the Twilight Zone . . . Very simply stay home. Nothing has changed. People are still getting infected, people are still dying. We don't have a cure to this virus. The only thing that's helped us is we have stayed apart from one another and I'm simply asking people to continue to do that. I think as leaders we have to make it easier for people to stay home. We've got to get money into the pockets of people who are concerned about putting food on the table and paying their rent. That's where we should be putting our energy.

Pew Research Center: The number of Americans who have filed first-time claims for unemployment benefits has blown past previous records—more than 24 million have filed since mid-March.

Gov. Kim Reynolds (IA): If you're an employer and you offer to bring your employee back to work and they decide not to, that's a voluntary quit . . . Therefore, they would not be eligible for the unemployment money.

Judy Conti, National Employment Law Project: We live in a country generally where employers have an awful lot of rights and workers have very few and as long as something isn't discriminatory in terms of laws that are already passed . . . employers have a lot of latitude to order you back to work.

Rodney A. Brooks, *National Geographic*: In urban centers large and small across the U.S., the novel coronavirus is devastating African American communities. The environments where most live, the jobs they have, the prevalence of health conditions such as high blood pressure and diabetes, and how they are treated by the medical establishment have created a toxic storm of severe illness and death. (These common, underlying conditions make coronavirus more severe.)

CDC: Globally, more than 2.7 million confirmed cases of coronavirus disease (Covid-19) have been reported, including more than 190,000 deaths in over 180 countries. In the United States, there have been more than 870,000 confirmed cases, with cases in all 50 states, District of Columbia, Puerto Rico, Guam, the Northern Mariana Islands and US Virgin Islands.

Dr. Michael Osterholm, Director, Center for Infectious Disease Research and Policy: We are gonna see it [in the fall]. It's like gravity . . . There is not a debate here. If you want someone to debate you on gravity, then you can have this debate.

Apoorva Mandavilli, *New York Times*: For the past few weeks, more than 50 scientists have been working diligently to do something that the

Food and Drug Administration mostly has not: Verifying that 14 coronavirus antibody tests now on the market actually deliver accurate results. These tests are crucial to reopening the economy, but public health experts have raised urgent concerns about their quality. The new research, completed just days ago and posted online Friday, confirmed some of those fears: Of the 14 tests, only three delivered consistently reliable results. Even the best had some flaws.

Rep. Nancy Pelosi (CA), Speaker of the House: It is just a necessary connection for the American people, especially our seniors, who get their drugs through the post office, who get their communications—for many of them—in that way. Right now, I see a very big danger for our country in the form of the Trump administration's interest in privatizing the post office.

Gov. Cuomo (NY): I've been talking about this for how long? Two months. I said, "How can you have a federal government in a position where they're not going to provide funding to state governments and local governments?" Small business, airlines, business program. Now some of these large corporations now apparently have been taking money from the government programs. And they're not funding state and local. When you don't fund state and local, you know who you don't fund? Police, fire, school teachers, school officials. What was the possible theory of funding large corporations, but not firefighters and not police and not healthcare workers? It boggles the mind.

Governor Bill Lee (TN): Part of this whole approach is the gradual lifting of mandates and restrictions and sanctions. That's how we want to get our economy started back. As businesses open and follow guidelines, customers will be safe to enter those businesses, and we'll feel safe, and we expect that businesses will take and commit to and post this pledge to take care of their customers, and that will provide a clearance for folks to know that this is a business that I can go into that's safe.

Gov. Cuomo (NY): I get inspired by the strength so I can tolerate the heartbreak of the weakness. Here's a letter that I received that just sums it up:

Dear Mr. Cuomo, I seriously doubt that you will ever read this letter, as I know you are busy beyond belief with the disaster that has befallen our country. We are a nation in crisis. Of that, there is no doubt. I am a retired farmer hunkered down in northeast Kansas with my wife, who has but one lung and occasional problems with her remaining lung. She also has diabetes. We are in our 70s now, and frankly, I am afraid for her. Enclosed, find a solitary N95 mask left over from my farming days. It has never been used. If you could, would you please give this mask to a nurse or doctor in your state? I have kept four masks for my immediate family. Please keep on doing what you do so well, which is to lead. Sincerely, Dennis and Sharon.

A farmer in northeast Kansas, his wife has one lung and diabetes. He has five masks. He sends one mask to New York for a doctor or a nurse, keeps four masks. You want to talk about a snapshot of humanity. You have five masks. What do you do? Do you keep all five? Do you hide the five masks? Do you keep them for yourselves or others? No. You send one mask to New York to help a nurse or a doctor. How beautiful is that? How selfless is that? How giving is that? That's the nursing home in Niskayuna that sent 100 ventilators down to New York City when they needed them. It's that love, that courage, that generosity of spirit that makes this country so beautiful and makes Americans so beautiful. It's that generosity of spirit, for me, makes up for all the ugliness that you see. Take one mask. I'll keep four. God bless America. Questions?

APRIL 25

Former Vice President Biden: Right now, there's no oversight. [Trump] made it real clear he doesn't have any damn interest in being checked. The last thing he wants is anyone watching that $500 billion going to corporate America, for God's sake.

Gov. Murphy (NJ): Let's also remind folks, 105,523. We don't know what the denominator is. We don't know how many people are infected in this, but we guarantee you that's not the number. We know that's the number of positive tests, but what exactly that denominator is, people around the world literally are trying to war game that . . . Sadly, with the heaviest hearts, we report an additional 249 deaths, meaning that we have now lost a total of 5,863 blessed souls from our New Jersey family. Just think about that. Let that sink in for a minute. It's an extraordinary loss of life by any measure.

Gov. Pritzker (IL): Chicago-land organizers at Off Their Plate have partnered with five area restaurants and 20 healthcare providers to advance their two-part mission, serving free meals to medical professionals while also supporting restaurant workers with donations. To date Off Their Plate has served nearly 2000 meals with thousands more set for distribution in the coming days. At Open Door Rehabilitation Center in Sandwich, Illinois, administrators paraded from group home to group home with a themed playlist blasting from a loudspeaker cheering their residents with "I Think We're Alone Now" by Tiffany, "U Can't Touch This" by MC Hammer and "Safety Dance" by Men Without Hats.

APRIL 26

Kevin Hassett, White House Economic Advisor: This is the biggest negative shock that our economy, I think, has ever seen. We're going to be looking at an unemployment rate that approaches rates that we saw during the Great Depression. During the Great Recession . . . we lost 8.7 million jobs in the whole thing. Right now, we're losing that many jobs about every ten days.

Gov. Cuomo (NY): I see no light at the end of the tunnel, and I'm cooped up in my home and I'm under tremendous stress, and then I have this added stress of being in this situation that I've never been before in my life. Yeah, that is a toxic mix. So when we talk about reopening, getting people out, some activities, places where people can walk, just something. I say tongue in cheek it's the sanity index, but people need to know that there's an opening, there is a future, that there's hope that somebody's doing something, and then you need a relief valve just on a day-to-day basis so people have some relief in their lives, some vent.

***Boston Globe*:** As the coronavirus continued to claim lives in the past week, the paid death notices in this Sunday's edition of *The Boston Globe* surged to 21 pages, up from 16 pages the Sunday before. For comparison, on the same Sunday last year—April 28, 2019—the *Globe* ran seven pages of death notices, according to an archive of the paper. Those seeking out the death notices might have noticed that they started on B-13 and B-14, with the Sports section interrupting until the notices picked back up on pages C-12 through C-31. The reason for that is as simple as it is devastating: *The Globe* ran out of room.

MONDAY, APRIL 27

***Washington Post*/Yale School of Public Health:** In the early weeks of the coronavirus epidemic, the United States recorded an estimated 15,400 excess deaths, nearly two times as many as were publicly attributed to Covid-19 at the time, according to an analysis of federal data conducted for *The Washington Post* by a research team led by the Yale School of Public Health. The excess deaths—the number beyond what would normally be expected for that time of year—occurred during March and through April 4, a time when 8,128 coronavirus deaths were reported.

Jennifer Miller, Spokeswoman, Wisconsin Department of Health Services: So far, 36 people who tested Covid-19 positive after April 9 have reported that they voted in person or worked the polls on election day.*

* This total was up to 67 people on May 8.

Steve Greenberg, Siena College Research Institute: Last month, fewer than one-third of New Yorkers knew someone who had tested positive for coronavirus. Today, 51 percent personally know someone who has been infected with Covid-19, including 60 percent from New York City, 67 percent from the downstate suburbs and 30 percent from upstate. The human toll is almost unfathomable as 46 percent of New York City voters personally know someone who has died from coronavirus, as do 36 percent of downstate suburbanites and 13 percent of upstaters. Half of Latino and black voters know someone who has passed away from this insidious virus . . . 48 percent of Latino voters say that they and/or someone in their household has been laid off, compared to 30 percent of both white and black voters affected by layoffs.

John Tyson, Chairman, Tyson Foods: In small communities around the country where we employ over 100,000 hard-working men and women, we're being forced to shutter our doors. This means one thing—the food supply chain is vulnerable. As pork, beef, and chicken plants are being forced to close, even for short periods of time, millions of pounds of meat will disappear from the supply chain. As a result, there will be limited supply of our products available in grocery stores until we are able to reopen our facilities that are currently closed . . . The food supply chain is breaking.

Gov. Abbott (TX): My executive order to stay at home that was issued last month is set to expire on April the 30th. That executive order has done its job to slow the growth of Covid-19 and I will let it expire as scheduled. Now, it's time to set a new course, a course that responsibly opens up business in Texas . . . With my new executive order, all retail stores, restaurants, movie theaters, and malls can reopen May the 1st. Now, to minimize the spread of Covid-19 during Phase 1, on the advice of doctors, I am limiting occupancy to no more than 25%.

Judge Clay Jenkins, Dallas County (TX): Just because something can be open doesn't mean it should be open, and just because something is open doesn't mean you should go there.

Gov. Reynolds (IA): The reality is that we cannot stop this virus. It will remain in our communities until a vaccine is available. Instead we must learn to live with coronavirus activity without letting it govern our lives . . . this level of mitigation is not sustainable for the long term and it has unintended consequences for Iowa families. So we must gradually shift from an aggressive mitigation strategy to focusing on containing and managing virus activity for the long term in a way that allows us to safely and responsibly balance the health of our people and the health of our economy.

Gov. DeWine (OH): The coronavirus is still here. It's just as dangerous as it has ever been. It's still living amongst us. I was thinking about this this weekend, and I thought back to when Fran and I were children growing up. Sunday morning we would go to St. Paul's Catholic Church, and the nuns taught us, and I remember, it is seared in my memory, the nuns talking about the devil, and the devil is roaming the world searching for souls. I'm not saying that the virus is the devil. I would describe it as a monster. But it is searching. And it is searching for bodies. And the way it does it is from going from one body to the other.

President Trump: There has been so much unnecessary death in this country. It could have been stopped and it could have been stopped short, but somebody a long time ago, it seems, decided not to do it that way. And the whole world is suffering because of it.

Greg Miller and Ellen Nakishima, *Washington Post*: U.S. intelligence agencies issued warnings about the novel coronavirus in more than a dozen classified briefings prepared for President Trump in January and February, months during which he continued to play down the threat, according to current and former U.S. officials.

Bill Barr, U.S. Attorney General: If a state or local ordinance crosses the line from an appropriate exercise of authority to stop the spread of

Covid-19 into an overbearing infringement of constitutional and statutory protections, the Department of Justice may have an obligation to address that overreach in federal court. I am therefore directing the Assistant Attorney General for Civil Rights, Eric Dreiband, and Matthew Schneider; the U.S. Attorney for the Eastern District of Michigan, to oversee and coordinate our efforts to monitor state and local policies and, if necessary, take action to correct them . . . Many policies that would be unthinkable in regular times have become commonplace in recent weeks, and we do not want to unduly interfere with the important efforts of state and local officials to protect the public. But the Constitution is not suspended in times of crisis. We must therefore be vigilant to ensure its protections are preserved, at the same time that the public is protected.

Rep. Eliot Engel (NY), Chair, House Committee on Foreign Affairs: President Trump's decision to halt funding for the World Health Organization (WHO) in the midst of a global pandemic is counterproductive and puts lives at risk. Attacking the WHO, rather than the Covid-19 outbreak, will only worsen an already dire situation by undermining one of our key tools to fight the spreading disease. The Administration's explanation for this decision is inadequate, and the Committee on Foreign Affairs is determined to understand the reasons behind this self-defeating withdrawal from global leadership.

Olivia Nuzzi, *New York*:* If an American president loses more Americans over the course of six weeks than died in the entirety of the Vietnam war, does he deserve to be reelected?

APRIL 28

NBC News: The total number of coronavirus cases in the United States reached 1 million on Tuesday afternoon, according to a tally compiled by

* Question to President Trump at that day's press conference

NBC News. The number stood at 1,100,037 just before 1:30 P.M. ET Tuesday. In all, 57,071 have died in the U.S.

Rob Nichols, President and CEO, American Bankers Association: Our member banks across the country are deeply frustrated at their inability to access @SBAGov's E-Tran system. We have raised these issues at the highest levels. Until they are resolved, #AmericasBanks will not be able help more struggling small businesses.

Jovita Carranza, Administrator, Small Business Association: More than $2 billion of the first round of #PaycheckProtectionProgram funding was either declined or returned and will be made available during the current application period.

Steve Mnuchin, Secretary of the Treasury: I never expected in a million years that the Los Angeles Lakers, which, I'm a big fan of the team, but I'm not a big fan of the fact that they took a $4.6 million loan. I think that's outrageous and I'm glad they returned it or they would have had liability.

Marc Perrone, President, UFCW: While we share the concern over the food supply, today's executive order to force meatpacking plants to stay open must put the safety of our country's meatpacking workers first. Simply put, we cannot have a secure food supply without the safety of these workers.

Sen. Mitch McConnell (KY), Senate Majority Leader: My red line going forward on this [next stimulus] bill is we need to provide protection, litigation protection, for those who have been on the front lines . . . We can't pass another bill unless we have liability protection.

Stuart Appelbaum, President, Retail, Wholesale and Department Store Union: We only wish that this administration cared as much about the lives of working people as it does about meat, pork, and poultry products.

Jamie Gulley, President, SEIU Healthcare: When Vice President Mike Pence ignores the safety policy and refuses to wear a face mask, he insults the hard work and sacrifice of all healthcare workers. Worse, he puts them, their patients, and their families at risk . . . We are deeply disappointed that Mayo [Clinic]* failed to enforce their own policy.

NPR: In not even three months since the first known U.S. deaths from Covid-19, more lives have now been lost to the coronavirus pandemic on U.S. soil than the 58,220 Americans who died over nearly two decades in Vietnam. Early Tuesday evening ET, the U.S. death toll reached 58,365, according to Johns Hopkins University.

President Trump: Tremendous progress has been made, we think, on a vaccine. You always have to say "think" and then you have to test it and that takes a period of time. But a lot of movement and a lot of progress has been made on a vaccine. But I think what happens is it's going to go away and this is going to go away and whether it comes back in a modified form in the fall, we'll be able to handle it. We'll be able to put out spurts and we're very prepared to handle it. We've learned a lot. We've learned a lot about it, the invisible enemy. It's a bad enemy. It's a very tough enemy, but we've learned a lot. It's in 184 countries, as you hear me say often. It's hard to believe, it's inconceivable. It should have been stopped at the source, which was China. Should have been stopped very much at the source, but it wasn't. Now we have 184 countries going through hell.

Dr. Fauci, Director, NIAID: I would love to be able to have all sports back, but as a health official and a physician and a scientist, I have to say, right now, when you look at the country, we're not ready for that yet. Safety, for the players and for the fans, trumps everything. If you can't guarantee

* Vice President Pence visited Covid-19 patients at the Mayo Clinic on April 28, without wearing a mask.

safety, then unfortunately you're going to have to bite the bullet and say, "We may have to go without this sport for this season." . . . If we let our desire to prematurely get back to normal, we can only get ourselves right back in the same hole we were in a few weeks ago.

Gov. Cuomo (NY): The person who delivers the groceries, the person who's driving the bus, the person who's driving the subway, the nurses, the doctors, the orderlies, all these people who are showing up every day, not because of the check. They could stay home too and file for unemployment. No, they're doing it out of their sense of honor and their sense of dignity and their sense of pride. This is their mission. This is their role. They're New Yorkers, they're Americans, and they're going to show up.

***New York Times*:** Total deaths in seven states that have been hard hit by the coronavirus pandemic are nearly 50 percent higher than normal for the five weeks from March 8 through April 11, according to new death statistics from the Centers for Disease Control and Prevention. That is 9,000 more deaths than were reported as of April 11 in official counts of deaths from the coronavirus. The new data is partial and most likely undercounts the recent death toll significantly.

Kristen Welker, NBC News: Sorry, are you saying you're confident you can surpass five million tests per day?

President Trump:* Well, we're going to be there very soon. If you look at the numbers, it could be that we're getting very close. I mean, I don't have the exact numbers. We would have had them if you asked me the same question a little while ago, because people with the statistics were there. We're going to be there very soon.

---

* Direct exchange

APRIL 29

Admiral Brett Giroir, M.D., Assistant Secretary for Health: There is absolutely no way on Earth, on this planet or any other planet, that we can do 20 million tests a day, or even five million tests a day.

U.S. Bureau of Economic Analysis, Department of Commerce: Real gross domestic product (GDP) decreased 4.8 percent in the first quarter of 2020, according to the "advance" estimate released by the Bureau of Economic Analysis. In the fourth quarter of 2019, real GDP increased 2.1 percent.

***The Hill*:** Members of the Congressional Black Caucus (CBC) are taking leading positions in the House Democratic response to the coronavirus as data shows African Americans are dying in disproportionate numbers across the country from the pandemic.

Rep. Karen Bass (CA): America is in shock to learn about all the inequities in health in our communities that we have known for all of these years.

Mayor Lori Lightfoot, Chicago: We knew that there were significant disparities in the way that people access health care, also healthy living, access to food, and all of that is around lack of investment and also poverty. And what this virus has shown is both how it has really ravaged communities and how the vulnerabilities that were there are flashing like a neon light.

Jerome Powell, Chair, Federal Reserve Bank: We are going to see economic data for the second quarter that is worse than any data we have seen for the economy. There are direct consequences of the disease and measures we are taking to protect ourselves from it.

Jared Kushner, Senior Advisor to the President: I think what you'll see in May as the states are reopening now is May will be a transition month, you'll see a lot of states starting to phase in the different reopening based on the safety guidelines that President Trump outlined on April 19. I think you'll see by June that a lot of the country should be back to normal, and the hope is that by July the country's really rocking again . . . This is a great success story, and I think that's really what needs to be told.

***Politico*/Morning Consult:** Nearly three-in-four voters, 73 percent, think Americans should continue social distancing, even if it means continued damage to the U.S. economy. Just 15 percent say social distancing should end to boost the economy, even if the virus spreads. Meanwhile, the poll also shows voters are girding for a second wave of cases. Nearly 8-in-10, 79 percent, say that a second wave is very or somewhat likely. Only 9 percent say it's unlikely.

Costco: To protect our members and employees, effective May 4, all Costco members and guests must wear a face covering that covers their mouth and nose at all times while at Costco . . . The use of a face covering should not be seen as a substitute for social distancing. Please continue to observe rules regarding appropriate distancing while on Costco premises.

Jared Kushner, Senior Advisor to the President: The eternal lockdown crowd can make jokes on late night television, but the reality is that the data is on our side.

Gov. Cuomo (NY): I know it is hard to communicate facts in this environment. But I know a lot of filters that don't communicate facts. They communicate spin now. Everybody has their own spin. There are still facts that are not political theater, right?

Elon Musk, CEO, Tesla Inc.: If somebody wants to stay in their house, that's great. They should be allowed to stay in their house and they should not be compelled to leave. But to say that they cannot leave their house, and they will be arrested if they do, this is fascist. This is not democratic. This is not freedom. Give people back their goddamn freedom.

Rep. Ilhan Omar (MN): Billionaires want to continue profiting off your labor even if it means risking millions of lives. They call this "freedom."

Sen. Lindsey Graham (SC): What have we learned? If you pay people 23 dollars an hour not to work they will take you up on it . . . So July the 31st is when this [unemployment benefit] expires and I promise you, over our dead bodies, this will get reauthorized. We've gotta stop this. You cannot turn on the economy until you get this aberration in the law fixed.

Gov. Cuomo (NY): [Republican senators] want to fund corporate America. That is who puts money in their pockets. And I say let's fund working Americans. That's the choice. Bailout, us, them. It's just theater. It's just smoke and mirrors to avoid the American people seeing the reality, which is whose pocket they want to put money in versus whose pocket state and local governments want to fund. The reason it is so disturbing to me—I am not surprised by anything and politics. I have seen the good, the bad, and the ugly for many, many years . . . But if there was ever a time that one could reasonably believe that you could put aside partisan politics, if there was ever going to be a moment where we could say—you know what? Let's stop, just for one moment, the partisanship, the ugliness, the anger, the deception—just stop for one moment. If there was going to be one moment to hit the pause button, the moment would be now.

Governor Gina Raimondo (RI): If you're planning a very large summer gathering, a Fourth of July parade, a large music festival, a huge cultural event with hundreds and hundreds of people, you are not going to be able to have that event in the state of Rhode Island with those people in person. That is a killer announcement for me to have to make. My stomach is in a knot . . . But in good conscience, I cannot stand here and tell you that you're going to be able to have those events in June, in July, in August, the way you had hoped to have.

President Trump: This is going away. This is going away. I think we're gonna come up with vaccines and all, but this is going away . . . It's gonna go. It's gonna leave. It's gonna be gone. It's gonna be eradicated.

Judge Christopher M. Murray, Court of Claims, Michigan: [An individual's] liberty interests are, and always have been, subject to society's interests—society being our fellow residents. They—our fellow residents—have an interest to remain unharmed by a highly communicable and deadly virus, and since the state entered the Union in 1837, it has had the broad power to act for the public health of the entire state when faced with a public crisis . . . The Court concludes that entry of a preliminary injunction [against Michigan's stay-at-home order] would be more detrimental to the public than it would to plaintiffs. Although the Court is painfully aware of the difficulties of living under the restrictions of these executive orders, those difficulties are temporary, while to those who contract the virus and cannot recover (and to their family members and friends), it is all too permanent.*

APRIL 30

State Senator Dayna Polehanki (MI): Directly above me, men with rifles yelling at us. Some of my colleagues who own bulletproof vests are wearing them. I have never appreciated our Sergeants-at-Arms more than today.

***Detroit News*:** Protesters, some carrying firearms, took their demonstration against Gov. Gretchen Whitmer's stay-home order inside the Michigan Capitol Thursday afternoon as lawmakers considered an expiring emergency

---

* Ruling in a lawsuit against Michigan Governor Whitmer regarding her "stay at home" order.

declaration. Dozens of protesters gathered outside the House chamber and demanded to be allowed in. As Michigan State Police troopers stood in a line outside the chamber, the protesters chanted, "Let us in."

Gov. Whitmer (MI): While some members of the legislature might believe this crisis is over, common sense and all of the scientific data tells us we're not out of the woods yet. By refusing to extend the emergency and disaster declaration, Republican lawmakers are putting their heads in the sand and putting more lives and livelihoods at risk. I'm not going to let that happen.

U.S. Department of Labor: In the week ending April 25, the advance figure for seasonally adjusted initial [unemployment] claims was 3,839,000, a decrease of 603,000 from the previous week's revised level . . . The advance seasonally adjusted insured unemployment rate was 12.4 percent for the week ending April 18, an increase of 1.5 percentage points from the previous week's revised rate. This marks the highest level of the seasonally adjusted insured unemployment rate in the history of the seasonally adjusted series.

Julie Su, Secretary of Labor, California: We're paying about $1 billion a day in unemployment insurance claims. In California just in the last six weeks alone, we had over 3.5 million people file for unemployment insurance. To put that in perspective, two weeks ago that was already more than we had in all of 2019.

President Trump: I think we did a spectacular job . . . And you shouldn't be hearing about testing, but that's the last thing they can complain about, I guess. If we do two million tests, they say 'how come you didn't do three?'

Gov. Hogan (MD): There had been reports—for example, in Massachusetts, Governor Charlie Baker told the story of his planeload came in with masks, was basically confiscated by the federal government . . . The National

Guard and the state police are both guarding these tests at an undisclosed location.*

President Trump: I'm just looking at the test numbers. We have more tests, we have given more tests, and the high-quality tests, than every other country combined.

Glenn Kessler, *Washington Post*: As of the end of April 28, the United States has conducted 5.9 million tests, according to one metric. The next five countries—Russia, Germany, Italy, Spain and United Arab Emirates—had conducted 10 million tests as of that date. The total for all non-U.S. countries is about 25 million. So Trump's bravado is ridiculously wrong. As we have repeatedly noted, what matters is the number of tests per million people. The United States, at about 17,855 per million, was the lowest of those five countries—Russia tested at a rate of 21,511, Germany at 24,748, Italy at 30,547, Spain at 28,799 and the UAE at 106,904.

Office of the Director of National Intelligence: The entire Intelligence Community has been consistently providing critical support to U.S. policymakers and those responding to the Covid-19 virus, which originated in China. The Intelligence Community also concurs with the wide scientific consensus that the Covid-19 virus was not manmade or genetically modified . . . The IC will continue to rigorously examine emerging information and intelligence to determine whether the outbreak began through contact with infected animals or if it was the result of an accident at a laboratory in Wuhan.

Mayor de Blasio, New York City: Now, this horrible situation† that occurred with the funeral home in Brooklyn, absolutely unacceptable. Let's be clear about this. Funeral homes are private organizations, private

* See Gov. Hogan on April 20, discussing tests he had purchased and flown in from South Korea.

† A Brooklyn funeral home was discovered to have "stored corpses in unrefrigerated storage vans as the city's death care system is overwhelmed with coronavirus patients" (CNBC).

businesses. They have an obligation to the people they serve to treat them with dignity. I have no idea in the world how any funeral home could let this happen. The city historically does not have a direct working relationship with funeral homes. They are regulated by the state of New York, so it's not an area that we work with a lot, but again, we all have to work together to solve problems I don't understand in this case, if the funeral home—I heard something about a driver didn't show up or something like that. Why on earth did they not either alert the state, who regulate them, or go to their NYPD precinct and ask for help, do something rather than leave the bodies there? It's unconscionable to me.

***U.S. News and World Report*:** Social distancing guidelines crafted by the federal government to stem the spread of coronavirus expire on Thursday, but President Donald Trump said Wednesday he has no intention of extending the measures.

Jeremy Konyndyk, Center for Global Development, WHO Independent Oversight and Advisory Committee: We have spent the month of April on a plateau. Daily counts fluctuating between 25-30k, no longer rising but not definitively declining. Testing has been stuck as well. After surging in March, growth slowed in the first week of April averaged 144k tests/day. Last week of April averaged 220k tests/day. At those levels, antibody surveys suggest we're only finding [less than] 1 in 10 cases.

Dr. Fauci, Director, NIAID: There's no doubt in my mind that when you pull back mitigation, you're going to start seeing cases crop up here and there. If you're not able to handle them, you're going to see another peak, a spike, and then you almost have to turn the clock back to go back to mitigation.

Jeremy Konyndyk, Center for Global Development:
U.S. cases, April 1: 25.1k
U.S. cases, April 30: 29.5k

David P. Gelles, CNN:
Total U.S. deaths as of April 1: 5,119
Total U.S. deaths as of April 30: 62,557

MAY 1

Gov. Newsom (CA): This disease doesn't know if you're a protester, a Democrat, a Republican. Protect yourself, protect your family, your kids, your parents, your grandparents, your neighbors.

Mayor Lyn Semeta, Huntington Beach, CA: Governor Newsom's mandate to close all beaches in Orange County today was a jarring decision that significantly impacts us here in Huntington Beach . . . The city was attempting to provide the community with the ability to safely experience the physical and mental health benefits associated with accessing the Pacific Ocean.

President Trump: The Governor of Michigan should give a little, and put out the fire. These are very good people, but they are angry. They want their lives back again, safely! See them, talk to them, make a deal.

Gov. Whitmer (MI): We're in the midst of a global pandemic that has already killed almost 4,000 people in our state. More people have died in Michigan from Covid-19 than died during the whole Vietnam conflict. The fact of the matter is, we have to listen not to pollsters and not to people with political agendas, but listen to epidemiologists and public healthcare experts, listen to our business leaders who are worried about making sure that they've got all the PPE and protocols to keep their employees safe. We will work together to determine when it is safe to start to re-engage. This is not a switch that we flip, this is a dial that we turn. We do the next right thing, and it's going to be driven by the data, and it's going to be driven by medical experts, not political polls, and not political posturing, and not political maneuvers like you saw yesterday at the Capitol.

Senator Kamala Harris (CA): As our nation continues to combat Covid-19, we know that the true death toll from the virus is likely far higher than the current count. An accurate count of the lives lost to the pandemic is critical to understanding the impact of the crisis, ensuring the federal government is held accountable for an adequate response, and providing information on rates and distribution of mortality and morbidity to inform public guidance as communities being to open up.

Mayor de Blasio, New York City: Like one continuous day from the beginning of this fight, and we know there's a lot up ahead. And I know all of you are dealing with the frustrations of everything we used to think was a routine being disrupted. And we're all trying to make sense of it and everyone's doing their best in trying to help each other through. So since it's hard to remember sometimes what day it is or what week it is, I thought at least I could do a service by telling you what month it is. Well this is an undeniable fact: it is now May.

Bob Hardt, Political Director, NY1: Over the last 20 years, 9,532 people have been murdered in New York City. In March and April of 2020, 18,231 New York City residents died from confirmed or suspected cases of Covid-19.

Dr. Michael Osterholm, Director, Center for Infectious Disease Research and Policy: The idea that this is going to be done soon defies microbiology . . . This is going to continue to be a rolling situation throughout the world, not just our country, for the months ahead. Expect many more New Yorks to occur. It's very likely they will.

***Washington Post*:** Publicly traded companies have received more than $1 billion in funds meant for small businesses from the federal government's economic stimulus package, according to data from securities filings compiled by *The Washington Post.* Nearly 300 public companies have reported receiving money from the fund, called the Paycheck Protection

Program, according to the data compiled by *The Post*. Recipients include 43 companies with more than 500 workers, the maximum typically allowed by the program. Several other recipients were prosperous enough to pay executives $2 million or more.

Kayleigh McEnany, White House Press Secretary:* I will never lie to you. You have my word on that.

Gov. Cuomo (NY): How do you operate a school that's socially distanced with masks, without gatherings, with a public transportation system that has a lower number of students on it? How would you get that plan up and running? We don't think it's possible to do that in a way that would keep our children and students and educators safe. So we're going to have the schools remain closed for the rest of the year.

Gov. Abbott (TX): How do we know reopening businesses won't result in faster spread of Covid-19? Listen, the fact of the matter is, pretty much every scientific and medical report shows that whenever you have a reopening . . . that it actually will lead to an increase in spread. It's almost ipso facto . . . The goal never has been to get Covid-19 transmission down to zero.†

State of the Nation Survey: More than 80% of Americans support closing non-essential businesses. Support for limiting restaurants, closing schools, canceling sporting and entertainment events, and group gatherings exceeds 90%. A total of 94% strongly or somewhat approve asking people to stay home and avoid gathering in groups; 92% support canceling major sports and entertainment events; 91% approve closing K-12 schools; 91% approve limiting restaurants to carry-out only; 83% approve closing businesses other

* First White House briefing since March 11, 2019, and the first for McEnany.

† Recording of call between Gov. Abbott and state legislators released by Progress Texas. May 1 was the same day that Abbott began to reopen businesses in his state.

than grocery stores and pharmacies. There are some partisan differences on these items—Republicans are somewhat less supportive, but even among Republicans large majorities support all of these measures; and, as summarized below, support is largely consistent across every state.

Raj Chetty, Economist, Harvard University: We illustrate the value of the tracker by analyzing the impacts of recent policy decisions in the Covid-19 crisis, focusing in particular on state shutdowns and re-openings. Perhaps surprisingly, we find these policies have little or no impact on economic activity. The decline in economic activity—consumer spending, the number of small business open, and employment—occurred in most cases before states "shut down" . . . Moreover, we show that recent policies ending these shut-downs in certain states such as Georgia and South Carolina have not been associated with significant increases in economic activity. These findings suggest that the primary barrier to economic activity is the threat of Covid-19 itself as opposed to legislated economic shutdowns.

Rep. Rosa DeLauro (CT): Too many people across the country are struggling to get food in their communities—at grocery stores and food banks. At the same time, farmers are plowing crops under, euthanizing pigs, and dumping milk. This is a massive failure in the food supply chain, and only the federal government has the scale and resources to solve the problem.

Dr. Amy Acton, Director, Ohio Department of Health: Today in Ohio, we now know that we have 18,743 cases. That's an increase of 716 since yesterday . . . It is the uncertainty of something like this virus that makes it so incredibly difficult. We receive a lot of calls. I've received a lot of letters throughout this. I can't read every single one. My staff reads them all, but I read some and I just want you to know that we listen, we hear you. If there's a hallmark of this administration that I could tell you about is that their goal is to listen and hear every Ohioan and I think one of the things that stood out to me today was the feeling of that uncertainty. How do I plan for that thing that was going to be an August? Can't you just tell me what that will look like? I think what we heard today is when we stick together, I feel that we are finding that sweet, sweet spot that helps propel us forward together and it's not an easy road.

State Rep. Nino Vitale (OH): Our basic human rights of life, liberty and the pursuit of happiness do not come from an unelected Globalist Health Director [Dr. Acton], who signed the order in the dark of night. Your basic human rights are inalienable and cannot be bought, sold, traded or taken from you.

Gov. DeWine (OH): This is not a popularity contest. That's not what this is about. We have lives at stake. We have an economy at stake. We have jobs at stake. I literally don't pay any attention to . . . people say, "You're doing a great job," I appreciate it. People say, "You're doing a bad job," I understand it. I try to listen. But ultimately, our job is to listen. Our job is to take all the input, but I'm ultimately responsible. And for those who want to say something about Dr. Acton, it's a cheap shot. Don't call them her orders. Call them my orders.

State Rep. Vitale (OH): The Ohio legislature is scheduled to be in session May 4th. It's time for every member of the Ohio House and Senate to go DO THEIR JOBS, get to the state house and vote on all these unconstitutional orders that defy your liberties and freedoms!

Gov. Inslee (WA): If we stick together for a while longer, we don't lose the gains we've already made. It's so frustrating, we don't want to do this twice.

Gov. Cuomo (NY): What keeps me up at night is the death toll I'm going to see the next morning. I feel good about everything we've done and where we are. I have anxiety about what tomorrow will bring.

MAY 2

Stephanie Kelton, Economist, former Bernie Sanders advisor: Over the last 6 weeks, nearly 30,000 people lost their jobs every hour.

Gov. Cuomo (NY): Transit workers have very much been at the frontline. We talk about essential workers, people who are out every day, running the buses, the subways all through this. We know there has been a very high infection rate among transit workers.* We have said thank you and we appreciate what you're doing 1000 times. I believe actions speak louder than words. If you appreciate what we are doing, help us do what we do and we are going to be doing that with more testing and resources that is going on right now. To keep our transit workers safe and to keep the public safe, the riding public, we are going to do something that has never been done before. The MTA [Metropolitan Transit Authority] is going to be disinfecting every train 24 hours. This is such a monumental undertaking I cannot begin to describe it to you. The New York City subway system has never been closed. It operates 24 hours a day because we have a 24 hour city. We are taking the unprecedented step during this pandemic of closing the system for 4 hours at night.

Sen. Patty Murray (WA): We all know the President hasn't told people the truth about this virus or his Administration's response, and late last night, he moved to silence an independent government† official who did. The President cannot be above oversight, no matter how he denies, attacks, and fights against it.

---

* Later that day MTA Chair Patrick J. Foye would announce there had been ninety-eight coronavirus deaths among MTA workers.

† Health and Human Services Inspector General Christi Grimm was replaced.

Jared Kushner, Senior Advisor to the President: When history looks back on this, they'll say, man, the federal government acted really quickly and creatively, they threw a lot at the problem and saved a lot of lives.

CNBC: The United States just had its deadliest day on record due to the coronavirus as states across the country begin to ease restrictions meant to curb the spread of the virus, according to data published by the World Health Organization. The U.S. saw 2,909 people die of Covid-19 in 24 hours.

Kevin Hassett, White House Economic Advisor: I think right now because there's been good news really, that the opening up is starting to happen faster than we expected, appears to be doing so safely, then there is a chance that we won't really need a phase four [stimulus package].

MAY 3

Mayor de Blasio, New York City: Well, let me tell you something, Kevin, why don't you come to New York City? Why don't you go to Elmhurst Hospital? Why don't you talk to our first responders? Why don't you talk to the families who have lost their loved ones, or go to the ICU where hundreds of people are still fighting for their lives? In terms of your desire, which is pretty transparent to save money rather than to protect people, to risk the future of New York City and this state and so many citizen states around the country, is outrageous that anyone with a position of authority in our federal government could even breathe these words, because it's disrespectful in every way, is an absolute misunderstanding of what has happened here and what continues to happen and the fight we're still waging, and how much it's going to take to get back on our feet this year and next year, and the years thereafter. I was disgusted when I heard these comments because it sounded like the comments not only of a cheapskate, but someone who just didn't care.

Dr. Gottlieb, Former Commissioner, FDA: When you look across the country, it's really a mixed bag. Certainly cases are falling in the Tri-State region around New York City. But when you back out what's happening in New York, and New York is really driving a lot of the national statistics because it was such a large outbreak, around the nation, hospitalizations and new cases continue to rise. So there's about 20 states where you see a rising number of new cases: Illinois, Texas, Maryland, Indiana, Virginia, North Carolina, Tennessee have a lot of new cases on a daily basis.

Max Roser, Founder, Our World in Data: Sunday update: All our #COVID19 charts & data are up to date for today 3rd May. The death rate by world region:

- staying high in North America.
- falling in Europe.
- rising in South America.
- comparatively low in Asia, Oceania, and Africa.

Caitlin Rivers, Epidemiologist, Johns Hopkins Center for Health Security: In April an average of ~2,000 people died of coronavirus in the US each day. That is more than daily average from cancer or heart disease. I fear there is growing complacency that this level of loss is a new normal. Are we really ready to add a new leading cause of death?

Rep. Alexandria Ocasio-Cortez (NY): New York City will be distributing over 100,000 face coverings in parks across the city free of charge from Saturday, May 2nd—Tuesday, May 5th. Use the map below to find the closest distribution location, date, and time.

Dr. Birx, White House Coronavirus Response Coordinator: It's devastatingly worrisome to me personally because if [protestors] go home and infect their grandmother or their grandfather who has a comorbid condition and they have a serious or a very . . . unfortunate outcome, they will feel guilty for the rest of our lives. So we need to protect each other at the same time we're voicing our discontent.

Warren Buffett: I don't believe anybody knows what the market is going to do tomorrow, next week, next month, next year. I know America is going to move forward over time, but I don't know for sure, and we learned this on September 10th, 2001, and we learned it a few months ago in terms of the virus. Anything can happen in terms of markets, and you can bet on America, but you got to have to be careful about how you bet, simply because markets can do anything.

Gov. Reeves (MS): Things can change quickly. We have to stay flexible. Today, I was prepared to announce further reopenings. That was the plan and I was excited to get more of our people back to work. This was a large enough change to make me take a step back . . . and I have come to the conclusion that I must hold on for now.

MONDAY, MAY 4

***Wall Street Journal*:** More than a quarter of a million people worldwide have died from the new coronavirus, a milestone in the pandemic, as several hard-hit countries took steps toward reopening. Globally, there have been 250,134 confirmed deaths, 68,387 of which were reported in the U.S., according to data from Johns Hopkins University. The U.S. accounts for 1.17 million of the 3.57 million cases world-wide. Experts say the reported figures likely undercount the extent of the pandemic.

White House Office of Legislative Affairs: For the month of May, no [Coronavirus] Task Force members may accept hearing invitations. Exceptions may be made only with the express approval of the White House Chief of Staff.

Institute for Health Metrics and Evaluation (IHME): New Covid-19 forecasts for the US project nearly 135,000 deaths through the beginning of August . . . The revised projections reflect rising mobility in most US states as well as the easing of social distancing measures expected in 31 states by May 11, indicating that growing contacts among people will promote transmission of the coronavirus. Increases in testing and contact tracing, along with warming seasonal temperatures—factors that could help slow transmission—do not offset rising mobility, thereby fueling a significant increase in projected deaths.

Sen. Mitch McConnell (KY), Majority Leader: The Senate is back in session because we have important work to do for the nation. Critical posts throughout the federal government, from public health to national security and beyond, remain vacant. Qualified nominees who have been held up for too long already have become even more necessary in these uncertain times.

Sen. Chuck Schumer (NY), Minority Leader: Mr. President, the Senate convenes a session this evening during a trying time for our nation. As we speak, millions of our citizens are respecting stay-at-home orders and doing their part to stop the spread of this pernicious disease . . . if we are going to be here, if we are going to make these fine people come in to work in these conditions, let the senate at least conduct the nation's business and focus like a laser on Covid-19. At the moment, the Republican leader has scheduled no significant Covid-related business for the floor of the Senate.

Dr. Fauci, Director, NIAID: Shame on us if we don't have enough tests by the time this so-called return might occur. I don't think there's a chance this virus is just going to disappear. It's going to be around, and if given the opportunity, it will resurge.

Sen. Schumer (NY): The President continues to pressure states and businesses to reopen, but he refuses to take responsibility for the one thing that would allow them to do it safely, testing . . . Do you know how the White House knows it's safe to hold a press conference? They test all the reporters before allowing them into the briefing room. What does the White House do before the President holds a meeting with business leaders? They take everyone's temperature and then administer a coronavirus test. Why on earth is there not a plan for the rest of the country, the whole country, not just the president and the White House?

Tim Bray, Vice President, Amazon: May 1st was my last day as a VP and Distinguished Engineer at Amazon Web Services, after five years and five months of rewarding fun. I quit in dismay at Amazon firing whistleblowers who were making noise about warehouse employees frightened of Covid-19 . . . Firing whistleblowers isn't just a side-effect of macroeconomic forces, nor is it intrinsic to the function of free markets . . . It's evidence of a vein of toxicity running through the company culture. I choose neither to serve nor drink that poison.

Gov. Cuomo (NY): By the way, you don't wear a mask for yourself. You wear a mask to protect me. I wear a mask to protect you. We owe each other a certain amount of reasonableness and respect in society. And I owe you that level of respect, that if I'm sick, I should wear a mask. Local governments have the ability to enforce and to penalize. That's up to local governments . . . I think local government should enforce it and I think there should be a penalty, because you could literally kill someone. You could literally kill someone because you didn't want to wear a mask. How cruel and irresponsible would that be?

State Senator Tom Barrett (MI): The governor's veto of SB 858* is extremely disappointing. This measure would have put several Covid-19

---

* "To reduce from 28 days to 14 days the duration of a disaster or emergency declaration by a governor, at which time the legislature may vote to extend it for a specific number of days."

executive orders into law and extended others to better fight the virus and deal with its impacts while simultaneously restoring constitutional governance to Michigan.

Gov. Whitmer (MI): I am happy to work with the legislature. I think, ideally, we all get on the same page here. What I can't do is negotiate like this is a political issue. This is a public health issue. I need to listen to the epidemiologists and the health experts in our state and across our country. That's precisely what I'm doing. I would welcome partnership from people of both sides of the aisle in every branch of government . . . This partisan conversation that has been started and inflamed is not something that is really constructive right now.

Josh Sharfstein, Vice Dean for Public Health Practice, Johns Hopkins University: The hospital system is not as robust in many of the [rural] places. Many of the hospitals have closed in rural areas, those that are open are very small and financially unstable. And so this has created an enormous challenge. It creates this dynamic where people go "We're never going to have a problem like New York," but it doesn't take a problem like New York to tip that entire local health care system over.

MAY 5

***Houston Chronicle* (TX):** The number of new reported Covid-19 cases and deaths last week was the largest since the pandemic began, suggesting that infections remain pervasive and much is still unknown about the size and scale of the Texas outbreak. The state reported more than 7,000 new cases and 221 deaths, an increase of 24 percent and 33 percent over the previous week, respectively, a Hearst Newspapers analysis shows.

Gov. Abbott (TX): How do I know that we are on an adequate trajectory and this plan fits within that trajectory? Dr. Birx herself has said it. All these other doctors have said it. And so, there's always going to be a difference of opinion among doctors.

Dr. Bright, Former Director, BARDA: It was my job to ensure that our country had life-saving tools to be as prepared as possible for a pandemic like Covid-19 . . . the past few years however, have been beyond challenging. Time after time I was pressured to ignore or dismiss expert and scientific recommendations and instead to award lucrative contracts based on political connections . . . ultimately I was removed from my position because of my continued insistence that the government invest funds allocated by Congress—hard-earned taxpayer dollars—to address the Covid-19 and invest them in safe and scientifically-vetted solutions instead of funding projects that were promoted by cronies or politically-connected companies.

Attorneys for Dr. Rick Bright:* It was obvious that Dr. Bright's persistent demands for urgent action to respond to the pandemic had caused a 'shit storm' and a 'commotion' and were unwelcome in the office of the HHS Secretary. As a result, HHS leadership excluded Dr. Bright and BARDA from these recurring meetings and from the critical discussions about addressing the Covid-19 pandemic.

***Arizona Republic*:** Just hours after [Governor] Ducey announced on Monday that he's accelerating the reopening of parts of the state's economy, state health officials told a team of university experts to stop working on models that project what will happen next. The universities' models had shown that the only way to avoid a dramatic spike in cases was to delay reopening the state until the end of May.

Brian Chesky, CEO, Airbnb: We don't know exactly when travel will return. When travel does return, it will look different. While we know

---

* Whistleblower complaint

Airbnb's business will fully recover, the changes it will undergo are not temporary or short-lived. Because of this, we need to make more fundamental changes to Airbnb by reducing the size of our workforce around a more focused business strategy. Out of our 7,500 Airbnb employees, nearly 1,900 teammates will have to leave Airbnb, comprising around 25% of our company.

Rep. Adam Schiff (CA): I don't think anyone anticipated that we would very soon lose more lives than we did during the Vietnam War, and it's due to the incompetence and maladministration of this president. We grossly underestimated the damage that he could do . . . House Republicans have become such a cult of the president that they're not even capable of acknowledging the facts staring them in the face.

Walt Disney Company: The Walt Disney Company today reported earnings for its second fiscal quarter ended March 28, 2020. Diluted earnings per share (EPS) from continuing operations for the quarter decreased 93% to $0.26 from $3.53 in the prior-year quarter . . . In total, we estimate that the Covid-19 impacts on our current quarter income from continuing operations before income taxes across all of our businesses was as much as $1.4 billion, inclusive of the impact at the Parks, Experiences and Products segment.

Gov. DeSantis (FL): It's interesting. I wonder whether people will say as Florida launches into phase one [of reopening], percentage positive tests plunged to record low. I don't think they will write that headline, because it's not going to generate the type of clicks, but the fact of the matter is, Florida has met all the gating criteria to be in the phase one obviously. We're doing it very judiciously.

***Tampa Bay Times*:** One day after reopening, Florida recorded a record number of new deaths Tuesday from the novel coronavirus, with 113 fatalities reported, including 11 in the Tampa Bay region. The new cases bring the state's total death count to 1,536. Tuesday is the first time since the epidemic took hold in Florida that the state reported more than 100 deaths in a single day.

***Houston Chronicle* (TX):** Since noon, the statewide Covid-19 case total rose from 32,813 to 34,134. That's an increase of 1,321 cases (4% increase). Another 36 deaths makes a total of 937 statewide (4% increase).

The single-day increase of more than 1,000 cases comes on the heels of two days that saw fewer than 1,000 cases reported.

Gov. Abbott (TX): Texas is in a position to continue opening parts of our economy because of the efforts and determination of the people of Texas. Over the past month, Texans have worked together to contain the spread of Covid-19 by following social distancing practices and staying at home whenever possible. As we move forward, I urge all Texans to continue following these social distancing guidelines and the health standards we have provided. With every Texan doing their part, we will contain Covid-19, we will unleash our entrepreneurs, and we will make it through this challenge together.

Gov. Cuomo (NY): There's no doubt that we're coming down the mountain. Only question is what trail we take, what path we take coming down the mountain. How fast does that decline continue? Does the decline continue? And that is purely a function of what we do. None of this is preordained. None of this is decided by any factor other than our own behavior.

Rep. Hakeem Jeffries (NY): Police officers aggressively "enforcing" social distancing in our community. This* occurred in East New York last evening. Why are sunbathers who violate social distancing guidelines

* This tweet was accompanied by a video of four police officers roughly handling a man on the ground.

treated one way and young men in certain communities another? This MUST end.

Vice President Pence: Conversations are being had about winding down the work for the [White House coronavirus] task force . . . I think we're having conversations about that and about what the proper time is for the task force to complete its work and for the ongoing efforts to take place on an agency-by-agency level. And we've already begun to talk about a transition plan with FEMA. But it's—it really is all a reflection of the tremendous progress we've made as a country.

President Trump: I'm viewing our great citizens of this country to a certain extent and to a large extent as warriors. They're warriors. We can't keep our country closed. We have to open our country . . . Will some people be badly affected? Yes. But we have to get our country open and we have to get it open soon.

MAY 6

Gregg Gonsalves, Epidemiologist, Yale School of Public Health: How many people will die this summer, before Election Day? What proportion of the deaths will be among African-Americans, Latinos, other people of color? This is getting awfully close to genocide by default. What else do you call mass death by public policy?

President Trump: So I call these people warriors, and I'm actually calling now, as you know, John,* the nation warriors. You have to be warriors. We can't keep our country closed down for years and we have to do something. And hopefully that won't be the case.

---

* Fox News's John Roberts, whose question he's answering.

Sen. Schatz (HI): Lotta tough talk about being a warrior for capitalism from people who don't pack meat or stock shelves or clean things or serve people.

Former Vice President Biden: You know, a president has a moral duty to protect the American people, to take responsibility, to tell the truth, without regard to political consequences. It's a responsibility that day after day is being ignored. He's ignored all the warnings, this president, having refused to prepare. We've now seen 70,000 Americans die on his watch. The president can't stop talking about himself.

President Trump: I thought we could wind it down sooner, but I had no idea how popular the task force is until actually yesterday when I started talking about winding down . . . So the Task Force will be around until we feel it's not necessary.

Kayleigh McEnany, White House Press Secretary: Let's dismiss a myth about tests right now. If we tested every single American in this country at this moment, we'd have to retest them an hour later and an hour later after that because at any moment, you could theoretically contract this virus. The notion that everyone needs to be tested is simply nonsensical.

President Trump: The media likes to say we have the most cases, but we do by far the most testing. If we did very little testing, we wouldn't have the most cases. So in a way, by doing all of this testing, we make ourselves look bad.

NPR: The Republican-led Michigan Legislature is suing Democratic Gov. Gretchen Whitmer, ratcheting their dispute over Covid-19 restrictions to a new level as lawmakers seek to force an end to orders that have closed down many nonessential businesses and largely confined residents to their homes. The legislators say the governor is acting illegally and overstepping her authority; Whitmer says she is protecting citizens from a global pandemic. The lawsuit was filed despite Michigan Attorney General Dana Nessel's recent affirmation that Whitmer is acting within the scope of the law.

Mike Pompeo, Secretary of State: We do not know, we don't have certainty about whether it began in the lab or whether it began someplace else . . . There's an easy way find out the answer to that—transparency, openness, the kinds of things that nations do when they really want to be part of solving a global pandemic, when they really want to participate in the things that keep human beings safe and get economies going back again.

Hua Chunying, Director, Foreign Ministry Information Department, China: I think this matter should be handed to scientists and medical professionals, and not politicians who lie for their own domestic political ends. Mr. Pompeo repeatedly spoke up but he cannot present any evidence. How can he? Because he doesn't have any.

Sen. Chris Murphy (CT): They're being terribly irresponsible because their statements on the origin of the virus are driven by political considerations. This administration is scurrying to try to deflect blame from a president who is floundering in his response to the epidemic. And China is a very convenient scapegoat. What worries me is that this escalation of rhetoric, back and forth, between the U.S. and China, it comes with consequences. We should call the Chinese out on what they've done wrong. But the hyperbole the administration is engaged in for political reasons hurts our efforts to try to fight the disease in the short term and long run. Ultimately, we need to have some cooperative relationship with the Chinese on battling pandemic diseases.

Utah County Health Department: During the tracing contacts conducted by the Utah County Health Department and Utah Department of Health, we found [two] businesses instructed employees to not follow quarantine guidelines after exposure to a confirmed case at work and required employees with a confirmed Covid-19 diagnosis to still report to work. This is completely unacceptable and resulted in a temporary full closure for one business along with heightened requirements for future cleaning and inspections.

President Trump: We want to terminate health care for, under Obamacare, because it's bad, and we're replacing it with a great health care at far less money and it includes pre-existing conditions . . . I don't view it as a termination. I view this as getting great health care.

Larry Levitt, Executive Vice President for Health Policy, Kaiser Family Foundation: President Trump is asking the Supreme Court to overturn the ACA (Affordable Care Act). He has never offered a plan to replace the ACA. While he has said he will protect coverage for pre-existing conditions, he has supported Congressional proposals to weaken those protections.

The Hamilton Project: Rates of food insecurity observed in April 2020 are also meaningfully higher than at any point for which there is comparable data (2001 to 2018). Looking over time, particularly to the relatively small increase in child food insecurity during the Great Recession, it is clear that young children are experiencing food insecurity to an extent unprecedented in modern times.

WBNS, Ohio: In an effort to stem the authority of Dr. Amy Acton, the Ohio House has passed an amendment that would limit the power of the Ohio Department of Health Director. The amendment proposed by Republican lawmakers would limit any stay-at-home order issued by the Ohio Department of Health to 14 days. It passed the House Wednesday 58-37, and now goes back to the Senate for approval.

Gov. DeWine (OH): My administration is focused on the important things we need to do to help businesses responsibly reopen while protecting Ohioans' health and safety. This week alone, this included increasing coronavirus testing and tracing, balancing Ohio's budget, and working on plans to move Ohio's economy forward. Ohioans need their legislators focused on these important issues. Creating more uncertainty regarding public health and employee safety is the last thing we need as we work to restore consumer confidence in Ohio's economy.

Dr. Scott Gottlieb, Former Commissioner, FDA: Ten days after Covid-19 infections peaked in Italy, Spain, and China; each nation showed declines in daily new cases. In U.S., ten days after infections peaked, we've showed few declines. Peak U.S. cases was 48,000 on April 26th. Since April 1st, average new cases are about 29,000.

Caitlin Rivers, Epidemiologist, Johns Hopkins Center for Health Security: It's clear to me that we are in a critical moment of this fight. We risk complacency and accepting the preventable deaths of 2,000 Americans each day. We risk complacency in accepting that our healthcare workers do not have what they need to do their jobs safely. And we risk complacency in recognizing that without continued vigilance in slowing transmission, we will again create the conditions that led to us being the worst-affected country in the world. And so, at this critical moment, it is important that we renew our focus on the public health actions that we know are effective in defeating Covid-19. These are the strategies of South Korea, Singapore, Taiwan, New Zealand, Germany, Iceland—all of which have successfully managed to slow their spread.

Gov. Cuomo (NY): A lot of people have been arguing where [the new cases] come from and where we should be focusing. But if you notice, 18% of the people came from nursing homes, less than 1% came from jail or prison, 2% came from the homeless population, 2% from other congregate facilities, but 66% of the people were at home, which is shocking to us.

Caitlin Rivers, Epidemiologist, Johns Hopkins Center for Health Security: Last week we performed around 1.6 million tests nationwide, an enormous improvement over the one million tests per week in early April. These gains are a testament to an impressive biomedical enterprise that we have built through sustained investments in science and medicine. But it is not enough. Estimates for the number of tests we need range from 3.5 million to tens of millions per week. While testing on the upper end of the range may not be logistically feasible any time soon, even increasing our testing capacity to 3–4 million tests per week would be enormously helpful to enable case-based interventions like contact tracing. We urgently need a national plan to close that gap.

Gov. Cuomo (NY): We were thinking that maybe we were going to find a higher percentage of essential employees who were getting sick because they were going to work. That these may be nurses, doctors, transit workers. That's not the case, and they were predominantly at home . . . But it reinforces what we've been saying, which is much of this comes down to what you do to protect yourself. Everything is closed down, government has done everything it could, society has done everything it could. Now it's up to you.

MAY 7

AP: A set of detailed documents created by the nation's top disease investigators meant to give step-by-step advice to local leaders deciding when and how to reopen public places such as mass transit, day care centers and restaurants during the still-raging pandemic has been shelved by the Trump administration. The 17-page report by a Centers for Disease Control and Prevention team, titled "Guidance for Implementing the Opening Up America Again Framework," was researched and written to help faith leaders, business owners, educators and state and local officials as they begin to reopen. It was supposed to be published last Friday, but agency scientists were told the guidance "would never see the light of day," according to a CDC official.

Mayor de Blasio, New York City: And the most essential question we all ask is, "Have I gotten this disease already or am I going to get this disease? If I have gotten it or if I do get it, do I put my family in danger, the people I love in danger?" The uncertainty is directly related to the lack of testing that's been the reality from day one. And this has been the central problem in this crisis.

Sen. Chris Murphy (CT): If you want to know why we have no national testing program, you just need to listen to what Trump said yesterday: "By doing all this testing," Trump said, "we make ourselves look bad." The lack of tests isn't accidental. It's by design.

Hogan Gidley, Deputy White House Press Secretary: We were recently notified by the White House Medical Unit that a member of the United States Military, who works on the White House campus, has tested positive for Coronavirus.

President Trump: They're doing everything that you can do, again, within the limits of testing, and you know what that is. We have the ultimate testing, we have the best tests in the world and we gave more than anybody else. And I've always said, testing is somewhat overrated because what happens after somebody takes a test, what's going on there?

Judd Deere, Deputy White House Press Secretary: Every staff member in close proximity to the President and Vice-President is being tested daily for Covid-19 as well as any guests.

President Trump: Right now we're all warriors. You're warriors, we're warriors. You could be with somebody, everything's fine and then something happens to that person and all of a sudden test positive and we're all warriors together. I am. You are. We all are.

Former State Rep. Stacey Abrams (GA): Black people are dying at a higher rate [from Covid-19]. Here in Georgia, 32% of the population, 54%

of the deaths. That's directly tied to identity and if we do not acknowledge it, we are never going to find the solutions to address it.

Former Vice President Biden: So this disease is not only tearing through the nation, devastating families, wrecking the economy, it's magnifying and exacerbating some of the worst systematic inequities exist. Counties with majority Black populations have Covid infections three times higher than majority white counties. Death rates nearly six times higher. Now that's inconceivable. It should never happen, but we know exactly why it has. People of color are less likely to have access to healthcare and health insurance. Therefore, they're less likely to go in for preventative efforts. They're less likely to have had treatment for underlying conditions that make them much more vulnerable to the virus now. And they're more likely to be exposed to pollutants tied to higher Covid death rates. Less likely to have a job they can just do from home, meaning they're more likely to have to choose between their lives and their livelihoods.

Adam Harris, *Atlantic*: Rural residents die at higher rates from heart disease, cancer, and stroke than those in cities, and black people in rural areas die at especially high rates. Roughly 75 percent of the areas most vulnerable to the coronavirus are in the South, according to the Surgo Foundation, a research group that built an index to survey Covid-19 vulnerability.

Rep. Terri Sewell (AL): This public-health crisis has really illuminated inherent structural inequities and disinvestment in health infrastructure. I'm most afraid that my Black Belt communities started on unequal footing and will just get left behind.

Gov. Abbott (TX): Basically, there's only three categories causing any type of outbreak. There are meatpacking plants, there are jails and there are senior centers. And so we have task forces that focus on those three areas. If it weren't for those three categories, the people in Texas testing positive would be very minimal.

Pew Research Center: A sizable majority of Americans (68%) continue to say their greater concern is that state governments will lift coronavirus-related restrictions on public activity too quickly. Fewer than half as many (31%) say their greater concern is that states will not lift restrictions quickly enough, according to a new Pew Research Center survey that comes as some states begin to ease the restrictions they put in place to combat the spread of Covid-19.

Gov. Cuomo (NY): I also think, and I do this for myself, any leader who makes a decision in this situation should be willing to participate in anything they authorize. So there is nothing that we are going to authorize or allow in this state that I myself will not be part of. It's too easy to say, "Okay, you can go do this, but I'm going to protect myself, and I'm going to stay behind the glass wall." No. If all human life has the same value, if I say something is safe for New Yorkers, then I will participate in it, because if it's safe for you, it's safe for me, right? That should be our standard, going forward. What we've been doing in New York is, look, make the decisions based on facts and data, not emotion and politics. I understand the emotion, and I understand the anxiety and the stress. I understand politics a little bit, but that's not the basis for making a decision. That was every leader who's told us that in different ways. That was John Adams. That was Lincoln. That was FDR. That was Teddy Roosevelt.

President Trump: I watch Fox News and I watch others and I read a lot of newspapers and I get a lot of information from my people. I think I'm very well versed when it comes to not only the pandemic, but everything. I enjoy that and I think I have an obligation to do it. But there's certainly a more honorable source than some. Some is fake. If you look at CNN, it's fake news. If you look at MSDNC, I call it MSDNC, you know what that means right? Democratic National Committee. You look at NBC. NBC to me is very dishonest news and that's why they fired Andy Lack, I guess. You'll have to ask them, but Andy Lack was a hack and they fired him and they did a big favor to the world and to this country. But no, I find NBC to be very dishonest, I find, which is a Comcast division. I call it Concast with an N. I don't use the M. I always call it Concast. ABC, I thought he* gave me a very fair interview the other night. Very good professional. I've had very good relationships with him, as you know. CBS is having a hard time, but they're not getting it straight. In fact, last night I read where they did a false report where they actually got people to make it look like it was—Did you see what happened? They got people, let's get some people because they want to make it look like it was turmoil. And they do that with this White House all the time. They love the word chaos when there's no chaos whatsoever. They love the word chaos, but what happened at CBS yesterday was terrible. Where they got a lot of people to try and pretend like it was a mass amount of chaos and disorder. You saw that, it was terrible. The news media in our country's a mess, but they fired Andy Lack and that was a good thing. That's a big step forward.

Johns Hopkins Coronavirus Resource Center

Global: 3,769,150 cases, 264,111 deaths

U.S.: 1,228,609 cases, 73,431 deaths†

Spain: 220,325 cases, 25,857 deaths

Italy: 214,457 cases, 29,684 deaths

United Kingdom: 202,359 cases, 30,150 deaths

Russia: 177,160 cases, 1,625 deaths

France: 174,224 cases, 25,812 deaths

Germany: 168,162 cases, 7,275 deaths

---

* David Muir, ABC anchor

† Dr. Anthony Fauci: "Almost certainly it's higher. There may have been people who died at home who were not counted as Covid because they never really got to the hospital." (Virtual Senate hearing, May 12, 2020)

Brazil: 126,611 cases, 8,588 deaths
South Korea: 10,810 cases, 256 deaths

MAY 8

U.S. Bureau of Labor Statistics: Total nonfarm payroll employment fell by 20.5 million in April, and the unemployment rate rose to 14.7 percent, the U.S. Bureau of Labor Statistics reported today. The changes in these measures reflect the effects of the coronavirus (Covid-19) pandemic and efforts to contain it. Employment fell sharply in all major industry sectors, with particularly heavy job losses in leisure and hospitality . . . In April, the unemployment rate increased by 10.3 percentage points to 14.7 percent. This is the highest rate and the largest over-the-month increase in the history of the series (seasonally adjusted data are available back to January 1948). The number of unemployed persons rose by 15.9 million to 23.1 million in April . . . Total nonfarm payroll employment fell by 20.5 million in April, after declining by 870,000 in March. The April over-the-month decline is the largest in the history of the series and brought employment to its lowest level since February 2011 (the series dates back to 1939).

Sen. Schumer (NY): No one could look at today's jobs report, the highest unemployment since the Great Depression, and say we should hit the pause button on further government action, as Leader McConnell, Leader McCarthy and the Trump White House have said. We need a big, bold approach now to support American workers and families. Republicans who choose inaction in the face of these historic economic and health crises will be taking the same misguided path as Herbert Hoover.

President Trump: We're in no rush, we're in no rush. The Democrats have to do what they have to do. We want to see what they have, but I can't say we're in a rush . . . This was an artificial turning off of a tremendous economy. When we turn it back on, which we've just started doing, I think it'll come back blazing.

Senator Pat Toomey (PA): Let me start with my starting premise and that is there was a very specific reason why we shut down our economy. Think about how drastic and draconian a step that was. It was completely unprecedented in American history to just forbid economic activity. We did it for one reason. That was to slow down the rate of the transmission of the virus, not to stop it altogether—nobody thought that was possible.

President Trump: These people want to get back to work. Everybody's done what they have done and you can only do that so long . . . You look at some cases, some people think they're doing it for politics, here we go again. But they think they're doing it because it'll hurt me—hurt me in the election—the longer it takes to open up. And I can see some of that. Because some of these people are being unrealistic. They're being ridiculous. I've looked at a couple of states that are being absolutely ridiculous. But ultimately the people are forcing it.

Marc Perrone, President, UFCW: Today's rush by the Trump Administration to re-open 14 meatpacking plants without the urgent safety improvements needed is a reckless move that will put American lives at risk and further endanger the long-term security of our nation's food supply Since the executive order was announced by President Trump, the Administration has failed to take the urgent action needed to enact clear and enforceable safety standards at these meatpacking plants.

Kayleigh McEnany, White House Press Secretary: We have put in place the guidelines that our experts have put forward to keep this building safe, which means contact tracing. All of the recommended guidelines we have for businesses that have essential workers, we are now putting them in place here in the White House. So as America reopens safely, the White House is continuing to operate safely.

***Des Moines Register*:** More than 1,000 workers at the Tyson Foods plant in Waterloo have tested positive for the coronavirus, a county public health leader said Thursday—more than double the number Gov. Kim Reynolds had said the day before.

The news came as the Arkansas-based company reopened the plant Thursday after a two-week closure following a spike in Covid-19 cases there.

Steven Dennis, Bloomberg News: Iowa now has had more confirmed Covid cases than South Korea.*

Timothy Egan, *New York Times*: Every 49 seconds or so, throughout the first week in May, an American has been dying of this disease. With 1.3 million reported cases, the United States, just five percent of the world's population, has nearly 33 percent of the sick. With more than 75,000 deaths, we're at the front of the pack as well. No country comes close on all three measures.

Globally, the average death rate is 34 people per million residents. In the United States, it's more than six times higher—232 per million.

Former President Obama: It would have been bad even with the best of governments. It has been an absolute chaotic disaster when that mindset—of "what's in it for me" . . . is operationalized in our government.

Douglas Christian, Talk Media News: Does the President see the CDC guidelines as an obstacle to getting the company—getting the country back up and running again? And if it does not see the CDC guidelines as an obstacle, why not release those guidelines to the public and also follow them as we move forward?

Kayleigh McEnany, White House Press Secretary:† No, those aren't CDC guidelines; those are guidelines in draft form that a

* South Korea: 51.6 million. Iowa population: 3.15 million.

† Direct exchange

> rogue employee has given you for whatever personal reason they've decided to do that . . . Those CDC guidelines are going through an editing process. And when we have those, you guys will be the first to know.

AP: White House spokeswoman Kayleigh McEnany said Friday that the documents had not been approved by CDC Director Robert Redfield. The new emails, however, show that Redfield cleared the guidance.

Dr. Bright, Former Director, BARDA: I am not disgruntled. I am frustrated at a lack of leadership. I am frustrated at a lack of urgency to get a head start on developing lifesaving tools for Americans. I'm frustrated at our inability to be heard as scientists. Those things frustrate me . . . We see too many doctors and nurses now dying. And I was thinking that we could have done more to get those masks and those supplies to them sooner. And if we had, would they still be alive today? It's a horrible thought to think about the time that passed where we could've done something and we didn't.

President Trump: I feel about vaccines like I feel about tests. This is going to go away without a vaccine, it's gonna go away, and we're not going to see it again, hopefully, after a period of time. You may have some flare-ups.

Michael Felberbaum, FDA spokesman: As [FDA Director] Dr. Hahn wrote in a note to staff today, he recently came into contact with an individual who has tested positive for Covid-19. Per guidelines, he is now in self-quarantine for the next two weeks.

MAY 9

CDC: CDC Director Dr. Robert Redfield has been determined to have had a low risk exposure on May 6 to a person at the White House who has Covid-19. He is feeling fine, and has no symptoms. He will be teleworking for the next two weeks . . . [I]n the event Dr. Redfield must go to the White House to fulfill any responsibilities as part of White House Coronavirus Task Force work, he will follow the safety practices set out by the CDC for those who may have been exposed.

CNN: Dr. Anthony Fauci, the director of the National Institute of Allergy and Infectious Diseases and member of the White House's coronavirus task force, told CNN he will begin a "modified quarantine" after making a "low risk" contact with the White House staffer who tested positive for the novel coronavirus.

Governor Newsom (CA): CA is now a vote-by-mail state. Every registered voter will receive a mail-in ballot for the Nov. election. We'll also provide safe in-person voting options. The right to vote is foundational to our democracy. No one should be forced to risk their health to exercise that right.

President Trump: So in California, the Democrats, who fought like crazy to get all mail in only ballots, and succeeded, have just opened a voting booth in the most Democrat area in the State. They are trying to steal another election. It's all rigged out there. These votes must not count. SCAM!

Gov. Cuomo (NY): The priority for us today is dealing with a new issue that has come up which is truly disturbing. And that is the issue on how the Covid virus may affect a young people, very young people. Infants, children in elementary school. We had thought initially and again so many of what the initial information we had turned out not to be correct or turned out to be modified, but we were laboring under the impression that young people were not affected by Covid-19. And that was actually good news, right? The vulnerable populations were older people, people with comorbidity. But one of the few rays of good news was young people weren't affected. We're not so sure that that is the fact anymore. Toddlers, elementary school children, our presenting symptoms similar to Kawasaki disease or toxic shock like syndrome.

Los Angeles Times**:** Nearly half of all deaths related to Covid-19 in California are linked to elder care facilities, a data analysis by the *Los Angeles Times* has found, with the state releasing new data suggesting that there have been many more outbreaks than previously disclosed. At least 1,276 people have died after being infected with the coronavirus in skilled nursing or assisted living facilities in California, accounting for more than 49% of total fatalities reported by the state.

Gov. Cuomo (NY): When you look at disasters, emergencies, I don't care if they're hurricanes, floods, whatever they are. Cruel irony is, the poorest people pay the highest price. I've seen this across the country when I was at HUD. You're there to take care of a flood or a storm, it's the poorer communities that get wiped out first, right. It's the lowland, it's the land that tends to flood that it has the lower value and that's where the lower community, lower-income community tends to locate . . . And today we're launching a new initiative, again to address exactly this which is to expand access to testing in low-income communities and communities of color.

MAY 10

Sen. Chris Murphy (CT): In the middle of a pandemic that has killed nearly 80,000 Americans, a normal president would try to expand health insurance. Donald Trump is in court right now trying to take health insurance away from 20 million of us. In the middle of a pandemic.

Steve Mnuchin, Secretary of the Treasury: Let me just emphasize first of all these numbers impact real people and I want to emphasize we understand what this is—how this is impacting real people. So they're not just numbers, it's impacting real people.

Dr. Christopher Murray, Director, IMHE: So our projections through till August 4th are up. We're up to 137,000 deaths that we expect to see and that's the effect of two things going in opposite directions. Some good-ish news coming out of New York and New Jersey and Michigan, where the death cases and death numbers are coming down faster than expected. Some other states where cases and deaths are going up more than we expected, Illinois and then Arizona, Florida, California as examples of that. And so it's the balancing of those that is driving our numbers. And then, of course, we're seeing just explosive increases in mobility in a number of states that we expect will translate into more cases and deaths, you know, in 10 days from now.

President Trump: We are getting great marks for the handling of the CoronaVirus pandemic, especially the very early BAN of people from China, the infectious source, entering the USA. Compare that to the Obama/Sleepy Joe disaster known as H1N1 Swine Flu. Poor marks, bad polls—didn't have a clue!

Dr. Murray, Director, IMHE: We're seeing increases in mobility, even in anticipation of the relaxation of social distancing. But there's definitely a correlation. The places that are taking off the social distancing mandate, the bump in mobility appears to be larger. So somewhere like Georgia, which was one of the first, we're seeing, in that category of a pretty big increase.

Dr. Michael Osterholm, Director, Center for Infectious Disease Research and Policy: We have to understand that we're riding this tiger; we are not directing it. This virus is going to do what it's going to do. What we can do is only nibble at the edges. And I think it's not a good message to send to the public that we can control this virus in a meaningful way.

Kevin Hassett, White House Economic Advisor: It is scary to go to work . . . I think that I'd be a lot safer if I was sitting at home than I would be going to the West Wing.

Dr. Osterholm, Director, Center for Infectious Disease Research and Policy: What we have to tell people honestly, what they want to hear, they don't want it sugarcoated and they do not want it coated in fear. But somewhere between now and tomorrow, next year, we're going to see 60–70% of Americans ultimately infected with this virus.

Steve Mnuchin, Secretary of the Treasury: If we do this carefully, working with the governors, I don't think there's a considerable risk. Matter of fact, I think there's a considerable risk of not reopening. You're talking about what would be permanent economic damage to the American public.

MAY 11

Peter Navarro, Director, White House Office of Trade and Manufacturing Policy: That was a pity party yesterday on the Sunday shows . . . It was a pity party. This is not the Great Depression. Anyone who thinks this is the Great Depression doesn't understand either history or economics.

Brian Kilmeade, Fox News: 78,000 are dead, we understand how many got the virus and will, I get it, but at the same time can you get the military mindset with the masses, of "take on the enemy because we have no choice," sitting on the sidelines will destroy the country.

Former Vice President Biden: Instead of unifying the country to accelerate our public health response and get economic relief to those who need it, President Trump is reverting to a familiar strategy of deflecting blame and dividing Americans . . . He hopes to split the country into dueling camps, casting Democrats as doomsayers hoping to keep America grounded and Republicans as freedom fighters trying to liberate the economy. It's a childish tactic—and a false choice that none of us should fall for.

NBC News: Coronavirus infection rates are spiking to new highs in several metropolitan areas and smaller communities across the country, according to undisclosed data the White House's pandemic task force is using to track rates of infection, which was obtained by NBC News. The data in a May 7 coronavirus task force report are at odds with President Donald Trump's declaration Monday that "all throughout the country, the numbers are coming down rapidly."

President Trump: The great people of Pennsylvania want their freedom now, and they are fully aware of what that entails. The Democrats are moving slowly, all over the USA, for political purposes. They would wait until November 3rd if it were up to them. Don't play politics. Be safe, move quickly!

Governor Tom Wolf (PA): To those politicians who decide to cave in to this coronavirus, they need to understand the consequences of their cowardly act. The funding we have put aside to help with fighting this crisis will go to the folks who are doing their part.

Bloomberg News: The coronavirus spread at more than twice the national rate in U.S. counties with major meatpacking plants during the first week after President Donald Trump issued an executive order directing that they be reopened. Confirmed Covid-19 cases jumped 40% during the week following the order in counties with major beef or pork slaughterhouses, compared with a 19% rise nationally, according to a Bloomberg News analysis of data compiled by Johns Hopkins University.

Sen. McConnell (KY): We're basically assessing what we've done already. I'm in constant communication with the White House and if we decide to go forward [on another stimulus bill] we'll go forward together. We have not yet felt the urgency of acting immediately. That time could develop, but I don't think it has yet.

Senator John Cornyn (TX): Now with the states beginning to gradually reopen their economies, we're staring down the barrel of a second epidemic, one generated by opportunistic lawsuits, crushing legal fees and drawn out court battles . . . more than 950 such lawsuits have already been filed in the United States. We've seen suits against healthcare workers, nursing homes, colleges, governments, retailers, you name it. As our economy begins to reopen, unfortunately so will the legal floodgates. The litigation epidemic is shaping up to be a big one.

Gov. Wolf (PA): If your county reopens prematurely and you don't feel comfortable returning to work, rest assured that the commonwealth will allow you to continue to receive unemployment compensation, even if your employer reopens.

Peter Navarro, Director, White House Office of Trade and Manufacturing Policy: It crossed me that Disneyland in Shanghai is opening this morning, while my own Disneyland in my own homeland in Orange County, in Anaheim, where Disneyland was born, is still shut because of the Chinese Communist Party. That makes me mad.

White House Office of Personnel Management: The CDC continues to encourage the use of facial coverings when social distancing is not an option. As an additional [layer] of protection, we are requiring everyone who enters the West Wing to wear a mask or facial covering.

President Trump: In the span of just a few short months we have developed a testing capacity unmatched and unrivaled anywhere in the world and it is not even close. This is a core element of our plan to safely and gradually reopened America, and we are opening and starting and there is enthusiasm like I haven't seen in a long time.

German Lopez, *Vox*: It's true that the US leads the world in total number of tests, in large part because it's a big country and has the most confirmed Covid-19 cases and deaths globally. But when controlling for population,

America is behind several countries in terms of Covid-19 testing: As of May 9, the US testing rate is roughly 26 per 1,000 people, according to Our World in Data; in comparison, Denmark's rate is 53, Italy's is 42, New Zealand's is 39, Germany's is 33 (as of May 3), and Canada's is 28.

President Trump: If somebody wants to be tested right now, they'll be able to be tested.

Adm. Giroir, Assistant Secretary for Health: So everybody who needs a test can get a test. We have plenty of tests for that. Right now in America anybody who needs a test can get a test in America with the numbers we have. If you are symptomatic with a respiratory illness, that is an indication for a test and you can get a test. If you need to be contact traced, you can get a test. And we hope and not hope, we are starting to have asymptomatic surveillance, which is very important.

President Trump: I really believe that as good as we've done and we've done great, we had the best economy in the history of the world, not just here, but anywhere in the world, you can talk China, you can talk any other country, we had the best economy anywhere in the world. We were going for numbers where there was unemployment numbers, where we had our best numbers, employment also numbers, little different where we had our best numbers, almost 160 million people. All of that, we had the greatest stock market numbers ever. I think we had 142 days where we set records in a short period of time, 152 days, we set records in the stock market.

Dr. Michael Ryan, Executive Director of Health Emergencies, WHO: Shutting your eyes and trying to drive through this blind is about as silly an equation as I've seen. And I'm really concerned that certain countries are setting themselves up for some seriously blind driving over the next few months.

Sen. Mitch McConnell (KY): I think President Obama should have kept his mouth shut. You know, we know he doesn't like much administration is doing, that's understandable. But I think it's a little bit classless, frankly, to critique an administration that comes after you. You had your shot, you were there for eight years.

Ben Rhodes, Former Deputy National Security Advisor: The maddening thing is Obama left them a WH office for pandemics, a literal playbook, a cabinet-level exercise, and a global infrastructure to deal with "something like this."

Michael Steele, Former Chair, Republican National Committee: I'm sure Mitch is aware that a grown ass black man who happens to be a former president has agency to speak his mind on how his successor is managing this crisis, especially since his successor has yet to keep "his mouth shut" about him.

Dr. Thomas Frieden, Former Director, CDC: We're not reopening based on science. We're reopening based on politics, ideology, and public pressure. And I think it's going to end badly . . . daring Mother Nature to kill you or someone you love. Mother Nature bats last, and she bats a thousand.

Johns Hopkins Coronavirus Resource Center:
United States: 80,239 deaths
United Kingdom: 32,141 deaths
Italy: 30,739 deaths
Spain: 26,744 deaths
France: 26,646 deaths
Brazil: 11,309 deaths
Belgium: 8,707 deaths
Germany: 7,653 deaths
China: 4,637 deaths
South Korea: 256 deaths

MAY 12

CNN: Four-in-10 Americans say that they personally know someone who has been diagnosed with coronavirus, a figure that has nearly doubled in the last month. And most say the government is not doing enough to address the growing death toll (56%), the limited availability of testing (57%) or the potential for a second wave of cases later this year (58%). The new poll finds President Donald Trump's overall approval rating holding about even at 45%. His rating now matches his high point in CNN polling dating back to the start of his term. But at the same time, the President's numbers for handling the coronavirus outbreak have worsened (55% now disapprove, up from 48% in early March and 52% last month), and only 36% say they consider Trump a trusted source of information about the outbreak.

Sen. Lamar Alexander (TN): This is a bipartisan hearing to examine how well we're preparing to go safely back to work and to school and to determine what else we need to do in the United States Senate. Such an exercise sometimes encourages finger pointing. Before we spend too much time finger pointing, I would like to suggest that almost all of us, the United States and almost every country so far as I can tell, underestimated this virus . . . Now while the crisis has our full attention, I believe we should put into law this year whatever improvements need to be made to be well-prepared for the next pandemic. If there is to be finger pointing, I hope they're pointed in that direction.

Dr. Fauci, Director, NIAID: When you talk about "will this virus just disappear"—as I've said publicly many times—that is just not gonna happen because it's such a highly transmissible virus . . . So my approach towards the possibility of a rebound, a second wave in the fall, is that a, it's entirely conceivable and possible it would happen. But b, I would hope that between now and then, given the capability of doing the testing that you heard from [Assistant Secretary for Health] Admiral Giroir and the ability of us to stock up on special protective equipment and the workforce that the CDC, under Dr. Redfield, will be putting forth to be able to identify, isolate, and contact trace, I hope that if we do have the threat of a second wave, we will be able to deal with it very effectively to prevent it from becoming an outbreak not only worse than now but much, much less.

Senator Rand Paul (KY): I think we ought to have a little bit of humility in our belief that we know what's best for the economy and as much as I respect you, Dr. Fauci, I don't think you're the end all. I don't think you're the one person that gets to make the decision. We can listen to your advice but there are people on the other side saying there's not going to be a surge and that we can safely open the economy. And the facts will bear this out, but if we keep kids out of school for another year, what's going to happen is the poor and underprivileged kids who don't have a parent that's able to teach them at home are not going to learn for a full year. And I think we ought to look at the Swedish model and ought to look at getting our kids getting back to school. I think it's a huge mistake if we don't open schools in the fall.

Dr. Fauci, NIAID:* First of all, Senator Paul, thank you for your comments. I never made myself to be out the end all. I'm a scientist, a physician, and a public health official. I give advice according to the best scientific evidence. A number of people come in to that and give advice to things more related to what you spoke about. The need to get the country back open again. I don't give advice about anything other than public health. I wanted to respond to that. The second the thing is that you used the word we should be humble about what we don't know. I think that falls under the fact that we don't know everything about this virus and we really better be very careful particularly when it comes to children because the more and more we learn, we're seeing things what this virus can do that we didn't

* Direct exchange

see from the studies in China or in Europe . . . I think we ought to be careful if we're not cavalier in thinking children are completely immune to the effects.

Sen. Patty Murray (WA): This is far from the first time this administration has silenced experts who were doing their job and putting public health first. The fact of the matter is, President Trump has been more focused on fighting against the truth than fighting this virus. and Americans have sadly paid the price.

Dr. Fauci, NIAID: My concern is that as states or cities or regions in their attempt, understandably, to get back to some form of normality disregard—to a greater or lesser degree—the checkpoints we put in our guidelines about when it's safe to proceed in pulling back on mitigation. Because I feel if that occurs, there is a real risk that you'll trigger an outbreak that you may not be able to control which, in fact, will set you back not only leading to some suffering and death that could be avoid but could even set you back on the road to get economic recovery. It would almost turn the clock back rather than going forward.

Sen. Chris Murphy (CT): Quarantine is relatively easy for people like you and me. We could still work and get paid, we could telework, but there are millions of other Americans who work jobs that can't be performed from home or are paid by the hour. And it is just remarkable to me that this administration has not yet developed a mechanism for states to implement and pay for a quarantine system that will work for all Americans. Your* plan to reopen America requires states develop that plan and yet my state has no clue how to implement and pay for that system without help from the federal government.

---

* Dr. Fauci, FDA Chair Stephen Hahn, and CDC Director Robert Redfield

Sen. Mitt Romney (UT): Admiral Giroir,* I'm going to take off where Senator Hassan spoke. I understand that politicians are going to frame data in a way most positive politically; of course, I wouldn't expect that from admirals. But yesterday you celebrated we had done more tests per capita than South Korea but ignored fact that they accomplished theirs at the beginning of the outbreak while we treaded water in February and March and, as a result, by March 6th the U.S. had completed just 2,000 tests whereas South Korea had conducted more than 140,000 tests. So partially as a result of that they have 256 deaths and we have almost 80,000 deaths. I find our testing record nothing to celebrate whatsoever. The fact is their test numbers are going down, down, down, down now because they don't have the kind of outbreak we have. Ours are going up, up, up as they have to.

Sen. Murphy (CT): Dr. Fauci, Dr. Redfield, you've made news today by warning us appropriately of the dangers of states opening too early. But as Senator Murray mentioned, this is infuriating to many of us because it comes hours after the President declared that we have prevailed over coronavirus and I'm going to tell you is going to make it much harder on state leaders to keep social distancing restrictions in place. It comes days after the President called on citizens to liberate their states from social distancing orders and I think you're all noble public servants but I worry that you're trying to have it both ways. You say the states shouldn't open too early. But then you don't give us the resources to succeed. You work for a President who is frankly undermining our efforts to comply with the guidance that you've given us and then the guidance that you have provided is criminally vague.

Sen. Kamala Harris (CA): Thank God for Dr. Fauci. Thank God for him to having the courage to speak truth. God only knows what kind of

* Adm. Brett Giroir, Assistant Secretary for Health

repercussion he's going to face for speaking the truth—but obviously he has the well-being of the American people as his priority.

Sen. McConnell (KY): If we want even an outside shot at the kind of risk rehiring that American workers deserve, we have to make sure our opportunistic trial lawyers are not lurking on the sidewalk outside every small business waiting to slap them with a lawsuit if they turn the lights back on. Our legislation is going to create a legal safe harbor for businesses and nonprofits, governments and workers and schools who are following public health guidelines to the best of their ability . . . If we want American workers the clock back in we need employers to know if they follow the guidelines they will not be left to drown in opportunistic litigation.

Marquette University Law School Poll: In March, 83% of Republicans said closures were appropriate; in new poll, it's 49%. Among Democrats, in March 95% said closures were appropriate; in new poll, it is 90%.

Timothy P. White, Chancellor, California State University System: Our university, when open without restrictions and fully in person, as is the traditional norm of the past, is a place where over 500,000 people come together in close and vibrant proximity with each other on a daily basis. That approach, sadly, just isn't in the cards now.

Adrian Wojnarowski, ESPN: Participants on a board of governors call Tuesday with NBA [National Basketball Association] commissioner Adam Silver left the virtual meeting feeling increasingly positive about the league's momentum toward a resumption of play this season, sources told ESPN.

Eric Holder, Former U.S. Attorney General: Can you imagine Ronald Reagan, can you imagine Bill Clinton, either of the Bushes, Barack Obama saying that this is something for the states to work out as opposed to leading an effort by the federal government to mobilize the people, mobilize the instruments of government to deal with this pandemic. This president, he's not up to the job. His incompetence is going to cost us.

Jeremy Konyndyk, Center for Global Development: [The U.S. Coronavirus response] has certainly damaged America standing in the world. Both in terms of our reputation for being able to competently manage some of our own problems. being unable to get it under control some of our own problems. The fact that we have the worst outbreak in the world—and are continuing to be unable to get it under control, I think it does damage the perception of American competence.

MAY 13

Dr. Osterholm, Director, Center for Infectious Disease Research and Policy: You can't be in lockdown for 18 months. We'll destroy society as we know it, and we don't know what we'll accomplish with it [but] can't just let the virus go. Lots of people will die and it'll shut down our health system, not just for Covid patients, but for anyone with a health problem. What we need is a plan.

Senator Mike Braun (IN): The White House and its Task Force have been beyond transparent in the midst of this outbreak, indeed holding an unprecedented amount of daily press briefings and allowing for a free flow of information that has been central to the White House's reopening efforts. This is not about transparency. The White House is always gonna be in favor of transparency. The President comes from a world of entrepreneurs where we embrace it in competition. This is about the minority leader trying to use the bureaucracy at the CDC to bog down the economy.

***Daily Beast*:** President Donald Trump and members of his coronavirus task force are pushing officials at the Centers for Disease Control and Prevention to change how the agency works with states to count coronavirus-related deaths. And they're pushing for revisions that could lead to far fewer deaths being counted than originally reported, according to five administration officials working on the government's response to the pandemic . . . Officials inside the CDC, five of whom spoke to The Daily Beast, said they are pushing back against that request, claiming it could falsely skew the mortality rate at a time when state and local governments are already struggling to ensure that every person who dies as a result of the coronavirus is counted.

Sen. Braun (IN): Are we really going to let the CDC shutter the economy a second time, like they did with testing, by dictating overly prescriptive guidelines?

Gov. Cuomo (NY) and Gov. Hogan (MD): Each day that Congress fails to act, states are being forced to make cuts that will devastate the essential services the American people rely on and destroy the economic recovery before it even gets off the ground. With widespread bipartisan agreement on the need for this assistance, we cannot afford a partisan process that turns this urgent relief into another political football. This is not a red state and blue state crisis. This is a red white and blue pandemic. The coronavirus is apolitical. It does not attack Democrats or Republicans. It attacks Americans. The nation's governors are counting on our leaders in Washington to come together, put partisanship aside, and to get this done for the American people. This is why the National Governors Association continues to call for the passage of critical priorities that will help states and territories lead us through this pandemic response and get America moving again: $500 billion in fiscal support for state budgetary shortfalls resulting from the pandemic, enhanced FMAP funding to provide healthcare to our most vulnerable, and 100 percent federal cost share for FEMA response and recovery efforts.

Jerome Powell, Chair, Federal Reserve System: Among people who were working in February, almost 40% of those in households making less than

$40,000 a year had lost a job in March. This reversal of economic fortune has caused a level of pain that is hard to capture in words as lives are upended and made great uncertainty about the future. This downturn is different from those that came before it . . . The record shows that deeper and longer recessions can leave behind lasting damage to the productive capacity of the economy . . . Additional fiscal support could be costly but worth it if it helps avoid long term damage and leaves us with a stronger recovery.

United Nations Department of Economic and Social Affairs: The world economy is expected to lose nearly $8.5 trillion in output in 2020 and 2021, nearly wiping out the cumulative output gains of the previous four years . . . According to baseline estimates, 34.3 million additional people—including millions working in the informal sector—will fall below the extreme poverty line this year, with African countries accounting for 56 per cent of this increase.

Delegate Lamont Bagby (VA), Chair, Virginia Legislative Black Caucus: Under the current plan, and with the already existent racial disparities that this pandemic and economic crisis are perpetuating, we will be creating a situation where Black and Brown Virginians outside of Northern Virginia will become guinea pigs for our economy. We've already seen this take place in Georgia, where that state's premature reopening resulted in a huge spike in Covid-19 cases, with the overwhelming majority being Black people and People of Color . . . Throughout our country's history, Black and Brown people have been experimented on and used as unwilling test subjects before—we cannot allow that to be repeated here.

Ken Paxton, Attorney General (TX): Unfortunately, a few Texas counties and cities seem to have confused recommendations with requirements and have grossly exceeded state law to impose their own will on private citizens and businesses. These letters* seek to avoid any public confusion as we reopen the state. I trust that local officials will act quickly to correct any orders that unlawfully conflict with Texas law and Governor Abbott's Executive Orders.

President Trump: Now, will you have an incident, one out of a million, one out of 500,000, will something happen? Perhaps. But you know, you can be driving to school and some bad things can happen too.

Gov. Pritzker (IL): I want this to end just as much as you do. If I could take away the pain and the loss you're feeling right now, I would do it in a heartbeat. But this virus is still among us. This pandemic is not over. And to pretend otherwise in a misguided attempt to reclaim what we've lost will only make this last longer. For leaders, there are no easy decisions in a pandemic. Every choice, every choice, has consequences. And I know leaders across the state are struggling with these choices, and I have sympathy for them in that struggle. But what I don't have sympathy for is those so intent on disregarding science and logic, so afraid to tell their constituents what they may not want to hear, that they put more people's lives at risk. You weren't elected to do what's easy. You were elected to do what's right.

***Guardian*:** Rightwing militia groups in Michigan plan to rally at the state capitol building on Thursday to protest Democratic governor Gretchen Whitmer's stay-at-home orders that she put in place to slow the deadly spread of the coronavirus pandemic.

Thursday's demonstration will be the latest in a series of protests that started as a demonstration against the lockdown policy but are now generating fears of an eruption of political violence.

---

* Texas AG Office: "Attorney General Ken Paxton today issued letters to three Texas counties (Dallas, Bexar, and Travis) and two mayors (San Antonio and Austin), warning that some requirements in their local public health orders are unlawful and can confuse law-abiding citizens."

Gov. Whitmer (MI): I do think that the fact of the matter is these protests, in a perverse way, make it likelier that we're going to have to stay in a stay-at-home posture . . . This is not appropriate in a global pandemic, but it's certainly not an exercise of democratic principles where we have free speech. This is calls to violence. This is racist and misogynistic.

***Milwaukee Journal Sentinel*:** The Wisconsin Supreme Court has struck down Gov. Tony Evers' order shutting down daily life to limit the spread of coronavirus—marking the first time a statewide order of its kind has been knocked down by a court of last resort. The state's highest court, which is controlled by conservatives, sided with Republican lawmakers Wednesday in a decision that curbed the Evers administration's power to act unilaterally during public health emergencies.

MAY 14

Gov. Evers (WI): In this one fell swoop, four judges, who didn't really care about what the statutes talk about, have thrown our state into chaos . . . When you have no requirements anymore, that's a problem. We're going to have more cases. We're going to have more deaths. And it's a sad occasion for the state.

Becky Bratu, Bloomberg News: Although most Americans are in favor of maintaining lockdowns, their commitment to social distancing seems to be waning—even as top doctors warn of uncontrollable outbreaks in areas that reopen too soon. In April, people in the U.S. moved around 41% less than normal. Now, distancing in nearly every state is on the decline, especially on the weekends.

President Trump: The less successful we are in reopening, the better they [Democrats] are, maybe for an election . . . They would rather see our country fail, and you know what that means, because part of failure is death, than have me get elected.

Governor Andy Beshear (KY): Remember, if you're in a workplace making fun of somebody for wearing a mask, you're not being a very good neighbor. You know somewhere deep down that this could help them. So let's encourage each other to do the right things and not the wrong things.

Rep. Anna Eshoo (CA), Chair, Energy and Commerce; Subcommittee on Health: Our country is in pain. Americans are afraid. They're sick. They're hungry and jobless. And over 80,000 souls have been lost. And the government that was supposed to protect them has failed . . . Regular Americans have risen when their leaders have not. We are the greatest country on earth, and, yet, we have the most cases and the most deaths from Covid-19 of any nation in the world. Why? First, it's the inept, ineffective and extremely late effort to respond to what was clear to many scientists and public health experts in January . . . Frankly, I'm tired of those who bear the responsibility accepting none of it while deflecting blame on others, the previous administration, the World Health Organization, the Wuhan lab, anywhere but where the blame belongs.

Dr. Rick Bright, Former Director, BARDA: Our window of opportunity is closing. If we fail to improve our response now, based on science, I fear the pandemic will get worse and be prolonged. There will likely be a resurgence of Covid-19 this fall and it'll be greatly compounded about the challenges of seasonal influenza. Without better planning, 2020 could be the darkest winter in modern history.

Rep. Michael Burgess (TX), Ranking Member, Energy and Commerce Subcommittee on Health: I ask why is this the first official hearing that we're having on this topic? To say this is a disappointment would be an understatement. But not only disappointment, but quite frankly, I'm concerned it took five months to have a hearing on this novel coronavirus. Instead of tackling any of the issues suggested in the letters that I've sent to you this week, we are examining a whistleblower complaint that is only one week old before a proper investigation.

Mike Bowen, Vice President, Prestige Ameritech: The government sits around, doesn't buy American-made products, comes to me in a pandemic, buys millions of masks in 2010, and you know what they did with those masks? They stored them for 10 years, then they auctioned them to some knucklehead who put them on eBay and sold them for 10 times what they were worth. So not only have I not seen the government in 10 years, I got to compete with my own masks.

Rep. Kathy Castor (FL): Is there not something more insidious here when you had an administration that downplayed it, said it would disappear, did not follow the scientists, told Dr. Bright, we will can you, reassign you, because you are speaking truth to power? Isn't that a little bit different right now?

> **Mike Bowen, Vice President, Prestige Ameritech:*** Now that you ask. Again, I'm a Republican. I've been a lifelong Republican and I'm embarrassed on how that's been handled. Like Rick Bright said, it's the scientists we need to be listening to. And we're not. That has got to change or more lives are going to be lost.

Dr. Rick Bright, Former Director, BARDA: I will never forget the emails I received from Mike Bowen, indicating our mask supplier, our n95 mask supplier, was decimated. And he said, "We are in deep shit, the world is, and we need to act." I pushed it forward to the highest level I could and got no response.

Rep. Frank Pallone (NJ): For months, the president has refused to develop and implement a national testing program. For months, we've been promised millions of tests were right around the corner. The promises have been hollow. Testing is getting better, but nowhere near what it needs to be. It

---

* Direct exchange

doesn't help that the president proclaimed about testing earlier this week, and I quote, "We have met the moment and we have prevailed." That could not be further from the truth, Mr. President.

Dr. Bright, Former Director, BARDA: First and foremost, we need to be truthful with the American people. Americans deserve the truth. The truth must be based on science. We have the world's greatest scientists. Let us lead. Let us speak without fear of retribution. We must listen. Each of us can and must do our part now . . . The virus is here, it's everywhere. We need to be able to find it, isolate it and stop it. We need to have the right testing for everyone who needs it. We need to be able to trace contacts, isolate, quarantine appropriately while striving to develop a cure. Initially, our nation was not as prepared as we should have been, as we could have been. Some scientists raised early warning signals that were overlooked and pages from our pandemic playbook were ignored by some in leadership . . . We will either be remembered for what we did or what we failed to do to address this crisis. I call on all of us to act, to ensure the health, safety, and prosperity of all Americans.

President Trump: The Great State of Wisconsin, home to Tom Tiffany's big Congressional Victory on Tuesday, was just given another win. Its Democrat Governor was forced by the courts to let the State Open. The people want to get on with their lives. The place is bustling!

Bloomberg News: Michigan closed down its capitol in Lansing on Thursday and canceled its legislative session rather than face the possibility of an armed protest and death threats against Democratic Governor Gretchen Whitmer. The gathering, meant to advocate opening the state for business despite the coronavirus pandemic, followed one April 30 that resulted in pictures of protesters clad in military-style gear and carrying long guns crowding the statehouse. They confronted police and taunted lawmakers.

The shutdown was done with little fanfare at the end of Wednesday's State Senate session.

Sen. Lindsey Graham (SC): The closer you can have it to 120 [thousand deaths], I think you can say you limited the casualties in this war.

CNN: Cook County in Illinois has replaced Queens County in New York as the single US county with the highest number of coronavirus cases, according to data generated by Johns Hopkins University. Cook County, which includes Chicago and surrounding areas, has reported 58,457 cases. It is the largest county by population in Illinois, and the second largest in the country.

Mayor Lori Lightfoot, Chicago: It's not a secret that there are health care disparities in our city. It's not a secret that way too many people live in poverty. That Black and Brown communities have a much higher rate of these underlying conditions that we now know are the death knell for Covid. You know, 93% or higher than that of the people who have died had underlying medical conditions like diabetes, heart disease, upper respiratory disease. That is a haunting statistic.

Gov. Pritzker (IL): There are people who live in one area who say, "Gee, I don't know anybody who's been—who's contracted Covid-19 and therefore my little area should be let out of some region." But the reality is this is about healthcare resources and making sure that if something bad happens, like a surge* . . . Remember that this is about healthcare regions and the availability of healthcare. Look at each of those metrics, and you'll take note of what we were counting here. So I would just remind everybody that yes, there will be some areas that will be a bigger hot spot than another area within a region. But we didn't want to hold back a region because there's one hotspot. What we do want to do is make sure everybody in that region has access to health care.

Sen. Mitch McConnell (KY): I was wrong. [The Obama Administration] did leave behind a plan. So I clearly made a mistake in that regard. As to

* Pritzker's video feed froze here and had to be reconnected.

whether or not the plan was followed and who is the critic and all the rest, I don't have any observation about that because I don't know enough about the details of it to comment on it in any detail.

Rob Manfred, Commissioner, Major League Baseball: Well, I think it's hopeful that we will have some major league baseball this summer. We are making plans by playing in empty stadiums.

President Trump: Could be that testing's, frankly, overrated. Maybe it is overrated . . . We have more cases than anybody in the world, but why? Because we do more testing. When you test, you have a case. When you test you find something is wrong with people. If we didn't do any testing, we would have very few cases. They don't want to write that. It's common sense. We test much more.

Rep. Ted Lieu (CA): Dear @realDonaldTrump: Without testing, we would have even more infections. Testing lets us see the hidden enemy and isolate those who are infected to prevent further spread of #Covid19. That's why your own @WhiteHouse tests regularly and often. Get it?

MAY 15

Joanne Freeman, Professor of History, Yale University: This makes my brain explode. If you didn't do testing, you wouldn't know how many cases you have. THE CASES WOULD STILL BE THERE. It's all numbers to him. Ratings. Low Covid numbers. Stock market numbers. All numbers.

Sen. Kamala Harris (CA):* Over the past two weeks, we have seen a misinformation campaign coming from the White House surrounding the

---

* Letter to HHS Sec Alex Azar and FEMA Administrator Peter Gaynor also signed by Senators Richard Blumenthal (CT), Mazie Hirono (HI), Ed Markey (MA), and Sherrod Brown (OH).

Covid-19 death numbers, claiming the death count has been inflated. President Trump has publicly suggested that there are far fewer deaths than currently reported and reports indicate that administration officials asked Centers for Disease Control and Prevention (CDC) officials to exclude individuals from the official death count who were presumed positive or who may not have died as a direct result of contracting the virus. The misinformation surrounding the Covid-19 death count is not a new tactic from President Trump. This is the exact behavior that led to an extreme undercount in Puerto Rico after Hurricane Maria.

President Trump: There's never been a vaccine project anywhere in history like this. And I just want to make something clear. It's very important, vaccine or no vaccine, we're back.

Mark Esper, Secretary of Defense: Winning matters, and we will deliver by the end of this year a vaccine at scale to treat the American people and our partners abroad.

Gov. Cuomo (NY): And how this goes is up to all of us, stone to stone across the morass, as my father used to say. You're going through a morass, and we are in a morass, there's no doubt about that. Find the stone, find firm footing and step onto that stone. Then you find the next stone. Then you find the next stone. That's what we have been doing. This reopening is the most data-driven, fact specific, science driven reopening that has been done, period. It's all about the numbers and the facts. That's right.

President Trump: We read about all of the very sad, very tragic. I've lost friends. Many of us have lost friends. We read about that and we see that, and that's what the news covers, but it's a very small percentage. It's a very, very small percentage. I say it all the time. It's a tiny percentage. The vast majority, many people don't even know they have it. They have it or they have sniffles or they have a very minor sign and they recover. Not only recover, they probably have immunity, whether it's short term, long term, but they have probably immunity. And I think people have to understand that. That's why I think the schools should be back in the fall.

Gov. Cuomo (NY): Second stone is, now you start to reopen, do it intelligently and do it with discipline and not with emotion. And government has to be there. And government has to perform. But to be up to all of us, it means it has to be up to each of us at the same time. Right? And that is very important here, that each of us understands our responsibility. And that's how this has worked from day one. Government, government, government, it's not about government. It's about what people have decided to do in this situation.

Katie Shepherd and Moriah Balingit, *Washington Post*: Rain drizzled as a crowd of about 200 people gathered in front of the Michigan State Capitol in Lansing on Thursday to urge Gov. Gretchen Whitmer (D) to lift coronavirus restrictions. The protesters—some carrying guns, few wearing masks—held up signs that said, "Stop Whitmer now," and, "Dangerous safety is better than safe tyranny." Near the capitol steps, one man had strung an American flag onto a fishing rod. Below the flag, a brunette doll dangled from a noose tied to the pole.

Gov. Whitmer (MI): These are not just citizens who are unhappy about having to stay home. This is a political rally . . . When people are showing up with guns, when people are showing up with things like confederate flags, it tells you that this really isn't about the lockdown.

AP: As businesses reopened Friday in more of the U.S., an overwhelming majority of states still fall short of the Covid-19 testing levels that public health experts say are necessary to safely ease lockdowns and avoid another deadly wave of outbreaks, according to an Associated Press analysis. Rapid, widespread testing is considered essential to tracking and containing the coronavirus. But 41 of the nation's 50 states fail to test widely enough to drive their infections below a key benchmark, according to an AP analysis of metrics developed by Harvard's Global Health Institute.

Among the states falling short are Texas and Georgia, which recently moved aggressively to reopen stores, malls, barbershops and other businesses.

***Austin-American Statesman* (TX):** The new cases Thursday marked the seventh day in a row that Texas saw more than 1,000 Covid-19 cases in a single day, bringing the total number of known cases to 43,851.

Kayleigh McEnany, White House Press Secretary: Recognizing the seriousness of biological threats, President Trump released a series of strategic documents to transform our preparedness for biological incidents, including pandemics. In September of 2018, President Trump released the national biodefense strategy, in May of 2019, he released the global health security strategy, and in September of 2019, he signed an EO to modernize influenza vaccines. His leadership is evident in the early days of this pandemic and in the preparation before that. These actions I've outlined today, these plans I noted, helped us as we approached what was an unprecedented crisis. It helped us to deploy our resources and to deliver what I believe is one of the best responses we've seen in this country's history.

Rep. Greg Walden (OR): It's totally surreal. There are signs of hope, but I really think for many, it really hasn't sunk in yet the depths of this problem. As Americans, we're pretty hopeful, we think we'll bounce right out of this and be fine. But I'm not sure we will be right away, or maybe even years.

Rep. Val Demings (FL): My Republican colleagues are deeply misguided when they say that no additional help is needed by Americans. The truth is that people are struggling. Either we help now, or America is facing a dark, deep depression which will last for years. That's not an option, so I and my Democratic colleagues are taking action.

Rep. Jodey Arrington (TX): Mr. Speaker, Democratic leadership has established in this piece of legislation* a new pandemic protocol for the United States Congress, the practice of reality distancing. Reality distancing is the unhealthy distance between politicians and their policies and the people they were elected to serve.

Rep. Tim Ryan (OH): I've got to tell you this is absolutely unbelievable. Just a few years ago, the stock market's at 25,000, corporate profits are the highest they've been in decades, the rich keep getting richer and our friends on the other side say, what do we do now? Let's do a tax cut—where 83% of it goes to the top 1% of the wealthiest people. Fast forward a few months: Global pandemic. 36 million unemployed. 40% of families who have a worker that makes $40,000 a year or less lose their job last month. Four million people didn't pay their rent. And the Republican party said we don't have any money to help you. Are you kidding me? Where do you guys live? Food lines around the blocks at our food banks in the United States of America. One in five kids are going hungry. Your party can't even get food to them. This isn't a wish list. If it's a wish list it's for the working-class people. How about the teamsters that are going to get a pension when this bill passes? If we don't act, their pension gets cut in half. This is ridiculous. Your turn your back on the American people.

MAY 16

Former President Obama: More than anything, this pandemic has fully, finally torn back the curtain on the idea that so many of the folks in charge know what they're doing. A lot of them aren't even pretending to be in charge. If the world's going to get better, it's going to be up to you.

---

* Health and Economic Recovery Omnibus Emergency Solutions Act or the HEROES Act

Sen. Ben Sasse (NE): We will bring the economy back. We are going to beat the virus. We're going to have to have a serious reckoning with the thugs in China who let this mess spiral out of control by lying about it.

Former President Obama: So much of your generation has woken up to the fact that the status quo needs fixing; that the old ways of doing things don't work . . . That our society and democracy only works when we think not just about ourselves, but about each other . . . Do what you think is right. Doing what feels good, what's convenient, what's easy—that's how little kids think. Unfortunately, a lot of so-called grown-ups, including some with fancy titles and important jobs, still think that way, which is why things are so screwed up.

MAY 17

Alex Azar, Secretary of HHS: Reopen we must, because it's not health versus the economy. It's actually health versus health. There are serious health consequences to keeping us shut down, whether it's the suicidality rates or cardiac procedures not being received, pediatric vaccinations declining. All of these are critical health needs that are part of reopening the economy.

Senator Mark Warner (VA): There is a recognition that this event is more transformative than 2008, more transformative than 9/11, more transformative than the fall of the Berlin Wall.

Peter Loftus, *Wall Street Journal*: Governments and drugmakers are weighing how to roll out coronavirus vaccines, including reserving the first batches for health-care workers, as several shots race to early leads. Of more than 100 vaccines in development globally, at least eight have started testing in humans.

David Fahrenthold, *New York Times*: The state of Georgia made it look like its Covid cases were going down ***by putting the dates out of order on its chart*** May 5 was followed by April 25, then back to May again, whatever made it look like a downslope.

Unnamed Senior CDC Official: This administration has shown time and time again that it has a problem with science. We are giving them science and they don't seem to want it.

Gov. Cuomo (NY): Today is day 78. Day 78, 78 days, a long time or a short time? You can argue both. When you shut down everything and you've gone through the trauma that we've gone through, 78 days is a long time. And people are feeling it, and they're feeling it in a number of ways. We've talked about it, but I don't know that any of us have really explored the depths of the mental health issues that have been created inadvertently through these 78 days. We've been so anxious about the day to day and operationally oriented, we've been talking about hospitalizations, talking about death, talking about infection rates, but there's also a more subtle but very present mental health crisis that has been going on. Don't underestimate the trauma that this has created for people. Out of the blue comes this virus, something we've never seen before. You're living a science fiction movie.

MAY 18

Gov. Inslee (WA): We have to make smart decisions based on science and data and the status of this virus. And the reason we need to do that is if we were to make the wrong decision, a premature decision, this thing could just bounce right back up. And we would be right back in the soup where we were a couple of months ago.

President Trump: I happened to be taking it. Hydroxychloroquine. Right now, yeah. A couple of weeks ago, I started taking it. I've heard a lot of good stories. And if it is not good, I will tell you right. I'm not going to get hurt by it . . . Here's my evidence: I get a lot of positive calls about it. The only negative I've heard was the study where they gave it, was it the VA? With people that aren't big Trump fans gave it.

Neil Cavuto, Fox News: Trump just acknowledged he's taking hydroxychloroquine . . . The fact of the matter is though, when Trump said, "What do you got to lose?"—in a number of studies the vulnerable population have one thing to lose, their lives . . . I cannot stress enough, This. Will. Kill. You.

Bloomberg News: The first Covid-19 vaccine to be tested in humans appears safe and able to generate coronavirus-killing antibodies in test subjects, Moderna said Monday. The findings are just a sample from its phase one clinical trial in which eight volunteers who were given two doses of the vaccine in March developed antibodies on par with recovered virus patients.

MAY 19

Jerome Powell, Chair, Federal Reserve System: This is the biggest shock we've seen in living memory, and the question looms in the air of: Is it enough?

President Trump: It is clear the repeated missteps by you [W.H.O.] and your organization in responding to the pandemic have been extremely costly for the world. The only way forward for the World Health Organization is if it can actually demonstrate independence from China. If the World Health Organization does not commit to major substantive improvements within the next 30 days, I will make my temporary freeze of United States funding to the World Health Organization permanent and reconsider our membership in the organization

Sen. Chuck Schumer (NY): When you don't believe in truth, you can't solve the problem. And the President avoids truth in every way.

***USA Today*:** The scientist who created Florida's Covid-19 data portal [Rebekah Jones] wasn't just removed from her position on May 5, she was fired on Monday by the Department of Health, she said, for refusing to manipulate data . . . she was fired because she was ordered to censor some data, but refused to "manually change data to drum up support for the plan to reopen."

Senator Sherrod Brown (OH): How many workers should give their lives to increase the GDP or the Dow Jones by 1,000 points?

> **Steve Mnuchin, Secretary of the Treasury:*** No workers should give their lives to do that, Mr. Senator, and I think your characterization is unfair.

Gov. Beshear (KY): Coming together at a time where it's very difficult to get together. It's about sharing our anxieties, it's about sharing our fears, it's about letting ourselves be vulnerable because we all feel the same. And it's about recommitting to defeating this virus, but also remembering that we're going to get through this and we're going to get through it together. So say it with me, "We're going to get through this. We're going to get through this together." One last time, "We're going to get through this. We're going to get through this together."

Rep. Ayanna Pressley (MA): MA isn't ready to 'reopen.' Policy decisions that offer a false choice between public health & economic recovery will hurt our communities. I urge @MassGovernor to re-evaluate his timeline & invest in the supports needed to keep our families safe.

Gov. DeSantis (FL): Look, no unemployment system in the country's an ideal system. There's all kinds of things, there's myriad of rules and regulations. And there are people that could get caught up in that. That's why

* Direct exchange

I want them to be very proactive in reaching out and they have done that for time. So we want to continue to do it, but I can tell you if you go through and you apply and you're valid and you're eligible as of right now, we're about 97% of all those folks have received at least one payment. And that's a heck of a lot better than it was six weeks ago.

President Trump: So when we have a lot of cases, I don't look at that as a bad thing; I look at that as—in a certain respect, as being a good thing because it means our testing is much better. So if we were testing a million people instead of 14 million people, we would have far fewer cases. Right? So, I view it as a badge of honor. Really, it's a badge of honor. It's a great tribute to the testing and all of the work that a lot of professionals have done. Okay?

MAY 20

Dr. Ryan, Executive Director, Health Emergencies, WHO: I would point out, however, that at this stage, hydroxychloroquine nor chloroquine have been as yet found to be effective in the treatment of Covid-19, or in the prophylaxis against coming down with the disease. In fact, the opposite, in that warnings have been issued by many authorities regarding the potential side effects of the drug.

***New York Times*:** If the United States had begun imposing social distancing measures one week earlier than it did in March, about 36,000 fewer people would have died in the coronavirus outbreak, according to new estimates from Columbia University disease modelers. And if the country had begun locking down cities and limiting social contact on March 1, two weeks earlier than most people started staying home, the vast majority of the nation's deaths—about 83 percent—would have been avoided, the researchers estimated. Under that scenario, about 54,000 fewer people would have died by early May.

Rep. Nancy Pelosi (CA), Speaker of the House: You're asking me about the appropriateness of the actions of this president of the United States?* So completely inappropriate in so many ways that it's almost a given. It's like a child who comes in with mud on their pants or something. That's the way it is. They're outside playing. That's what it—He comes in with doggy doo on his shoes and everybody who works with him has that on their shoes, too, for a very long time to come. I don't know. I hear doctors talk to me about saying, "What's the matter with him?"

Ed Yong, *Atlantic*: Stay-at-home orders were necessary but ruinous, economically and emotionally. Their purpose was to buy time for the country to catch its breath, steel its hospitals, and roll out a public-health plan capable of quashing the virus. Many such plans exist. Umpteen think tanks and academics have produced their own road maps for dialing society back up. These vary in their details, but are united in at least having some. By contrast, the Trump administration's guidelines for "opening up America again" are so bereft of operational specifics that they're like a cake recipe that simply reads, "Make cake."

Caitlin Rivers, Epidemiologist, Johns Hopkins Center for Health Security: The talk of a second wave as if we've exited the first doesn't capture what's really happening.

Gov. Cuomo (NY): People ask all the time, well now we're reopening, what's going to happen? What's going to happen is what we make happen. There is no predestined course here. There is nothing that is pre-ordained. What is going to happen is a consequence of our choices and a consequence of our action. It's that simple. If people are smart and if people are

---

* A reporter asked Speaker Pelosi if it was appropriate for President Trump to tweet accusations of murder about MSNBC host Joe Scarborough.

responsible and if the employers who are opening those businesses do it responsibly, if employees are responsible, if individuals are responsible, then you will see the infection rates stay low. If people get arrogant, if people get cocky, if people get casual, if people become undisciplined, you will see that infection rate go up. It is that simple. This has always been about what we do. It's never been about what government mandated. Government cannot mandate behavior of people, and it certainly can't mandate behavior of 19 million people. It can give you the facts. It can give you the facts that lead to an inevitable conclusion, and New Yorkers have been great about following the facts. But we're at another pivot point.

AP: The [AP/NORC Center for Public Affairs Research] poll finds that 83% of Americans are at least somewhat concerned that lifting restrictions in their area will lead to additional infections, with 54% saying they are very or extremely concerned that such steps will result in a spike of Covid-19 cases . . . close to half say it is essential that a vaccine be available before public life resumes. Another third say that's important, although not essential.

Dana Nessel, Attorney General (MI): Dear President Trump . . . While my Department will not act to prevent you from touring Ford's plant, I ask that while you are on tour you respect the great efforts of the men and women at Ford—and across this State—by wearing a facial covering. It is not just the policy of Ford . . . It is currently the law of this State. Michigan has been hit especially hard by the virus, with more than 50,000 confirmed cases and 5,000 deaths. Therefore, we must all do our part to stop the spread of Covid-19. Anyone who has potentially has been recently exposed, including the President of the United States, has not only a legal responsibility, but also a social and more responsibility, to take reasonable precautions to prevent further spread of the virus.

Dr. Tedros, Director-General, WHO: We still have a long way to go in this pandemic. In the last 24 hours, there have been 106,000 cases reported to WHO, the most in a single day since the outbreak began. Almost two-thirds of these cases were reported in just four countries.

President Trump: Maybe that's what we should've done. If I would've done 3 million [tests] they would've said, "oh, they have very few cases. The US is doing well."

National Nurses United: Nurses and other health care workers continue to find themselves abandoned at Covid-19's front lines, without PPE. Despite nurses' demands, President Trump has made no effort to mass produce N95 respirators using the Defense Production Act. Many hospitals still keep PPE under lock and key when they have it, and the Occupational Safety and Health Administration never addressed nurses' demands to pass emergency temporary standards that would have mandated employers provide optimal PPE.

Bonnie Castillo, RN, Executive Director, National Nurses United: Dr. Rick Bright's testimony to Congress last week came as no surprise to us. Nurses on the front lines are dying as evidence of it. He calls it indifference—we call it willful negligence. We can't even say they failed, because that would imply they tried.

Quinnipiac University: Former Vice President Joe Biden leads President Trump 50–39 percent in a head-to-head matchup in the election for president, according to a Quinnipiac University national poll of registered voters released today . . . More than two months into the coronavirus crisis in the U.S., President Trump's job approval rating ticks lower. 42 percent of voters approve of the job President Trump is doing, while 53 percent disapprove. That's compared to a 45–51 percent job approval rating he received in April, his highest ever. On the president's response to the coronavirus, 41 percent of voters approve and 56 percent disapprove. That is down from a 46–51 percent approval rating in April.

MAY 21

Alexis C. Madrigal and Robinson Meyer, *Atlantic*: The Centers for Disease Control and Prevention is conflating the results of two different types of coronavirus tests, distorting several important metrics and providing the country with an inaccurate picture of the state of the pandemic . . . The agency confirmed to *The Atlantic* on Wednesday that it is mixing the results of viral and antibody tests, even though the two tests reveal different information and are used for different reasons.

Megan Cassella, *Politico*: Georgia's early move to start easing stay-at-home restrictions nearly a month ago has done little to stem the state's flood of unemployment claims—illustrating how hard it is to bring jobs back while consumers are still afraid to go outside.

Weekly applications for jobless benefits have remained so elevated that Georgia now leads the country in terms of the proportion of its workforce applying for unemployment assistance. A staggering 40.3 percent of the state's workers—two out of every five—has filed for unemployment insurance payments since the coronavirus pandemic led to widespread shutdowns in mid-March, a POLITICO review of Labor Department data shows.

Rep. Debbie Dingell (MI): Mr. President, I just hope you'll wear that mask so people know that it's important, and your wearing that mask can save lives.

Unidentified White House Reporter: Are you going to wear a mask today at the Ford plant?

President Trump: Well, I don't know. We're going to look at it. A lot of people have asked me that question. I want to get our country back to normal. I want to normalize.

Dana Nessel, Attorney General (MI): If he fails to wear a mask, he's going to be asked not to return to any enclosed facility inside our state.

President Trump: Well, I had one on before. I wore one in this back area, but I didn't want to give the press the pleasure of seeing it, but no, where I had it in the back area, I did put a mask on.

Sen. Brian Schatz (HI): Trump not wearing a mask is not a sign of toughness. It's a sign of vanity. It's a sign he thinks he's better and more important than everyone else. And it is this ignorance, selfishness, and anti-science attitude that brought preventable mass death to America.

Ford Motor Company: Bill Ford encouraged President Trump to wear a mask when he arrived. He wore a mask during a private viewing of three Ford GTs from over the years. The President later removed the mask for the remainder of the visit.

Dana Nessel, Attorney General (MI): In Michigan, of course, now that is the law. And in fact, a court just upheld that, just upheld the governor's orders just hours ago. And even in Ford, it is their own policy. So the president is like a petulant child who refuses to follow the rules. And I have to say, this is no joke. I mean, you just reported that 93,000 people have died in the United States. He is in a county right now where over a hundred people have died. I am 20 minutes away from him in Wayne County where we've had him over 2,300 people die. This is not a joke. And he's conveying the worst possible message to people who cannot afford to be on the receiving end of terrible misinformation and it's very, very concerning.

***Detroit News*:** A Court of Claims judge ruled Thursday that [Michigan] Gov. Gretchen Whitmer had the legal authority to extend Michigan's state of emergency under the Emergency Powers of the Governor Act, calling claims to the contrary "meritless" in a ruling GOP leaders vow to appeal . . . The ruling overrides the argument from the Republican-led House and Senate that Whitmer had no authority to extend the coronavirus state of emergency past April without legislative approval.

***Des Moines Register*:** An Iowa agency's order of nearly 100,000 high-quality masks to aid in its coronavirus response was canceled last month after President Donald Trump invoked his authority to give the federal government priority for obtaining and distributing those supplies, according to a top state official and documentation obtained by the Des Moines Register.

Larry Kudlow, Director, National Economic Council: Look, it's really hard to model a virus, a pandemic, the likes of which we have not seen for 100 years. The numbers coming in are not good. In fact, they are downright bad in most cases. But we are seeing some glimmers, perhaps . . . there's a lot of heartbreak here. There's a lot of hardship here. There's a lot of anxiety here. It's a very difficult situation.

CNN: Of the 2,200 employees at Tyson Foods' Wilkesboro, North Carolina, poultry facility, 570 employees tested positive or Covid-19. That's a quarter of the staff.

Governor Kay Ivey (AL): Our numbers are not as good as we would hope. But we cannot sustain a delayed way of life as we search for a vaccine. It's not realistic to believe we're going to keep everyone totally isolated from each other.

President Trump: A permanent lockdown is not a strategy for a healthy state or a healthy country. Our country wasn't meant to be shut down. We did the right thing, but now it's time to open it up. A never-ending lockdown would invite a public health calamity.

Anna Wilde Mathews, *Wall Street Journal*: A recently launched federal effort to collect data on the impact of the coronavirus in nursing homes will leave the full toll unclear, because a new rule doesn't require facilities to report deaths and infections that occurred before early May.

The new rule, issued May 8, compels nursing homes to submit data on coronavirus cases and associated deaths to the Centers for Disease Control and Prevention. According to a form posted on the CDC website, the information only has to go back to the week leading up to their first filing, which was supposed to occur by May 17, while older data is optional. Nursing homes will provide current data at least weekly going forward.

John Holdren, Former White House Science Advisor:* It is possible that the 2020 phase of the Covid-19 epidemic will decrease during the late spring, but it also may well be that there is a resurgence in the fall. Preparation for such a resurgence needs to be initiated now. It needs to be at a national level, in close collaboration and coordination with state and local officials. Even after this current phase tails off (if in fact it does so), focus on curtailing the disease needs to be maintained as the country pursues its financial recovery. Indeed, the second requires the first.

MAY 22

President Trump: Some governors have deemed liquor stores & abortion clinics essential, but have left out churches . . . it's not right. So I am correcting this injustice & am calling houses of worship essential. I call upon governors to allow churches & places of worship to open right now . . . If they don't do it, I will override the governors.

***Washington Post*:** The coronavirus may still be spreading at epidemic rates in 24 states, particularly in the South and Midwest, according to new research that highlights the risk of a second wave of infections in places that reopen too quickly or without sufficient precautions. Researchers at Imperial College London created a model that incorporates cellphone data showing that people sharply reduced their movements after stay-at-home orders were broadly imposed in March. With restrictions now easing and mobility

---

* Along with other former members of President Obama's Council of Advisors on Science and Technology (OPCAST)

increasing with the approach of Memorial Day and the unofficial start of summer, the researchers developed an estimate of viral spread as of May 17.

Governor Doug Burgum (ND): If someone is wearing a mask, they're not doing it to represent what political party they're in, or what candidates they support. They might be doing it because they have a five-year-old child who's going through cancer treatments. They might have vulnerable adults in their life who currently have Covid.

Carnegie Mellon University School of Computer Science: Carnegie Mellon researchers have discovered that much of the discussion around the pandemic and stay-at-home orders is being fueled by misinformation campaigns that use convincing bots. To analyze bot activity around the pandemic, CMU researchers since January have collected more than 200 million tweets discussing coronavirus or Covid-19. Of the top 50 influential retweeters, 82% are bots, they found. Of the top 1,000 retweeters, 62% are bots.

Dr. Deborah Birx, White House Coronavirus Response Coordinator: We have concerns of where cities have remained closed and metros that have remained closed but have still persistent high number of cases.

***New York Times*:** Last Friday, Mr. Trump told reporters that he accepted the current death toll, but that the figures could be "lower than" the official count, which now totals nearly 95,000. Most statisticians and public health experts say he is wrong; the death toll is probably far higher than what is publicly known. People are dying at their houses and nursing homes without ever being tested, and deaths early this year were likely misidentified as influenza or described only as pneumonia.

MAY 24

David Aaro, Fox News: Researchers have found that wearing surgical masks can significantly reduce the rate of airborne Covid-19 transmission, according to a study released on Sunday. The study, conducted by a team of scientists in Hong Kong, found the rate of non-contact transmission through respiratory droplets or airborne particles dropped by as much as 75 percent when masks were used, "The findings implied to the world and the public is that the effectiveness of mask-wearing against the coronavirus pandemic is huge," said Dr. Yuen Kwok-yung, a leading microbiologist from Hong Kong University who helped discover the SARS virus back in 2003.

Robert O'Brien, National Security Advisor: The guy [President Trump] has got more energy than anyone I've ever seen. He works 16–18 hours a day. I don't see any change in his strong performance.

Anne Gearan, *Washington Post*: As the death toll in the coronavirus pandemic neared 100,000 Americans this Memorial Day weekend, President Trump derided and insulted perceived enemies and promoted a baseless conspiracy theory, in between rounds of golf. In a flurry of tweets and retweets Saturday and Sunday, Trump mocked former Georgia gubernatorial candidate Stacey Abrams's weight, ridiculed the looks of House Speaker Nancy Pelosi (D-Calif.) and called former Democratic presidential rival Hillary Clinton a "skank." He revived long-debunked speculation that a television host with whom Trump has feuded may have killed a woman and asserted without evidence that mail-in voting routinely produces ballot stuffing. He made little mention of the sacrifice Americans honor on Memorial Day or the grim toll of the virus. In fact, Trump's barrage of social media attacks stood in sharp contrast to a sober reality on a weekend for mourning military dead—the number of Americans whose lives have been claimed by the novel coronavirus has eclipsed the combined total of U.S. deaths from wars in Vietnam, the Persian Gulf, Iraq and Afghanistan.

Gov. Cuomo (NY): We've never been here before. We've never been here before in our lifetimes. That's true, but the country has been through this before and you learn from the past so you don't make the same mistakes. When we went through this in the 1918 pandemic, you go back and you look at the places that opened in an uncontrolled way, and you see that the virus came back, and came back with a fury. So again, it's not about what you think, ideology. This is what we know. These are facts. You go back and you look at what happened in the 1918 pandemic in St. Louis. Go look at Denver where they loosened up too quickly and the virus came back.

Reis Thebault and Abigail Hauslohner, *Washington Post*: The pandemic that first struck in major metropolises is now increasingly finding its front line in the country's rural areas; counties with acres of farmland, cramped meatpacking plants, out-of-the-way prisons and few hospital beds.

Chicago Urban League: According to the Centers for Disease Control and Prevention, about 30% of confirmed cases of Covid-19 in the United States have occurred among Black people, despite the fact that Blacks comprise just 13% of the national population. Blacks also make up about 33% of hospitalized Covid-19 patients, and those patients tend to be younger overall than White patients and more likely to die from the disease. The national picture is indicative of what is occurring in major cities and states that track racial data on the pandemic . . . Simply put: Black people are overrepresented in Covid-19 cases and deaths. Blacks die disproportionately from Covid-19 as compared to their share of the total population in 19 of the 24 states race data is available for deaths. The worst disparities in death rates occurred in states with the most segregated cities in the nation.

Leah Richier, Historian, University of North Florida: As a death historian, I feel like I'm going *mad* watching the United States stumble through a mass death event, pushing aside elderly folks & poor folks & people of color in pursuit of normalcy, summertime, & instant gratification. We are utterly grotesque. This is horrifying.

THE RECKONING

MAY 25–JUNE 5

MAY 25

Gov. Cuomo (NY): And this Memorial Day, I think it's especially poignant and powerful when this country is going through what it's going through. And we know something about loss because we're living it again. Over 100,000 Americans will lose their lives to this Covid virus.

Kevin Hassett, White House Economic Advisor: Our capital stock hasn't been destroyed. Our human capital stock is ready to go back to work. So there are lots of reasons to believe that we can get going way faster than we have in previous crises.

Justin Wolfers, Economist, University of Michigan: When you don't think of them as people, you're probably also doing the economics wrong.

Aaron Rupar, *Vox*: The AP/NORC Center polling dovetails with a *Washington Post*/Ipsos poll taken from April 27 to May 4 that found 74 percent of Americans want the US to focus on controlling the virus instead of reopening businesses—and that 54 percent felt Trump is doing too little to ensure people can safely return to work. Other recent polls, from Citrix and Qualtrics, have found about two-thirds of Americans saying they are not yet ready to return to work.

***Ocean Star* (NJ):** As many as 500 demonstrators, some bearing American flags and Trump 2020 campaign banners, crowded into the parking lot at Little Silver Lake on Monday, protesting—and defying—Gov. Phil Murphy's Covid-19 emergency restrictions. Speakers at the largely peaceful rally included a Bellmawr gym owner who had captured national attention by opening his establishment in violation of the governor's executive order closing non-essential businesses. Other speakers included members of the New Jersey state legislature, a congressional candidate and a former American Idol contestant and local veterans. Most of the demonstrators were not wearing face masks, despite the general absence of social distancing.

Gov. Murphy (NJ): I don't begrudge their right to protest, but they don't sway me. The only thing that sways me are the facts and the data and the science. And listen, I want to open salons and gyms . . . I want to do it responsibly. I don't want to kill anybody.

Dr. Maria Van Kerkhove, Head, Emerging Diseases, WHO: All countries need to remain on high alert here. All countries need to be ready to rapidly detect cases, even countries that have had success in suppression . . . Even countries that have seen a decline in cases must remain ready.

A hallmark of coronaviruses is its ability to amplify in certain settings, its ability to cause transmission—or super spreading events. And we are seeing in a number of situations in these closed settings. When the virus has an opportunity, it can transmit readily.

Dory MacMillan, Spokesperson for Governor Roy Cooper (NC): State health officials are working with the RNC [Republican National Committee] and will review its plans as they make decisions about how to hold the convention in Charlotte, North Carolina is relying on data and science to protect our state's public health and safety.

President Trump: I love the Great State of North Carolina, so much so that I insisted on having the Republican National Convention in Charlotte at the end of August. Unfortunately, Democrat Governor, @RoyCooperNC is still in Shutdown mood & unable to guarantee that by August we will be allowed full attendance in the Arena.

Gov. Whitmer (MI): I'm never going to apologize for the fact that because there was a vacuum of leadership at the federal level, we had to take action to save people here in Michigan . . . It has not come without a cost. I recognize that. I know a lot of people are stressed about the job they lost or the business that might not open. But there's also over 5,000 families that are mourning the loss of a loved one. And I'm grateful that it's not 8,000 or more.

Dr. Michael Ryan, Executive Director, of Health Emergencies, WHO: We need to be also cognizant of the fact that the disease can jump up at any time. We cannot make assumptions that just because the disease is on the way down now that it's going to keep going down, and the way to get a number of months to get ready for a second wave—we may get a second peak in this way.

MAY 26

***Politico*:** Glenn Fine, who was ousted last month as the Pentagon's acting watchdog by President Donald Trump, has resigned from the Defense Department inspector general's office in the latest of a series of departures across the executive branch.

Christi Grimm, Principal Deputy Inspector General, Department of Health and Human Services (HHS): I personally and professionally cannot let the idea of providing unpopular information drive decision-making in the work that we do . . . We are plowing ahead.

President Trump: Stock Market up BIG, DOW crosses 25,000. S&P 500 over 3000. States should open up ASAP. The Transition to Greatness has started, ahead of schedule. There will be ups and downs, but next year will be one of the best ever!

Kayleigh McEnany, White House Press Secretary: I think—look, you know, the President is excited to see that Joe [Biden] emerged from the basement. It is a bit peculiar though that, in his basement, right next to his wife, he's not wearing a mask, but he's wearing one outdoors when he's socially distanced. So I think that there was a discrepancy there. He is not shaming anyone.

Former Vice President Biden: He's a fool. An absolute fool to talk that way. I mean, every leading doctor in the world is saying we should wear a mask when you're in a crowd . . . Presidents are supposed to lead, not engage in folly and be falsely masculine . . . It's costing people's lives.

Libor Jany, *Star Tribune* (MN): Federal authorities are investigating a white Minneapolis police officer for possible civil rights violations, after a video surfaced Monday that showed him kneeling on a handcuffed African American man's neck and ignoring the man's protests that he couldn't breathe. The man later died. The four officers involved in the incident have been fired, Minneapolis mayor Jacob Frey said Tuesday afternoon . . . An attorney for the man's family identified him as George Floyd.

President Trump: Great News: The boring but very nasty magazine, The Atlantic, is rapidly failing, going down the tubes, and has just been forced to announce it is laying off at least 20% of its staff in order to limp into the future. This is a tough time to be in the Fake News Business!

Aaron Rupar, *Vox*: It's a bad look for the American president to dunk on Americans for losing jobs amid an economic crisis created by a pandemic he was unprepared for.

Dr. Christopher Murray, Director, Institute for Health Metrics and Evaluation (IMHE): We continue to forecast, really, an awful lot of deaths right through to August. And if we think past August, the total will continue well past that date as well.

CNN: Packing pool parties and other Memorial Day events, many Americans marked the unofficial start of summer just like they did before coronavirus. But while the revelers shunned face masks and ignored social distancing guidelines, the virus keeps spreading unabated, killing both the elderly and the young. By Tuesday morning, more than 1,660,000 Americans have been infected with the coronavirus, and more than 98,000 have died, according to Johns Hopkins University. The number of new cases keeps rising in 18 states—including Georgia, Arkansas, California and Alabama. In 22 states, the numbers appear to be holding steady. And only 10 states are seeing declines in the numbers of new cases.

MAY 27

AP: U.S. death toll from the coronavirus has surpassed 100,000, according to a tally by Johns Hopkins University.

Dr. Sara Cody, Public Health Director, Santa Clara County, CA: We all want to reopen our economy, get back to our lives, get back to work, send our kids to school, visit our extended families, host parties, have celebrations and put this behind us as some sort of strange, long and very bad dream. But the truth is we're in the greatest global crisis since the Second World War and all of the choices before us here, in our county and everywhere, are extraordinarily difficult . . . This announcement to authorize county health officers to allow religious, cultural and political gatherings of 100 people poses a very serious risk of the spread of Covid-19. [California] has shifted away from the stay-at-home model and has made significant modifications with increasing frequency. The pace at which the state has made these modifications is concerning to me.

Sen. Mitch McConnell (KY): There is no stigma attached to wearing a mask . . . You have an obligation to others in case you might be a carrier to take the advice we've all been given by people like Dr. Birx and Dr. Fauci and be responsible.

Former Vice President Biden: There are moments in our history so grim, so heart-rending, that they're forever fixed in each of our hearts as shared grief. Today is one of those moments. 100,000 lives have now been lost to this virus. To those hurting, I'm so sorry for your loss. The nation grieves with you.

Sen. Kamala Harris (CA): As we remember the more than 100,000 people in the United States who we have lost to Covid-19, we must recognize that much of this suffering was preventable . . . This administration's glaring failures made this pandemic worse than it had to be.

Gov. Cuomo (NY): We want to reopen the economy. We want to get this national economy better than ever. Fine. Then act accordingly and act appropriately. This hyper-partisan Washington environment is toxic for this country. You have people saying, well, we don't want to pass a bill that helps Democratic states. It would be a blue state bailout, is what some have said. Senator McConnell, stopping blue state bailouts. Senator Scott, "We're supposed to go bail them out? That's not right." On Fox TV, Laffer,* "You want us to give our money to Cuomo and New York? Hello, not this week." First of all, this is really an ugly, ugly sentiment. It is an un-American response. We're still the United States of America. Those words meant something. United States of America. First of all, Mr. Federal Legislator, you are nothing without the states, and you represent the United States. Not only is it ugly. It is false.

---

* Sen. Kelly Loeffler (GA)

Gov. Jay Inslee (WA): And as I've said before, this crisis may affect our physical connections, but we should not allow it to stop our emotional connections. And that is one reason why we deliberately meet our prohibitions in this area flexible as to meet the needs of different organizations. So I'm pleased today to announce that we will be able to ease some of the restrictions on religious gatherings, in a safe way as our state continues on this journey forward . . . Clear on this, that this virus is transmitted of course, through our exhalations. And the louder we project our voices, the farther this virus travels. So we're also encouraging congregations to see if they can maintain a voluntary log of attendees at these services and try to retain it for a couple of weeks.

Gov. Greg Abbott (TX): While so many people in this state are suffering from the coronavirus, there are so many more people in the state who are suffering economically. Their businesses are being shuttered, their paychecks are being lost, their ability to feed their families is being compromised, and they need help. They need to get back to work. One thing about Texans is they're not looking for a handout, they're looking to get back to work.

Gov. Larry Hogan (MD): Effective Friday, May 29th at 5:00 PM, restaurants, as well as social organizations, such as American Legions, VFWs, or Elks Clubs, et cetera, will be able to begin safely reopening for outdoor dining, following strict public health requirements, consistent with the CDC, the FDA and the National Restaurant Association. Restaurant patrons must be appropriately distanced with no more than six people seated at a table. Restaurants are required to either use single use disposable paper menus or sanitize reusable menus between each use. And to sanitize the outdoor tables and chairs between each customer seating.

Gov. Andrew Cuomo (NY): Today I am signing an Executive Order authorizing businesses to deny entry to those who do not wear masks or face-coverings. No mask—No entry.

Rep. Nancy Pelosi (CA): With all these deaths and the need for us to pass so that as law more specific prescribed direction to the administration who should have done this on their own. Mitch McConnell says no, we need a pause. We need a pause? Tell that to the virus. Is the virus taking a pause? Is hunger in America taking a pause? . . . We need more resources, and that's in the HEROES Act as well. The HEROES Act is an answer, it has a strategy.

Dr. Anthony Fauci, Director, NIAID: I still think that we have a good chance—if all the things fall in the right place—that we might have a vaccine that would be deployable by the end of the year.

U.S. Federal Reserve: Employment continued to decrease in all Districts, including steep losses in most Districts, as social distancing and business closures affected employment at many firms. Securing PPP loans helped many businesses to limit or avoid layoffs, although employment continued to fall sharply in retail and in leisure and hospitality sectors. Contacts cited challenges in bringing employees back to work, including workers' health concerns, limited access to childcare, and generous unemployment insurance benefits.

CNBC: Black Americans continue to make up a disproportionate share of Covid-19 fatalities as the number of deaths from the coronavirus pandemic exceeds 100,000 in the U.S., according to an analysis of CDC data. Nearly 23% of reported Covid-19 deaths in the U.S. are African American as of May 20, even though black people make up roughly 13% of the U.S. population, according to the data.

MAY 28:

NPR: More than 1 in 4 U.S. workers have lost their jobs since the coronavirus crisis shut down much of the economy in March. Just last week, another 2.1 million people filed for unemployment benefits, the Labor

Department said Thursday. That's down 323,000 from the previous week but brings the total for the past 10 weeks to 40.8 million, which represents 26% of the civilian labor force in April.

Sen. Warren (MA): 100,000 people are dead. 1 in 4 people are unemployed. Donald Trump's response to this pandemic has been a leadership failure, a policy failure, and a moral failure of historic proportions.

***Washington Post*:** The Trump administration mishandled the initial distribution of the only approved coronavirus medication, delaying treatment to some critically ill patients with Covid-19, the disease caused by the virus, according to nine current and former senior administration officials. The first tranche of 607,000 vials of the antiviral medication remdesivir, donated to the government by drugmaker Gilead Sciences, was distributed in early May—in some cases to the wrong hospitals, to hospitals with no intensive care units and therefore no eligible patients, and to facilities without the needed refrigeration to store it, meaning some had to be returned to the government, said the officials familiar with the distribution effort.

Erica MacDonald, U.S. Attorney for Minneapolis (MN): On May 25th of 2020, George Floyd was arrested and detained by Minneapolis police officer . . . we are conducting a robust and meticulous investigation into the circumstances surrounding the events of May 25th, 2020, and the police officer's actions on that evening. I really probably don't need this to say this to all of you, but Minneapolis, our nation, really the world, has witnessed this incredibly and disturbing loss of life. My heart goes out to George Floyd.

***Star-Tribune* (MN):** Anger over the death of George Floyd under a police officer's knee spilled into the streets of Minneapolis for a second night Wednesday, intensifying well beyond Tuesday night's unrest with a shooting death, widespread looting and a fire that shrouded the Lake Street neighborhood in smoke.

Mayor Jacob Frey, Minneapolis, MN: What we've seen over the last two days and the emotion ridden conflict over last night is the result of so much built up anger and sadness. Anger and sadness that has been ingrained in our Black community not just because of five minutes of horror, but 400 years. If you're feeling that sadness and that anger, it's not only understandable, it's right . . . And at this time when one crisis is sandwiched against another, this could be the marker. This could be a point in time when several years from now, we can look back to know that we rose to right the wrongs of the past.

MAY 29

President Trump: We have detailed the reforms that [the World Health Organization] must make and engage with them directly, but they have refused to act. Because they have failed to make the requested and greatly needed reforms, we will be today terminating our relationship with the World Health Organization and redirecting those funds to other worldwide and deserving urgent global public health needs. The world needs answers from China on the virus. We must have transparency.

Gov. Cuomo (NY): We know where the hot spots are in the city. We want to focus on them next week, be ready to open. We are on track to open on June 8th, which is one week from Monday, and next week, as I mentioned, we'll be following up on these issues. Phase one should bring about 400,000 employees back to work in New York City. Remember that reopening does not mean we're going back to the way things were. Life is not about going back. Nobody goes back. We go forward.

***Springfield News Leader* (MO):** A week after images of Memorial Day weekend revelers jammed into a Lake of the Ozarks pool party at Backwater Jack's Bar & Grill in Osage Beach made international headlines, the Camden County Health Department announced that a Boone County resident tested positive for the novel coronavirus after visiting the Lake of the Ozarks area over the holiday weekend. The Boone County subject arrived at the lake on Saturday, May 23 and "developed illness" on Sunday . . . The infected person "was likely incubating illness and possibly infectious at the time of the visit," the health department said.

Rep. Val Demings (FL): As a former woman in blue, let me begin with my brothers and sisters in blue: What in the hell are you doing? . . . We all know that the level of force must meet the level of resistance. We all can see that there was absolutely zero resistance from George Floyd. He posed no threat to anyone, especially law enforcement.

CNN: Protesters took to the streets across America over the death of George Floyd on Friday night. Some of the protests have been peaceful, while others have been destructive. Here are the cities where protesters gathered:

California: Los Angeles, Bakersfield, Sacramento, San Jose, Oakland, San Francisco
Colorado: Denver
Georgia: Atlanta
Illinois: Chicago
Iowa: Des Moines
Indiana: Indianapolis, Fort Wayne
Kentucky: Louisville (Related to the death of Breonna Taylor)
Louisiana: New Orleans
New York: New York City
Massachusetts: Boston
Michigan: Detroit
Minnesota: Minneapolis
Nevada: Las Vegas
North Carolina: Charlotte
Ohio: Columbus, Cincinnati

Texas: Dallas, Houston
Virginia: Richmond
Washington, D.C.

Mayor Keisha Lance Bottoms, Atlanta: This is not a protest. This is not in the spirit of Martin Luther King Jr. This is chaos . . . If you want change in America, go and register to vote! Show up at the polls on June 9. Do it in November. That is the change we need in this country. You are disgracing our city, you are disgracing the life of George Floyd and every other person who has been killed in this country. We are better than this! We're better than this as a city, we are better than this as a country. Go home. Go home! And in the same way I couldn't protect my son on yesterday, I cannot protect you out in those streets.

Gov. Tim Walz (MN): It's time to rebuild our community and that starts with safety in our streets. Thousands of Minnesotans have expressed their grief and frustration in a peaceful manner. But the unlawful and dangerous actions of others, under the cover of darkness, has caused irreversible pain and damage to our community. This behavior has compromised the safety of bystanders, businesses, lawful demonstrators, and first responders. Now, we come together to restore the peace.

President Trump: These THUGS are dishonoring the memory of George Floyd, and I won't let that happen. Just spoke to Governor Tim Walz and told him that the Military is with him all the way. Any difficulty and we will assume control but, when the looting starts, the shooting starts. Thank you!

Twitter: This Tweet violated the Twitter Rules about glorifying violence. However, Twitter has determined that it may be in the public's interest for the Tweet to remain accessible.

Keith Ellison, Attorney General (MN): Violence begets violence and Trump's angry words just feed an ugly cycle that is going on in my beloved city.

Gov. Walz (MN): These are things that have been brewing in this country for 400 years. We have people out there putting themselves on the line to try and put out fires and our firefighters that are under attack. Those are the things I'm asking you. Help me restore that order.

Former Vice President Joe Biden: None of us can be silent. None of us can any longer can we hear the words I can't breathe and do nothing. We can't fail victims like what Martin Luther King called "The appalling silence of good people." Every day African Americans go about their lives with a constant anxiety and trauma wondering, who would be next?

MAY 30

***Washington Post*:** Two to four weeks after many states began lifting restrictions on restaurants, bars and larger gatherings, cases are rising in areas that had previously dodged the worst of the virus's impact. Arizona, Mississippi, South Carolina, Utah and Wisconsin all set record highs for new cases reported Friday. Restaurants, gyms, and other businesses have been allowed open for at least two weeks in all of the states.

Mayor Bill de Blasio, New York City: I would still wish that everyone would realize that when people gather it's inherently dangerous in the context of this pandemic and I'm going to keep urging people not to use that approach and if they do they focus on social distancing and wearing face coverings . . . you cannot see overt racism, you cannot see overt racist murder and not feel something profoundly deep, so I understand that. But the last thing we would want to see is members of our community harmed because the virus spread in one of these settings. It's a very, very complicated reality.

President Trump: Big crowd, professionally organized, but nobody came close to breaching the fence. If they had they would have been greeted with the most vicious dogs, and most ominous weapons, I have ever seen. That's when people would have been really badly hurt, at least.

Mayor Muriel Bowser, Washington, D.C.: People are tired, sad, angry, and desperate for change. And we need leaders who recognize this pain and in times of great turmoil and despair, can provide us a sense of calm and a sense of hope. Instead what we've got in the last two days from the White House is the glorification of violence against American citizens. What used to be heard in dog whistles, we now hear from a bullhorn. So, to everyone hurting and doing our part to move this country forward, we will look to ourselves and our own communities for this leadership and this hope. Our power, we know, is in peace, in our voices, and ultimately at the ballot box.

Gov. Cuomo (NY): For 90 days we were just dealing with the Covid crisis. On the 91st day, we had the Covid crisis and we have the situation in Minneapolis with the racial unrest around the George Floyd death. Those are not disconnected situations. One looks like a public health system issue—Covid—but it is getting at the inequality in healthcare also on a deeper level. And then the George Floyd situation, which gets at the inequality and discrimination in the criminal justice system. They are connected.

MAY 31

President Trump: Other Democrat run Cities and States should look at the total shutdown of Radical Left Anarchists in Minneapolis last night. The National Guard did a great job, and should be used in other States before it is too late!

Mayor Keisha Lance Bottoms, Atlanta: He should just stop talking. This is like Charlottesville all over again. He speaks and he makes it worse. There are times when you should just be quiet and I wish that he would just be quiet. Or if he can't be silent, if there is somebody of good sense and good conscience in the White House, put him in front of a teleprompter and pray he reads it and at least says the right things, because he is making it worse.

Jack Healy and Dionne Searcey, *New York Times*: By one estimate, black people accounted for at least 29 percent of known Covid-19 cases in Minnesota, despite making up about 6 percent of the state's population. African-Americans make up 35 percent of coronavirus cases in Minneapolis, though they are less than 20 percent of the city's population.

Rep. Ilhan Omar (MN): What we are seeing, the unrest we are seeing in our nation, isn't just because of the life that was taken. It's also because so many people have experienced this, so many people have experienced injustices within our system, so many people know the social and economic neglect. We are living in a country that has a two-tiered justice system. And people are tired of the—people are sick and tired of being sick and tired. And we need to really step back and say to ourselves, where do we actually go from here? And that can't just be getting justice for George Floyd. It needs to be bigger than that.

Sen. Kamala Harris (CA): Black communities have not received equal justice under law for centuries. Black blood has stained America's sidewalks. The pain is real. It's deep. It's legitimate. We must listen, acknowledge that, and take action to transform our communities.

Sen. Cory Booker (NJ): This is a moment in America that can't just lead to a momentary outrage. We have to begin to do the concerted things that so many of our great heroes—Ella Baker, Fannie Lou Hamer, Fred Shuttlesworth—tried to demand. That the conscience of this country remains disturbed and uncomfortable until actual laws are changed that bring more justice to our country.

Mayor London Breed, San Francisco: The murder of George Floyd is only the latest in a long history of African American men who have lost their lives as a result of police violence. There is a lot of pain right now here in San Francisco and across the country . . . Peaceful protests in San Francisco will continue to have my full support and the full support of the City.

Unfortunately, some of the violence and vandalism we saw last night is unacceptable, and we will be instituting a curfew beginning tonight.

Jonathan Lemire and Zeke Miller, AP: Protesters started fires near the White House as tensions with police mounted during a third straight night of demonstrations held in response to the death of George Floyd at police hands in Minnesota. An hour before the 11 P.M. curfew, police fired a major barrage of tear gas stun grenades into the crowd of more than 1,000 people, largely clearing Lafayette Park across the street from the White House and scattering protesters into the street.

JUNE 1:

Mayor Jenny Durkan, Seattle, WA: It is striking how many of the people who were doing the looting and stealing and the fires over the weekend were young white males.

Mayor Melvin Carter, St. Paul, MN: Folks in St. Paul, just like folks across the country, are traumatized right now. We are, I think, doubly traumatized, as we're in the midst of this Covid-19 pandemic, as 40% of low-income workers have lost their jobs and the economic realities of this year before George Floyd was killed.

Former President Barack Obama: I recognize that these past few months have been hard and dispiriting—that the fear, sorrow, uncertainty, and hardship of a pandemic have been compounded by tragic reminders that prejudice and inequality still shape so much of American life. But watching the heightened activism of young people in recent weeks, of every race and every station, makes me hopeful. If, going forward, we can channel our justifiable anger into peaceful, sustained, and effective action, then this moment can be a real turning point in our nation's long journey to live up to our highest ideals.

CNN: As California continues to reopen, coronavirus cases are mounting with an 11% increase over just five days. Sunday's report from California Department of Public Health marked yet another single-day high with 3,705 cases. The total number of confirmed cases in the state is 110,583. That's an increase of more than 11,000 cases since Wednesday.

Mayor LaToya Cantrell, New Orleans: Orleans Parish will not move into "Phase Two" this Friday. As we have said throughout this pandemic: we are watching the data, not the date. We don't yet have sufficient data to authorize opening up further at this point.

***Washington Post*:** A recent *Washington Post*-Ipsos poll found that blacks reported being furloughed and laid off at higher rates than whites, underlining the disproportionate toll of the pandemic on African American communities. And this is all happening at a time when black Americans are also dying of Covid-19, the disease caused by the virus, at much higher rates than whites, according to the Centers for Disease Control and Prevention.

Gov. Phil Murphy (NJ): The fact that so many came forward in peace, and common ground to fight for the most basic principle of human dignity is a powerful reminder of the Black and Brown experience in America today, and the fact that so many others who do not live this reality would join them. Making these protests powerful displays of our great diversity should be a point of pride for our state. People with privilege are now recognizing the pain of those without. We are seeing our common humanity, and so, I watched as an example with tremendous pride to see the chief of police in Camden march in lockstep with residents on Saturday and to help them hold their banner.

Karen Attiah, *Washington Post*: When white men march armed with their privilege and guns,/America doesn't do much, perhaps a little shrug./When black people march, armed with anger and grief/America unleashes all hell, just to suppress our speech.

Maimuna Majumder, Epidemiologist, Harvard University: The same broad-sweeping structural racism that enables police brutality against black Americans is also responsible for higher mortality among black Americans with Covid-19. One in every 1,000 black men and boys can expect to be killed by police in this country. To me, this clearly illustrates why police brutality is a public health problem; anything that causes mortality at such a scale is a public health problem.

Cornel West, Activist, Author, and Professor, Harvard University: There's no doubt that this is America's moment of reckoning . . . The catalyst was certainly Brother George Floyd's public lynching, but the failures of the predatory capitalist economy to provide the satisfaction of the basic needs of food and healthcare and quality education, jobs with a decent wage, at the same time the collapse of your political class, the collapse of your professional class. Their legitimacy has been radically called into question.

Mark Esper, Secretary of Defense:* I think the sooner that you mass and dominate the battlespace, the quicker this dissipates and we can get back to the right normal.

President Trump:† You have to get much tougher. Someone throwing a rock is like shooting a gun. You have to do retribution . . . You have to dominate. If you don't dominate, you're wasting your time. They're going to run all over you, you'll look like a bunch of jerks. You have to dominate, and you have to arrest people, and you have to try people and they have to go to jail for long periods of time.

---

* Phone call between Trump, Secretary of Defense Mark Esper, and U.S. governors

† Same phone call

Gov. Pritzker (IL):* I wanted to take this moment—and I can't let it pass—to speak up and say that I've been extraordinarily concerned about the rhetoric that's been used by you. It's been inflammatory. We have to call for calm. We have to have police reform called for. We've called out our national guard and our state police, but the rhetoric that's coming out of the White House is making it worse. And I need to say that people are feeling real pain out there and we've got to have national leadership in calling for calm and making sure that we're addressing the concerns of the legitimate peaceful protesters. That will help us to bring order.

Gov. Charlie Baker (MA): I heard what the president said today about "dominating" and "fighting." I know I should be surprised when I hear incendiary words like this from him, but I'm not. At so many times during these past several weeks, when the country needed compassion and leadership the most, it was simply nowhere to be found. Instead we got bitterness, combativeness, and self-interest. That's not what we need in Boston, it's not what we need right now in Massachusetts, and it's definitely not what we need across this country of ours either.

President Trump: First, we are ending the riots and lawlessness that has spread throughout our country. We will end it now. Today I have strongly recommended to every governor to deploy the national guard in sufficient numbers that we dominate the streets, mayors and governors must establish an overwhelming law enforcement presence until the violence has been quelled. If a city or state refuses to take the actions that are necessary to defend the life and property of their residents, then I will deploy the United States military and quickly solve the problem for them.

Sen. Kamala Harris (CA): Let's be clear: when Trump says "dominate" he's talking about supremacy.

---

* Same phone call

Yamiche Alcindor, PBS: Here is what was happening outside the White House as President Trump was giving his Rose Garden address and saying he is an "ally of all peaceful protestors." Peaceful protestors being tear gassed outside of the WH gates. I confirmed because I was teargassed along with them.

Mayor Muriel Bowser, Washington, D.C.: I imposed a curfew at 7pm. A full 25 minutes before the curfew & w/o provocation, federal police used munitions on peaceful protestors in front of the White House, an act that will make the job of @DCPoliceDept officers more difficult. Shameful! D.C residents—Go home. Be safe.

Rep. Hakeem Jeffries (NY): Peaceful protestors were tear-gassed outside of the White House this evening. Trump's inhumanity does not surprise me. The willingness of others to follow him should. It's time to get this guy's finger off the nuclear button.

Ben Rhodes, Former Deputy National Security Advisor: More than 100,000 Americans are dead in no small part because of his incompetence and Trump is waving a bible and declaring war against Americans.

JUNE 2

Rep. Bennie Thompson (MS), Chair, House Committee on Homeland Security: I write to you* stunned, disturbed, and furious at the sight of federal authorities teargassing peaceful protesters in Lafayette Park, outside the White House, last night, in order to clear the way for the President to walk over and hold a Bible in front of St. John's Episcopal Church. It is shameful that the President used the power of the federal government to

---

* Letter to U.S. Secret Service Director James Murray.

attack Americans exercising their Constitutional right to protest just so he could stage a photo opportunity.

Sen. Cory Booker (NJ): Every member of this co-equal body should condemn what this President did, trampling upon the most sacred right of this nation to assemble, to petition, to protest. What this President did was to make a mockery of our civil rights.

Anne Milgram, Former Attorney General (NJ): What we're seeing is something that we know exists, but it has been in many ways, I think, below the surface of American consciousness and what we have seen in this past week is that the George Floyd murder has pushed it over—it's bubbled out into our collective consciousness.

Sen. Kamala Harris (CA): In the last couple of days, I've been saying America is raw right now, her wounds are exposed. The reality of it is that the life of a Black person in America, historically, and even most recently with Mr. Floyd, has never been treated as fully human. And it is time that we come to terms with the fact that America has never fully addressed the systemic racism that has existed in our country. That's just a fact. And so the people protesting on the street are protesting understanding that we have yet to fulfill that promise of equal justice under the law. And there is a pain that is present that is being expressed in their Constitutional right to march and to shout.

Mayor Eric Garcetti, Los Angeles: And while not every death is as visible and as vicious as George Floyd's, we have to own those deaths that come from the diabetes, and that come from Covid-19, and all of the things that visit Black Americans disproportionately because of where they start life, and where this society values their life. The schools that they are born into, and the neighborhoods where they live that have been discarded and efforts to fund those schools rejected, the moments in which we see that racial justice can't be the work of 10% of a nation. It has to be the work of a 100% of the nation.

Ken Klippenstein, *Nation*: The FBI's Washington Field Office "has no intelligence indicating Antifa involvement/presence" in the violence that occurred on May 31 during the D.C.-area protests over the murder of George Floyd, according to an internal FBI situation report obtained exclusively by *The Nation*. That same day, President Donald Trump announced on Twitter that he would designate "Antifa" a terrorist organization, even though the government has no existing authority to declare a domestic group a terrorist organization, and antifa is not an organized group.

Mayor Lori Lightfoot, Chicago: Block by block what I saw, even amidst damage, was a sense of pride and work in communities and families. And people who know their neighbors and know how to take care of them. And what I saw yesterday was also the power in the bond that truly... exemplifies what it means to be a neighbor, particularly in this time of need. That was a humbling experience to bear witness to the resolve in a simple notion shown in these incredibly compassionate gestures that I saw all over the city.

Former Vice President Biden: The country is crying out for leadership. Leadership that can unite us. Leadership that brings us together. I look at the presidency as very big job and nobody will get it right every time. And I won't either, but I promise you this, I won't traffic in fear and division. I won't fan the flames of hate. I'll seek to heal the racial wounds that have long plagued our country, not use them for political gain. I'll do my job and I will take responsibility. I won't blame others. I promise you, this job is not about me. It's about you. It's about us to build a better future. That's what America does.

Mayor Lightfoot, Chicago: After a lot of conversation with people on the ground whose lives had been shattered, and after a lot of consultation with local businesses, local chambers, local alderman and other elected officials, everywhere I went, I asked the question, should we open? Or should we delay? And to universal acclaim emphatically what I heard from people is, "Mayor, we have to step forward."

JUNE 3

Gov. Cuomo (NY): You have the Covid crisis, you have the murder of Mr. Floyd, two very different situations, but both critical in and of themselves, and both happening at the same time. It's then wrapped in an environment and a dynamic that is racially charged, and politically charged. It makes it a very, very perilous time in this country, and we have to be careful. We have to be very careful, because the consequences are steep on both sides of this equation, so leadership, good government, responsibility is more important than ever before, especially, in these divided times. Covid-19 is still a real threat. We're still battling that.

Luke Kemp, University of Cambridge: The U.S. is at risk of a downfall over the coming decade. There are early warning signals and the different contributors to collapse are rising.

Gov. Walz (MN): Tomorrow, the world will turn its focus, and the space will be created for the Floyd family. But it's also going to be very clear if the belief is, is that this will finally just kind of calm down, and everything will go back, I certainly don't believe it. If you're out there listening to people, I don't believe it. And I certainly don't think the young people that are our future believe it.

Adam Serwer, *Atlantic*: A different president might have tried to quell the unrest and unify the nation, but Trump is incapable of that. He cannot rally Americans around a common identity or interest, because his presidency is a rejection of the concept, an affirmation of the conviction that America's traditional social hierarchies are good and just.

James Mattis, Former Secretary of Defense: Donald Trump is the first president in my lifetime who does not try to unite the American people—does not even pretend to try. Instead he tries to divide us. We are witnessing the consequences of three years of this deliberate effort. We are witnessing the consequences of three years without mature leadership. We can unite without him, drawing on the strengths inherent in our civil society. This will not be easy, as the past few days have shown, but we owe it to our fellow citizens; to past generations that bled to defend our promise; and to our children.

***New York Times*:** In California, daily case reports exceeded 3,000 twice in the past week, a threshold the state had not crossed before . . . Arizona, Tennessee, Wisconsin, at least 12 other states and Puerto Rico are also seeing an upward trend of newly reported cases, and some are reaching new highs. In Mississippi, the 439 cases announced Saturday were the most yet on a single day. In Alaska, which has so far avoided the worst of the virus, cases have soared to their highest levels in recent days.

Charles Ornstein, ProPublica: Worrying trend: ICUs across the country are pretty full. In 10 states, plus DC, more than 70% of beds in ICUs are occupied, per @CDCgov.

Gov. Cuomo (NY): Today is day 95 of the situation dealing with the Coronavirus pandemic, and it is day 10 of the situation dealing with the civil unrest after the murder of Mr. Floyd that we all saw on TV. The president held up the Bible the other day in Washington, DC. Here in New York, we actually read the Bible, and there were some passages that I think are especially appropriate for today, and this time of where we are. "Blessed are the peacemakers for they will be called children of God." Matthew 5, "If a house be divided against itself, that house cannot stand." That was Mark 3. Actually, before Abraham Lincoln . . ."You can't set fire to the house, and then, claim you are the one trying to put out the flames." Do you know who said that? You guys are not well-read, that I can tell you. A.J Parkinson said that.

JUNE 4:

***Washington Post*:** Unemployment claims for the last week of May totaled 1.9 million, a painfully high number, but the lowest since the novel coronavirus started spreading widely back in March, a sign the economy may no longer be in free fall. The Department of Labor, which released the data, also noted gig and self-employed workers filed fewer initial claims last week—620,000 compared with 1.2 million the previous week—under the expanded federal program that grants them benefits. The slowing in jobless claims doesn't mean the United States has any less deep of a hole to dig itself out of.

Mayor Dan Gelber, Miami, FL: It's almost as if [the CDC] just said, "Open up and figure out whether it's a good idea or not afterward."

Dr. Francis Collins, Director, NIH: I'm a bit concerned to see there's a fair amount of skepticism in the American public about whether or not they would take such a vaccine We won't get past Covid-19 unless we have a substantial majority of our public ultimately rendered immune . . . Because we have a number of these, and they all use a different strategy, I am optimistic that at least one maybe two, maybe three will come through looking like what we need. We want to hedge our bets by having a number of different approaches, so that it's very likely that at least one of them and maybe more will work.

Former Vice President Biden: If we just let this wound scab over again, it's never going to heal. As I said, George Floyd's last words didn't die with him. They're echoing all across the country. And I think they speak onto to a nation where you have over 108,000 people who've lost their lives to a virus now. 40 million Americans have filed for—over 40 million for unemployment. A disproportionate number of the coronavirus cases and job losses are on African American and Latino communities. Matter of fact, Latino community even have a higher unemployment rate, lost jobs. The moment, it seems to me, it's a wake up call for everybody, for all of us.

Kyung Lah, CNN: It's just past 8:30 P.M. in Los Angeles, where protests are still continuing in full force. There is no curfew in the city today, and demonstrations have stayed peaceful all day, without violent confrontations or clashes . . . Protesters chant slogans as they march, with music and drum beats blaring in the background. Cars are slowly moving through the tunnel along with marchers, with many drivers and passengers holding protest signs or raised fists out of their windows to show support.

Mark Berman and Emily Wax-Thibodeaux, *Washington Post*: While most protests have been peaceful, President Trump and other officials in government and law enforcement have focused on the groups setting fires, looting and causing destruction in footage also relayed across cable news and social media. Observers say they fear these attacks could escalate the tension on American streets, concerns they say are amplified by Trump's repeated calls for officials to use much greater force on demonstrators.

Mayor Keisha Lance Bottoms, Atlanta: For every single second that I give energy to [Trump] is wasted energy. This president is a lost cause . . . America is a tinder box right now, and his tongue is a match.

JUNE 5

AP: Unemployment dips to 13.3% as U.S. adds 2.5 million jobs in May as impact from virus eases.*

---

* On June 8, the Department of Labor will admit a mistake in the unemployment numbers: "BLS has admitted that government household survey takers mistakenly counted about 4.9 million

President Trump: Really Big Jobs Report. Great going President Trump (kidding but true)!

Former Vice President Biden: It's time for him to step out of his own bunker. A president who takes no responsibility for costing millions and millions of Americans their jobs deserves no credit when a fraction of them return.

President Trump: This is a very big day for our country. It's affirmation of all the work we've been doing, really for three and a half years. This isn't just over the last few months. This is for three and a half years. And it's a great thing. We were very strong. We had the greatest economy in the history of our country. We had the greatest economy in the history of the world. And that strength let us get through this horrible pandemic, largely through.

***New York Times*:** These figures released Friday reflect the employment situation for May, specifically the week of May 10-16. A more recent data set released Thursday, initial claims for unemployment benefits, indicates that while job losses have slowed, layoffs continued last week even as businesses have begun to reopen.

President Trump: Hopefully George [Floyd] is looking down right now and saying, "This is a great thing that's happening for our country." This is a great day for him. It's a great day for everybody. This is a great day for everybody.

Nikole Hannah-Jones, *New York Times*: I am looking for all of their posts about why black small business owners are only getting 2 percent of

---

people as employed, although they were unemployed. Had the mistake been corrected, the unemployment rate would have risen to 16.1% in May." (Jack Kelly, "There's a Glaring, Misleading Error in the May Jobs Report: U.S. May Be at 20% Unemployment," Forbes.com, June 8, 2020.)

PPE funding and why 2 of 5 black small businesses will likely shutter permanently because of Covid.

President Trump: We have a lot of protestors and we have something else. We have something else. We have a pandemic, we've made tremendous progress really on both if you look at where we've come on, both, we've made tremendous progress on both, tremendous progress. But you're looking and the people are now starting to return to work. So it's been an incredible thing to see. It's been a beautiful thing to see.

Andrew Restuccia, *Wall Street Journal*: The White House coronavirus task force is meeting less frequently, the government's top infectious disease expert is getting little face time with President Trump, and the administration's virus-testing coordinator is returning to his previous job.

President Trump: But we're going to be back and we're opening our country. And I hope that the lockdown governors, I don't know why they continue to lock down. Because if you look at Georgia, if you look at Florida, if you look at South Carolina, if you look at so many different places that have opened up, I don't want to name all of them, but the ones that are most energetic about opening, they are doing tremendous business.

NPR: In the South, the timing of new cases appears to be linked to the reopening of restaurants, barber shops and gyms, which started in most states more than a month ago. Figures tracked by NPR show the number of cases in North Carolina and South Carolina this week is up by roughly 60% from two weeks ago. In Tennessee, that increase is 75%.

***Miami Herald*:** Florida's Department of Health on Friday morning confirmed 1,305 additional cases of Covid-19, bringing the state's total to 61,488 confirmed cases. There were also 53 new deaths announced, raising the statewide toll to 2,660. This is the third day this week that the state's daily total of newly confirmed cases surpassed 1,000. On Thursday, the state recorded 1,413 additional cases, the highest daily count since Florida's Department of Health began providing daily updates on the novel coronavirus in March.

Johns Hopkins Coronavirus Resource Center:
875,402 confirmed U.S cases
108,278 confirmed U.S deaths

President Trump: So it's been a really a terrific thing. It's now time for us to work together as we rebuild, renew and recover the great promise of America, and that's true, we're going to work together. It'll all work out. It'll all work out.

ACKNOWLEDGMENTS

First off, I want to give thanks and credit to all the hardworking journalists whose work is included in this book. Without a rigorous and free press, our country is nowhere. The toxic nature of the discussion of the news media in the current administration, along with the blatant distrust and disregard of fact-based institutions, is frightening. I can only hope that the pandemic has shown the danger of "alternative facts" and that books like this will help along the process of self-correction.

Thanks to the very wise Anton Mueller, who came up with the idea for the book and selected me to write it, and who directed this project from start to finish, to the incomparable Morgan Jones, who helped every step of the way, to Suzanne Keller and to the entire team at Bloomsbury, who did a phenomenal job bringing it to publication. Thank you so much to Tim Egan for agreeing to be part of the project and lending his genius to it.

Thanks to early draft readers Justin Gricus, George Gierer, and Evan Gottfried, whose comments and perspectives were invaluable.

Thanks to Aaron Rupar of *Vox*, whose Twitter account showed me that the most damning evidence is always just people's words.

Special thanks to my wife, Lydia, whose support makes any book I write possible, and to my children, Lucy and Arlo, for being their curious and understanding selves.

Finally, to all those who have been ill, who have lost loved ones, or whose lives have been upended by the coronavirus pandemic, this book is dedicated to you. I hope your stories will continue to be told as an integral and necessary part of history.

NOTES

iv **Everyone now asks** Mukherjee, Siddhartha. "What the Coronavirus Crisis Reveals About American Medicine," *New Yorker*, April 27, 2020.

THE ARRIVAL

3 **7 confirmed cases** WeChat message, December 31, 2019

3 **Recently some medical institutions** Hubei Daily, "Wuhan Municipal Health and Health Commission Informs of Pneumonia," January 1, 2020. Accessed April 30, 2020 (Google Translate).

4 **According to official** "Wuhan South China Seafood Market Closed for Official Response in Response to Opening Time," *Beijing News Express*, January 2, 2020 (Google Translate).

4 **According to a report** Via *Chutian Dushi Bao*, January 3, 2020. Translation from https://crofsblogs.typepad.com.

4 **As of 8:00 on January 5** Wuhan Municipal Health Committee, press release.

5 **The cause of mysterious** Helen Braswell, "Cause of Wuhan's Mysterious Pneumonia Cases Still Unknown, Chinese Officials Say," *Scientific American*, January 6, 2020.

5 **Chinese authorities have made** "WHO Statement Regarding Cluster of Pneumonia Cases in Wuhan, China," January 9, 2020.

5 **According to the risk assessment** Ministry of Health, Labor and Welfare, Japan, "Outbreak of Patients with Pneumonia Associated with New Coronavirus (1st Case)," January 16, 2020. Accessed April 28, 2020 (Google Translate).

5 **According to the current data** "China Biodiversity Conservation and Green Development Foundation," CBCGDF, January 21, 2020.

6 **The World Health Organization will** "Coronavirus in China Spreads by Human-to-Human Transmission," NPR, January 21, 2020.

6 **Coronaviruses are a large** Centers for Disease Control and Prevention, "First

Travel-related Case of 2019 Novel Coronavirus Detected in United States," press release, January 21, 2020.

6 **As of today 21 January** Ministry of Health and Welfare, South Korea, "Update on the Confirmed Case of the Novel Coronavirus (2019-nCoV) in Korea," press release, January 21, 2020.

7 **The Centers for Disease** Centers for Disease Control and Prevention, "First Travel-related Case of 2019 Novel Coronavirus Detected in United States."

7 **From November to January 15** Jay Inslee, January 21, 2020.

7 **While originally thought** Centers for Disease Control and Prevention, January 21, 2020.

7 **This is certainly** Jay Inslee, January 21, 2020.

7 **We have it totally** Donald Trump, January 22, 2020.

7 **Currently, we use** Sylvie Briand, "World Health Organization Coronavirus Update Transcript—January 23, 2020," Rev.com.

8 **The data we presented** Michael Ryan, ibid.

8 **Make no mistake** Tedros Adhanom Ghebreyesus, "WHO Director-General's Statement on the Advice of the IHR Emergency Committee on Novel Coronavirus," January 23, 2020.

8 **IATA is closely** International Air Transport Association (IATA), "Statement on Coronavirus Outbreak in Wuhan (China)," press release, January 25, 2020.

8 **Experts from the World Health Organization** "China Novel Coronavirus: National Health Commission Press Conference Transcript," press release, *Outbreak News Today*, January 26, 2020.

9 **We understand that the public** Interview with China Central Television, reported in Yang Zekun, "Wuhan Mayor Says Will Resign If It Helps Control Outbreak," *China Daily*, January 27, 2020. Accessed June 2, 2020.

9 **Global spread appears inevitable** Scott Gottleib, "Op-ed: We Need to Prepare for US Outbreak of Wuhan Coronavirus," CNBC.com, January 27, 2020.

9 **A man from the district** Bavarian Ministry of Health, Germany, "Confirmed Corona Virus Case in Bavaria—Infection Control Measures in Progress," press release. Accessed April 28, 2020 (Google Translate).

9 **The virus is a devil** "Fighting the Covid-19 Outbreak: Important Remarks by General Secretary Xi Jinping," Permanent Mission of the People's Republic of China to the United Nations Office at Geneva and Other International Organizations in Switzerland, January 28, 2020.

10 **With well over** Elizabeth Warren, "Preventing, Containing, and Treating Infectious Disease Outbreaks at Home

and Abroad," elizabethwarren.com (former presidential candidate site, now Warren Democrats), January 28, 2020

10 **The idea that we could create** Brenda Goodman, "Can the New Coronavirus Be Stopped?" *Medscape*, January 28, 2020.

10 **The outbreak of a new** "Joe Biden: Trump Is Worst Possible Leader to Deal With Coronavirus Outbreak," *USA Today*, January 29, 2020.

10 **The threat of the coronavirus** "Minutes of the Federal Open Market Committee January 28–29, 2020."

11 **I'm declaring a public** "Transcript: World Health Organization Declares Coronavirus a Global Health Emergency," Rev.com, January 30, 2020.

11 **We have two confirmed** Giuseppe Conte, press conference, January 30, 2020.

11 **I don't want to talk** Wilbur Ross, interview with Maria Bartiromo, Fox Business, January 30, 2020.

11 **The 2019 novel coronavirus** Centers for Disease Control and Prevention, "CDC Confirms Person-to-Person Spread of New Coronavirus in the United States," press release, January 30, 2020.

12 **We only have five** Iowa Campaign Rally

12 **There are now 98 cases in 18 countries** "Transcript: World Health Organization Declares Coronavirus a Global Health Emergency," Rev.com, January 30, 2020.

12 **After receiving the new** Weibo.

THE EMERGENCY

15 **I have today declared** Alex Azar, "Secretary Azar Delivers Remarks on Declaration of Public Health Emergency for 2019 Novel Coronavirus," Department of Health and Human Services, January 31, 2020.

15 **Yesterday, after 10 pm** Salvador Illa, public statement, "Spain: Health Minister Confirms First Case of Coronavirus in Canary Islands," February 1, 2020.

16 **Today the nucleic acid test** Weibo

16 **We take a situation** Andrew Cuomo, "Governor Cuomo Issues Update on Novel Coronavirus and Announces New Hotline Staffed by State Health Department," February 2, 2020.

16 **We pretty much shut it down** Donald Trump, interview with Sean Hannity, Fox News, February 3, 2020.

16 **The Wuhan coronavirus spreading** Donald G. McNeil Jr., "Wuhan Coronavirus Looks Increasingly Like a Pandemic, Experts Say," *New York Times*, February 2, 2020.

17 **The total number of confirmed cases** James Griffiths, "China Marks Deadliest Day of Outbreak, with Confirmed Cases Topping 20,000," CNN.com, February 4, 2020.

17 **Protecting Americans' health** The State of the Union Address

17 **The total number of confirmed positives** Nancy Messonnier, "Transcript for CDC Telebriefing: CDC Update on Novel Coronavirus," Centers for Disease Control and Prevention, February 5, 2020.

17 **All of the evidence we have indicates** Shannon Firth, "Travel Bans Can't Stop Coronavirus, Public Health Experts Tell Congress," Medpage Today, February 7, 2020.

18 **Just had a long and very good conversation** Donald Trump, @realDonaldTrump, Twitter, 5:31 A.M., February 7, 2020.

18 **Although the virus** Alex Azar, "Remarks at Briefing by Members of the President's Coronavirus Task Force," February 7, 2020.

18 **Nonfarm payroll employment rose by 225,000** U.S. Bureau of Labor Statistics, "Employment Situation News Release," February 7, 2020.

18 **Economists surveyed by Dow Jones** Jeff Cox, "January Adds a Much Stronger-Than-Expected 225,000 Jobs, with a Boost from Warm Weather," CNBC, February 7, 2020.

18 **In the fight against** Dr. Li passed away in the early hours of Friday, Feb. 7 in China, Feb. 6 in America. This message was released on the social messaging service Weibo.

18 **CDC today confirmed another** Centers for Disease Control and Prevention, "CDC Confirms 13th Case of 2019 Novel Coronavirus," media statement, February 10, 2020.

19 **They're working hard** Donald Trump, "President Trump Rally in Manchester, New Hampshire," C-SPAN, February 10, 2020.

19 **There've been some concerning** Tedros Adhanom Ghebreyesus, @DrTedros, Twitter, 5:06 P.M., February 9, 2020.

19 **I had a long talk** Donald Trump, "Remarks by President Trump at the White House Business Session with our Nation's Governors," February 10, 2020.

19 **First of all** Tedros Adhanom Ghebreyesus, "WHO Director-General's Remarks at the Media Briefing on 2019-nCoV on 11 February 2020," February 11, 2020.

19 **Scientists have done** Sylvia Briand, "Coronavirus Press Conference 11 February, 2020," February 11, 2020.

20 **Princess Cruises confirms** Princess Cruises, "Additional Cases Confirmed by Ministry of Health," February 11, 2020.

20 **The number of cases** Tedros Adhanom Ghebreyesus, "Coronavirus Press Conference 11 February, 2020."

20 **If fires are left** Michael Ryan, "Coronavirus Press Conference 11 February, 2020."

20 **There are more than 600** Nancy Messonnier, "Transcript for CDC Media Telebriefing: Update on Covid-19," Centers for Disease Control and Prevention, February 14, 2020.

20 **In the past 24 hours** Tedros Adhanom Ghebreyesus, "World Health Organization Coronavirus Update Transcript—February 18, 2020," Rev.com.

21 **People on a large ship** "Threats to Global Health and Bio Security," Council on Foreign Relations, February 18, 2020.

21 **It takes a huge effort** Michael Ryan, "World Health Organization Coronavirus Update Transcript—February 18, 2020."

21 **Well, it's even more** Anthony Fauci, "Threats to Global Health and Bio Security," Council on Foreign Relations, February 18, 2020.

21 **The coronavirus is our** "Finding Solid Footing for the Global Economy," February 19, 2020.

21 **We believe the greater** Fred Imbert, "Goldman Says Market Underestimating Coronavirus Risk: 'Correction Is Looking Much More Probable,'" CNBC, February 19, 2020.

22 **Irrational exuberance** Kevin Stankiewicz, "Markets May Face 'Pretty Serious Reckoning' as Coronavirus Slows Growth, Yale's Stephen Roach Says," CNBC, February 19, 2020.

22 **S&P 500** "Stock Market News February 20, 2020," The Stock Market on the Internet, February 20, 2020.

22 **U.S. equities slumped** Vildana Hajric and Claire Ballentine, "Tech Leads Stock Slide on Virus Fears; Gold Gains: Markets Wrap," Bloomberg, February 19, 2020.

22 **There's a high probability** Jeff Cox, "Expectations for a Rate Cut Will Fade as Coronavirus Fear Eases, Fed's James Bullard Says," CNBC, February 21, 2020.

22 **Authorities in northern Italy** Daniele Lepido, "Italy Regions Close Universities as Coronavirus Reaches Milan," Bloomberg, February 22, 2020.

23 **The contagiousness of** Giulio Galleria, public statement, reported in Eric Reguly, "Northern Italy Shut Down as Coronavirus Death Toll Climbs," *Globe and Mail*, February 24, 2020.

23 **I've wondered myself** Giuseppe Conte, press conference, in Valentina Za and Riccardo Bastianello, "Update: 5-Two Dead, 79 Infected in Italy as Govt Fights to Contains Coronavirus Outbreak," Reuters, February 22, 2020.

23 **There is an increasing probability** Peter Navarro, Memo to the President, reported in Jonathan Swan and Margaret Talev, "Navarro Memos Warning of Mass Coronavirus Death Circulated in January," *Axios*, April 7, 2020.

23 **We have it very much** Donald Trump, "Remarks by President Trump before Marine One Departure," February 3, 2020.

24 **The sudden increase of cases in Italy** Tedros Adhanom Ghebreyesus, "World Health Organization Coronavirus Update Transcript February 24: WHO Addresses Spread into Europe & Middle East," February 24, 2020, Rev.com.

24 **Pandemic comes, I think** Michael Ryan, ibid.

24 **The quarantine has been** Ron Nirenberg, press conference, reported in Carma Hassan, "San Antonio Reports 6 Cases of Coronavirus," CNN, February 24, 2020.

24 **The Coronavirus is very much** Donald Trump, @realDonaldTrump, Twitter, 4:42 P.M., February 24, 2020.

24 **It's now clear that the epidemic** Michael D. Osterholm and Mark Olshaker, "Is It a Pandemic Yet?" *New York Times*, February 24, 2020.

25 **As mayor of the great** "A Special Invitation from the Honorable LaToya Cantrell," MardiGrasNewOrleans.com.

25 **While large crowds** Anthony McAuley, Katelyn Umholtz, and Nicholas Reimann, "Fat Tuesday Goes Off without a Hitch After a Tragic Mardi Gras Season," Nola.com, February 25, 2020.

25 **As of this morning** Alex Azar, "Transcript: U.S. Health Officials on Response to Coronavirus February 25, 2020," Rev.com.

25 **We have contained this** Fred Imbert, "Larry Kudlow Says US Has Contained the Coronavirus and the Economy Is Holding Up Nicely," CNBC, February 25, 2020.

26 **The president's budget** Brian Schatz, ibid.

26 **Of course, we've been watching** Anne Schuchat, ibid.

26 **We have very few** Donald Trump, "Remarks by President Trump in Press Conference," February 25, 2020.

26 **Now, it's not so much** Anne Schuchat, "Transcript: U.S. Health Officials on Response to Coronavirus February 25, 2020," Rev.com.

27 **A standard flu season** Anthony Fauci, ibid.

27 **We're trying to engage** Alex Azar, ibid.

27 **I think that whole** Trump, "Remarks by President Trump in Press Conference," February 25, 2020.

27 **It's time to turn down** Giuseppe Conte, press conference, in Holly Ellyatt, "'We Need to Stop the Panic': Italy's Prime Minister Calls for Calm as Virus Spikes," February 26, 2020.

27 **The Centers for Disease Control and Prevention (CDC) has confirmed** Centers for Disease Control and Prevention, "CDC Confirms Possible Instance of Community Spread of Covid-19 in U.S.," media statement, February 26, 2020.

28 **Today we learned** University of California Davis, "Coronavirus Patient and Precautions at UC Davis Medical Center," press release, February 26, 2020.

28 **As of today** Alex Azar, "Remarks by President Trump, Vice President Pence, and Members of the Coronavirus Task Force in Press Conference," whitehouse.gov, February 27, 2020.

28 **We're rapidly developing** Donald Trump, ibid.

28 **So although this is the fastest** Anthony Fauci, ibid.

29 **Johns Hopkins, I guess** Donald Trump, ibid.

29 **National health security is** Elizabeth Cameron, Jennifer B. Nuzzo, and Jessica A. Bell, "GHS Index: Global Health Security Index," Johns Hopkins Bloomberg School of Public Health, October 2019.

29 **As more and more** Nancy Messonnier, "Transcript for the CDC Telebriefing Update on Covid-19," Centers for Disease Control and Prevention, February 26, 2020.

29 **I don't think it's inevitable** Donald Trump, "Remarks by President Trump, Vice President Pence, and Members of the Coronavirus Task Force in Press Conference," white house.gov, February 27, 2020.

29 **I don't think the president** Nancy Pelosi, February 29, 2020.

30 **Maybe it's going** Trump, "Remarks by President Trump, Vice President Pence, and Members of the Coronavirus Task Force in Press Conference," February 27, 2020.

30 **As of today** Gavin Newsom, "Governor Gavin Newsom Coronavirus Update Transcript: California Governor Holds Press Conference on Coronavirus," Rev.com, February 27, 2020.

30 **It's going to disappear** Donald Trump, "Remarks by President Trump in Meeting with African American Leaders," whitehouse.gov, February 28, 2020.

31 **It's very easy for me** Newsom, "Governor Gavin Newsom Coronavirus Update Transcript: California Governor Holds Press Conference on Coronavirus," February 27, 2020.

31 **This narrowing window** Tedros Adhanom Ghebreyesus, "WHO Coronavirus Update Transcript February 27, 2020," Rev.com.

31 **The testing protocol** Newsom, "Governor Gavin Newsom Coronavirus Update Transcript: California Governor Holds Press Conference on Coronavirus," February 27, 2020.

31 **I think Maria** Michael Ryan, "WHO Coronavirus Update Transcript February 27, 2020."

31 **I just received a call** Jay Inslee, @JayInslee, Twitter, 11:09 P.M., February 27, 2020.

31 **Testing for Coronavirus** Caroline Chen, Marshall Allen, Lexi Churchill, and Isaac Arnsdorf: "Key Missteps at

the CDC Have Set Back Its Ability to Detect the Potential Spread of Coronavirus," ProPublica, February 28, 2020.

32 **As the highly infectious** Ibid.

32 **I'm going to South Carolina** Donald Trump, "Remarks by President Trump Before Marine One Departure," whitehouse.gov, February 28, 2020.

32 **The World Health Organization (WHO) has shipped** Jon Cohen, "United States Badly Bungled Coronavirus Testing—But Things May Soon Improve," *Science*, February 28, 2020.

32 **While there have been** Gretchen Whitmer, public statement, reported in "Governor Outlines Plan for Coronavirus Response," Woodtv .com, February 28, 2020.

33 **We took extraordinary steps** Interview at Conservative Political Action Conference (CPAC)

33 **There have been no deaths** Trump, "Remarks by President Trump Before Marine One Departure," February 28, 2020.

33 **Democrats have dangerously** Kelly Loeffler, @KLoeffler, Twitter, 2:20 P.M., February 20, 2020.

33 **Well, I think that the media** Donald Trump, "President Trump White House Departure," C-SPAN, February 28, 2020.

34 **To be prepared, you have** Andrew M. Cuomo, "Governor Cuomo Is a Guest on Long Island News Radio with Jay Oliver," February 24, 2020, rush transcript.

34 **Let me be clear** Kate Brown, public statement, "Governor Kate Brown Convenes Coronavirus Response Team," Oregon.gov, February 28, 2020.

34 **One of my people** Rally in South Carolina

35 **Today Public Health of** Jeff Duchin, "First Death Due to Novel Coronavirus (Covid-19) in a Resident of King County," King County, February 29, 2020.

35 **I know the news** Jay Inslee, ibid.

35 **We've taken the most** Donald Trump, "Remarks by President Trump, Vice President Pence, and Members of the Coronavirus Task Force in Press Conference," whitehouse.gov, February 29, 2020.

36 **And as the president** Mike Pence, ibid.

36 **At this moment we have** Donald Trump, ibid.

36 **The risk to any average** Alex Azar, ibid.

36 **We're going to continue** Robert Redfield, ibid.

36 **This evening we learned** Andrew Cuomo, "Governor Cuomo Issues Statement Regarding Novel Coronavirus in New York," March 1, 2020.

37 **The virus is not going** Interview at CPAC

37 **Here we have** Michael Ryan, "WHO Press Conference on Covid-19,"

World Health Organization, March 2, 2020.

37 **We're extrapolating from** Andrew Cuomo, "At Novel Coronavirus Briefing, Governor Cuomo Announces State Is Partnering with Hospitals to Expand Novel Coronavirus Testing Capacity in New York," March 2, 2020.

37 **We know that there's** Oxiris Barbot, "Transcript: Mayor de Blasio, Governor Cuomo Hold Media Availability on the First Confirmed Case of Coronavirus in New York State," nyc.gov, March 2, 2020.

38 **Though health officials have** Elisabeth Buchwald, "U.S. Health Officials Say Americans Shouldn't Wear Face Masks to Prevent Coronavirus—Here Are 3 Other Reasons Not to Wear Them," *MarketWatch*, March 2, 2020

38 **I remember once** Tedros Adhanom Ghebreyesus, "World Health Organization Briefing Update Transcript: March 2, 2020," Rev.com.

38 **At the present moment** Mike Pence, "Mike Pence Coronavirus Update Transcript: Pence & Task Force Hold Briefing," Rev.com.

38 **We spend quantums more** Ryan, "World Health Organization Briefing Update Transcript: March 2, 2020."

39 **The risk to the American** Robert Redfield, "Mike Pence Coronavirus Update Transcript: Pence & Task Force Hold Briefing," March 2, 2020.

39 **If you talk about** Anthony Fauci, "Mike Pence Coronavirus Update Transcript: Pence & Task Force Hold Briefing," March 2, 2020.

39 **I don't think you'll** Donald Trump, "Remarks by President Trump and Members of the Coronavirus Task Force in Meeting with Pharmaceutical Companies," whitehouse.gov, March 2, 2020.

40 **Around the world** Lamar Alexander, "CDC Official Testimony Transcript to Senate on Coronavirus," Rev.com, March 3, 2020.

40 **Over the weekend, multiple** Nancy Messonnier, "Transcript for the CDC Telebriefing Update on Covid-19," Centers for Disease Control and Prevention, March 3, 2020.

40 **WHO has no national** Michael Ryan, "WHO Coronavirus Update Transcript March 3, 2020." Rev.com.

41 **And as is so often** Patty Murray, "CDC Official Testimony Transcript to Senate on Coronavirus," March 3, 2020.

41 **We're obviously concerned** Paul Molinaro, "WHO-AUDIO Emergencies Coronavirus Press Conference 03 March 2020," World Health Organization.

41 **High percentages of hospitals** National Nurses United, "Press Conference to Release Results of National Nurse Survey About Covid-19 Preparedness," press release, March 4, 2020.

41 **This crisis highlights** Ibid.

42 **The administration has had months** Murray, "CDC Official Testimony Transcript to Senate on Coronavirus," March 3, 2020.

42 **I do think it's worth** Chris Murphy, "CDC Official Testimony Transcript to Senate on Coronavirus," March 3, 2020.

42 **We've heard so much misinformation** Tina Smith, "CDC Official Testimony Transcript to Senate on Coronavirus," March 3, 2020.

42 **There are always conspiracy** Anthony Fauci, "CDC Official Testimony Transcript to Senate on Coronavirus," March 3, 2020.

43 **There's a lot of partisan** Pat Roberts, "CDC Official Testimony Transcript to Senate on Coronavirus," March 3, 2020.

43 **This is a brand-new** Fauci, "CDC Official Testimony Transcript to Senate on Coronavirus," March 3, 2020.

43 **Should our flight attendants** Mitt Romney, "CDC Official Testimony Transcript to Senate on Coronavirus," March 3, 2020.

43 **The number of cases** Gavin Newsom, public statement, "California Governor Declares Statewide Emergency Due to Threat of New Coronavirus, Becoming Third US State to Do So," 23ABC News Bakersfield, March 4, 2020, and "Listen to Governor Newsom Make Emergency Proclamation and Find Out What That Means," *Sacramento Bee*, March 4, 2020.

44 **There is a lot of overlap** Andrew Cuomo, "Governor Cuomo Confirms 5 Additional Cases of Coronavirus in Westchester County, Bringing Statewide Total to 11," ny.gov, March 4, 2020.

44 **I know you're not supposed** Lois Frankel, "Anthony Fauci Testimony Transcript on NIH Budget Amid Coronavirus Outbreak," Rev.com, March 4, 2020.

44 **The current challenge** Tom Cole, ibid.

44 **Microsoft has asked** Ashley Stewart, "Microsoft Has Asked All Seattle and Bay Area Employees to Work from Home until March 25 Due to Coronavirus Fears," *Business Insider*, March 4, 2020.

45 **When the President says** Nancy Pelosi, "Nancy Pelosi Weekly News Conference Transcript: March 5, 2020," Rev.com.

45 **While other countries** Neel V. Patel, "Why the CDC Botched Its Coronavirus Testing," *MIT Technology Review*, March 5, 2020.

45 **Well, actually, we were given** Donald Trump, town hall, Fox News, March 5, 2020.

46 **We're very proud** Nancy Pelosi, "Nancy Pelosi Weekly News Conference Transcript: March 5, 2020," Rev .com, March 5, 2020.

46 **It's going to all** Trump, town hall, Fox News, March 5, 2020.

46 **So I told Mike not to be** Donald Trump, "Transcript: Donald Trump Visits CDC, Calls Jay Inslee a 'Snake,'" Rev.com, March 6, 2020.

46 **The City of Austin** "March 6, 2020: City of Austin Cancels SXSW March Events," South by Southwest.

47 **Once a contagious** Maria Morris, "Are Our Prisons and Jails Ready for Covid-19?" American Civil Liberties Union, March 6, 2020.

47 **They would like to have** Trump, "Transcript: Donald Trump Visits CDC, Calls Jay Inslee a 'Snake,'" March 6, 2020.

47 **As I said yesterday** Mike Pence, "Press Briefing by Vice President Pence and Members of the White House Coronavirus Task Force," whitehouse.gov, March 6, 2020.

48 **Anybody that wants a test** Trump, "Transcript: Donald Trump Visits CDC, Calls Jay Inslee a 'Snake,'" March 6, 2020.

48 ***The Atlantic* could only verify** Robinson Meyer and Alexis C. Madrigal, "Exclusive: The Strongest Evidence Yet That America Is Botching Coronavirus Testing," *Atlantic*, March 6, 2020.

48 **Total nonfarm payroll** "Employment Situation News Release," U.S. Bureau of Labor Statistics, March 6, 2020.

48 **The spread of the novel** Sarah Chaney, "Coronavirus Spread Could Halt Robust U.S. Job Gains," *Wall Street Journal*, March 6, 2020.

48 **Italy's government early** Jason Horowitz, "Italy Locks Down Much of the Country's North Over the Coronavirus," *New York Times*, March 7, 2020.

49 **As of February 19** Tim Killian, "Life Care Center Covid-19 Press Conference," Q13 Fox.

49 **No, [the testing system is]** Donald Trump, "Remarks by President Trump After Tour of the Centers for Disease Control and Prevention | Atlanta, GA." whitehouse.gov, March 7, 2020.

49 **You may not get** Alex Azar, "Anyone Who Wants a Coronavirus Test Can Have One, Trump Says. Not Quite, Says His Administration," *New York Times*, March 7, 2020.

49 **There were manufacturing** Stephen Hahn, "Coronavirus (Covid-19) Update: White House Press Briefing by FDA Commissioner Stephen M. Hahn, M.D.," U.S. Food & Drug Administration, March 7, 2020.

50 **We still have only** Robert Redfield, "Remarks by President Trump After Tour of the Centers for Disease Control and Prevention | Atlanta, GA," whitehouse.gov, March 7, 2020.

50 **The other confusion** MSNBC interview with David Gura.

50 **Sir** Press conference at Mar-a-Lago with Brazilian President Jair Bolsonaro.

51 **As of yesterday** Bill de Blasio, "Transcript: Mayor de Blasio Holds Media Availability on Covid-19," nyc.gov, March 8, 2020.

51 **We are trying to contain** Andrew Cuomo, "Governor Cuomo Confirms 16 Additional Coronavirus Cases in New York State—Bringing Statewide Total to 105," nystate.gov, March 8, 2020.

51 **I am about to sign** Giuseppe Conte, "Coronavirus Death Toll Tops 4,000 with Over 113,000 Confirmed Infections as Italy Goes into Nationwide Lockdown," *Democracy Now!*, March 10, 2020.

51 **Over the weekend we** Tedros Adhanom Ghebreyesus, "WHO Director-General's Opening Remarks at the Media Briefing on Covid-19—9 March 2020."

52 **Just minutes ago** John Bel Edwards, "Gov. Edwards' 2020 Regular Session Remarks," Office of the Governor, March 9, 2020.

52 **As I stand before you** Mike Pence, "Remarks by President Trump, Vice President Pence, and Members of the White House Coronavirus Task Force in Press Briefing," whitehouse.gov, March 9, 2020.

52 **We now have a total** Alex Azar, ibid.

52 **Nearly two weeks after** Robinson Meyer and Alexis C. Madrigal, "The Dangerous Delays in U.S. Coronavirus Testing Haven't Stopped," *Atlantic*, March 9, 2020.

52 **So last year** Donald Trump, @realDonaldTrump, Twitter, 10:47 A.M., March 9, 2020.

52 **Certainly a lot** Bill de Blasio, "Transcript: Mayor de Blasio Updates New Yorkers on City's Covid-19 Response," nyc.gov, March 9, 2020.

53 **Think about the insanity** Rally in St. Louis, Missouri. (Sen. Sanders was running for the Democratic Presidential nomination at the time. He would drop out April 8.)

53 **This was something** Donald Trump, "Remarks by President Trump After Meeting with Republican Senators," whitehouse.gov, March 10, 2020.

53 **Thousands have died** Hakeem Jeffries, @RepJeffries, Twitter, 2:38 P.M., March 10, 2020.

53 **The Executive Office for Immigration** Subcommittee on Labor, Health and Human Services, Education, and Related Agencies Appropriations Hearing regarding coronavirus budget.

54 **We obviously got first** Ibid.

54 **I'm very concerned** Ibid.

54 **As of this morning,** Anthony Fauci, "Press Briefing by Vice President Pence and Members of the Coronavirus Task Force," whitehouse.gov, March 10, 2020.

55 **As of noon Pacific** Alex Azar, ibid.

55 **Know your circumstances** Jerome Adams, ibid.

55 **As the President said** Mike Pence, ibid.

55 **I mean I think** Fauci, ibid.

56 **Let me just say** Larry Kudlow, ibid.

56 **We have 173 cases** Andrew Cuomo.

56 **Well, look, as the President** Mike Pence, "Press Briefing by Vice President Pence and Members of the Coronavirus Task Force," March 10, 2020.

56 **The period would be from** Andrew Cuomo, "Governor Cuomo Accepts Recommendation of State Health Commissioner for New Emergency Measures to Contain Novel Coronavirus Cluster in New Rochelle," ny.gov, March 10, 2020.

57 **In the past two weeks** Tedros Adhanom Ghebreyesus, "WHO Director-General's Opening Remarks at the Media Briefing on Covid-19–11 March 2020," World Health Organization.

57 **When the virus is** Angela Merkel, reported in Paul Carrel and Thomas Escritt, "Two-thirds of Germans May Get Coronavirus, Merkel Says," Reuters, March 11, 2020.

58 **Was it a mistake** House Committee on Oversight and Government Reform Hearing on Coronavirus Response.

58 **We are worse off** Peter Bergen, "The Disease Expert Who Warned Us," CNN Opinion, March 11, 2020.

58 **Governor Inslee has ordered** Dow Constantine, "Inslee Issues Emergency Proclamation That Limits Large Events to Minimize Public Health Risk during Covid-19," March 11, 2020.

58 **You don't get this disease** Bill de Blasio, "Transcript: Mayor de Blasio Hosts Roundtable for Ethnic and Community Media on Covid-19," nyc.gov, March 11, 2020.

59 **While the risk to** Andrew Cuomo, "During Novel Coronavirus Briefing, Governor Cuomo Announces New York State Will Contract with 28 Private Labs to Increase Coronavirus Testing Capacity," ny.gov, March 11, 2020.

59 **Nearly 80 million** "Congress Must Strengthen First Responder Designation and Paid Leave," UFCW for Local Unions blog, March 16, 2020.

59 **I think you set** House Committee on Oversight and Reform Hearing

60 **Chicken Little has** Matt Bevin, @MattBevin, Twitter, 5:35 P.M., March 11, 2020.

60 **Mayor London N. Breed** Office of the Mayor, "San Francisco Issues Moratorium on Gatherings of 100 or More to Slow Spread of Covid-19," news release, March 13, 2020.

60 **Due to escalating concerns** Golden State Warriors, @warriors, Twitter, 2:10 P.M., March 11, 2020.

60 **Taking early intense** Donald Trump, "Remarks by President Trump in Address to the Nation," whitehouse.gov, March 11, 2020.

61 **Today, President Donald J. Trump** Department of Homeland Security, "Homeland Security Acting Secretary Chad F. Wolf's Statement on

Presidential Proclamation to Protect the Homeland from Travel-Related Coronavirus Spread," March 11, 2020.

61 **We have today again** Mike DeWine, @GovMikeDeWine, Twitter, 2:48 P.M., 2;49 P.M., 2:50 P.M., 2:50 P.M., 3:14 P.M., March 12, 2020.

61 **The logic here** "Mayor Fulop Signs Executive Order to Proactively Establish a Curfew on Liquor Establishments to Control Crowds at Bars and Nightclubs," press release, Insider N.J., March 12, 2020, and Tom Bergeron, "Fulop Urges Taking Attendance at Private Events in Case Coronavirus Is Linked to Gathering," ROI-NJ.com, March 12, 2020.

62 **I said yesterday** Mike Duggan, "Mayor Duggan's Covid-19 Update: March 12, 2020," City of Detroit, Channel 21.

62 **The system is not** Anthony Fauci, "Fauci Testifies Coronavirus Testing System 'Not Really Geared to What We Need Right Now,'" House Committee on Oversight and Reform, March 12, 2020.

62 **They have a million** "Remarks by President Trump and Prime Minister Varadkar of Ireland Before Bilateral Meeting," White House Remarks, March 12, 2020.

62 **As of March 11** Alice Park, "Why It's So Hard to Get Coronavirus Testing in the U.S. Right Now," *Time*, March 12, 2020.

63 **Our system has** Haley Byrd, Lauren Fox, Manu Raju, and Ted Barrett, "'We Are Flying Blind': Lawmakers Fume Amid Lack of Coronavirus Testing and Answers," CNN.com, March 12, 2020.

63 **I am appalled** Ibid.

63 **One of the reasons why** Senate Small Business and Entrepreneurship Committee Hearing.

63 **These are extraordinary** Alexandre de Juniac, "IATA Warns US-EU Market Restrictions 'Will Create Enormous Cash-Flow Pressures for Airlines,'" Aviation Agency, March 12, 2020.

63 **While there have been** Disney World Resorts, press release.

64 **U.S. stocks plunged** Caitlin McCabe and Caitlin Ostroff, "Stocks Plunge 10% in Dow's Worst Day Since 1987," *Wall Street Journal*, March 12, 2020.

64 **To unleash the full power** Donald Trump, "Remarks by President Trump, Vice President Pence, and Members of the Coronavirus Task Force in Press Conference," whitehouse.gov, March 13, 2020.

64 **Sadly and prayerfully** Nancy Pelosi, "Pelosi Remarks on the Families First Coronavirus Response Act," press release, March 13, 2020.

64 **Senate Majority Leader** Colby Itkowitz, "McConnell Absent as Pelosi, White House Reach Deal on Coronavirus Economic Relief Package," *Washington Post*, March 13, 2020.

64 **Today we are announcing** Trump, "Remarks by President Trump, Vice President Pence, and Members of the Coronavirus Task Force in Press Conference," March 13, 2020.

65 **After you tapped me** Mike Pence, ibid.

65 **U.S. Tests as of** The Covid Tracking Project at the *Atlantic*, March 13, 2020.

65 **Google is helping** Trump, "Remarks by President Trump, Vice President Pence, and Members of the Coronavirus Task Force in Press Conference," March 13, 2020.

66 **The containment, the mitigation** Anthony Fauci, ibid.

66 **Dr. Fauci said** Kristen Welker and Donald Trump, ibid.

66 **If you go back to the Swine** Donald Trump, ibid.

67 **My first question** Yamiche Alcindor and Donald Trump, ibid.

68 **On March 11, 2020** Pedro Sánchez, Universidad de Las Palmas de Gran Canaria, March 17, 2020.

68 **From my point of view** Andrew Cuomo, "Governor Cuomo Gives Novel Coronavirus Briefing," ny.gov, March 14, 2020.

68 **I was honored** Donald Trump, "Remarks by President Trump, Vice President Pence, and Members of the Coronavirus Task Force in Press Briefing," whitehouse.gov, March 14, 2020.

THE LOCKDOWN

71 **I think Americans should** Anthony Fauci, *Meet the Press*, March 15, 2020.

71 **We are calling for** Gavin Newsom, "California Governor Gavin Newsom Coronavirus Press Conference: Announces Closure of Bars Across State," Rev.com, March 15, 2020.

71 **This is a decision** Bill de Blasio, "Mayor de Blasio Holds Media Availability on Covid-19," nyc.gov, March 15, 2020.

72 **Number two, we are** Newsom, "California Governor Gavin Newsom Coronavirus Press Conference: Announces Closure of Bars Across State," March 15, 2020.

72 **Eating with my kids** Zack Budryk, "Oklahoma Governor Will Continue to 'Take His Family Out to Dinner' Amid Pandemic," *The Hill*, March 16, 2020.

72 **There's a lot of concerns** Devin Nunes, interview with Maria Bartiromo. "Rep. Nunes on National Emergency, Congressional Response to Coronavirus," Fox News, March 15, 2020.

72 **In the (unlikely) absence** Neil M. Ferguson et al, "Report 9: Impact of Non-Pharmaceutical Interventions (Npis) to Reduce Covid-19 Mortality and Healthcare Demand," Imperial College Covid-19 Response Team, March 16, 2020.

73 **So, we had new** Deborah Birx, "Remarks by President Trump, Vice President Pence, and Members of the Coronavirus Task Force in Press Briefing," whitehouse.gov, March 16, 2020.

73 **Social distancing is** University of Washington (UW) Health, Facebook video.

73 **You cannot fight** Tedros Adhanom Ghebreyesus, "WHO Director-General's Opening Remarks at the Media Briefing on Covid-19—16 March 2020," World Health Organization.

73 **Every American adult** Mitt Romney, "Romney Calls for Urgent Action on Additional Coronavirus Response Measures," press release, March 16, 2020.

74 **Remember those snow globe** Andrew Cuomo, "During Coronavirus Briefing, Governor Cuomo Calls for National Unity in Face of Historic Coronavirus Pandemic," ny.gov, March 17, 2020.

74 **I've always known this is a** Donald Trump, "Remarks by President Trump, Vice President Pence, and Members of the Coronavirus Task Force in Press Briefing," whitehouse .gov, March 17, 2020.

74 **I said to the President** Cuomo, "During Coronavirus Briefing, Governor Cuomo Calls for National Unity in Face of Historic Coronavirus Pandemic," March 17, 2020.

74 **I think our economy** Trump, "Remarks by President Trump, Vice President Pence, and Members of the Coronavirus Task Force in Press Briefing," March 17, 2020.

75 **Is it three months?** Cuomo, "During Coronavirus Briefing, Governor Cuomo Calls for National Unity in Face of Historic Coronavirus Pandemic," March 17, 2020.

75 **If you look at a swine flu** Trump, "Remarks by President Trump, Vice President Pence, and Members of the Coronavirus Task Force in Press Briefing," March 17, 2020.

75 **There is something to this** Cuomo, "During Coronavirus Briefing, Governor Cuomo Calls for National Unity in Face of Historic Coronavirus Pandemic," March 17, 2020.

75 **By the way, for the markets** Trump, "Remarks by President Trump, Vice President Pence, and Members of the Coronavirus Task Force in Press Briefing," March 17, 2020.

76 **Realize the time frame** Cuomo, "During Coronavirus Briefing, Governor Cuomo Calls for National Unity in Face of Historic Coronavirus Pandemic," March 17, 2020.

76 **I don't think in terms of** Trump, "Remarks by President Trump, Vice President Pence, and Members of the Coronavirus Task Force in Press Briefing," March 17, 2020.

76 **This is an extraordinary** Cuomo, "During Coronavirus Briefing,

Governor Cuomo Calls for National Unity in Face of Historic Coronavirus Pandemic," March 17, 2020.

76 **Our task force** Mike Pence, "Remarks by President Trump, Vice President Pence, and Members of the Coronavirus Task Force in Press Briefing," March 17, 2020.

77 **Frankly, we're focused** J. B. Pritzker, "Illinois Governor J. B. Pritzker Coronavirus News Conference Transcript," Rev.com, March 17, 2020.

77 **We've ordered a massive** Trump, "Remarks by President Trump, Vice President Pence, and Members of the Coronavirus Task Force in Press Briefing," March 17, 2020.

77 **I can tell you** Larry Hogan, "Transcript: Covid-19 Press Conference March 17," Southern Maryland Online, March 19, 2020.

77 **Since German unification—no** Angela Merkel, reported in Justin Davidson, "The Leader of the Free World Gives a Speech, and She Nails It," *New York* magazine, March 18, 2020.

78 **There are people right** Gretchen Whitmer, "Michigan Governor Gretchen Whitmer Coronavirus News Briefing Transcript," Rev.com, March 18, 2020.

78 **I would like to begin** Donald Trump, "Remarks by President Trump, Vice President Pence, and Members of the Coronavirus Task Force in Press Briefing," whitehouse.gov, March 18, 2020.

78 **We know that something** Jay Inslee, "Washington Governor Jay Inslee Coronavirus Update March 18," Rev .com, March 18, 2020.

78 **You might not get** Suzy Khimm, "Who Gets a Ventilator? Hospitals Facing Coronavirus Surge Are Preparing for Life-Or-Death Decisions," NBC News, March 18, 2020.

79 **Based on our information** Justine Coleman, "Health Official: One Person Dying Every 10 Minutes from Coronavirus in Iran," *The Hill*, March 19, 2020.

79 **China has exonerated** "China Exonerates Doctor Reprimanded for Warning of Virus," Associated Press, March 19, 2020.

79 **I have to say I think** Trump, "Remarks by President Trump, Vice President Pence, and Members of the Coronavirus Task Force in Press Briefing," March 18, 2020.

79 **I really thought that we** London Breed, "San Francisco Mayor London Breed Coronavirus Briefing Transcript," Rev.com, March 19, 2020.

80 **First of all, governors are** Trump, "Remarks by President Trump, Vice President Pence, and Members of the Coronavirus Task Force in Press Briefing," March 18, 2020.

80 **I think every governor** Charlie Baker, "Massachusetts Governor Charlie

Baker March 19 Coronavirus Update," Rev.com, March 19, 2020.

80 **I have to say if chloroquine** Trump, "Remarks by President Trump, Vice President Pence, and Members of the Coronavirus Task Force in Press Briefing," March 18, 2020.

80 **Look, I haven't seen** Baker, "Massachusetts Governor Charlie Baker March 19 Coronavirus Update," Rev .com, March 19, 2020.

81 **The number one opportunity** Andrew Cuomo, "Andrew Cuomo Orders New York 'On Pause': Transcript of March 20 Briefing," Rev.com, March 20, 2020.

81 **We can say 10,000** Michael Ryan, "World Health Organization March 20 Coronavirus Briefing Transcript: Warn Health Systems Are 'Collapsing' under Covid-19," Rev .com, March 20, 2020.

81 **We've gotten a hundred** Andy Grimm, "Public Defender: Release Cook County Jail Inmates Who Aren't a Threat," *Chicago Sun-Times*, March 20, 2020.

82 **We're going to be talking** Donald Trump, "Remarks by President Trump, Vice President Pence, and Members of the Coronavirus Task Force in Press Briefing," whitehouse .gov, March 20, 2020.

82 **What do you say** Peter Alexander and Donald Trump, ibid.

82 **Stay home, save lives** Jacinda Ardern, "Prime Minister Jacinda Ardern Statement to the Nation on Covid-19, March 21," RNZ.

83 **Italy, at the heart** "The Latest: Japan Urges Against Nonessential Travel to US," Associated Press, March 22, 2020.

83 **What is happening** Gary Fineout, Alexandra Glorioso, and Ben Schreckinger, "Will Spring Breakers Become Super-spreaders?" *Politico*, March 21, 2020.

83 **As the number of** Robin Foster and E. J. Mundell, "U.S. Coronavirus Cases Pass 26,000, with 1 in 4 Americans under 'Shelter-in-Place' Orders," *U.S. News and World Report*, March 22, 2020.

83 **I'm really happy** Donald Trump, "Remarks by President Trump, Vice President Pence, and Members of the Coronavirus Task Force in Press Briefing," whitehouse.gov, March 22, 2020.

83 **Extreme measures to flatten** Lloyd Blankfein, @lloydblankfein, Twitter, 9:59 P.M., March 22, 2020.

84 **Today I'm issuing a stay** John Bel Edwards, "Louisiana Governor Issues Statewide 'Stay at Home' Order," Associated Press, March 22, 2020.

84 **WE CANNOT LET** Donald Trump, @realDonaldTrump, Twitter, 11:50 P.M., March 22, 2020.

84 **This is a war on** Amy Acton, reported in "Editorial: This Is a Character Test," *Roanoke Times*, March 24, 2020.

84 **The pandemic is accelerating** Tedros Adhanom Ghebreyesus, "WHO Director-General's Opening Remarks at the Media Briefing on Covid-19—23 March 2020," World Health Organization.

84 **We know that the** Andrew Capps, "Louisiana Experiences Fastest Covid-19 Case Increase in The World in First Weeks," *Lafayette Daily Advertiser*, March 24, 2020.

84 **It is outrageous** National Nurses United, "Nurses Send Petition to Congress Demanding Immediate Protections During Covid-19 Outbreak," press release, March 23, 2020.

85 **And you know, Tucker** Dan Patrick, interview with Tucker Carlson, Fox News, March 23, 2020.

85 **In just 13 days** Gretchen Whitmer, "Michigan Governor Gretchen Whitmer Coronavirus Briefing Transcript March 23," Rev.com, March 23, 2020.

86 **And we're going to be opening** Fox Town Hall event

86 **There will be no** Liz Cheney, @Liz_Cheney, Twitter, 10:30 A.M., March 24, 2020.

86 **The question of whether** Gavin Newsom, "Governor Gavin Newsom of California Coronavirus Briefing Transcript March 24," Rev.com, March 24, 2020.

86 **Look: Easter's a very** Fox News interview

87 **What we're seeing at Rikers** Josiah Bates, "'We Feel Like All of Us Are Gonna Get Corona.' Anticipating Covid-19 Outbreaks, Rikers Island Offers Warning for U.S. Jails, Prisons," *Time*, March 24, 2020.

87 **New York City jails** Ibid.

87 **After sleep-deprived** Chuck Schumer, "Schumer Floor Remarks Announcing Bipartisan Agreement on Coronavirus Response Legislation That Puts Workers and Public Health First," Senate Democrats, March 25, 2020.

87 **We remain very concerned** Jennifer Avegno, reported in Patrick Madden and Ashley Dean, "New Orleans Officials Point to Increasing Spread of Covid-19 Cases," NPR, March 27, 2020.

87 **The first case confirmed** John Bel Edwards, reported in Greg Hilburn, "Coronavirus: Gov. John Bel Edwards Believes Mardi Gras Elevated Infection in Louisiana," *Monroe News-Star*, March 24, 2020.

88 **Now you have to** Andrew Cuomo, "Amid Ongoing Covid-19 Pandemic, Governor Cuomo Announces 40,000 Health Professionals Have Signed Up to Volunteer as Part of the State's Surge Healthcare Force," ny.gov, March 25, 2020.

88 **Sir, lawmakers and economists** Paula Reid and Donald Trump, "Remarks by President Trump, Vice President Pence, and Members of

the Coronavirus Task Force in Press Briefing," whitehouse.gov, March 25, 2020

89 **[President Trump] has been so attentive** Interview with Christian Broadcast Network

89 **We need substantially** Kate Brown.

89 **The second answer is** Cuomo, "Amid Ongoing Covid-19 Pandemic, Governor Cuomo Announces 40,000 Health Professionals Have Signed Up to Volunteer as Part of the State's Surge Healthcare Force," March 25, 2020.

90 **I have no doubt** Joe Biden, "Joe Biden Coronavirus Online News Conference Transcript," Rev.com, March 25, 2020.

90 **I can see how New Yorkers** Cuomo, "Amid Ongoing Covid-19 Pandemic, Governor Cuomo Announces 40,000 Health Professionals Have Signed Up to Volunteer as Part of the State's Surge Healthcare Force," March 25, 2020.

90 **Although both countries** Kimberly Hickock, "No, the US Has Not Tested More People in 8 Days Than South Korea Did in 8 Weeks," Live Science, March 26, 2020.

90 **Widespread diagnostic testing** Elizabeth Warren, "Medium Post: Congress Must Move to Rapidly Increase Our Coronavirus Testing Capacity," warren .senate.gov, March 26, 2020.

91 **It is with deep sadness** Lori Bassani, reported in Herb Scribner, "An American Airlines Flight Attendant Died of Coronavirus. Now, Industry Experts Are Worried," *Deseret News*, March 27, 2020.

91 **The federal government's** Jesse Drucker, "Bonanza for Rich Real Estate Investors, Tucked into Stimulus Package," *New York Times*, March 26, 2020.

91 **It's wrong. It's outrageous** Muriel Bowser, in "Bowser Slams D.C. Aid Package," ABC 7 WJLA and Associated Press, March 26, 2020.

92 **No, we're not going** Charlie Baker, "Massachusetts Governor Baker Coronavirus News Conference," C-SPAN, March 27, 2020.

92 **We have now lost** Phil Murphy, "Transcript: March 27th, 2020 Coronavirus Briefing Media," nj.gov, March 28, 2020.

92 **We've had great success.** Donald Trump, "Remarks by President Trump, Vice President Pence, and Members of the Coronavirus Task Force in Press Briefing," whitehouse .gov, March 28, 2020.

92 **The US now has** "Coronavirus: US Overtakes China with Most Cases," BBC, March 27, 2020.

92 **I mentioned at the end of my** Murphy, "Transcript: March 27th, 2020 Coronavirus Briefing Media," March 28, 2020.

93 **I represent one of** Alexandria Ocasio-Cortez, "House Debate on

Coronavirus Economic Relief Bill," C-SPAN, March 27, 2020

93 **Government can do some** Denver Riggleman, ibid

93 **The House just passed** Hakeem Jeffries, @RepJeffries, Twitter, 1:37 P.M., March 27, 2020.

94 **I think they [Democratic governors] should be** Trump, "Remarks by President Trump, Vice President Pence, and Members of the Coronavirus Task Force in Press Briefing," March 28, 2020.

94 **25,573 cases in** Bill de Blasio, "Transcript: Mayor de Blasio Holds Media Availability on Covid-19," nyc.gov, March 27, 2020.

94 **So look, hydroxychloroquine** Trump, "Remarks by President Trump, Vice President Pence, and Members of the Coronavirus Task Force in Press Briefing," March 28, 2020.

94 **[I] want to take a moment** de Blasio, "Transcript: Mayor de Blasio Holds Media Availability on Covid-19," March 27, 2020.

95 **Boy, I follow a lot** Charlie Baker, "Massachusetts Governor Charlie Baker Press Conference Transcript March 27," Rev.com, March 27, 2020.

95 **Just finished a very** Donald Trump, @realDonaldTrump, Twitter, 1:19 A.M., March 27, 2020.

95 **On Friday at 7 P.M.** Jen Carlson, "Videos: New Yorkers Are Clapping for the Helpers," *Gothamist*, March 28, 2020.

96 **When we discussed** Trump, "Remarks by President Trump, Vice President Pence, and Members of the Coronavirus Task Force in Press Briefing," March 28, 2020.

96 **The Covid-19 Outbreak** Matt Berger, "How South Korea Successfully Battled Covid-19 While the U.S. Didn't," Healthline, March 30, 2020.

96 **US Cases 139,099** Johns Hopkins Coronavirus Resource Center, March 29, 2020.

96 **Because the "Ratings"** Donald Trump, @realDonaldTrump, Twitter, 1:06 P.M., March 29, 2020.

97 **The environment** Brett Crozier, letter printed in Matthias Gafni and Joe Garofoli, "Exclusive: Captain of Aircraft Carrier with Growing Coronavirus Outbreak Pleads for Help from Navy," *San Francisco Chronicle*, March 31, 2020.

97 **Most impacted states** Andrew Cuomo, "Governor Andrew Cuomo New York Covid-19 Press Conference Transcript March 30," Rev.com, March 30, 2020.

97 **It is disgraceful** Letitia James, "AG James' Statement on Firing of Amazon Worker Who Organized Walkout," press release, New York Office of the Attorney General, March 30, 2020.

98 **Let me just make my plea** Sylvester Turner, reported in Michael Berry, "Mayor Turner to Criminals: 'Chill' &

'Wait Until' the Pandemic Is Over," AM740 KTRH, March 31, 2020.

98 **The nationwide Janta Curfew** "Impact of Janta Curfew & Lockdown on Air Quality," India Environment Portal, March 31, 2020.

98 **One of the [pieces of] information** Sam Whitehead and Carrie Feibel, "CDC Director on Models for the Months to Come: 'This Virus Is Going to Be with Us,'" NPR, March 31, 2020.

98 **I want every American** Donald Trump, "Remarks by President Trump, Vice President Pence, and Members of the Coronavirus Task Force in Press Briefing," March 31, 2020, transcript issued April 1, 2020.

98 **Due to the closure of** "Temporary Homeless Shelter to Open at Cashman Center," City of Las Vegas, Nevada, March 30, 2020.

99 **The marked squares** Jace Radke, reported in Ed Komenda, "Las Vegas Homeless Forced to Sleep in Painted Squares for 'Social Distancing Requirements,'" *Reno Gazette Journal*, March 31, 2020.

99 **I've had many friends** Donald Trump, "Donald Trump Coronavirus Task Force Briefing Transcript March 31: 'Painful' Weeks Ahead," Rev.com, March 31, 2020.

99 **In general, I am tired** Andrew Cuomo, "Amid Ongoing Covid-19 Pandemic, Governor Cuomo Announces New Hospital Network Central Coordinating Team," ny.gov, March 31, 2020.

99 **In a perfect world** Anthony Fauci, "Remarks by President Trump, Vice President Pence, and Members of the Coronavirus Task Force in Press Briefing," March 31, 2020.

99 **And also we need a social** Cuomo, "Amid Ongoing Covid-19 Pandemic, Governor Cuomo Announces New Hospital Network Central Coordinating Team," March 31, 2020.

100 **15 days ago we published** Trump, "Donald Trump Coronavirus Task Force Briefing Transcript March 31: 'Painful' Weeks Ahead," March 31, 2020.

100 **So you have** Andrew Cuomo, "Governor Andrew Cuomo NY Covid-19 Briefing Transcript March 31: Discusses His Brother Chris Cuomo's Coronavirus Diagnosis," Rev.com, March 31, 2020.

100 **Coronavirus Death Toll, United States** "Americans Warned That as Many as 240,000 May Die," NBC News, April 1, 2020.

101 **Simply. Stop. Moving** Silveria Jacobs, April 1, 2020 speech, reported in Jennifer Hassan and Siobhan O'Grady, "Female World Leaders Hailed as Voices of Reason Amid the Coronavirus Chaos," *Washington Post*, April 20, 2020.

101 **Over the past 48 hours** Brian Kemp, "Governor Brian Kemp Georgia Covid-19 Briefing Transcript:

Shelter-in-Place Ordered, Schools Closed for the School Year," Rev.com, April 1, 2020.

101 **Yeah, that's not going to work** Devin Nunes, "Nunes: US Must Focus More on Employment Numbers During Coronavirus Contagion," Fox News, April 1, 2020.

101 **To drive down the street** Rhonda Colvin, "Rep. Karen Bass on What Concerns Her Most About Coronavirus in Los Angeles," *Washington Post*, April 1, 2020.

102 **Let me just put on** Phil Murphy, "Transcript: April 1st, 2020 Coronavirus Briefing Media," nj.gov, April 1, 2020.

102 **It's social media** Donald Trump, "Donald Trump Coronavirus Task Force Briefing Transcripts April 1," Rev.com, April 1, 2020.

102 **The new documents** Carolyn Maloney, in House Committee on Oversight and Reform, "New FEMA Documents Show Critical Shortages of Medical Supplies," press release, April 2, 2020.

103 **So, it's a very simple** Jared Kushner, "Remarks by President Trump, Vice President Pence, and Members of the Coronavirus Task Force in Press Briefing," whitehouse.gov, April 3, 2020.

103 **More beds will still** Charlie Baker, "Massachusetts Gov Charlie Baker Covid-19 Briefing April 2," Rev.com, April 2, 2020.

103 **What a lot of the voters** Jared Kushner, "Remarks by President Trump, Vice President Pence, and Members of the Coronavirus Task Force in Press Briefing," whitehouse .gov, April 3, 2020.

103 **We have repeatedly requested** Marilyn Sudders, "Massachusetts Gov Charlie Baker Covid-19 Briefing April 2," April 2, 2020.

104 **You also have a situation** Kushner, "Remarks by President Trump, Vice President Pence, and Members of the Coronavirus Task Force in Press Briefing," April 3, 2020.

104 **Senator Menendez and I** Cory Booker, "NJ Senators Cory Booker and Bob Menendez Covid-19 Press Conference April 2," Rev.com, April 2, 2020.

104 **The President must act** Carolyn Maloney, in House Committee on Oversight and Reform, "New FEMA Documents Show Critical Shortages of Medical Supplies," April 2, 2020.

105 **It is critical** Letter to HHS Secretary Alex Azar. Other Democratic lawmakers signed onto the letter.

105 **Two months before the novel** Emily Baumgaertner and James Rainey, "Trump Administration Ended Early Warning Pandemic Program to Detect Coronaviruses," *Los Angeles Times*, April 2, 2020.

105 **Our country is in crisis** Alphonso David, reported in Lucas Acosta,

"HRC Responds to Trump Refusing to Reopen Obamacare Exchanges," Human Rights Campaign, April 2, 2020.

106 **We are the wealthiest country** Cory Booker, "NJ Senators Cory Booker and Bob Menendez Covid-19 Press Conference April 2," April 2, 2020.

106 **On Monday we announced** Marty Walsh, "Boston Mayor Marty Walsh Covid-19 Briefing April 2," Rev.com, April 2, 2020.

106 **Let us try** Pope Francis, "In Video, Pope Greets Families at 'Difficult,' 'Unusual' Time," Catholic News Service, April 4, 2020.

106 **So with the masks** Trump, "Remarks by President Trump, Vice President Pence, and Members of the Coronavirus Task Force in Press Briefing," April 3, 2020.

107 **Many of the ways** David Scharfenberg, "A Quarter Million Americans Could Die from the Coronavirus. Maybe More. How Do We Absorb That Much Death?" *Boston Globe*, April 3, 2020.

107 **In March, the unemployment rate** "Employment Situation News Release," U.S. Bureau of Labor Statistics. April 3, 2020.

107 **No. Me sign?** Trump, "Remarks by President Trump, Vice President Pence, and Members of the Coronavirus Task Force in Press Briefing," April 3, 2020.

107 **A federal TSA employee** Transportation Security Administration, "Statement on the Passing of First Federal TSA Employee to Pass Away Due to Covid-19," press release, April 3, 2020.

108 **A rapidly escalating** Filed in class action lawsuit against Cook County Sheriff Thomas Dart on the conditions and Covid risks at Cook County Jail, Chicago, Illinois.

108 **The previous administration** Trump, "Remarks by President Trump, Vice President Pence, and Members of the Coronavirus Task Force in Press Briefing," April 3, 2020.

108 **More than once** D'Angelo Gore, "Trump Falsely Claims He Inherited 'Empty' Stockpile," Factcheck.org, April 3, 2020.

109 **As the disease spread** Akilah Johnson and Talia Buford, "Early Data Shows African Americans Have Contracted and Died of Coronavirus at an Alarming Rate," ProPublica, April 3, 2020.

109 **I came to NIH** Anthony Fauci, "Remarks by President Trump, Vice President Pence, and Members of the Coronavirus Task Force in Press Briefing," April 4, 2020, transcript issued April 5, 2020.

109 **And I hope they** Donald Trump, ibid.

110 **Personal opinion, look** Andrew Cuomo, "Andrew Cuomo Covid-19 Briefing Transcript April 4: China

Donating 1,000 Ventilators to NY," Rev.com, April 4, 2020.

110 **Remember Washington State** Fauci, "Remarks by President Trump, Vice President Pence, and Members of the Coronavirus Task Force in Press Briefing," April 4, 2020.

110 **Since Chinese officials** Steve Eder, Henry Fountain, Michael H. Keller, Muyi Xiao, and Alexandra Stevenson, "430,000 People Have Traveled from China to U.S. Since Coronavirus Surfaced," *New York Times*, April 4, 2020.

110 **I don't know much about** Donald Trump, "Remarks by President Trump, Vice President Pence, and Members of the Coronavirus Task Force in Press Briefing," April 4, 2020.

111 **Across the Commonwealth** Queen Elizabeth II, "Queen Elizabeth II Coronavirus Speech Transcript," Rev .com, April 5, 2020.

111 **Given the surge** Federal Bureau of Prisons, "Update on Covid-19 and Home Confinement," April 5, 2020.

111 **Like everyone, this is a challenging** Gretchen Whitmer, "Michigan Governor Whitmer Coronavirus News Conference," C-SPAN, April 6, 2020.

112 **This Administration's alarming** Kristen Clarke, reported in Reis Thebault, Andrew Ba Tran, and Vanessa Williams, "The Coronavirus Is Infecting and Killing Black Americans at an Alarmingly High Rate," *Washington Post*, April 7, 2020.

112 **Disturbingly, this information** John Bel Edwards, reported in Jason Lemon, "70 Percent of Coronavirus Deaths in Louisiana Are African Americans, Despite Being 33 Percent of the Population," *Newsweek*, April 7, 2020.

112 **Chronic Absenteeism is** Dana Goldstein, Adam Popescu, and Nikole Hannah-Jones, "As School Moves Online, Many Students Stay Logged Out," *New York Times*, April 8, 2020.

112 **States can do their own testing** Donald Trump, "Remarks by President Trump, Vice President Pence, and Members of the Coronavirus Task Force in Press Briefing," April 6, 2020, transcript issued April 7, 2020.

113 **The White House is just simply** Elizabeth Warren, "Elizabeth Warren Has a Plan for This, Too," *The Ezra Klein Podcast*, April 6, 2020.

113 **While fighting Covid-19** Gretchen Whitmer, "Gretchen Whitmer Michigan Covid-19 Briefing Transcript April 6," Rev.com, April 6, 2020.

114 **Due to the overwhelming demand** "Locations for Unemployment Forms," City of Hialeah, April 6, 2020.

114 **We're heard stories** Whitmer, "Gretchen Whitmer Michigan Covid-19 Briefing Transcript April 6," April 6, 2020.

114 **People at home. You are** Amy Acton, "Covid-19 in Ohio: Dr. Amy Acton Provides Update on Coronavirus Cases," WBNS 10 TV, April 6, 2020.

114 **Today, I signed an executive** Tony Evers, "Gov. Evers Suspends In-Person Voting," *On Focus*, April 6, 2020.

115 **Wisconsin has decided** United States Supreme Court Ruling, Majority Opinion, reported in Adam Liptak, "Supreme Court Blocks Extended Voting in Wisconsin," *New York Times*, April 6, 2020.

115 **Tomorrow in Wisconsin** Tony Evers, "Gov. Evers Statement on Supreme Court of Wisconsin Ruling Allowing In-Person Voting Tomorrow," press release, Office of the Governor, State of Wisconsin, April 6, 2020.

115 **It is unconscionable** Josh Gerstein, "Liberals Recoil at SCOTUS' Wisconsin Primary Decision," *Politico*, April 7, 2020. (Ifill released a near identical statement on Twitter).

115 **The city has only** "Election Day Blog Recap: Milwaukee Releases Tuesday's Voter Turnout; Late Lines After Polls Closed," *Milwaukee Journal Sentinel*, April 7, 2020.

116 **People seem to literally** Ibid.

116 **We have moved forward with an election** "State Debate: 'We Moved Forward with an Election, But We Haven't Moved Forward with Democracy,' Election Official Says," Madison.com, April 8, 2020.

116 **We want to look into it** Donald Trump, "Remarks by President Trump, Vice President Pence, and Members of the Coronavirus Task Force in Press Briefing," whitehouse .gov, April 7, 2020.

116 **So far, we've been talking** Roge Karma, "Michael Lewis Explains How the Trump Administration Puts Us All at Risk of Catastrophe," *Vox*, April 7, 2020.

116 **An apparent wiring short** Jim Shay and John Nickerson, "Fire Erupts from Crematorium at Stamford Funeral Home," *Stamford Advocate*, April 7, 2020.

117 **Since the Covid-19 crisis** Lori Lightfoot, "Chicago Mayor Lori Lightfoot Press Conference Transcript April 7," Rev.com, April 7, 2020.

117 **I know a lot of people** Eric Garcetti, "Los Angeles Mayor Eric Garcetti Covid-19 Briefing Transcript April 7," Rev.com, April 7, 2020.

117 **I used to run a hospital** Mike Duggan, "Detroit Mayor Mike Duggan Covid-19 Briefing Transcript April 8," Rev.com, April 8, 2020.

118 **I've never seen anything** Nicholas Kulish, "'Never Seen Anything Like It': Cars Line Up for Miles at Food Banks," *New York Times*, April 8, 2020.

118 **One wonders if** Sarah Ferris and Heather Caygle, "Democrats Urge

White House to Step Up as Minority Communities Hit Hard by Coronavirus," *Politico*, April 8, 2020.

118 **The Radical Left Democrats** Donald Trump, @realDonaldTrump, Twitter, 10:42 A.M., April 8, 2020.

118 **What I'd like to do** Duggan, "Detroit Mayor Mike Duggan Covid-19 Briefing Transcript April 8."

119 **All across Illinois** J. B. Pritzker, "Illinois Governor J.B. Pritzker Briefing Transcript April 9," Rev.com, April 9, 2020.

119 ***Wall Street Journal*** Donald Trump, @realDonaldTrump, Twitter, 3:35 P.M., April 9, 2020.

119 **This has been a hard month** Gretchen Whitmer, "Gov. Gretchen Whitmer Coronavirus Briefing Transcript April 9," Rev.com, April 9, 2020.

119 **Now I've told you** Mike DeWine, "Gov. Mike DeWine Ohio Coronavirus Briefing Transcript April 9," Rev.com, April 9, 2020.

120 **I am worried about** Pritzker, "Illinois Governor J.B. Pritzker Briefing Transcript April 9," April 9, 2020.

120 **I think that it's important** Whitmer, "Gov. Gretchen Whitmer Coronavirus Briefing Transcript April 9," April 9, 2020.

120 **Well, first of all** Mike DeWine, "Gov. Mike DeWine Ohio Coronavirus Briefing Transcript April 9," April 9, 2020.

121 **The Postal Service** Carolyn Maloney, in Angélica Acevedo, "The Postal Service Is Holding On for Dear Life': Maloney Calls on Federal Government to Provide Relief for USPS," April 10, 2020.

121 **Every day, the dedicated** Brenda Lawrence, "Postmaster General Warns Committee of Dire Consequences without Congressional Action," House Committee on Oversight and Reform, April 9, 2020.

121 **In perhaps the most sobering** Tom Orsborn, "We Just Can't Feed This Many," *San Antonio Express-News*, April 9, 2020.

121 **To help reduce** United Food and Commercial Workers International Union, "UFCW Urges Easter Grocery Shoppers to Exercise Caution as Coronavirus Outbreak Continues," UFCW.org, April 10, 2020.

122 **At the onset** Rashida Tlaib, "Tlaib, Dingell Lead 63 Members of Congress in Introducing Federal Ban on Water Shutoffs During Covid—19 Crisis," press release, April 10, 2020.

122 **Since I addressed** Gretchen Whitmer, "Michigan Reports 205 New Coronavirus Deaths, Nearly Double Previous Daily Peak," MLive, April 11, 2020.

122 **OUR Governor IS** "Sen. Shirkey Says Whitmer Is 'Killing Our Livelihoods' with Stay-at-Home Extension," mlive, April 11, 2020.

122 **April 9, 2020. 7,096 uniformed members** NYPD News, @NYPD news, Twitter, 6:52 P.M., April 10, 2020.

122 **Next week I will be** "Texas Gov. Greg Abbott Coronavirus Press Conference Transcript April 10: Hints at Reopening Businesses Next Week," Rev.com, April 10, 2020.

123 **Because the T.V. Ratings** Donald Trump, @realDonaldTrump, Twitter, 10:36 A.M., April 10, 2020.

123 **Today, New Mexico's public order** Michelle Lujan Grisham, reported in Patrick Cornell, "New Mexico Adds Houses of Worship to Ban on Mass Gatherings," CNN.com, April 11, 2020.

123 **I'm going to** Ted Cruz, @tedcruz, Twitter, 3:34 P.M., April 11, 2020.

123 **There are additional** J. B. Pritzker, "Illinois Governor J.B. Pritzker Coronavirus Briefing Transcript April 11," Rev.com, April 11, 2020.

124 **In these weeks** Easter Address

124 **In a world** Trey Haddon, reported in Antonia Ayres Brown, "Honks Instead of 'Hallelujahs.' Bloomington Church Offers Drive-In Easter Service with Worshippers Confined to Their Cars," *Chicago Tribune*, April 12, 2020.

124 **The U.S. now** Jeffrey Sachs, "Why the US Has the World's Highest Number of Covid-19 Deaths," CNN.com, April 12, 2020.

125 **Somebody asked the question once** Andrew Cuomo, "Amid Ongoing Covid-19 Pandemic, Governor Cuomo Issues Executive Order Directing Employers to Provide Masks to Employees Who Interact with the Public," ny.gov, April 12, 2020.

125 **Again, to put it in context** Cuomo, "Amid Ongoing Covid-19 Pandemic, Governor Cuomo Issues Executive Order Directing Employers to Provide Masks to Employees Who Interact with the Public," April 12, 2020.

126 **These masks are actually now** Amy Acton, "Dr. Amy Acton: General Public Could Be Wearing Masks for the Next Year," WKYC Studios, April 13, 2020.

126 **In a time where full-on** Andrew Carter, "Ohio Senate Candidate Attacks DeWine's 'Tyranny' in Coronavirus Response," *Marion Star*, April 14, 2020.

126 **We need to get the economy** J. Edward Moreno, "Protesters, Anti-Quarantine Groups Call for End Coronavirus Closures," *The Hill*, April 14, 2020.

126 **It's disappointing that so many** Peter Navarro, interview with Alan Rappeport, "Navarro Calls Medical Experts 'Tone Deaf' Over Coronavirus Shutdown," *New York Times*, April 13, 2020.

126 **I'm glad to be able to** Jay Inslee, "Gov. Jay Inslee Washington Coronavirus Briefing Transcript April 13," Rev.com, April 13, 2020.

127 **One thing that's undeniable** Ned Lamont, "Massachusetts Joins New

York, New Jersey, Connecticut, Pennsylvania, Delaware and Rhode Island's Multi-State Council to Get People Back to Work and Restore the Economy," nystate.gov, April 13, 2020.

127 **When you say my authority** Donald Trump, "Remarks by President Trump, Vice President Pence, and Members of the Coronavirus Task Force in Press Briefing," whitehouse .gov, April 13, 2020, transcript issued April 14, 2020.

127 **As far as who has** Jay Inslee, "Gov. Jay Inslee Washington Coronavirus Briefing Transcript April 13," April 13, 2020.

127 **A quick question on** Kaitlan Collins and Donald Trump, "Remarks by President Trump, Vice President Pence, and Members of the Coronavirus Task Force in Press Briefing," April 13, 2020.

128 **We also have to be clear** Andrew Cuomo, "Governor Cuomo Holds a Briefing on New York's Covid-19 Response," ny.gov, April 14, 2020.

128 **The plans to reopen** Donald Trump, "Remarks by President Trump in Press Briefing," whitehouse.gov, April 14, 2020.

128 **This has been a topic** Cuomo, "Governor Cuomo Holds a Briefing on New York's Covid-19 Response," April 14, 2020.

129 **The day will be very close** Trump, "Remarks by President Trump in Press Briefing," April 14, 2020.

129 **Let me make a personal point** Cuomo, "Governor Cuomo Holds a Briefing on New York's Covid-19 Response," April 14, 2020.

129 **Let me start by saying** Barack Obama, "Full Text: Read Barack Obama's Endorsement of Joe Biden for President," NBC 4 New York, April 14, 2020.

130 **Sometimes it takes more** Cuomo, "Governor Cuomo Holds a Briefing on New York's Covid-19 Response," April 14, 2020.

130 **If there's one thing** Barack Obama, "Full Text: Read Barack Obama's Endorsement of Joe Biden for President," April 14, 2020.

130 **Today, I'm instructing my** Trump, "Remarks by President Trump in Press Briefing," April 14, 2020.

130 **50 years ago this week** Cuomo, "Governor Cuomo Holds a Briefing on New York's Covid-19 Response," April 14, 2020.

131 **The number of "probable"** Jesse Rodriguez and Tom Winter, "'Probable' Coronavirus Deaths in New York City Would Push Toll over 10,000," NBC News, April 14, 2020.

131 **Behind every death** Oxiris Barbot, reported in Quil Lawrence, "New York City's Covid-19 Death Toll Soars Past 10,000," NPR, April 14, 2020.

131 **Obviously, WWE** Ron DeSantis, "Gov. DeSantis Responds to WWE Being Deemed an 'Essential

Business,'" WKMG News 6 Click Orlando, April 14, 2020.

132 **So we have a lot of patients** Donald Trump, "Donald Trump Coronavirus Press Briefing Transcript April 15," Rev.com, April 15, 2020.

132 **Our numbers yesterday** Gavin Newsom, "Gov. Gavin Newsom California Covid-19 Briefing Transcript April 15," Rev.com, April 15, 2020.

132 **Everyone, every citizen** Operation Gridlock, Facebook public event page, details. Accessed on June 9, 2020.

133 **I was really disappointed** Gretchen Whitmer, "Governor Whitmer on Protest: 'We Know That This Rally Endangered People,'" Fox17 West Michigan, April 15, 2020.

133 **This is Covid-19, not Covid-1** Interview on *Fox & Friends*

133 **This is a big part** Amy Acton, "Mike DeWine Ohio Coronavirus Briefing Transcript April 16," Rev.com, April 16, 2020.

133 **This morning's unemployment** Steny Hoyer, "Hoyer Statement on the Unemployment Insurance Claims Report," press release, April 16, 2020.

134 **We simply cannot take** Kristalina Georgieva, IMF/IMFC Press Conference, "IMFC Calls on Private Creditors to Join Debt Standstill," *News Market*, April 16, 2020.

134 **As you know, Covid-19** J. B. Pritzker, "Illinois Gov. J.B. Pritzker Press Conference Transcript April 16," Rev.com, April 16, 2020.

134 **What we're watching, potentially** Chris Murphy, interview with Alex Ward, "The Senator of State," *Vox*, April 16, 2020.

134 **This is now a matter of life** Marc Perrone, "UFCW: Amazon and Whole Foods Must Take Immediate Action to Protect Workers from Coronavirus," UFCW, April 16, 2020.

135 **I'll confess, myself included** Gavin Newsom, "Gov. Gavin Newsom California Covid-19 Briefing Transcript April 16," Rev.com, April 16, 2020.

135 **In our suburban communities** Lauren Underwood, interview with Mandy Oaklander, "The Coronavirus Is a Wake-Up Call for Racial Inequality. It's Time to Change the System," *Time*, April 16, 2020.

135 **We're going to be helping** Donald Trump, "Donald Trump Coronavirus Press Conference Transcript April 16: Guidelines to Reopen Parts of US in Phases," Rev.com, April 16, 2020.

136 **It's been confirmed by** Jay Inslee, "Washington Governor Jay Inslee Coronavirus Press Briefing Transcript April 16," Rev.com, April 16, 2020.

136 **Based on the latest data** Trump, "Donald Trump Coronavirus Press Conference Transcript April 16: Guidelines to Reopen Parts of US in Phases," April 16, 2020.

136 **On what we need to do better** Interview on *The View*, ABC

136 **We are a thousand miles** Jay Inslee, "Washington Governor Jay Inslee Coronavirus Press Briefing Transcript April 16," April 16, 2020.

137 **As of 5 P.M. tomorrow** "Coronavirus: Jacksonville Beaches and Parks to Reopen Friday with Time, Activity Restrictions," *Florida Times-Union*, April 16, 2020

137 **There have been 3,423,034 total** "This Week in Coronavirus: April 10 to April 17," Kaiser Family Foundation, April 17, 2020.

137 **Let's be honest, it's up to the states** Andrew Cuomo, "Andrew Cuomo New York Covid-19 Briefing Transcript April 17: 'Don't Pass the Buck without Passing Bucks,'" Rev.com, April 17, 2020.

137 **Governor Cuomo should** Donald Trump, @realDonaldTrump, Twitter, 12:11 P.M., April 17, 2020.

138 **Let's respond to the president** Andrew Cuomo, "Andrew Cuomo New York Covid-19 Briefing Transcript April 17: 'Don't Pass the Buck without Passing Bucks,'" Rev.com, April 17, 2020.

138 **So we're helping people** Donald Trump, "Remarks by President Trump, Vice President Pence, and Members of the Coronavirus Task Force in Press Briefing," whitehouse .gov, April 17, 2020.

138 **I don't know what I'm supposed to do** Cuomo, "Andrew Cuomo New York Covid-19 Briefing Transcript April 17: 'Don't Pass the Buck without Passing Bucks.'"

138 **There's a tremendous amount of unused** Trump, "Remarks by President Trump, Vice President Pence, and Members of the Coronavirus Task Force in Press Briefing," April 17, 2020.

138 **The president doesn't want to help** Cuomo, "Andrew Cuomo New York Covid-19 Briefing Transcript April 17: 'Don't Pass the Buck without Passing Bucks.'"

139 **As some governors** Keith Collins, "Coronavirus Testing Needs to Triple Before the U.S. Can Reopen, Experts Say," *New York Times*, April 17, 2020.

139 **Well, this is an important moment** Cuomo, "Andrew Cuomo New York Covid-19 Briefing Transcript April 17: "Don't Pass the Buck without Passing Bucks."

139 **I want to remind Marylanders** Larry Hogan, "Maryland Gov. Larry Hogan Coronavirus Briefing Transcript April 17," Rev.com, April 17, 2020.

140 **LIBERATE MINNESOTA** Donald Trump, @realDonaldTrump, Twitter, 11:21 A.M., April 17, 2020.

140 **If we just said let's go back** Tim Walz, "4-17-2020 Covid-19 Update from Mn Governor Tim Walz and Mdh," CCX Media, April 17, 2020.

140 **LIBERATE MICHIGAN** Donald Trump, @realDonaldTrump, Twitter, 11:22 A.M., April 17, 2020.

140 **I hope that it's not encouraging** Gretchen Whitmer, "Michigan Governor Gretchen Whitmer Press Conference Transcript April 17," Rev .com, April 17, 2020.

140 **LIBERATE VIRGINIA** Donald Trump, @realDonaldTrump, Twitter, 11:25 A.M., April 17, 2020.

140 **As the Governor of the Commonwealth** Ralph Northam, "Ralph Northam Virginia Covid-19 Press Conference Transcript April 17," Rev .com, April 17, 2020.

141 **Let me just say a few things** Muriel Bowser, "Washington D.C. Mayor Muriel Bowser Covid-19 Briefing April 17," Rev.com, April 17, 2020.

141 **I wanted to come here today** Tate Reeves, reported in Patrice Boykin, "Governor Extends Shelter-in-Place," *Magee News*, April 17, 2020.

141 **In South Dakota, it looks** Kristi Noem, "South Dakota Governor Kristi Noem Covid-19 Briefing April 17," Rev.com, April 17, 2020.

141 **We made it through another week** Robert F. Hill, "Distance Learning Update for April 17, 2020," Springfield City School District (OH), April 17, 2020.

142 **Good morning. Okay, let's start** Andrew Cuomo, "Amid Ongoing Covid-19 Pandemic, Governor Cuomo Calls for Federal Coordination of Supply Chain to Bring Testing to Scale," ny.gov, April 18, 2020.

142 **You don't hear anymore about** Donald Trump, "Remarks by President Trump and Members of the Coronavirus Task Force in Press Briefing," whitehouse.gov, April 18, 2020.

142 **We did 500,000 tests** Cuomo, "Amid Ongoing Covid-19 Pandemic, Governor Cuomo Calls for Federal Coordination of Supply Chain to Bring Testing to Scale," April 18, 2020.

143 **My administration has also** Trump, "Remarks by President Trump and Members of the Coronavirus Task Force in Press Briefing," April 18, 2020.

143 **Last point, personal opinion** Cuomo, "Amid Ongoing Covid-19 Pandemic, Governor Cuomo Calls for Federal Coordination of Supply Chain to Bring Testing to Scale," April 18, 2020.

144 **We have a tremendous lab** Trump, "Remarks by President Trump and Members of the Coronavirus Task Force in Press Briefing," April 18, 2020.

144 **This has been the number one** Larry Hogan, "Maryland Governor: Goal Is to Reopen State 'in a Safe Way,'" *Today*, April 16, 2020.

144 **I've always promoted** Ron DeSantis, "Coronavirus Update: Florida Governor Ron DeSantis Encourages Outdoor Activity," CBS Miami, April 17, 2020.

144 **Atlantic County Officials** Molly Bilinski and Zac Spencer, "Murphy Calls Out Atlantic County Surrogate for Post Demanding State Reopen Immediately," *The Press of Atlantic City*, April 18, 2020.

144 **That is irresponsible** Phil Murphy, "New Jersey Governor Phil Murphy Coronavirus Briefing April 18," Rev .com, April 18, 2020.

145 **Today is Sunday** Andrew Cuomo, "Andrew Cuomo New York Covid-19 Briefing Transcript April 19," Rev.com, April 19, 2020.

145 **[T]here are three ways** Deborah Birx, "Transcript: Dr. Deborah Birx Discusses Coronavirus on "Face the Nation," April 19, 2020

145 **The federal government at the** Mike Pence, interview, *Meet the Press*, April 19, 2020.

145 **That's just delusional** Ralph Northam, interview with Jake Tapper, "Northam: 'Delusional' to Claim US Has Enough Tests," *State of the Union*, April 19, 2020.

146 **One's a swab, one's a Q-Tip** Donald Trump, "Donald Trump Coronavirus Press Conference Transcript April 19," Rev.com, April 19, 2020.

146 **It's not accurate** Larry Hogan, interview with Jake Tapper, *State of the Union*, April 19, 2020.

146 **Some people believe in testing** Trump, "Donald Trump Coronavirus Press Conference Transcript April 19," April 19, 2020.

146 **To try to push this off** Hogan, interview with Jake Tapper, *State of the Union*, April 19, 2020.

146 **I've seen the [protestors]** Trump, "Donald Trump Coronavirus Press Conference Transcript April 19," April 19, 2020.

147 **I don't want to have** Cuomo, "Andrew Cuomo New York Covid-19 Briefing Transcript April 19," April 19, 2020.

THE OPENING

151 **Given the favorable data** Brian Kemp, "Gov. Kemp Updates Georgians on Covid-19," Office of the Governor, April 20, 2020.

151 **My phone has** Manuel's Tavern, Facebook post, April 20, 2020. Accessed June 9, 2020.

152 **If you're looking for** Andrew Cuomo, "Video, Audio, Photos and Rush Transcript: Amid Ongoing Covid-19 Pandemic, Governor Cuomo Calls on Federal Government to Provide Hazard Pay to

Essential Public Workers," ny.gov, April 20, 2020

152 **South Carolina's business is business** Henry McMaster, "SC Gov. McMaster Allows Some Stores to Reopen 2 Weeks After Closing due to Covid-19," *The State*, April 20, 2020.

152 **To the citizens of New Orleans** LaToya Cantrell, reported in Jessica Williams and Tyler Bridges, " 'I Will Not Be Bullied': Latoya Cantrell Firm in Decisions About Coronavirus Stay-Home Orders," Nola.com, April 20, 2020.

152 **What I said when** Dan Patrick, interview with Tucker Carlson, "Texas Lt. Gov. Dan Patrick Responds to Criticism for Questioning America's Economic Shutdown," Fox News, interview on April 20, 2020, posted April 21, 2020.

153 **Who in this great state** Gretchen Whitmer, "Michigan Governor Gretchen Whitmer Press Conference Transcript April 20," Rev.com, April 20, 2020.

153 **As the experts** Donald Trump, "Remarks by President Trump, Vice President Pence, and Members of the Coronavirus Task Force in Press Briefing," whitehouse.gov, April 20, 2020

153 **We need to deliver** "Roadmap to Pandemic Resilience" report

154 **This weekend** "Maryland Gov. Larry Hogan Coronavirus Briefing Transcript April 20," Rev.com, April 20, 2020.

154 **We'll give you** Donald Trump, "Remarks by President Trump, Vice President Pence, and Members of the Coronavirus Task Force in Press Briefing," whitehouse.gov, April 20, 2020.

154 **The 500,000 test** "Maryland Gov. Larry Hogan Coronavirus Briefing Transcript April 20," Rev.com, April 20, 2020.

154 **Some states** Donald Trump, "Remarks by President Trump, Vice President Pence, and Members of the Coronavirus Task Force in Press Briefing," whitehouse.gov, April 20, 2020.

155 **The truth of** J. B. Prtizker, "Transcript: Leadership During Crisis: A Conversation with Governors Gretchen Whitmer and J.B. Pritzker," *Washington Post*, April 21, 2020.

155 **There's no legitimate** Stacey Abrams, reported in Elizabeth Elkind, "Stacey Abrams Says There's 'No Legitimate Reason' for Georgia Governor to Lift Virus Restrictions," CBS News, April 21, 2020.

155 **We really are at a loss** Interview on *Cuomo Prime Time*, reported in Quint Forgey, " 'There's Nothing About This That Makes Sense': Georgia Democrats Rail Against Kemp's Move to Reopen State," *Politico*, April 21, 2020.

155 **There's no social** Hannah Dreier, " 'A Recipe for Disaster': American Prison

Factories Becoming Incubators for Coronavirus," *Washington Post*, April 21, 2020.

156 **Black people represent** Collin Marozzi, "Covid-19 Highlights Long-Known Issues of Systemic Racism," ACLU Ohio, April 21, 2020.

156 **The Trump Administration is currently** Joe Biden, "Biden Campaign: Statement on the Trump Administration's Failure to Deliver for Wisconsin Families Impacted by the Covid-19 Pandemic," Wispolitics.com, April 21, 2020.

156 **To highlight** Press Release, "Enloe Medical Center Nurses to Hold Candlelight Vigil at Shift Change to Demand Protections When Treating Patients With Covid-19." California Nurses Association, National Nurses United, April 21, 2020.

157 **Since we announced** Donald Trump, "Remarks by President Trump and Members of the Coronavirus Task Force in Press Briefing," whitehouse.gov, April 21, 2020.

157 **I am concerned** Ron Wyden, "Wyden Requests Answers on Trump Signature on Checks," United States Senate Committee on Finance, April 21, 2020.

157 **Now let me make** Steve Mnuchin, "Remarks by President Trump and Members of the Coronavirus Task Force in Press Briefing," whitehouse.gov, April 21, 2020.

157 **There's a possibility** Robert Redfield, reported in Lena H. Sun, "CDC Director Warns Second Wave of Coronavirus Is Likely to Be Even More Devastating," *Washington Post*, April 21, 2020.

157 **Global cases** Johns Hopkins University, Coronavirus Resorce Center, accessed April 22, 2020.

158 **I'd like to remember** Phil Murphy, "TRANSCRIPT: April 22nd, 2020 Coronavirus Briefing Media," nj.gov.

158 **We've actually directed** Gavin Newsom "Gov. Gavin Newsom California Covid-19 Briefing Transcript April 22," Rev.com, April 22, 2020.

159 **I'd love everything** Carolyn Goodman, interview with Anderson Cooper, "Anderson Cooper Presses Las Vegas Mayor Over Wish to Reopen," CNN, April 22, 2020.

159 **If you jump the gun** Anthony Fauci, interview on *Today*, reported in Savannah Behrmann, "Fauci Takes Heat from Protesters of Stay-at-Home Orders, Says Ignoring Guidelines Will 'Backfire,'" *USA Today*, April 20, 2020.

159 **The government models** Udi Ofer and Lucia Tan, "New Model Shows Reducing Jail Population Will Lower Covid-19 Death Toll for All of Us," ACLU, April 22, 2020.

159 **Yesterday, I was removed** Rick Bright, "Read: Statement from Leader of Federal Vaccine Agency About His Reassignment," CNN, April 22, 2020.

160 **We all hope** Adam Schiff, @RepAdamSchiff, Twitter, 6:00 P.M., April 22, 2020.

160 **I think this whole** Interview with Hugh Hewitt.

160 **[McConnell] represents the state** Andrew Cuomo, "Andrew Cuomo New York Covid-19 Briefing Transcript April 23," Rev.com, April 23, 2020.

161 **I think by Memorial Day weekend** Interview with Geraldo Riviera, "Pence Says Coronavirus Could Be 'Largely' Behind Us by Memorial Day Weekend," Fox News, April 23, 2020.

161 **I agree you don't** Alice Park, "Dr. Anthony Fauci 'Not Overly Confident' with U.S. Covid-19 Testing Capabilities," *Time*, April 23, 2020.

161 **No, I don't agree with** Donald Trump, "Donald Trump Coronavirus Press Conference Transcript April 23," Rev.com, April 23, 2020.

161 **Removing Dr. Bright in the midst** Frank Pallone, "Pallone Calls for Inspector General Investigation into Circumstances Surrounding Dr. Bright's Reassignment," House Energy and Commerce Committee, April 23, 2020.

162 **In the week ending** U.S. Department of Labor, "Unemployment Insurance Weekly Claims," April 23, 2020.

162 **Shares of Zoom** Jessica Bursztynsky, "Zoom Shares Pop After Users Grow from 200 Million to 300 Million in a Matter of Days," CNBC, April 23, 2020.

162 **Last month, Congress** Ben Sasse, "Sasse Calls on Pelosi and Sanders to Fix Unemployment Insurance," April 23, 2020.

162 **I'd just encourage everybody** Pete Ricketts, "Gov's: People Won't Get Unemployment Money If They Refuse to Work," 3 News Now, April 23, 2020.

163 **My oldest brother, Don Reed** Elizabeth Warren, in Quint Forgey, "Elizabeth Warren's Brother Dies from Coronavirus," *Politico*, April 23, 2020.

163 **I'm going to take a moment** Maxine Waters, speech on House floor, reported in "Maxine Waters Dedicates Legislation to Sister Dying of Coronavirus," *The Hill*, April 23, 2020.

163 **Senator McConnell, who is the head** Cuomo, "Andrew Cuomo New York Covid-19 Briefing Transcript April 23," April 23, 2020.

163 **It is a joke** Alexandria Ocasio-Cortez, speech on House floor, "Alexandria Ocasio-Cortez Accuses GOP of Lacking Urgency on Passing Emergency Relief Bill," C-SPAN, April 23, 2020.

164 **It is interesting that the states** Trump, "Remarks by President Trump, Vice President Pence, and Members of the Coronavirus Task Force in Press Briefing," April 23, 2020.

164 **Vicious is saying** Cuomo, "Andrew Cuomo New York Covid-19 Briefing Transcript April 23," April 23, 2020.

164 **Recent incidents and arrests** Natasha Bertrand, "DHS Warns of Increase in Violent Extremism Amid Coronavirus Lockdowns," *Politico*, April 23, 2020.

164 **Supposedly when we hit the body** Trump, "Remarks by President Trump, Vice President Pence, and Members of the Coronavirus Task Force in Press Briefing," April 23, 2020.

165 **I certainly wouldn't** Stephen Hahn, interview with Anderson Cooper and Dr. Sanjay Gupta, "FDA Commissioner Weighs in on Trump's Disinfectant Claim," CNN, April 23, 2020.

165 **It is unfortunate that I** Patrice Harris, "Trump Floats Another Bogus Coronavirus Cure—and His Administration Scrambles to Stop People from Injecting Disinfectants," *Washington Post*, April 24, 2020.

165 **In addition to advising** CNN interview with Wolf Blitzer, *The Situation Room*, April 24, 2020.

165 **The number of Americans** Drew DeSilver, "Not All Unemployed People Get Unemployment Benefits; in Some States, Very Few Do," Pew Research Center, April 24, 2020.

166 **If you're an employer** Kim Reynolds, reported in Brendan Cole, "Employees Face 'Really Tough Choice' as States Say Return to Work or Lose Unemployment Benefits," *Newsweek*, April 29, 2020.

166 **We live in a country** Courtney Vinopal, "Watch: 5 Questions Answered About Workers' Rights During the Coronavirus Pandemic," *Newshour*, April 24, 2020.

166 **In urban centers large and small** Rodney A. Brooks, "African Americans Struggle with Disproportionate Covid Death Toll," *National Geographic*, April 24, 2020.

166 **Globally, more than 2.7 million** CDC Foundation, "Making an Impact: The CDC Foundation Responds to Covid-19," April 24, 2020.

166 **We are gonna see it** Michael Osterholm, "Dr. Michael Osterholm Says High Amount of Transmission to Come," interview on *Morning Joe*, April 23, 2020.

166 **For the past few weeks** Apoorva Mandavilli, "Coronavirus Antibody Tests: Can You Trust the Results?" *New York Times*, April 28, 2020.

167 **It is just a necessary connection** Nancy Pelosi, "Nancy Pelosi Speech on Coronavirus Relief Bill April 24," Rev.com, April 24, 2020.

167 **I've been talking about this for how** Andrew Cuomo, "Andrew Cuomo New York Covid-19 Briefing Transcript April 24," Rev.com, April 24, 2020.

167 **Part of this whole approach** Bill Lee, "Tennessee Governor Lee Coronavirus News Conference," C-SPAN, April 24, 2020.

168 **I get inspired by the strength** Cuomo, "Andrew Cuomo New York Covid-19 Briefing Transcript April 24," April 24, 2020.

168 **Right now, there's no oversight** Michael Grunwald, "Biden Wants a New Stimulus 'a Hell of a Lot Bigger' Than $2 Trillion," *Politico*, April 25, 2020.

169 **Let's also remind folks** Phil Murphy, "Transcript: April 25th, 2020 Coronavirus Briefing Media," nj.gov, April 25, 2020.

169 **Chicago-land organizers at Off Their Plate** J. B. Pritzker, "Illinois Gov. J.B. Pritzker Press Conference Transcript April 25," Rev.com, April 25, 2020.

169 **This is the biggest negative** Kevin Hassett, "*This Week* Transcript 4-26-20: Gov. Larry Hogan, Gov. Gretchen Whitmer, Kevin Hassett, Sen. Amy Klobuchar," ABC News, April 26, 2020.

169 **I see no light at the end** Andrew Cuomo, "Andrew Cuomo New York covid-19 Briefing Transcript April 26," Rev.com, April 26, 2020.

170 **As the coronavirus continued** Jaclyn Reiss, "Sunday's Boston Globe Runs 21 Pages of Death Notices as Coronavirus Continues to Claim Lives," *Boston Globe*, April 26, 2020.

170 **In the early weeks** Emma Brown, Andrew Ba Tran, Beth Reinhard, and Monica Ulmanu, "U.S. Deaths Soared in Early Weeks of Pandemic, Far Exceeding Number Attributed to Covid-19," *Washington Post*, April 27, 2020.

170 **So far, 36 people** Jennifer Miller, "Wisconsin Health Department: 36 People Positive for Coronavirus After Primary Vote," *Politico*, April 27, 2020.

171 **Last month, fewer than one third** Steve Greenberg, "Coronavirus Pandemic Pushes Cuomo to Record High Ratings; Voters Trust Cuomo over Trump on NY Reopening 78-16%," Siena College Research Institute, April 27, 2020.

171 **In small communities around** John Tyson, "Feeding the Nation and Keeping Our Team Members Healthy," Tyson, April 26, 2020.

171 **My executive order** Greg Abbott, "Gov. Greg Abbott Texas Coronavirus Press Conference Transcript April 27," Rev.com, April 27, 2020.

171 **Just because something can be open** Clay Jenkins, interview with Erin Burnett, *Outfront*, April 27, 2020.

172 **The reality is that we** Kim Reynolds, reported in Nikoel Hytrek, "Reynolds: Iowa 'Must Learn to Live' with

Coronavirus, 77 Counties to Reopen," *Iowa Starting Line*, April 27, 2020.

172 **The coronavirus is still here** Mike DeWine, "Ohio Governor DeWine Coronavirus News Conference," C-SPAN, April 27, 2020.

172 **There has been so much unnecessary** Donald Trump, "Donald Trump Coronavirus Press Conference Transcript April 27," Rev.com, April 27, 2020.

172 **U.S. intelligence agencies** Greg Miller and Ellen Nakishima, "President's Intelligence Briefing Book Repeatedly Cited Virus Threat," *Washington Post*, April 27, 2020.

172 **If a state or local ordinance** Bill Barr, reported in Matt Zapotosky, "Barr Tells Prosecutors to 'Be On the Lookout' for State, Local Coronavirus Orders That May Violate Constitution," *Washington Post*, April 27, 2020.

173 **President Trump's decision** Elliot Engel, in U.S. House of Representatives Committee on Foreign Affairs, "Engel Launches Inquiry into Trump Decision to Halt WHO Funding," press release, April 27, 2020.

173 **If an American president** Olivia Nuzzi, "Remarks by President Trump, Vice President Pence, and Members of the Coronavirus Task Force in Press Briefing," whitehouse.gov, April 27, 2020.

173 **The total number of coronavirus** Daniel Arkin, "Grim Milestone: Total Number of U.S. Coronavirus Cases Hits 1 Million," NBC News, April 28, 2020.

174 **Our member banks** Rob Nichols, @BankersPrez, Twitter, 12:26 P.M., April 27, 2020.

174 **More than $2 billion** Jovita Carranza, @SBAJovita, Twitter, 11:09 A.M., April 27, 2020.

174 **I never expected** Steve Mnuchin, "CNBC Transcript: Treasury Secretary Steven Mnuchin Speaks to CNBC's 'Squawk Box' Today," *Squawk Box*, April 28, 2020.

174 **While we share the concern** Marc Perrone, "UFCW: Trump Order to Keep Meatpacking Plants Open Must Include Immediate Action to Strengthen Coronavirus Testing and Safety Measures," United Food and Commercial Workers, April 28, 2020.

174 **My red line going forward** Mitch McConnell, interview, "McConnell Says US Needs to Provide Protection for Businesses and Employees," Fox News, April 28, 2020.

174 **We only wish that this administration** Stuart Appelbaum, "Statement from RWDSU President Stuart Appelbaum on Trump Invoking the Defense Production Act Mandating Poultry and Meat Processors Remain Open," Retail, Wholesale, and Department Store Union, April 28, 2020.

175 **When Vice President** "SEIU Healthcare Minnesota Respond to Vice President Pence Ignoring Safety Policies During Mayo Visit," SEIU Minnesota, April 28, 2020

175 **In not even three months** David Welna, "Coronavirus Has Now Killed More Americans Than Vietnam War," NPR, April 28, 2020.

175 **Tremendous progress has been made** Donald Trump, "President Trump on Covid-19 Paycheck Protection Program," C-SPAN, April 28, 2020.

175 **I would love to be able** James Wagner and Ken Belson, "Some Sports May Have to Skip This Year, Fauci Says," *New York Times*, April 28, 2020.

176 **The person who delivers** Andrew Cuomo, "Andrew Cuomo New York Covid-19 Briefing Transcript April 28," Rev.com, April 28, 2020.

176 **Total deaths in 7 states** Josh Katz, Denise Lu, and Margot Sanger-Katz, "U.S. Coronavirus Death Toll Is Far Higher Than Reported, C.D.C. Data Suggests," *New York Times*, April 28, 2020.

176 **Sorry, are you saying** Kristen Welker and Donald Trump, "Donald Trump Small Business Relief Speech Transcript April 28," Rev.com, April 28, 2020.

177 **There is absolutely no way** Brett Giroir, in W. J. Hennigan, "Trump Says U.S. Will Run 5 Million Daily Virus Tests 'Very Soon.' His Testing Chief Says That's Impossible," *Time*, April 28, 2020.

177 **Real gross domestic product** "Gross Domestic Product, First Quarter 2020," Bureau of Economic Analysis, Department of Commerce, April 29, 2020.

177 **Members of the Congressional** Scott Wong, "Black Caucus Moves to Front and Center in Covid Fight," *The Hill*, April 29, 2020.

177 **America is in shock** Wong, "Black Caucus Moves to Front and Center in Covid Fight."

177 **We knew that there** Jonathan Capeheart, "For Chicago, the Coronavirus Is 'The Perfect Storm,' Mayor Lori Lightfoot Says," *Washington Post*, April 29, 2020.

177 **We are going to see economic** Jerome Powell, "Transcript of Chair Powell's Press Conference April 29, 2020."

177 **I think what you'll** Jared Kushner, interview, "Kushner: I'm very confident we have all the testing we need to reopen the country," Fox News, April 29, 2020

178 **Nearly three-in-four voters** Myah Ward, "Poll: Voters Expect Second Wave of Coronavirus Cases," *Politico*, April 29, 2020.

178 **To protect our members and** "Costco Customers Will Be Required to Wear Masks Beginning Monday," *Triad Business Journal*, April 30, 2020.

178 **The eternal lockdown crowd** Jared Kushner, interview, "Kushner: I'm

very confident we have all the testing we need to reopen the country," Fox News, April 29, 2020

178 **I know it's hard to communicate** Andrew Cuomo, "Amid Ongoing Covid-19 Pandemic, Governor Cuomo Announces 35 Counties Approved to Resume Elective Outpatient Treatments," ny.gov, April 29, 2020.

178 **If somebody wants to stay** Elon Musk, in Lauren Feiner, "Elon Musk Says Orders to Stay Home Are 'Fascist' in Expletive-Laced Rant During Tesla Earnings Call," CNBC, April 29, 2020.

179 **Billionaires want to continue** Ilhan Omar, @Ilhan, Twitter, 11:54 A.M., April 29, 2020.

179 **What have we learned** Lindsey Graham, reported in Kay Jones, "Sen. Lindsey Graham Says He Will Not Vote to Authorize More Money for Unemployment Benefits," CNN, April 29, 2020.

179 **[Republic Senators] want to fund** Cuomo, "Amid Ongoing Covid-19 Pandemic, Governor Cuomo Announces 35 Counties Approved to Resume Elective Outpatient Treatments," April 29, 2020.

179 **If you're planning a very large** Gina Raimondo, "Gov. Raimondo Says No to Newport Folk Festival, Other Large Gatherings Due to Coronavirus," NewportRI.com, April 29, 2020.

180 **This is going away** Donald Trump, reported in Libby Cathey, "Coronavirus Government Response Updates: Trump Rejects a New Normal: 'This Is Going Away,'" ABC News, April 29, 2020.

180 **[An individual's] liberty interests are** Christopher M. Murray, reported in Melissa Hudson, "Judge Upholds Governor's Stay at Home Order in Constitutional Challenge,"ABC57, April 30, 2020.

180 **Directly above me** Dayna Polehanki, @SenPolehanki, Twitter,12:38 A.M., April 30, 2020.

180 **Protestors, some carrying firearms** Craig Mauger, "Protesters, Some Armed, Enter Michigan Capitol in Rally Against Covid-19 Limits," *Detroit News*, April 30, 2020.

181 **While some members of the legislature** Gretchen Whitmer, "After GOP Legislature Declares 'Mission Accomplished' on Covid-19, Governor Whitmer Signs New Executive Orders to Save Lives, Protect Michiganders," Michigan.gov, April 30, 2020.

181 **In the week ending April 25** Department of Labor, Unemployment Insurance Weekly Claims, April 30, 2020.

181 **We're paying about** Lucy Bayly, "Jobless Claims Top 30 Million as Coronavirus Continues to Devastate Economy," NBC News, April 30, 2020.

181 **I think we did** Donald Trump, "Remarks by President Trump and Vice President Pence in Roundtable

with Industry Executives on the Plan for Opening Up America Again," whitehouse.gov, April 29, 2020.

181 **There had been reports** Larry Hogan, in interview with Paul LeBlanc, "Hogan: Maryland Protected Coronavirus Tests It Secured from South Korea 'Like Fort Knox,'" April 30, 2020.

182 **I'm just looking at the test** Donald Trump, "Remarks by President Trump on Protecting America's Seniors," whitehouse.gov, April 30, 2020, transcript issued May 1, 2020.

182 **At the end of April 28** Glenn Kessler, "Fact Check: Trump's Triumphant Rhetoric on Coronavirus Testing," *Washington Post*, April 30, 2020.

182 **The entire intelligence community** Office of the Director of National Intelligence, "Intelligence Community Statement on Origins of Covid-19," press release, April 30, 2020.

182 **Now, this horrible situation** Bill de Blasio, "Bill de Blasio NYC Covid-19 Press Briefing Transcript April 30," Rev.com, April 30, 2020.

183 **Social distancing guidelines** Robin Foster and E. J. Mundell, "Trump Says Federal Guidelines on Social Distancing Set to Expire," *U.S. News and World Report*, April 30, 2020.

183 **We have spent the month** Jeremy Konynydk, @JeremyKonynydk, Twitter, 1:17 A.M., May 1, 2020.

183 **There's no doubt in my** Anthony Fauci, CNN interview, "Fauci Says He's Concerned That Some US States and Cities Are 'Leapfrogging' Guidelines," CNN.com, April 30, 2020.

183 **US Cases** Jeremy Konyndyk, @JeremyKonyndyk, Twitter, 1:17 A.M., May 1, 2020

184 **US Deaths** David P. Gelles, @Gelles, Twitter, 3:42 P.M., April 30, 2020

184 **This disease doesn't know** Gavin Newsom, "Gov. Gavin Newsom California Covid-19 Briefing Transcript May 1," Rev.com, May 1, 2020.

184 **Governor Newsom's mandate** Lyn Semeta, reported in Marc Cota-Robles, "Judge Denies Request to Overturn Gov. Newsom's Orange County Beach Closure for Now," ABC 7, May 1, 2020.

184 **The Governor of Michigan** Donald Trump, @realDonaldTrump, Twitter, 8:42 P.M., May 1, 2020.

184 **We're in the midst of a global** Gretchen Whitmer, "Michigan Governor Gretchen Whitmer Press Conference Transcript May 1," Rev.com, May 1, 2020.

185 **As our nation continues** Letter to HHS Sec. Azar and FEMA administrator Gaynor

185 **Like one continuous day** Bill de Blasio, "Bill de Blasio NYC Covid-19 Briefing Transcript May 1," Rev.com, May 1, 2020.

185 **Over the last 20 years** Bob Hardt, @bobhardt, Twitter, 1:37 P.M., May 1, 2020.

185 **The idea that this** Michael Osterholm, interview with Jim Sciutto, "Expert Report Predicts Up to Two More Years of Pandemic Misery," CNN.com, May 1, 2020.

185 **Publicly traded companies** Jonathan O'Connell, Steven Rich, and Peter Whoriskey, "Public Companies Received $1 Billion in Stimulus Funds Meant for Small Businesses," *Washington Post*, May 1, 2020.

186 **I will never lie to you** Kayleigh McEnany, "White House Press Secretary Kayleigh McEnany Briefing Transcript: First Press Conference," Rev.com, May 1, 2020.

186 **How do you operate a school** Andrew Cuomo, "Andrew Cuomo New York Covid-19 Briefing Transcript May 1," Rev.com, May 1, 2020.

186 **How do we know reopening** Greg Abbott, May 1, 2020, call, reported in Daniel Villarreal, "Texas Governor Abbott Caught on Recording Saying Reopening Will Escalate Coronavirus Spread on Same Day State Businesses Open," *Newsweek*, May 5, 2020.

186 **More than 80%** Matthew Baum and John Della Volpe, "The State of the Nation: a 50-State Covid-19 Survey," Harvard Kennedy School, Mossavar-Rahmani Center for Business and Government, April 30, 2020.

187 **We illustrate the value** Raj Chetty, John N. Friedman, Nathaniel Hendren, and Michael Stepner, "Real-Time Economics: A New Platform to Track the Impacts of Covid-19 on People, Businesses, and Communities Using Private Sector Data," Opportunity Insights, Harvard University, May 2020.

187 **Too many people** Rosa DeLauro, "DeLauro, House Ag Chairman Peterson, Fmr. USDA Secretaries Vilsack and Glickman, Chef José Andrés, Consumer Reports Announce Release of Action Plan to Safeguard America's Food Supply," press release, May 1, 2020.

187 **Today in Ohio, we now know** Amy Acton, "Mike DeWine Ohio Coronavirus Briefing Transcript May 1," Rev .com, May 1, 2020.

188 **Our basic human rights of life** Nino Vitale, Facebook post, May 1, 2020.

188 **This is not a popularity contest** Mike DeWine, "Mike DeWine Ohio Coronavirus Briefing Transcript May 1," Rev.com, May 1, 2020.

188 **The Ohio legislature** Nino Vitale, Facebook post, May 1, 2020.

188 **If we stick together for** Jay Inslee, public statement, reported in Joseph O'Sullivan, "Inslee Extends Coronavirus Stay-Home Order Through May 31, Outlines Plan to Reopen Washington in Phases," *Seattle Times*, May 1, 2020.

188 **What keeps me up** Alan Chartock, "Gov. Cuomo on WAMC's Northeast Report 5/1/20," WAMC Northeast Public Radio, May 1, 2020.

189 **Over the last 6 weeks** Stephanie Kelton, @StephanieKelton, Twitter, 10:30 A.M., May 2, 2020.

189 **Transit workers have very much** Andrew Cuomo, "Andrew Cuomo New York Covid-19 Briefing Transcript May 2," Rev.com, May 2, 2020.

189 **We all know the President hasn't** Patty Murray, public statement, reported in Jason Slotkin, "Trump Moves to Replace Watchdog Who Reported Medical Shortages," NPR, May 2, 2020.

190 **When history looks back** Philip Rucker, Josh Dawsey, Yasmeen Abutaleb, Robert Costa, and Lena H. Sun, "34 Days of Pandemic: Inside Trump's Desperate Attempts to Reopen America," *Washington Post*, May 2, 2020.

190 **The United States just had** William Feuer, "The US Just Reported Its Deadliest Day for Coronavirus Patients as States Reopen, According to WHO," CNBC, May 2, 2020.

190 **I think right now** Kevin Hassett, interview, "Kevin Hassett on Economy: by the End of May, Hopefully Every State Will Be Open," Fox News, May 2, 2020.

190 **Well, let me tell you** Bill de Blasio, "Bill de Blasio NYC Covid-19 Briefing Transcript May 3," Rev.com, May 3, 2020.

191 **When you look across** "Transcript: Scott Gottlieb Discusses Coronavirus on *Face the Nation*," May 3, 2020," CBS News, May 3, 2020.

191 **Sunday update** Max Roser, @MaxCRoser, Twitter, 7:23 A.M., May 3, 2020.

191 **In April an average** Caitlin Rivers, @cmyeaton, Twitter, 12:28 P.M. May 3, 2020.

191 **New York City** Alexandria Ocasio-Cortez, @RepAOC, Twitter, 9:05 A.M., May 3, 2020

191 **It's devastatingly worrisome** Deborah Birx, "Birx Says Protesters Not Practicing Social Distancing Are 'Devastatingly Worrisome,'" NBC News, May 3, 2020.

192 **I don't believe anybody** Annual Berkshire Hathaway shareholders meeting

192 **Things can change** Tate Reeves, public statement, May 1, 2020, reported in Christina Carrega, "Mississippi Governor Reconsiders Reopening State After Its Largest Spike of Covid-19 Deaths and Cases," ABC News, May 2, 2020.

192 **More than a quarter of a million** Jennifer Calfas, Arian Campo-Flores, and Eric Sylvers, "Global Deaths from Coronavirus Pass 251,000," *Wall Street Journal*, May 4, 2020.

192 **For the month of May** May 4, 2020, statement reported in Andrew

Restuccia, "White House Coronavirus Task Force Team Restricted from Congressional Hearings," *Wall Street Journal* May 5, 2020.

193 **New Covid-19 forecasts** "New IHME Forecast Projects Nearly 135,000 Covid-19 Deaths in US," May 4, 2020. Institute for Health Metrics and Evaluation.

193 **The Senate is back in session** Mitch McConnell, speech on the Senate floor, "In an 87-0 vote, the Senate Confirmed Robert Feitel's Nomination for Inspector General of the Nuclear Regulatory Commission (NRC)," C-SPAN, May 4, 2020.

193 **Mr. President, the Senate convenes** Chuck Schumer, speech on the Senate floor, ibid.

193 **Shame on us if** Nsikan Akpan and Victoria Jaggard, "Fauci: No Scientific Evidence the Coronavirus Was Made in a Chinese Lab," *National Geographic*, May 4, 2020.

193 **The president continues** Chuck Schumer, speech on the Senate floor, "In an 87-0 vote, the Senate Confirmed Robert Feitel's Nomination for Inspector General of the Nuclear Regulatory Commission (NRC)," C-SPAN, May 4, 2020.

194 **May 1st was my last** Tim Bray, "Bye, Amazon," May 4, 2020.

194 **By the way, you don't wear** Andrew Cuomo, "Andrew Cuomo New York Covid-19 Briefing Transcript May 4," Rev.com, May 4, 2020.

194 **The governor's veto of** Tom Barrett, "Barrett Responds to Governor's Veto of SB 858," MI Senate GOP, May 4, 2020.

195 **I am happy to work** Gretchen Whitmer, "Michigan Governor Gretchen Whitmer Press Conference Transcript May 4," Rev.com, May 4, 2020.

195 **The hospital system is not** Josh Sharfstein, interview, "Covid-19 at a Plateau, Not Going Down in U.S.: Johns Hopkins," Bloomberg, May 4, 2020.

195 **The number of new reported** Jeremy Blackman, Stephanie Lamm, Jordan Rubio, "Last Week Was the Worst Yet for Texas Covid-19 Deaths and Infections," *Houston Chronicle*, May 5, 2020.

195 **How do I know that we** Greg Abbott, "Gov. Greg Abbott Texas Coronavirus Press Conference Transcript May 5: Governor Allowing Salons, Pools to Open This Week," Rev.com, May 5, 2020.

196 **It was my job to ensure** Rick Bright, reported in Hilary Brueck, "A Top US Scientist Who Was Pushed Out of His Job Says He Was 'Pressured to Let Politics and Cronyism Drive Decisions' in the Nation's Coronavirus Response," *Business Insider*, May 5, 2020.

196 **It was obvious that Dr. Bright** Rick Bright Whistleblower Complaint, published by Brandon Carter, NPR.

196 **Just hours after [Governor] Ducey** Laurie Roberts, "Gov. Doug Ducey Fires the Scientists Who Warn He's Making a Mistake by Reopening Arizona," *Arizona Republic*, May 6, 2020.

196 **We don't know exactly** Brian Chesky, "A Message from Co-Founder and CEO Brian Chesky," Airbnb, May 5, 2020.

197 **I don't think anyone** Sam Van Pykeren, "Adam Schiff Says Trump's 'Cult of the President' Has Infected the Republican Party," *Mother Jones*, May 5, 2020.

197 **The Walt Disney Company today** Walt Disney Company, "The Walt Disney Company Reports Second Quarter and Six Months Earnings for Fiscal 2020," May 5, 2020.

197 **It's interesting. I wonder** Ron DeSantis, "Florida Governor Ron DeSantis Covid-19 Briefing May 5," Rev.com, May 5, 2020.

197 **One day after reopening** Rebecca Woolington, Langston Taylor, and Allison Ross, "Florida Adds 113 Coronavirus Deaths, a New One-Day Record," *Tampa Bay Times*, May 5, 2020.

198 **Since noon, the statewide** Robert Downe and Julian Gill, "Houston Coronavirus Updates: May 5, 2020," *Houston Chronicle*, May 5, 2020.

198 **Texas is in a position** Greg Abbott, "Governor Abbott Expands Business Openings in Texas, Announces Surge Response Teams to Combat Covid-19," press release, Office of the Texas Governor, May 5, 2020.

198 **There's no doubt that** Andrew Cuomo, "Andrew Cuomo New York Covid-19 Briefing Transcript May 5," Rev.com, May 5, 2020.

198 **Police officers aggressively** Hakeem Jeffries, @RepJeffries, Twitter, 10:05 A.M., May 5, 2020.

199 **Conversations are being had** Mike Pence, Ben Tracy, Kathryn Watson, and Paula Reid, "Winding Down Coronavirus Task Force Is Under Discussion by Trump Administration," CBS News, interview, May 5, 2020, report May 6, 2020.

199 **I'm viewing our great citizens** Donald Trump, "Donald Trump Press Conference & Speech Transcript at Arizona Mask Factory May 5," Rev.com, May 5, 2020.

199 **How many people** Gregg Gonsalves, @gregggonsalves, Twitter, 6:19 A.M., May 6, 2020.

199 **So I call these people warriors** Donald Trump, "Transcript: Donald Trump Signs Nurse's Day Proclamation, Contradicts Nurse on PPE," Rev.com, May 6, 2020.

200 **Lotta tough talk** Brian Schatz, @brianschatz, Twitter, 6:41 P.M., May 6, 2020.

200 **You know, a president** Joe Biden, Virtual Fundraiser, leaked audio, May 6, 2020.

200 **I thought we could wind it down** Trump, "Transcript: Donald Trump Signs Nurse's Day Proclamation, Contradicts Nurse on PPE," May 6, 2020.

200 **Let's dismiss a myth about tests** Kayleigh McEnany, "White House Kayleigh McEnany Press Conference Transcript May 6," Rev.com, May 6, 2020.

200 **The media likes to say** Donald Trump, "Remarks by President Trump and Vice President Pence at a Meeting with Governor Reynolds of Iowa," whitehouse.gov, May 6, 2020.

200 **The Republican-led** Bill Chappell, "Michigan Legislature Sues Gov. Whitmer, Seeking to End Coronavirus Emergency Orders," NPR, May 6. 2020.

201 **We do not know** Mike Pompeo, news conference, reported in Carol Morello, "Pompeo Accuses China of Withholding Vital Information on Coronavirus," *Washington Post*, May 6, 2020.

201 **I think this matter should** Hua Chunying, reported in Matt Perez, "White House Characterizes China Relationship as One of 'Disappointment and Frustration,'" *Forbes*, May 6, 2020.

201 **They're being terribly** Nahal Toosi and Natasha Bertrand, "Democrats Demand Intel on Coronavirus Origins," *Politico*, May 6, 2020.

201 **During the tracing contacts** Public statement, reported in Connor Richard, "2 Utah County Businesses Told Staff to Ignore Covid-19 Guidelines, Resulting in 68 Positive Cases," *Standard Examiner*, May 6, 2020.

202 **We want to terminate** Trump, "Transcript: Donald Trump Signs Nurse's Day Proclamation, Contradicts Nurse on PPE," May 6, 2020.

202 **President Trump is asking** Larry Levitt, @larry_levitt, Twitter, 2:49 P.M., May 6, 2020.

202 **Rates of Food Insecurity** Lauren Bauer, "The Covid-19 Crisis Has Already Left Too Many Children Hungry in America," The Hamilton Project, May 6, 2020.

202 **In an effort to stem** "Ohio Senate Unanimously Rejects Amendment to Limit Dr. Amy Acton's Power," Associated Press and WBNS.

202 **My administration is focused** Mike DeWine, "Mike DeWine Ohio Coronavirus Briefing Transcript May 6," Rev.com, May 6, 2020.

203 **Ten days after covid19** Scott Gottlieb, @ScottGottliebMD, Twitter, 5:28 P.M., May 6, 2020.

203 **It's clear to me** Testimony to U.S. House Appropriations Subcommittee

203 **A lot of people have been** Cuomo, "Andrew Cuomo New York Covid-19 Briefing Transcript May 6," May 6, 2020.

203 **Last week we performed** Caitlin Rivers, Testimony to the United States

House of Representatives Committee on Appropriations, Johns Hopkins Center for Health Security, May 6, 2020.

204 **We're thinking that maybe** Cuomo, "Andrew Cuomo New York Covid-19 Briefing Transcript May 6," May 6, 2020.

204 **A set of detailed** Jason Dearen and Mike Stobbe, "Trump Administration Buries Detailed CDC Advice on Reopening," Associated Press, May 7, 2020.

205 **And the most essential** Bill de Blasio, "Bill de Blasio NYC Covid-19 Press Conference Transcript May 7," Rev .com, May 7, 2020.

205 **If you want to know** Chris Murphy, @ChrisMurphyCT, Twitter, 11:47 A.M., May 7, 2020.

205 **We were recently notified** Hogan Gidley, statement, reported in Grace Segers, "Military Aide Assigned to White House Tests Positive for Coronavirus," CBS News, May 7, 2020.

205 **They're doing everything** Donald Trump, "Transcript: Donald Trump Meeting with Texas Governor Greg Abbott on Coronavirus," Rev.com, May 7, 2020.

205 **Every staff member in close** Judd Deere, public statement, reported in Michael Crowley and Michael D. Shear, "White House Rattled by a Military Aide's Positive Coronavirus Test," *New York Times*, May 7, 2020.

205 **Right now, we're all warriors** Trump, "Transcript: Donald Trump Meeting with Texas Governor Greg Abbott on Coronavirus," May 7, 2020.

205 **Black people are dying** Bill Barrow and Hilary Powell, "Q&A: Stacey Abrams Is Ready to Serve but Not on Top Court," Associated Press, May 7, 2020.

206 **So this disease is not only** Joe Biden, "Transcript: Joe Biden Virtual Roundtable with African American Florida Representatives," Rev.com, May 7, 2020.

206 **Rural residents die** Adam Harris, "Rural Southerners Take on the Coronavirus," *Atlantic*, May 7, 2020.

206 **The public-health crisis** Ibid.

206 **Basically, there's only three** Greg Abbott, "Transcript: Donald Trump Meeting with Texas Governor Greg Abbott on Coronavirus," May 7, 2020.

207 **A sizable majority** Andrew Daniller, "Americans Remain Concerned That States Will Lift Restrictions Too Quickly, But Partisan Differences Widen," Pew Research Center, May 7, 2020.

207 **I also think, and I do this** Andrew Cuomo, "Andrew Cuomo New York Covid-19 Press Conference Transcript May 7," Rev.com, May 7, 2020.

207 **I watch Fox News** Trump, "Transcript: Donald Trump Meeting with Texas Governor Greg Abbott on Coronavirus," May 7, 2020.

208 **Global 3,769,150 cases** Johns Hopkins University and Medicine, Coronavirus Resource Center. Accessed May 7, 2020.

209 **Total nonfarm payroll** U.S. Bureau of Labor Statistics, "Employment Situation Summary," economic news release, June 5, 2020.

209 **No one could look at today's** Chuck Schumer, "Schumer Statement on Record High Unemployment in April," Senate Democrats, May 8, 2020.

209 **We're in no rush** Donald Trump, "Transcript: Donald Trump Meets with Republican Members of Congress," Rev.com, May 8, 2020.

210 **Let me start with my** Pat Toomey, "Exclusive: Toomey Calls for Reopening America Faster: Virus 'Danger' to Most Overstated," American Priority, May 8, 2020.

210 **These people want to get back** *Fox & Friends* interview

210 **Today's rush by the Trump** United Food and Commercial Workers, "Trump Order to Re-Open 14 Meatpacking Plants Fails to Increase Coronavirus Testing and Safety Measures Needed to Protect Food Supply & Workers," press release, May 8, 2020.

210 **We have put in place** Kayleigh McEnany, "Press Briefing by Press Secretary Kayleigh McEnany," whitehouse.gov, May 8, 2020.

210 **More than 1,000 workers** Donnelle Eller, "Number of Workers with Coronavirus at Waterloo Tyson Plant More Than Double Earlier Figure," *Des Moines Register*, May 7, 2020.

211 **Iowa now has** Steven Dennis, @StevenTDennis, Twitter, 3:44 P.M., May 8, 2020.

211 **Every 49 seconds or so** Timothy Egan, "The World Is Taking Pity on Us," *New York Times*, May 8, 2020.

211 **It would have been bad** Barack Obama.

211 **Does the President see** Douglas Christian and Kayleigh McEnany, "Press Briefing by Press Secretary Kayleigh McEnany," May 8, 2020.

212 **White House Spokeswoman** Jason Dearen and Mike Stobbe, "Trump Administration Buries Detailed CDC Advice on Reopening," Associated Press, May 7, 2020.

212 **I am not disgruntled** Interview with Norah O'Donnell, "The Government Whistleblower Who Says the Trump Administration's Coronavirus Response Has Cost Lives," *60 Minutes*, May 18, 2020.

212 **I feel about vaccines** Trump, "Transcript: Donald Trump Meets with Republican Members of Congress," May 8, 2020.

212 **As [FDA Director] Stephen Hahn** Michael Felberbaum, public statement, reported in Grace Segers, "FDA Commissioner Self-Quarantines After Contact with Person Who Tested Positive for Covid-19," CBS News, May 9, 2020.

212 **CDC Director Dr. Robert Redfield** Public statement, reported in Wesley Breuer and Jeremy Diamond, "CDC Director Self-Quarantining After Exposure to Person at the White House Who Tested Positive for Covid-19," CNN, May 9, 2020.

213 **Dr. Anthony Fauci, the director** Jake Tapper, "Fauci to Begin 'Modified Quarantine,'" CNN.com, May 10, 2020.

213 **CA is now a vote** Gavin Newsom, @GavinNewsom, Twitter, 6:01 P.M., May 8, 2020.

213 **So in California** Donald Trump, @realDonaldTrump, Twitter, 11:45 A.M., May 9, 2020.

213 **The priority for us** Andrew Cuomo, "Amid Ongoing Covid-19 Pandemic, Governor Cuomo Launches New Initiative to Expand Access to Testing in Low-Income Communities and Communities of Color," ny.gov, May 9, 2020.

214 **Nearly half of all deaths** Anita Chabria, Ben Welsh, Jack Doland, Richard Winton, "Senior Care Homes Source of Nearly Half of All California Coronavirus-Related Deaths, Data Show," *Los Angeles Times*, May 8, 2020.

214 **When you look at disasters** Cuomo, "Amid Ongoing Covid-19 Pandemic, Governor Cuomo Launches New Initiative to Expand Access to Testing in Low-Income Communities and Communities of Color," May 9, 2020.

214 **In the middle** Chris Murphy, @ChrisMurphyCT, Twitter, 11:08 A.M., May 10, 2020.

214 **Let me just emphasize** Fox interview

215 **So our projections through till** "Transcript: Christopher Murray Discusses Coronavirus Models on *Face the Nation*," CBS News, May 10, 2020.

215 **We are getting** Donald Trump, @realDonaldTrump, Twitter, 7:48 A.M., May 10, 2020.

215 **We're seeing increases** "Transcript: Christopher Murray Discusses Coronavirus Models on *Face the Nation*," May 10, 2020.

215 **We have to understand** Michael Osterholm, interview with Chuck Todd, *Meet the Press*, May 10, 2020.

215 **It is scary to** Interview on *Face the Nation*, CBS News

216 **What we have to tell** Osterholm, interview with Chuck Todd, *Meet the Press*, May 10, 2020.

216 **If we do this carefully** Steve Mnuchin, interview, "Mnuchin Remains Confident in Bounce-Back Later This Year, But Unemployment Will 'Get Worse' Before It Happens," *Fox News Sunday*, May 10, 2020.

216 **That was a pity party** Peter Navarro, "Peter Navarro Pushes Back on Economic 'Pity Party': This Is Not the Great Depression," Fox News, May 11, 2020.

216 **78,000 are dead** Brian Kilmeade, *Fox & Friends*, reported in Roger

Sollenberg, "*Fox & Friends* Hosts Urge Americans to Adopt 'Military Mindset' to Reopen Economy 'Right Now,'" *Salon*, May 11, 2020.

216 **Instead of unifying the country** Joe Biden, op-ed, "Joe Biden: How the White House Coronavirus Response Presents Us with a False Choice," *Washington Post*, May 11, 2020.

216 **Coronavirus infection rates** Jonathan Allen, Phil McCausland, and Cyrus Farivar, "Unreleased White House Report Shows Coronavirus Rates Spiking in Heartland Communities," NBC News, May 11, 2020.

217 **The great people of** Donald Trump, @realDonaldTrump, Twitter, 10:26 A.M., May 11, 2020.

217 **To those politicians** Tom Wolf, "Gov. Wolf May 11 Remarks on Staying the Course, Following the Law," May 11, 2020.

217 **The coronavirus spread** Mike Dorning, Dominic Carey, and Dave Merrill, "Infections Near U.S. Meat Plants Rise at Twice the National Rate," *Bloomberg*, May 12, 2020.

217 **We're basically assessing** Mitch McConnell, reported in Manu Raju and Claire Foran, "Democrats Plot Massive Stimulus Plan Amid Stiff White House and GOP Resistance," CNN, May 11, 2020; "House Democrats' Coronavirus Relief Bill Expected to Cost $3T," *The Hill*, May 12, 2020.

217 **Now with the states** John Cornyn, speech on Senate floor, "Senate Session," C-SPAN, May 11, 2020.

218 **If your country reopens** Tom Wolf, @GovernorTomWolf, Twitter, 12:37 P.M., May 11, 2020.

218 **It crossed me that** *Fox & Friends* interview

218 **The CDC continues to encourage** Staff email, reported in Libby Cathey, "Coronavirus Government Response Updates: Americans Returning to Work Can Get Tested 'Very Soon,' Trump Claims," ABC News, May 11, 2020.

218 **In the span of just** Donald Trump, "Donald Trump Press Conference Transcript on Coronavirus Testing—May 11," Rev.com, May 11, 2020.

218 **It's true that the U.S.** German Lopez, "Trump's White House Banner Claims 'America Leads the World in Testing.' That's Wrong," *Vox*, May 11, 2020.

219 **If somebody wants to be tested** Trump, "Donald Trump Press Conference Transcript on Coronavirus Testing—May 11."

219 **So everybody who needs a** Brett Giroir, ibid.

219 **I really believe that as good** Donald Trump, ibid.

219 **Shutting your eyes and trying** Michael Ryan, "World Health Organization Coronavirus Press Conference Transcript May 11," Rev.com, May 11, 2020.

220 **I think President Obama should have** Mitch McConnell, interview with Lara Trump, "Trump Online Campaign Event with Senate Majority Leader Mitch McConnell," C-SPAN, May 11, 2020.

220 **The maddening thing** Ben Rhodes, @BRhodes, Twitter, 9:10 P.M., May 11, 2020.

220 **I'm sure Mitch is aware** Michael Steele, @MichaelSteele, Twitter, 2:17 P.M., May 12, 2020.

220 **We're not reopening based** Donald G. McNeil Jr., "As States Rush to Reopen, Scientists Fear a Coronavirus Comeback," *New York Times*, May 11, 2020.

220 **United States 80,239 deaths** Johns Hopkins Coronavirus Resource Center. Accessed May 11, 2020.

221 **Four-in-10 Americans** Jennifer Agiesta, "CNN Poll: Negative Ratings for Government Handling of Coronavirus Persist," CNN.com, May 12, 2020.

221 **This is a bipartisan hearing** Senate Health, Education, Labor, and Pensions (HELP) Committee Hearing

221 **When you talk about** Ibid.

222 **I think we ought to have** Ibid.

223 **This is far from** Ibid.

223 **My concern is that** Ibid.

223 **Quarantine is relatively easy** Ibid.

224 **Admiral Giroir, I'm** Ibid.

224 **Dr. Fauci, Dr. Redfield, you've** Ibid.

224 **Thank god for** Kamala Harris, "'Thank God for Dr. Fauci': Sen. Harris on Fauci's Courage to Speak the Truth," *All In with Chris Hayes*, May 12, 2020.

225 **If we want even an outside** Mitch McConnell, speech on Senate floor, "Senators Grassley and McConnell on Coronavirus Impact," C-SPAN, May 12, 2020.

225 **In March, 83%** Marquette University Law School Poll, @MULawPoll, Twitter, 1:19 P.M., May 12, 2020.

225 **Our university, when open** Timothy P. White, public statement, May 12, 2020, "California Moving University Classes Online as Fauci Warns of Reopening Too Soon," Reuters, May 13, 2020.

225 **Participants on a board** Adrian Wojnarowski, "NBA Owners, Execs Hopeful for Return after Call with Adam Silver, Sources Say," ESPN, May 12, 2020.

225 **Can you imagine Ronald Reagan** "'Not Up to the Job': Fmr. AG Holder on Trump's Failed Coronavirus Response," *All In with Chris Hayes*, May 12, 2020.

226 **[The U.S. coronavirus response] has certainly damaged** Jon Snow, "Fact We Have Worst Outbreak in World Damages Perception of American Competence"—Jeremy Konyndyk, Center for Global Development," 4 News (UK), May 12, 2020.

226 **You can't be in lockdown** Ezra Klein, "We Don't Have a President, or a Plan," *Vox*, May 13, 2020.

226 **The White House and its Task Force** Mike Braun, speech on Senate floor, "Senators Schumer and Braun on Coronavirus Response," C-SPAN, May 13, 2020.

226 **President Donald Trump and** Eric Banco and Asawin Suebsaeng, "Team Trump Pushes CDC to Revise Down Its Covid Death Counts," *Daily Beast*, May 13, 2020.

227 **Are we really going** Mike Braun, speech on Senate floor, "Senators Schumer and Braun on Coronavirus Response," May 13, 2020.

227 **Each Day that Congress** Joint Written Statement

227 **Among people who were** Webcast hosted by the Peterson Institute for International Economics.

228 **The world economy is expected** "Covid-19 to Slash Global Economic Output by $8.5 Trillion Over Next Two Years," United Nations, May 13, 2020.

228 **Under the current plan** Lamont Bagby, letter to Gov. Northam from the Virginia Legislative Black Caucus, reported in Mel Leonor, "Black Caucus Opposes Northam's Decision to Begin Reopening in All but Northern Virginia," *Roanoke Times*, May 14, 2020.

228 **Unfortunately, a few Texas counties** Ken Paxton, letters to three Texas counties, "AG Paxton Warns County Judges and Local Officials on Unlawful Covid-19 Orders," News Channel 6, May 13, 2020.

229 **Now, will you have an incident** Donald Trump, "President Trump Meeting with Colorado and North Dakota Governors," C-SPAN, May 13, 2020.

229 **I want this to end** J. B. Pritzker, public statement, reported in Andrew Carrigan, "Pritzker Tells Officials to 'Step Up and Lead,' Says Counties Reopening Early May Face Consequences," WREX 13, May 13, 2020.

229 **Rightwing Militia Groups** Tom Perkins, "Michigan: Rightwing Militia Groups to Protest Stay-At-Home Orders," The Guardian, May 13, 2020.

230 **I do think that the fact** Interview on *The View*, ABC, May 13, 2020

230 **The Wisconsin Supreme Court** Molly Beck and Patrick Marley, "Wisconsin Supreme Court Strikes Down Wisconsin's Stay-at-Home Order That Closed Businesses to Limit Spread of Coronavirus," *Milwaukee Journal Sentinel*, May 13, 2020.

230 **In this one fell swoop** "Wisconsin Supreme Court Strikes Down State's Stay-at-Home Order," NBC News, May 13, 2020.

230 **Although most Americans** Becky Bratu, "Social Distancing in America Appears to Be on the Decline," Bloomberg, May 14, 2020.

230 **The less successful** "Interview: Maria Bartiromo Interviews Donald Trump on Fox Business," Fox Business, May 14, 2020.

231 **Remember, if you're in a workplace** Andy Beshear, "Kentucky Governor Andy Beshear Covid-19 Briefing Transcript May 14," Rev.com, May 14, 2020.

231 **Our country is in pain** House Committee on Energy and Commerce, Subcommittee on Health Hearing

231 **Our window of opportunity is closing** Ibid.

231 **I ask why is this** Ibid.

232 **The government sits around** Ibid.

232 **Is there not something** Ibid.

232 **I will never forget the emails** Ibid.

232 **For months the president has** Ibid.

233 **First and Foremost** Ibid.

233 **The Great State of Wisconsin** Donald Trump, @realDonaldTrump, Twitter, 8:11 A.M., May 14, 2020.

233 **Michigan closed down its** David Welch, "Michigan Cancels Legislative Session to Avoid Armed Protesters," Bloomberg, May 14, 2020.

234 **The closer you can** Ryan Lizza and Daniel Lippman, "A Metrics-Obsessed White House Struggles to Define Success on Coronavirus," *Politico*, May 14, 2020.

234 **It's not a secret** Lori Lightfoot, interview with David Axelrod, *The Axe Files*, CNN Audio (taped May 14, aired May 18).

234 **There are people who live** J. B. Pritzker, "Illinois Governor J.B. Pritzker Coronavirus Press Conference Transcript May 14," Rev.com, May 14, 2020.

234 **I was wrong** Mitch McConnell, interview, "Sen. Mitch McConnell on Additional Coronavirus Economic Relief, Michael Flynn Saga, November Election," Fox News, May 14, 2020.

235 **Well, I think it's hopeful** CNN interview.

235 **Could be that testing's** Donald Trump, "Donald Trump Speech Transcript at PA Distribution Center for Coronavirus Relief Supplies," Rev .com, May 14, 2020.

235 **Dear @realDonaldTrump** Ted Lieu, @tedlieu, Twitter, 6:51 P.M., May 14, 2020.

235 **This makes my brain** Joanne Freeman, @joannefreeman, Twitter, 12:28 P.M., May 15, 2020.

236 **Over the past two weeks** Kamala Harris, "Harris Leads Call for Accurate Count of Fatalities and Consistent Statistics During Covid-19 Pandemic," Kamala D. Harris, U.S. Senator for California, May 15, 2020.

236 **There has never been a vaccine project** Donald Trump, "Remarks by President Trump on Vaccine Development," whitehouse.gov, May 15, 2020.

236 **Winning matters and we will deliver** Mark Esper, press conference, "Defense Secretary Esper Pledges Vaccine by Year's End to Treat Coronavirus," C-SPAN, May 15, 2020.

236 **And how this goes up** Andrew Cuomo, "Andrew Cuomo New York

May 15 Covid-19 Press Conference Transcript," Rev.com, May 15, 2020.

236 **We read about all of the very sad** Trump, "Remarks by President Trump on Vaccine Development," May 15, 2020.

237 **Second stone is** Cuomo, "Andrew Cuomo New York May 15 Covid-19 Press Conference Transcript."

237 **Rain drizzled as a crowd** Katie Shepherd and Moriah Balingit "A Noose, an Ax and Trump-Inspired Insults: Anti-Lockdown Protesters Ratchet up Violent Rhetoric." *Washington Post*, May 15, 2020.

237 **These are not just citizens** Adrienne Vogt, "Michigan Governor Says Reopening Protests Are 'Essentially' Political Rallies." CNN. May 15, 2020

237 **As businesses reopened** Matthew Perrone, Brian Witte, and Nicky Forster, "Most US States Fall Short of Recommended Testing Levels," Associated Press, May 15, 2020.

238 **The new cases Thursday** Nicole Cobler, "Texas Sees Highest Single-Day Hike in Coronavirus Deaths, Cases," *Austin American-Statesman*, May 14, 2020.

238 **Recognizing the seriousness** Kayleigh McEnany, "Press Briefing by Press Secretary Kayleigh McEnany Issued on: May 15, 2020," whitehouse.gov, May 15, 2020.

238 **It's totally surreal** Sarah Ferris and John Bresnahan, "As Crisis Continues, an Anxious House Returns to Washington," *Politico*, May 15, 2020.

238 **My Republican colleagues are** Val Demings, "Rep. Demings to Support 'The Heroes Act,'" press release, May 15, 2020.

239 **Mr. Speaker, Democratic Leadership** Jodey Arrington, "House Session, Part 2," C-SPAN, May 15, 2020.

239 **I've got to tell you** Speech on House floor

239 **More than anything, this** HBCU Commencement 2020, "Show Me Your Walk."

240 **We will bring the economy** Commencement Speech to Fremont High School, NE

240 **So much of your generation** Commencement Address, #Graduate Together

240 **Reopen we must** Alec Azar, interview with Jake Tapper, *State of the Union*, May 17, 2020.

240 **There is a recognition** Alexander Burns, "Seeking: Big Democratic Ideas That Make Everything Better," *New York Times*, May 17, 2020.

240 **Governments and drugmakers** Peter Loftus, "Coronavirus Vaccine Front-Runners Emerge, Rollouts Weighed," *Wall Street Journal*, May 17, 2020.

241 **The state of Georgia** David Fahrenthold, @Fahrenthold, Twitter, 10:39 A.M., May 17, 2020.

241 **This administration has shown** Interview with Nick Valencia, CNN.

241 **Today is day 78** Andrew Cuomo, "Amid Ongoing Covid-19 Pandemic, Governor Cuomo Announces New York State Has Doubled Testing Capacity to Reach 40,000 Tests Per Day, Encourages Eligible New Yorkers to Get Tested for Covid-19," ny.gov, May 17, 2020.

241 **We have to make smart** Jay Inslee, "Washington Governor Jay Inslee Coronavirus Press Briefing Transcript May 18," Rev.com, May 18, 2020.

241 **I happened to be taking it** Donald Trump, "Donald Trump Says He's Taking Hydroxychloroquine to Prevent Coronavirus in Press Conference," Rev.com, May 18, 2020.

242 **Trump just acknowledged** Neal Cavuto, "President Trump: I've Taken Hydroxychloroquine for about a Week-and-a-Half Now," *Your World*, Fox News, May 18, 2020.

242 **The first Covid-19 vaccine** Becky Bratu, "Moderna's Coronavirus Vaccine Shows Early Progress," *Bloomberg*, May 18, 2020.

242 **This is the biggest shock** Jerome Powell, "Fed Reserve Chair and Treasury Secretary Testimony on Coronavirus Relief Bill," C-SPAN, May 19, 2020.

242 **It is clear the repeated** Donald Trump, letter to WHO Director-General Tedros Adhanom Ghebreyesus, reported in Andrew Restuccia, Gordon Lubold, and Drew Hinshaw, *Wall Street Journal*, May 19, 2020.

242 **When you don't believe in truth** Interview with CNN's Manu Raju.

243 **The scientist who** Alessandro Marazzi Sassoon, "Florida's Scientist Was Fired for Refusing to 'Manipulate' Covid-19 Data," *USA Today*, May 19, 2020.

243 **How many workers . . . No workers should**: Senate Banking Committee Hearing

243 **Coming together at a time** Andy Beshear, "Kentucky Governor Andy Beshear Covid-19 Briefing Transcript May 19," Rev.com, May 19, 2020.

243 **MA isn't ready** Ayanna Pressley, @AyannaPressley, Twitter, 9:53 A.M., May 19, 2020.

243 **Look, no unemployment system** Ron DeSantis, "Florida Governor Ron DeSantis May 19 Coronavirus Press Conference Transcript," Rev.com, May 19, 2020.

244 **So when we have** Donald Trump, "Remarks by President Trump in Cabinet Meeting," whitehouse.gov, May 19, 2020.

244 **I would point out** Michael Ryan, "World Health Organization Coronavirus Press Conference Transcript May 20," Rev.com.

244 **If the United States** James Glanz and Campbell Robertson, "Lockdown Delays Cost at Least 36,000 Lives, Data Show," *New York Times*, May 20, 2020.

245 **You're asking me about** Nancy Pelosi, "Transcript of Pelosi Weekly Press

Conference Today," Congressman Nancy Pelosi, California's 12th District, Pelosi.house.gov, May 20, 2020.

245 **Stay-at-home orders** Ed Yong, "America's Patchwork Pandemic Is Fraying Even Further," *Atlantic*, May 20, 2020.

245 **The talk of a second wave** Caitlin Rivers quoted in ibid.

245 **People ask all the time** Andrew Cuomo, "Video, Audio, Photos & Rush Transcript: Amid Ongoing Covid-19 Pandemic, Governor Cuomo Announces Results of State's Antibody Testing Survey at Churches in Lower-income NYC Communities of Color Show 27 Percent of Individuals Tested Positive for Covid-19 An,"[sic], ny.gov, May 20, 2020.

246 **The [AP/NORC Center for Public Affairs Research]** Thomas Beaumont and Hannah Fingerhut, "AP-NORC Poll: Americans Harbor Strong Fear of New Infections," Associated Press, May 20, 2020.

246 **Dear President Trump** Dana Nessel, "Open Letter to President Donald J. Trump," Michigan.gov, May 20, 2020.

246 **We still have a long way** Tedros Adhanom Ghebreyesus, "World Health Organization Coronavirus Press Conference Transcript May 20," Rev.com.

247 **Maybe that's what we should have done** Donald Trump, "Donald Trump Meeting Transcript with Kansas, Arkansas Governors," Rev.com, May 20, 2020.

247 **Nurses and other health care** National Nurses United, "New Survey of Nurses Provides Frontline Proof of Widespread Employer, Government Disregard for Nurse and Patient Safety, Mainly Through Lack of Optimal PPE," press release, May 20, 2020.

247 **Dr. Rick Bright's testimony** Bonnie Castillo, "New Survey of Nurses Provides Frontline Proof of Widespread Employer, Government Disregard for Nurse and Patient Safety, Mainly Through Lack of Optimal PPE," National Nurses United, May 20, 2020.

247 **Former Vice President Joe Biden leads** "Biden Holds 11 Point Lead as Trump Approval on Coronavirus Dips, Quinnipiac University National Poll Finds; Almost Half Say Second Wave of Coronavirus 'Very Likely' in Fall," Quinnipiac University/Poll, May 20, 2020.

248 **The Centers for Disease Control and Prevention is** Alexis C. Madrigal and Robinson Meyer, "'How Could the CDC Make That Mistake?'" *Atlantic*, May 21, 2020.

248 **Georgia's early move** Megan Cassella, "Reopening Reality Check: Georgia's Jobs Aren't Flooding Back," *Politico*, May 21, 2020.

248 **Mr. President, I just hope** Debbie Dingell, interview on MSNBC,

reported in Dan Mangan, "Trump Doesn't Wear Coronavirus Mask in Public at Ford Plant," CNBC, May 21, 2020.

248 **Are you going to wear** Donald Trump, "Remarks by President Trump Before Marine One Departure," whitehouse.gov, May 21, 2020.

248 **If he fails to wear** Interview on *New Day*, "Michigan Attorney General: We Ask You Wear a Mask," CNN .com.

249 **Well, I had one on before** Donald Trump, "Donald Trump Tours the Ford Plant Without a Mask, Explains Why," Rev.com, May 21, 2020.

249 **Trump not wearing** Brian Schatz, @brianschatz, Twitter, 4:16 P.M., May 21, 2020.

249 **Bill Ford encouraged** Public statement, reported in John Fritze and Courtney Subramanian, "Ford 'Encouraged' Trump to Wear Mask During Factory Tour, but It Came Off for the Cameras," *USA Today*, May 21, 2020.

249 **In Michigan, of course** CNN interview with Wolf Blitzer.

249 **A Court of Claims judge** Beth LeBlanc, "Judge Affirms Whitmer's Authority to Extend Covid-19 Emergency; Legislature to Appeal," *Detroit News*, May 21, 2020.

250 **An Iowa agency's order** Barbara Rodriguez, "Iowa Agency's Order for Nearly 100,000 Masks for Covid-19 Response Canceled under FEMA Directive, State Official Says," *Des Moines Register*, May 21, 2020.

250 **Look, it's really hard** Jeff Stein and Robert Costa, "Top White House Economic Adviser Expresses Uncertainty About Recovery Despite Trump's Confidence," *Washington Post*, May 21, 2020.

250 **Of the 2,200 employees** Jordan Valinsky, "1 in 4 Tyson Employees in a North Carolina Plant Tested Positive for Covid-19," CNN Business, May 22, 2020.

250 **Our numbers are not as good** Kay Ivey, "Alabama Governor Ivey Coronavirus News Conference," C-SPAN, May 21, 2020.

250 **A permanent lockdown is not** Donald Trump, "Remarks by President Trump at Ford Rawsonville Components Plant," whitehouse.gov, May 21, 2020.

250 **A recently launched federal effort** Anna Wilde Mathews, "Nursing Homes Don't Have to Report Pre-May Covid-19 Deaths to U.S. Officials," *Wall Street Journal*, May 21, 2020.

251 **It is possible** Christine Cassel, Christopher Chyba, Susan L. Graham, John P. Holdren, Eric S. Lander, Ed Penhoet, William Press, Maxine Savitz, Harold Varmus, "Recommendations for the National Strategic Pandemic-Response Stockpile," May 20, 2020.

251 **Some governors have deemed** Donald Trump, "Donald Trump

Coronavirus Press Conference Transcript May 22: Says Places of Worship Must Open Immediately," Rev.com, May 22, 2020.

251 **The coronavirus may still** Joel Achenbach, Rachel Weiner, and Isaac Stanley-Becker, "Study Estimates 24 States Still Have Uncontrolled Coronavirus Spread," *Washington Post*, May 22, 2020.

252 **If someone is wearing a mask** Doug Burgum, "ND Governor Doug Burgum Press Conference: Burgum Makes Emotional Plea Over Masks," Rev.com, May 23, 2020.

252 **Carnegie Mellon Researchers** Virginia Alvino Young, "Nearly Half of the Twitter Accounts Discussing 'Reopening America' May Be Bots," Carnegie Mellon University School of Computer Science, May 20, 2020.

252 **We have concerns** Deborah Birx, "Press Briefing by Press Secretary Kayleigh McEnany," whitehouse.gov, May 23, 2020.

252 **Last Friday, Mr. Trump** "As Death Toll Nears 100,000, Some in White House Question the Math," *New York Times*, May 22, 2020.

252 **Researchers have found** David Aaro, "Wearing a Surgical Mask Can Reduce Coronavirus Transmission by Up to 75 Percent, Study Says," Fox News, May 20, 2020.

253 **The guy has got more** "Transcript: Robert O'Brien on *Face the Nation*," May 24, 2020.

253 **As the death toll** Anne Gearan, "On Weekend Dedicated to War Dead, Trump Tweets Insults, Promotes Baseless Claims and Plays Golf," *Washington Post*, May 24, 2020.

253 **We've never been here before** Andrew Cuomo, "NY Governor Andrew Cuomo May 24 Press Conference Transcript," Rev.com, May 24, 2020.

254 **The pandemic that first struck** Reis Thebault and Abigail Hauslohner, "A Deadly 'Checkerboard': Covid-19's New Surge Across Rural America," *Washington Post*, May 24, 2020.

254 **According to the Centers** Chicago Urban League, "An Epidemic of Inequities: Structural Racism and Covid-19 in the Black Community," n.d.

254 **As a death historian** Leah Richier, @CallMeRichier, Twitter, 11:46 A.M., May 24, 2020.

THE RECKONING

257 **And this Memorial Day** Andrew Cuomo, "NY Governor Andrew Cuomo Memorial Day Press Conference Transcript," Rev.com, May 25, 2020.

257 **Our capital stock** CNN interview

257 **When you don't think** Justin Wolfers, @JustinWolfers, Twitter, 10:44 P.M., May 25, 2020.

257 **The AP/NORC Center polling** Aaron Rupar, "'Human Capital Stock': White House Adviser Kevin Hassett

Uses Dehumanizing Term for US Workers," *Vox*, May 26, 2020.

258 **As many as 500** Michael Nunes, "Hundreds Gather in Point Beach to Protest Covid-19 Lockdown," *Ocean Star*, May 25, 2020.

258 **I don't begrudge their** CNN interview

258 **All countries need to remain** Maria Van Kerkhove, media briefing, reported in Amanda Watts, "WHO Warns There Could Be a Second Peak, Not a Second Wave," CNN, May 25, 2020.

258 **State health officials** Dory MacMillan, public statement, reported in Maggie Haberman, "Trump Threatens to Pull Republican National Convention from North Carolina," *New York Times*, May 25, 2020.

259 **I love the Great State** Twitter

259 **I'm never going to apologize** "Michigan Governor Won't Apologize for Coronavirus Lockdown," *Axios*, May 26, 2020.

259 **We need to be also cognizant** Michael Ryan, media briefing, reported in Amanda Watts, "WHO Warns There Could Be a Second Peak, Not a Second Wave," CNN, May 25, 2020.

259 **Glenn Fine, who** Connor O'Brien, "Pentagon Watchdog Resigns after Being Sidelined by Trump," *Politico*, May 26, 2020.

259 **I personally and professionally** House Committee on Oversight Reform Hearing

260 **Stock Market up** Donald Trump, @realDonaldTrump, Twitter, 9:45 A.M., May 26, 2020

260 **I think—look, you know** Kayleigh McEnany, "Press Secretary Kayleigh McEnany Press Conference Transcript May 26," Rev.com, May 26, 2020.

260 **He's a fool** Joe Biden, interview with Dana Bash, reported in Eric Bradner, "Biden Blasts Trump for Mocking Face Masks," CNN, May 26, 2020.

260 **Federal authorities are investigating** Libor Jany, "4 Police Officers Fired as FBI Investigates In-Custody Death of Man in Minneapolis," *Star Tribune*, May 26, 2020.

260 **Great News, the** Donald Trump, @realDonaldTrump, Twitter, 10:16 P.M., May 26, 2020.

260 **It's a bad look** Aaron Rupar, @atrupar, Twitter, 10:22 P.M., May 26, 2020.

261 **We continue to forecast** "May 25 Coronavirus News," CNN, May 25, 2020.

261 **Packing pool parties** Holly Yan and Christina Maxouris, "The Numbers of New Covid-19 Cases Are Rising in 17 States," CNN.com, May 27, 2020.

261 **U.S. death toll** "U.S. Death Toll from the Coronavirus Has Surpassed 100,000, According to a Tally by Johns Hopkins University," Associated Press, May 27, 2020.

261 **We all want to reopen** Santa Clara County Public Health, Facebook video.

262 **There is no stigma attached** Mitch McConnell, public statement, reported in Caitlin Oprysko, "'There's No Stigma Attached to Wearing a Mask': McConnell Makes Plea in Favor of Face Masks," *Politico*, May 27, 2020.

262 **There are moments in our history** Joe Biden, video address, reported in Tim Reid, "Biden on 100,000 Coronavirus Deaths: 'To Those Hurting, the Nation Grieves with You,'" Reuters, May 27, 2020.

262 **As we remember** Kamala Harris, "Harris Statement as US Surpasses 100,000 Covid-19 Deaths," Kamala D. Harris, May 27, 2020.

262 **We want to reopen** Andrew Cuomo, "NY Governor Andrew Cuomo May 27 Press Conference Transcript," Rev.com, May 27, 2020.

263 **And as I've said before** Jay Inslee, "Washington Gov. Jay Inslee Press Conference Transcript May 27," Rev .com, May 27, 2020.

263 **While so many people** Greg Abbott, "Gov. Greg Abbott Texas Press Conference Transcript May 27," Rev .com, May 27, 2020.

263 **Effective Friday, May 29** Larry Hogan, "Maryland Gov. Larry Hogan Coronavirus Briefing Transcript May 27," Rev.com, May 27, 2020.

264 **With all these deaths and the need** Nancy Pelosi, "House Speaker Weekly Briefing," C-SPAN, May 28, 2020.

264 **I still think** CNN interview with Jim Sciutto.

264 **Employment continued to** "Beige Book—May 27, 2020," Board of Governors of the Federal Reserve System, May 27, 2020.

264 **Black Americans continue** Berkeley Lovelace Jr., "As U.S. Coronavirus Deaths Cross 100,000, Black Americans Bear Disproportionate Share of Fatalities," CNBC.com, May 27, 2020.

264 **More than 1 in 4** Avie Schneider, "40.8 Million Out of Work in the Past 10 Weeks—26% of Labor Force," NPR, May 28, 2020.

265 **100,000 people are dead** Elizabeth Warren, @ewarren, Twitter, 7:18 P.M., May 28, 2020.

265 **The Trump Administration** Yasmeen Abutaleb, Josh Dawsey, Lena H. Sun, and Laurie McGinley, "Administration Initially Dispensed Scarce Covid-19 Drug to Some Hospitals That Didn't Need It," *Washington Post*, May 28, 2020.

265 **On May 25th of 2020, George Floyd** Erica McDonald, "FBI News Conference Transcript on the Death of George Floyd Investigation," Rev .com, May 28, 2020.

265 **Anger over the death** Ryan Faircloth, Liz Navratil, Liz Sawyer, and Matt McKinney, "Looting and Flames Erupt in Minneapolis Amid Growing Protests Over George Floyd's Death," *Star Tribune*, May 28, 2020.

266 **What we've seen over the last two days** Jacob Frey, "Minneapolis Police Press Conference Transcript on

George Floyd Death Investigation," Rev.com, May 28, 2020.

266 **We have detailed the reforms** Donald Trump, "Donald Trump Press Conference Transcript on China, Hong Kong, and the WHO," Rev.com, May 29, 2020.

266 **We know where the hot spots** Andrew Cuomo, "NY Governor Andrew Cuomo May 29 Press Conference Transcript," Rev.com, May 29, 2020.

266 **A week after images** Gregory J. Holman, "Boone County Resident Positive for Covid-19 After Visiting Lake of the Ozarks Pool Party Venue," *Springfield News-Leader*, May 29, 2020.

267 **As a former woman** Val Demings, "My Fellow Brothers and Sisters in Blue, What the Hell Are You Doing?" *Washington Post*, May 29, 2020.

267 **Protestors took to the streets** Melissa Macaya, Mike Hayes, Fernando Alfonso III, Daniella Diaz, Jessie Yeung, Steve George, Ivana Kottasová, and Nick Thompson, "George Floyd Protests Spread Nationwide," CNN.com, May 30, 2020.

268 **This is not a protest** Keisha Lance Bottoms, public statement, reported in Jim Galloway, "On What Keisha Lance Bottoms Said Last Night," *Atlanta Journal-Constitution*, May 30, 2020.

268 **It's time to rebuild** Tim Walz, "Minnesota Governor Walz News Conference," C-SPAN, May 29, 2020.

268 **These thugs** The White House, @WhiteHouse, Twitter, 8:17 A.M. May 29, 2020.

268 **Violence begets violence** Keith Ellison, interview, "Protests Continue Over George Floyd's Death," *CBS This Morning*, CBS, May 29, 2020.

269 **These are things** Walz, "Minnesota Governor Walz News Conference," May 29, 2020.

269 **None of us can be silent** Joe Biden, interview, "'None of Us Can Be Silent': Biden Responds to Outrage Over George Floyd's Death | MSNBC," MSNBC, May 29, 2020.

269 **Two to four weeks** Karen DeYoung, Chelsea Janes, Gregory S. Schneider, and Scott Farwell, "Social Distancing Strictures Fall Away as Crowds Gather to Party and Protest," *Washington Post*.

269 **I would still wish** Bill de Blasio, "Transcript: Mayor de Blasio, Police Commissioner Shea Hold Media Availability," nyc.gov, May 30, 2020.

269 **Big crowd, professionally** Donald Trump, @realDonaldTrump, Twitter, 8:41 A.M., May 30, 2020.

270 **People are tired, sad** Muriel Bowser, "Mayor Bowser Responds to the President's Tweets," Office of the Mayor, Government of the District of Columbia, May 30, 2020.

270 **For 90 days** Andrew Cuomo, "Governor Cuomo Signs into Law New Measure Providing Death Benefits for Families of Frontline

Government Workers Who Lost Their Lives Due to Covid-19," ny.gov, May 30, 2020.

270 **Other Democrat run cities** Donald Trump, @realDonaldTrump, Twitter, 12:12 P.M., May 31, 2020.

270 **He should just stop** Keisha Lance Bottoms, interview with Jake Tapper, *State of the Union*, May 31, 2020.

271 **By one estimate** Jack Healy and Dionne Searcey, "Two Crises Convulse a Nation: A Pandemic and Police Violence," *New York Times*, May 31, 2020.

271 **What we are seeing** Ilhan Omar, interview with George Stephanopoulos, "*This Week* Transcript 5-31-20: House Speaker Nancy Pelosi, Rep. Ilhan Omar, Amb. Robert O'Brien," ABC News, May 31, 2020.

271 **Black communities have** Kamala Harris, @KamalaHarris, Twitter, 11:11 A.M., May 31, 2020.

271 **This is a moment in America** Cory Booker, interview with Jake Tapper, *State of the Union*, May 31, 2020.

271 **The murder of George Floyd** London Breed, "Mayor London Breed and Public Safety Officials Announce Curfew in San Francisco to Begin Tonight at 8 PM," press release, Office of the Mayor, City and County of San Francisco, May 31, 2020.

272 **Protestors started fires** Jonathan Lemire and Zeke Miller, "Protesters Start Fires Near White House," Associated Press, May 31, 2020.

272 **It is striking** Isaac Stanley-Becker, "White Instigators to Blame for Mayhem in Some Protests, Local Officials Say," *Washington Post*, June 1, 2020.

272 **Folks in St. Paul** Interview with *Today*.

272 **I recognize that these** Barack Obama, "How to Make this Moment the Turning Point for Real Change," Medium.

273 **As California continues** Cheri Mossburg, "Coronavirus Cases in California Climb 11% in Just Five Days," CNN.com.

273 **Orleans Parish will not move** LaToya Cantrell, "Orleans Parish Monitoring Data Closely, Will Remain under 'Phase One' Guidelines beyond June 5," press release, Mayor's Office, NOLA.gov, June 1, 2020.

273 **A recent *Washington Post*-Ipsos** Eli Rosenberg, "An Undercurrent of the Protests: African Americans Are Struggling More Economically from This Pandemic," *Washington Post*, June 1, 2020.

273 **The fact that so many** Phil Murphy, "New Jersey Governor Phil Murphy Briefing Transcript June 1," Rev.com, June 1, 2020.

273 **When white men march** Karen Attiah, @KarenAttiah, Twitter, 1:53 A.M., June 1, 2020.

274 **The same broad-sweeping** Maimuna Majumder, interviewed in Brian Resnick, "Police Brutality Is a Public Health Crisis," *Vox*.

274 **There's no doubt that this** Cornel West, interview with Nermeen Shaikh, "'America's Moment of Reckoning': Cornel West Says Nationwide Uprising Is Sign of 'Empire Imploding,'" *Democracy Now!*, June 1, 2020.

274 **I think the sooner** Mark Esper, leaked phone call, "Full Call Audio: Trump Berates Governors Over Protests," *Washington Post*, June 1, 2020.

274 **You have to get much tougher** Donald Trump, leaked phone call, ibid.

275 **I wanted to take this** J. B. Pritzker, leaked phone call, ibid.

275 **I heard what the president** Charlie Baker, in Katie Rogers, Jonathan Martin, and Maggie Haberman, "As Trump Calls Protesters 'Terrorists,' Tear Gas Clears a Path for His Walk to a Church," *New York Times*, June 1, 2020.

275 **First, we are ending** Donald Trump, "Statement by the President," whitehouse.gov, June 1, 2020.

275 **Let's be clear** Kamala Harris, @KamalaHarris, Twitter, 10:42 P.M., June 1, 2020.

276 **Here is what was happening** Yamiche Alcindor, @Yamiche, Twitter, 7:07 P.M., June 1, 2020.

276 **I imposed a curfew** Muriel Bowser, @MurielBowser, Twitter, 8:40 P.M., June 1, 2020.

276 **Peaceful protestors were** Hakeem Jeffries, @RepJeffries, Twitter, 8:41 P.M., June 1, 2020.

276 **More than 100,000 Americans** Ben Rhodes, @BRhodes, Twitter, 8:26 P.M., June 1, 2020.

276 **Bennie Thompson** Letter to James M. Murray, Director of Secret Service.

277 **Every member of this co-equal** Cory Booker, "Cory Booker & Kamala Harris Speech Transcript on George Floyd & Racial Injustice," Rev.com, June 2, 2020.

277 **What we're seeing is something** Anne Milgram, "CAFE Insider 6/2: George Floyd & America in Turmoil," *CAFE Insider*, June 2, 2020.

277 **In the last couple of days** Kamala Harris, ibid.

277 **And while not every death** Eric Garcetti, "LA Mayor Eric Garcetti Speech Transcript While Protestors Outside His House," Rev.com, June 2, 2020.

278 **The FBI's Washington Field Office** Ken Klippenstein, "The FBI Finds 'No Intel Indicating Antifa Involvement' in Sunday's Violence," *Nation*, June 2, 2020.

278 **Block by block what I saw** Lori Lightfoot, "Chicago Mayor Lori Lightfoot Press Conference Transcript June 2," Rev.com, June 2, 2020.

278 **The country is crying out** Joe Biden, public statement, "Read: Joe Biden's Remarks on Civil Unrest and Nationwide Protests," CNN, June 2, 2020.

278 **After a lot of conversation** Lightfoot, "Chicago Mayor Lori Lightfoot Press

Conference Transcript June 2," June 2, 2020.

279 **You have the Covid-19 crisis** Andrew Cuomo, "NY Governor Andrew Cuomo June 3 Press Conference Transcript," Rev.com, June 3, 2020.

279 **The U.S. is at risk** Bryan Walsh, "American Society Is Teetering on the Edge," *Axios*, June 3, 2020.

279 **Tomorrow, the world will** Tim Walz, "Minnesota Governor Tim Walz June 3 Press Conference Transcript," Rev.com, June 3, 2020.

279 **A different president might have** Adam Serwer, "Trump Gave Police Permission to Be Brutal," *Atlantic*, June 3, 2020.

280 **Donald Trump is** Jeffrey Goldberg, "James Mattis Denounces President Trump, Describes Him as a Threat to the Constitution," *Atlantic*, June 3, 2020.

280 **In California, daily case reports** "U.S. Roundup: The Number of Confirmed Cases Is Rising in 16 States, Partly a Consequence of Expanded Testing," *New York Times*, June 3, 2020.

280 **Worrying trend** Charles Ornstein, @charlesornstein, Twitter, 3:20 P.M., June 3, 2020.

280 **Today is Day 95** Andrew Cuomo, "Video, Audio, Photos & Rush Transcript: Governor Cuomo Holds Briefing on George Floyd Protests & Provides Update on Covid-19 Progress," ny.gov, June 3, 2020.

281 **Unemployment claims for the last** Eli Rosenberg and Heather Long, "Nearly 2 Million People Applied for Unemployment Last Week, Even as Economy Shows Signs of Reopening," *Washington Post*, June 4, 2020.

281 **It's almost as if** Dan Gelber, interviewed in Michael D. Shear, "'They Let Us Down': 5 Takeaways on the C.D.C.'s Coronavirus Response," *New York Times*, June 3, 2020.

281 **I'm a bit concerned** Francis Collins, interviewed in Elizabeth Cohen, "NIH Chief Worried Vaccine 'Skepticism' Might Cause Some to Skip Coronavirus Vaccine," CNN.com, June 4, 2020.

281 **If we just let this wound scab** Joe Biden, "Joe Biden Town Hall Transcript with Young Americans: Says 10-15% of Americans 'Not Very Good People,'" Rev.com, June 4, 2020.

282 **It's just past 8 30 P.M. in Los Angeles** Report by Kyung Lah, "Los Angeles Has Lifted Its Curfew, and Protesters Are Peacefully Marching Through Downtown," CNN.com, June 4, 2020.

282 **While most protests** Mark Berman and Emily Wax-Thibodeaux, "Police Keep Using Force Against Peaceful Protesters, Prompting Sustained Criticism About Tactics and Training," *Washington Post*, June 4, 2020.

282 **For every single second** Keisha Lance Bottoms, interview with Ellen DeGeneres, "Mayor Keisha Lance Bottoms

on the President," *The Ellen DeGeneres Show*, June 4, 2020.

282 **Unemployment dips** "Unemployment Dips to 13.3% as US Added 2.5 Million Jobs in May as Impact from Virus Eases," Associated Press, June 5, 2020.

283 **Really big jobs report** Donald Trump, @realDonaldTrump, Twitter, 8:33 A.M., June 5, 2020

283 **It's time for him** Joe Biden, "Joe Biden Remarks in Dover, Delaware," C-SPAN, June 5, 2020.

283 **This is a very big day** Donald Trump, "Donald Trump Press Conference Transcript on Jobs Report: Says This Is a Great Day for George Floyd," Rev .com, June 5, 2020.

283 **These figures released** Alicia Palapiano, "The Economic Pain That the Unemployment Rate Leaves Out," *New York Times*, June 5, 2020.

283 **Hopefully George [Floyd] is** Trump, "Donald Trump Press Conference Transcript on Jobs Report: Says This Is a Great Day for George Floyd," June 5, 2020.

283 **I am looking for all of their** Nikole Hannah-Jones, @nhannahjones, Twitter, 3:21 P.M., June 5, 2020.

284 **We have a lot of protestors** Trump, "Donald Trump Press Conference Transcript on Jobs Report: Says This Is a Great Day for George Floyd," June 5, 2020.

284 **The White House Coronavirus Task Force** Andrew Restuccia, "Trump's Focus Shifts away from Coronavirus," *Wall Street Journal*, June 5, 2020.

284 **But we're going to be back** Trump, "Donald Trump Press Conference Transcript on Jobs Report: Says This Is a Great Day for George Floyd," June 5, 2020.

284 **In the South** Martha Bebinger, Blake Farmer, and Jackie Fortier, "New Coronavirus Hot Spots Emerge Across South and in California, as Northeast Slows," NPR, June 5, 2020.

284 **Florida's Department of Health** Michelle Marchante, "Florida Sees 1,300 New Cases of Covid-19, Another Big Jump, as State Tests More People," *Miami Herald*, June 5, 2020.

285 **875,402** Johns Hopkins Coronavirus Resource Center. Accessed June 5, 2020.

285 **So it's been a really terrific** Trump, "Donald Trump Press Conference Transcript on Jobs Report: Says This Is a Great Day for George Floyd," June 5, 2020.

A NOTE ON THE AUTHORS

Jon Sternfeld is a former editor and the coauthor of *Crisis Point*, with Senator Tom Daschle and Senator Trent Lott; *A Stone of Hope*, with Jim St. Germain; and *A Forever Family* with Rob Scheer, among other nonfiction books. He lives in New York.

Timothy Egan is a Pulitzer Prize–winning reporter and the author of nine books, most recently *The Immortal Irishman*, a *New York Times* bestseller. His book on the Dust Bowl, *The Worst Hard Time*, won a National Book Award for nonfiction and was named a *New York Times* Notable Book of the Year, a Washington State Book Award winner, and a Book Sense Book of the Year Honor Book. He writes a weekly opinion column for the *New York Times* and lives in Seattle.